JEWISH FOUNDATIONS OF
THE NEW TESTAMENT

Studies in Judaism and Christianity

Exploration of Issues in the Contemporary Dialogue between Christians and Jews

EDITORS

Michael McGarry, CSP

Mark-David Janus, CSP, PhD

Adam Gregerman, PhD

Yehezkel Landau, DMin

Peter Pettit, PhD

Elena Procario-Foley, PhD

Ellen M. Umansky, PhD

Rabbi Stephen Wylen

A STIMULUS BOOK

Jewish Foundations of the New Testament

Addressing the Roots of Antisemitism

JESPER SVARTVIK

A STIMULUS BOOK

PAULIST PRESS • NEW YORK • MAHWAH, NJ

Unless otherwise indicated, the Scripture quotations contained herein are from the New Revised Standard Version: Catholic Edition, Copyright © 1989 and 1993, by the Division of Christian Education of the National Council of the Churches of Christ in the United States of America. Used by permission. All rights reserved. All translations from other non-English texts are the author's own.

Cover art: *The Road to Emmaus* by Altobello Melone, courtesy Google Art Project
Cover design by Sharyn Banks
Book design by Lynn Else

Copyright © 2025 by the Stimulus Foundation, Inc.

All rights reserved. No part of this publication may be reproduced, stored in a retrieval system, or transmitted in any form or by any means, electronic, mechanical, photocopying, recording, scanning, or otherwise, without either the prior written permission of the Publisher, or authorization through payment of the appropriate per-copy fee to the Copyright Clearance Center, Inc., 222 Rosewood Drive, Danvers, MA 01923, (978) 750-8400, fax (978) 646-8600, or on the Web at www.copyright.com. Requests to the Publisher for permission should be addressed to the Permissions Department, Paulist Press, 997 Macarthur Boulevard, Mahwah, NJ 07450.

Library of Congress Cataloging-in-Publication Data
Names: Svartvik, Jesper, author
Title: Jewish foundations of the New Testament: addressing the roots of antisemitism / Jesper Svartvik.
Description: New York: Paulist Press, [2025] | Series: Studies in Judaism and Christianity | "A Stimulus Book." | Includes bibliographical references and index. | Summary: "This book provides a much-needed series of interpretations of thirty key passages in the New Testament that have played a crucial role in Jewish-Christian relations"—Provided by publisher.
Identifiers: LCCN 2024019659 (print) | LCCN 2024019660 (ebook) | ISBN 9780809157204 (paperback) | ISBN 9780809188826 (ebook)
Subjects: LCSH: Jews in the New Testament. | Bible. New Testament—Criticism, interpretation, etc. | Antisemitism—Biblical teaching. | Christianity and antisemitism—History. | Judaism (Christian theology)—History of doctrines—Early church, ca. 30-600.
Classification: LCC BS2545.J44 S83 2025 (print) | LCC BS2545.J44 (ebook) | DDC 225.6—dc23/eng/20240927
LC record available at https://lccn.loc.gov/2024019659
LC ebook record available at https://lccn.loc.gov/2024019660

ISBN 978-0-8091-5720-4 (paperback)
ISBN 978-0-8091-8882-6 (ebook)

Published by Paulist Press
997 Macarthur Boulevard
Mahwah, New Jersey 07430
www.paulistpress.com

Printed and bound in the
United States of America

CONTENTS

Preface ix

Introduction xi

    The Four-"A" Terminology. xiv

    The Seventy Faces of the Scriptures and Four Challenges. xx

        • The First Challenge: Pharisees in the Synoptic Gospels xxi

        • The Second Challenge: "Jews" in the Gospel of John xxviii

        • The Third Challenge: The Law in Pauline Theology xxxiii

        • The Fourth Challenge: "The New Covenant" in the
          Epistle to the Hebrews xxxviii

1. Who Is Heeding the Teaching of John the Baptist?
   (Matt 3:1–10, Mark 1:2–6, and Luke 3:1–9) 1

2. "An Eye for an Eye?...We Are Not Barbarians!"
   (Matt 5:38–48 and Luke 6:29f.) 8

3. The Golden Rule in the Royal Law
   (Matt 7:12 and Luke 6:31) 20

4. Should Auld Acquaintance Be Forgot, and Never Brought
   to Mind? (Matt 9:16f., Mark 2:21f., and Luke 5:36–39) 27

5. What Yoke Gives Rest for the Heavy-Burdened?
   (Matt 11:28–30) 32

6. A Snowball Rolling down a Hill in Galilee (Matt 12:1–8,
   Mark 2:23–28, and Luke 6:1–5) 37

7. Mustard: Tree, Weed, or Seed? (Matt 13:31f.,
   Mark 4:30–32, and Luke 13:18f.) 44

Contents

8. Bread (Unfit) for Passover or Heavenly Hospitality? (Matt 13:33 and Luke 13:20f.) 51
9. Is Noshing Sacred Anymore? (Matt 15:1–20 and Mark 7:1–23). 55
10. The Text about the Tenants in the Vineyard: Parable Proper or Yet Another Allegory? (Matt 21:33–46, Mark 12:1–12, and Luke 20:9–19) 68
11. A Commandment in Common? (Matt 22:34–40 and Mark 12:28–34). 80
12. The Good Samaritan and Bad Jews (Luke 10:25–37) 86
13. Why Commend a Dishonest Steward? (Luke 16:1–13) 92
14. Lazarus—"What's in a Name?" (Luke 16:19–31) 98
15. A Parable about Prayer or Politics? (Luke 18:1–8). 104
16. Justice in the Temple Court? (Luke 18:9–14). 111
17. Judas Iscariot: "I Know Who Everybody's Gonna Blame" (Matt 10:1–4, 26:14–16, 26:21–25, 27:3–10; Mark 3:13–19, 14:10f., 14:18–21, 14:43–45; Luke 6:12–16, 22:3–6, 22:21–33, 22:47f.; John 6:70f., 12:1–7, 13:2, 13:21–30, 17:12; and Acts 1:15–26) 116
18. Who Are Shouting: "His Blood Be on Us and on Our Children"? (Matt 27:25). 130
19. Rendering the Rending of the Veil (Matt 27:51, Mark 15:38, and Luke 23:45) 137
20. Is John's Pro-logue Anti-Logos? (John 1:1–18) 151
21. What Did Jesus Write in the Sand? (John 7:53—8:11). 159
22. Demonizing One's Spiritual Adversaries (John 8:31–59, esp. 8:44). 165
23. Paulus—Mädchen für alles? (1 Cor 9:19–23). 176
24. Reviewing Veils and Revelations (2 Cor 3:4–18). 181
25. Deciphering Sarah and Hagar in Genesis and Galatia (Gal 4:21—5:1). 188

Contents

26. "The Israel of God" in Galatians (Gal 6:16) 203
27. "Mr. G., Tear Down This Wall!" (Eph 2:11–22) 209
28. Paul and Profanity (Phil 3:7–14) 218
29. Did Paul the Persecutor Accuse the Jews of Persecuting?
    (1 Thess 2:13–16) 223
30. What Are the Membership Requirements for
    "the Synagogue of Satan"? (Rev 2:9 and 3:9) 230
Concluding Remarks 235
Notes 245
Bibliography 311
Names Index 337
Ancient Sources Index 343

PREFACE

This book has been in the making for more than thirty years. Ever since 1990, when I first studied in Jerusalem, I have been fascinated by the remarkable possibilities for New Testament scholarship to see farther, dig deeper, and understand more by continuously taking into consideration the Jewish content and context of the early Christian movement. Furthermore, I came to realize that we must reassess what has been written and said about Judaism—especially second-temple Judaism. During my studies in Jerusalem, I was struck, for the first time in my life, by the far-reaching consequences of Christian anti-Jewish teaching and preaching throughout history. Although I had already studied for five years, I felt like I had to start my theological studies all over again, this time with respect for Jewish tradition and self-understanding.

When Boston College offered me the Corcoran Visiting Chair for two consecutive years (2020–2022), I finally had the opportunity to write a book addressing the issues that have been on my mind for such a long time. It has been a profound pleasure and distinct privilege to serve as the visiting professor in Jewish-Christian relations, a topic that has been close to my heart for three decades, and I would like to express my deep gratitude for the remarkable opportunity that Boston College has provided me during this time. I am incredibly grateful for the stimulating cooperation with Ruth Langer and Camille Fitzpatrick Markey at the Center for Christian-Jewish Learning at Boston College. James Bernauer's term as director for the center had just ended and, as I departed, Daniel Joslyn-Siematkoski was appointed his successor and about to return to Boston College: to both of them I am most grateful for stimulating conversations. For ceaselessly exploring and finding ways for me to work at Boston College in the midst of—and in spite of—the pandemic, I am very grateful to the administrative staff at Boston College.

On this three-decade odyssey I have been no lone sailor on the sometimes stormy seas of scholarship, and it gives me great pleasure to express

Jewish Foundations of the New Testament

my profound thanks to several colleagues and friends for stimulating conversations: I would particularly like to mention Mary C. Boys and Marc Zvi Brettler, who, upon hearing about this book project, encouraged me to pursue it. I would also like to thank Lars M. Andersson, Judith H. Banki, Tina Haettner Blomquist, Gunnel Borgegård, Leif Carlsson, James Carroll, Philip A. Cunningham, Sören Dalevi, Per Eckerdal, Jonas Eek, Tamara Cohn Eskenazi, Adam Gregerman, Thomas Kazen, James A. Kelhoffer, Eugene B. Korn, Åse Lindberg, Barbara U. Meyer, Inger Nebel, Gunilla Ohlsson, John Stendahl, Peter Vale, Cecilia Wassén, Johanna van Wijk-Bos, and Sara and Ophir Yarden for stimulating conversations. I am particularly grateful to Peter A. Pettit for many engaging discussions about theology and language, and also for reviewing my English in this book. Göran Larsson, my professor when I studied in Jerusalem in 1990, was the first to give me the vantage point to "read the New Testament *within* Judaism"; I am deeply thankful for our numerous conversations for more than three (!) decades about the implications of this perspective for biblical studies, theology, and homiletics, and for his willingness to read and comment on the entire manuscript. Finally, and "the last will be first," from the bottom of my heart I wish to thank my very dear Annika Wenemark for vigorous discussions about the topics in this book, for reading and commenting on innumerous versions of the manuscript, and for her unfailing support in some of the most difficult moments in my life: for being my eyes when my health faltered and for renewing my thoughts when I was downtrodden, I am immensely grateful.

This book is a combination of four overlapping areas of research and interest: *New Testament studies*, *Jewish studies*, *hermeneutics*, and *homiletics*. It could be described as a handbook with hermeneutical strategies for those seeking to avoid the pitfalls of various anti-Jewish readings of the New Testament. In order to reach out to both the scholarly community and a wider audience, I have sought to avoid the heavy terminology that, although often helpful in its meticulousness, at times has the side-effect of making scholarly publications somewhat inaccessible. Whether I have succeeded in this endeavor is, of course, a matter only the readers can assess.

Over time, I have become increasingly aware of the fact that, in order to improve Jewish-Christian relations, we also have to bring our formative texts into our discussions and learn how to read them *differently*. It is my fervent hope that this book may contribute to that important endeavor.

Idus Martiae 2023
Jesper Svartvik

INTRODUCTION

Long before the first Christ followers began to reflect on any other issues, there was one specific topic to which their attention was drawn: *the covenant between the God of Israel and the Israel of God—and why and how Gentile Christ followers were related to the God of Israel and the Israel of God.* The early Christian movement was an intra-Jewish phenomenon: Jesus of Nazareth was a Jew and so were all his disciples, as were the crowds listening to his teaching.[1]

But the far-reaching consequences of this inherent Jewishness are only beginning to be explored. The purpose of this book is to read thirty key passages in the New Testament with this approach: the following thirty chapters will present and evaluate various ways to interpret New Testament passages that have played a crucial role in the history of Jewish-Christian relations. It is not a matter of establishing *the* correct interpretation of the various texts but more of providing the reader with brief summaries of lines of thought that range from *contrast* to *context*. Generally speaking, the first interpretations describe the New Testament texts in contradistinction to the Jewish "background," which more often than not has been depicted in gloomy colors in order to put the limelight on the protagonist in the Gospels. The other interpretations in each chapter gradually emphasize the Jewish context more and more, seeking to understand the New Testament texts not vis-à-vis Judaism but *within* a Jewish context. The German expression *Fingerspitzengefühl* (lit. "fingertips feeling") is of relevance here. The main purpose of this book is to help readers of the New Testament develop interpretive dexterity by improving their contextual awareness and cultivating a sensitivity for a theology that does not depict the Jewish tradition disgracefully and dishonestly. The sad fact is that an apologetic agenda has often governed readings of the New Testament. It is often taken for granted that the Jewish "background" by definition is gloomy, burdensome, and defective. In particular, there are four deceptive dichotomies that have been particularly common.[2] The word *they* here refers to the scribes and the Pharisees, and often Jews in general are "generously" included in this stereotyping:

(i) Whereas "they" are too strict in their religious observance, the teaching of Jesus is renewing and redemptive: his yoke is easy, and his burden is light.[3]
(ii) Whereas "they" are theologically indolent, Jesus is always radical, demanding that his audience turn the other cheek and go the second mile.[4]
(iii) Whereas "they" are too mundane and pettifogging in their teaching, Jesus's message is spiritual and cosmic, proclaiming the kingdom of heaven, which is not from this world.[5]
(iv) Whereas "they" are idealistic and uncompromising, Jesus is realistic and down-to-earth in his teaching, in which he refreshingly refers to the lilies in the field and things that matter to ordinary people.[6]

Needless to say, these four assertions are incompatible and do not do justice to ancient Judaism. Perhaps the gravest mistake of all is to think of textual interpretation as a contest, in which one's own religious tradition must necessarily compete, win, and triumph. Yet many interpretations of New Testament passages do display a clear theological triumphalism. As Amy-Jill Levine writes, it is as if the purpose of the parables of Jesus were to "show how bad Jewish Law is," and as if numerous readers "need to find some fault with Judaism in order to understand Paul and so their own theology."[7] This is not typically a matter of malice; far more often it is due to, firstly, an ignorance of the Jewish tradition and, secondly, the assertion that interpretation is necessarily a zero-sum game, in which one side has to lose in order for the other to proclaim itself victorious.

How on earth did this happen? How did it come about that Christians started to read the *Jewish* Scriptures—now known among Christians as the Old Testament—in *anti-Jewish* ways? And why do Christians so often read the New Testament without perceiving and appreciating the vibrant spirituality of the Jewish tradition? Even today, sadly, numerous Christian sermons present Judaism at the time of Jesus unfavorably. One would like to pose the question in Matthew 20:15 to the preacher: "Is thine eye evil, because I am good?"[8]

So—how on earth did this happen? The short answer to this complex question is that Christ followers started to assume that Christian faith necessarily excludes nonmessianic forms of Judaism, and eventually all varieties

Introduction

of Judaism. Over time, Christian theology has developed a hermeneutics that has not only decentered but also disinherited Jews and Judaism. Christian self-definitions became exclusive and excluding, and, consequently, religious beliefs were expressed at the expense of the self-understanding of the Other. The perspective in this book, however, is that the earliest Christian movement was *a Christ-centered worship of the God of Israel, with predominantly Gentile followers* rather than *an early form of the anti-Jewish Christendom that evolved more fully in the coming centuries.*

Supersessionism—and the synonym "replacement theology"—is the understanding both that Judaism is a separate religion from Christianity and also, in terms of chronology and quality, that it could and should be described as a *prologue* to Christianity: supersessionism argues that Judaism historically *preceded* Christianity and, therefore, Christianity should theologically *proceed* in the future without Judaism. Judaism *paved the way* for Christianity, and it should also *make way* for Christianity. The word *supersessionism* comes from two words in Latin: *super* ("above," "[up]on") and *sedere* ("to sit"); hence, this free translation nevertheless takes into consideration that the etymology is "to take someone else's place."[9]

As David Nirenberg has pointed out, supersessionism is not a minor or marginal phenomenon; instead, ever since it intruded into our thinking it has been at the very heart of Western culture:

> Because critical thought in the Western tradition has so often imagined itself as an overcoming of Judaism, it has the capacity to introduce Judaism in whatever it criticizes....And anti-Judaism is not simply an attitude toward the action of real Jews and their religion, but a way of critically engaging the world.[10]

What does this passage mean? Quite simply, if the Jewish tradition erred when it did not accept Jesus as the Messiah, then every error can be labeled "Jewish." Hence, Judaism can be inserted into any argument about any topic, and Jews can be presented as the scapegoats of all kinds of phenomena: "all capitalists are Jews," "all Bolsheviks are Jews," "all bankers are Jews," "all academicians are Jews," and so on. The accusations may vary over time, but the rationale—or should we rather say "irrationale"?—for the accusations is one and the same: the Jews erred at the time of Jesus, and therefore every error is, in effect, "Jewish."[11]

This way of thinking has also been extraordinarily influential in New Testament studies. Although Christianity evolved in the Western world, it is today a global phenomenon, on the rise predominantly outside of Europe and North America. Hence, supersessionism is now a global phenomenon. In other words, all parts of World Christianity have to address this problem.

It is therefore all the more gratifying that a growing number of scholars, as well as readers of the New Testament in general, are seeking other ways to describe the relationship between the Jewish and Christian traditions. They do this because they are convinced that the biblical texts may provide us with an earlier way—and one "less traveled by"—of relating the two traditions to each other.

Hence, many of the questions that are posed in this book are *old*, as old as the Christian tradition, and some of the answers that we articulate are *new*; they make it possible for us to read the texts in such a way that the inherent Jewishness of the early Christian movement is taken into consideration to a much higher extent than only a couple of decades ago. A growing number of scholars firmly situate both the historical Jesus and the historical Paul in late second-temple Judaism. When reading the New Testament texts in this way, Judaism is not portrayed as the gloomy background from which Christianity had to be *removed* in order to glow and grow. On the contrary, it is to the Jewish matrix we must *return* in order to appreciate the New Testament texts more fully. In short, it is a way of seeking to interpret the texts as they could have been understood before the supersessionist paradigm—which sets Christianity over against Judaism, as if they were two separate religious systems—began to govern most of the theological imagination. In that sense it is both a new and an old endeavor: it is *new* in the sense that it is only after the *Shoah* (the Holocaust) that Christians have started to reflect self-critically on the connection between Christian anti-Jewish teaching and secular anti-semitism.[12] Jews have suffered—and indeed still suffer—because of the way in which Christians have interpreted the New Testament. The way in which the New Testament *texts* have been interpreted cannot be isolated from the way in which Jews have been treated in Christian *contexts*. But, at the same time, the endeavor is also *old* because the meta-question goes all the way back to Pauline times: in his epistles Paul continuously pondered *the covenant between the God of Israel and the Israel of God—and especially why and how Gentile Christ followers were related to the God of Israel and the Israel of God.*

THE FOUR-"A" TERMINOLOGY

Four words are often used in discussions about Jewish-Christian relations, Jewish and Christian hermeneutics, and animosity against Jews:

Introduction

antisemitism, *anti-Judaism*, *allosemitism*, and *asemitism*. Any attempt to explore these topics comprehensively in a short introduction such as this must be limited, but a few aspects may nevertheless be mentioned here, with particular emphasis on the implications for the present study.

(i) *Antisemitism* is a notoriously challenging concept. It was coined about 1873 by the antisemite Wilhelm Marr to be worn by antisemites with pride. In addition, particularly in its hyphenated form, "anti-Semitic," it can be misleading ("How could I be an antisemite? I, too, am a Semite!"). It is therefore essential to remember that antisemitism is a euphemism for *Judenhaß* ("Jew-hatred"), which was meant to refer to—and should refer to—animosity against Jews only.[13] Helen Fein's definition is well-known and recognized by scholars and organizations alike:

> A persisting latent structure of hostile beliefs toward Jews as a collectivity manifested in individuals as attitudes, and in culture as myth, ideology, folklore, and imagery, and in actions—social or legal discrimination, political mobilization against the Jews, and collective or state violence—which results in and/or is designed to distance, displace, or destroy Jews as Jews.[14]

The dehyphenated spelling "antisemitism" is preferable (over "anti-Semitism"), simply because there is no "Semitism" of which one can be in favor. Although coined as an expression in the late nineteenth century, the phenomenon antisemitism has a long history; indeed, at times it is called "the longest hatred." It is often used in a narrow sense, to wit, for the *racial* antisemitism that thrived in the nineteenth century and peaked during the Third Reich era in the twentieth century. As we shall see in the following chapters, this racial antisemitism has at times alluded or even referred to a catalog of New Testament passages, especially in the Gospel of John, but generally speaking, Christians in history have been less interested in an alleged contamination of a Jewish "*race*" than in their allegedly contaminating *religion*. Indeed, to "Judaize" is a label that has often been put by *Christians* on other *Christians* that have another *Christian* theology or lifestyle—and therefore were described as being "too Jewish."[15] This takes us to the second technical term.

xv

(ii) *Anti-Judaism*: This term was coined by Bernard Lazare, who wished to distinguish antisemitism from Christian opposition to Judaism.[16] Theologians often hasten to distinguish between *antisemitism* and *anti-Judaism*, where the former refers to antipathy to Jews *qua* Jews, and the latter to antipathy to the Jewish religion. There is a wide variety of "Jew-hatreds," and there is a need for a well-defined terminology in order to analyze these phenomena. As we have already mentioned, Christendom has been teaching and preaching anti-Judaism rather than antisemitism, if understood in its narrow, racial sense. In one word, generally speaking, Christians have repudiated the Jewish *belief*, not Jewish *blood*.

There *is* a difference between, on the one hand, for example, Martin Luther's call for the destruction of synagogues in his notorious 1543 book *Von den Juden und ihren Lügen* (On the Jews and their lies) and, on the other hand, seeking to annihilate an entire people four hundred years later with the help of a state-of-the-art technology.[17] In the tsunami of anti-Jewish writings and images that flows in the Christian tradition, we do not find clear evidence for a justification of mass murder on traditional *religious* grounds.[18] But one cannot help but wonder if at times we discover an apologetic agenda when the distinction between these two concepts—anti-Judaism and antisemitism—is accentuated. To be blunt, to the Jews who are stigmatized, ostracized, and murdered, it may not be that important to know whether they are accused of killing Jesus, poisoning wells, controlling the media, or destroying the Aryan race. What matters far more is why Jew-hatred seems to be omnipresent and why it has such an intensity. In the language of theologians: there is an easily detectable *eschatological* fervor in certain strands of the animosity against Jews and Judaism. As some antisemites claimed in the 1930s and 1940s: without solving the so-called "Jewish question," one cannot solve the plight of humanity; *keine Erlösung der Menschheit ohne Lösung der Judenfrage* (no salvation for humanity without a solution to the Jewish question). So what is the background for such a discourse? And *that* question cannot be solved by using a sword that—simply and elegantly—cuts Jew-hatred into two distinct phenomena; dividing it into, on the one hand, anti-Judaism (which, it is stated, is not as bad

Introduction

as antisemitism) and, on the other hand, rabid racial antisemitism (which is supposed to be something quite different). But before there was a *racial antisemitism*, there was a *rhetorical anti-Judaism*. James Carroll writes in his book *Constantine's Sword* that the distinction between anti-Judaism and antisemitism became meaningless to him because the hatred of Jews had been made *holy* before it became *lethal*.[19] Jew-hatred was a virtue that Christians preached long before it became Nazi politics. And *that* is the key question. Rather than focusing on the distinction between antisemitism and anti-Judaism, we ought to pay much more attention to the *longue durée* of the teaching of contempt in the Christian tradition, as John Connelly does in his book *From Enemy to Brother*:

> Hitler could—and did—claim to be doing a service to Christianity by persecuting Jews, and *Christianity did not have a language with which to oppose him*. No matter how much Christians objected to violations of human dignity, the human person, or the sanctity of life, they were for the most part left speechless when it came to Hitler's target—the Jewish people.[20]

This is the decisive observation and assertion: "Christianity did not have a language with which to oppose him" because there was a widespread, rhetorical, Christian anti-Jewish teaching and preaching for many centuries long before there was a racial antisemitism. Once again, in Carroll's words: it was *holy* before it became *lethal*.

(iii) *Allosemitism*: Coined by Artur Sandauer but known first and foremost because of Zygmunt Bauman's publications, this term focuses on the idea of Jews as the perpetual "Other" (cf. Greek: *allos*, "other"), but not necessarily negatively. Bauman writes that allosemitism is "an intrinsically ambivalent attitude, able to embrace everything from love and respect to outright condemnation and genocidal hatred."[21] What is essential here is the notion that Jews are different from non-Jews and that, for this reason, Jews cannot be "measured by the same yardstick," as Ruth Gruber writes.[22] This terminology has obvious implications for biblical scholarship. Evidently, the Jewish Scriptures stem from the Jewish tradition but are read also by Christians. Indeed, given the statistic correlation between the number of Jews and Christians in the world, an overwhelming majority of readers of these texts about Jews are not Jews. When Jewish texts, which contain discussions about Jewish self-understanding ("Who are we?" "What went wrong?" "What should we do?"), are read by non-Jews (i.e., Christians), these texts about Jewish *self-understanding* are transformed into texts about "*other-standing*" ("Who were they?" "What have they done?" "What should they do?"). A Jewish soul-searching reflection on the destruction of the temple in 586 BCE may well end with self-critique: this happened *mi-pnei chataeinu* (because of our sins). But when Christians read the same texts, the *mea culpa* (my sin) perspective of the text is transformed into a *tua culpa* (your sin). The New Testament Gospels indicate that the historical Jesus criticized some of his fellow Jews—to state that "my Judaism is better than your Judaism" is a very typical Jewish thing to do. However, when the *insider* discourse is transferred outside of the Jewish context, it becomes an *outsider* discourse. In short, intra-Jewish debate mutates and becomes anti-Jewish condemnation. Furthermore, the key issue in the Pauline epistles is the relation between Jews and Gentiles, and, as we shall see in this book, Paul opposes the idea that Gentiles-in-Christ must observe the commandments in the Torah—not because the Torah is detrimental but because he wants to uphold the distinction between Jews and Gentiles. His is a distinctly positive invocation of allosemitism.

(iv) *Asemitism*, recently reintroduced as a concept by James Bernauer, is not as aggressive as antisemitism; in fact, it denounces all violent anti-Jewish hostilities. It is neither antisemitic nor philosemitic; instead, it is *nonviolent indifference* to Jews, the Jewish tradition, and any matter in which they, *quae* Jews, are involved.[23] In short, asemitism results in thinking, writing, and acting as if there were no Jews in the world: it is the ability to imagine a world without Jews, and it finds consolation in their disappearance. As Bernauer writes, "No attention is owed to those who failed to see [that Jesus of Nazareth is] the Messiah."[24]

The term *asemitism* provides us with an ideological background and a hermeneutical classification for what Abraham

Introduction

Joshua Heschel critiqued in his famous series of questions to Gustave Weigel in 1964:

> Is it really the will of God that there be no more Judaism in the world? Would it really be the triumph of God if the scrolls of the Torah were no longer taken out of the Ark and the Torah no longer read in the synagogue, our ancient Hebrew prayers in which Jesus himself worshipped no more recited, the Passover Seder no longer celebrated in our lives, the Law of Moses no longer observed in our homes? Would it really be *ad maiorem Dei gloriam* [for the greater glory of God] to have a world without Jews?[25]

Given the focus for the present study, the most obvious instance of asemitism in biblical scholarship is the Christian habit of reading and talking about the Scriptures as if they did not spring from the Jewish tradition, as if they were not written down, preserved, and cherished by Jews, long before there ever was a Jesus movement. Asemitism is similar to what R. Kendall Soulen calls *structural supersessionism*, the consequences of which he describes as "God's identity as the God of Israel and God's history with the Jewish people become largely indecisive for the Christian conception of God."[26]

As we have seen so far, these four concepts—*antisemitism*, *anti-Judaism*, *allosemitism*, and *asemitism*—are of relevance when studying the history of interpretation of the New Testament.

How, then, can Christians start reading the New Testament *differently*— *differently* in the sense that their interpretations are less triumphalistic and less contemptuous vis-à-vis the Jewish tradition; *differently* in the sense that the texts read with more care, that they are handled with care not because the texts per se are fragile but because people are both valuable and vulnerable? Jonathan Culler once wrote that "it seems an elementary and intuitively given fact that a story can be told in different ways and remain, in an important sense, the same story."[27] This is what the present book seeks to achieve: to tell the master narrative of the New Testament in new ways, without fearing that it will not remain the same story. Indeed, we may even go as far as to state that it is only when we read the texts without presupposing supersessionism that we will detect the hidden treasures in the texts.

THE SEVENTY FACES OF THE SCRIPTURES AND FOUR CHALLENGES

When interpreting the New Testament texts, this book focuses on several stumbling blocks and one major stepping stone. The stumbling blocks emerge from the anti-Jewish legacy of New Testament interpretation. In history as well as in our own times, they are indeed many, but it is nevertheless important to remember that they do not constitute the entire landscape. There are ways to avoid them, and it is the ambition of the present book that its thirty chapters will provide the readers with a hermeneutical toolbox to use also when interpreting texts that are not explicitly discussed here.

The major stepping stone is the celebration of the many ways to interpret the Scriptures. Among readers of the Bible there is at times an insistence on finding the one and only true interpretation, and this has contributed to a sense of *nervousness* among readers of the Bible: "How do I find *the* true interpretation?" Instead, this book celebrates the multiple meanings and many readings of the New Testament texts. In the Jewish tradition there is an expression: *shiv'im panim la-Torah* (Hebrew for "seventy faces in the Torah") meaning that the Scriptures can be interpreted in numerous ways, "seventy" being the biblical expression for a multitude (e.g., the *seventy* nations of the world, forgiving one's sibling *seventy* times, etc.). Whereas the Hebrew expression, obviously, refers to the Torah,[28] this book takes the liberty of also applying such a "polyinterpretive" approach to the texts in the New Testament. In each of the following thirty chapters the readers will not encounter as many as *seventy* interpretations of each text, but always *several* ways to read the texts. And if there are numerous interpretations, then some of them are better, and some are worse. What, then, characterizes a good interpretation? Some interpretations are not only *dear* to many readers of the Bible but, in addition, have proven to be *dangerous* to others. The two hermeneutical criteria in this particular book are, firstly, whether an interpretation does justice to the Jewish tradition, both at the time of Jesus and throughout history, and, secondly, whether the interpretation has proven to be harmful to Jews in history, depriving them of their self-understanding and of what is central to the Jewish tradition. Again, the interpretations are not scrutinized and problematized because they are *dear* to many Christians but because they are *dangerous* to Jews.

In biblical scholarship, homilies, and Bible study groups, there are four keywords that resurface over and over again. Be there Jews present or not, it does not matter—because when you open a New Testament, Jews are

Introduction

there. They are omnipresent as soon as Christians discuss theological issues. The four keywords are *Pharisees*, *Jews*, *Law*, and *Covenant*. There are, of course, additional topics and terms, but these four represent the four most fundamental challenges to renewed and reinvigorated Jewish-Christian relations.

The First Challenge: Pharisees in the Synoptic Gospels

Given the purpose of the present study, it is altogether fitting and proper that we first seek to understand more about the Pharisees, quite simply because the portrayal of the Pharisees in the New Testament has governed much of how people in general, especially in Christian contexts, have depicted Jews on the whole.[29] In short, if the Pharisees in antiquity were hypocrites, then are not all Jews—also today—hypocritical? If the Pharisees put heavy burdens on people's shoulders, is not the entire Jewish tradition unbearable? Furthermore, this alleged "Pharisaism" also lurks around the corner in Christian churches today. One particularly palpable example of this pattern is Gary Tyra's book *Defeating Pharisaism: Recovering Jesus' Disciple-Making Method*: "It has become more and more apparent that the Pharisaism we find Jesus wrestling with in the Gospels is alive and well in our evangelical churches."[30]

Hence, the task for Christians today, as Tyra presents it, is to discern the Pharisaism in Christian communities today—and to oppose it![31] This suggests the image of a four-stage rocket: firstly, the Pharisees as narrative characters in the Synoptic Gospels are taken out of the New Testament texts and presented as actual figures in a Jewish historical context; secondly, the Pharisees thus construed are presented as typical Jews in general in antiquity; thirdly, these alleged Pharisaic Jews in antiquity are transferred into our own times, displayed as being typical of contemporary Judaism; and, fourthly and finally, Pharisaism transmutes into a theological temptation for Christians. Everything Christians dislike tends to become typically "Pharisaic."

All this has to do with the fact that both Jews and Christians, generally speaking, have emphasized the bond between the Pharisees and subsequent forms of Judaism. On the one hand, a traditional *Jewish* understanding is that the Pharisees quite frankly saved Judaism. When the temple was destroyed in 70 CE, the temple-centered piety in Jerusalem vanished, and other "Judaisms"—for example, the Pharisees—emphasized studying the Torah, prayers, and good deeds, and this way of living a Jewish life, so to speak, substituted for the temple service.[32] It is quite striking that "priests" are not mentioned in the opening passage in the tractate *Mishnah Pirqei Avot*:

> Moses received the Torah at Sinai and transmitted it to Joshua, Joshua to the elders, and the elders to the prophets, and the prophets to the men of the great assembly.[33]

The most probable reason for not mentioning the priests in this chain of the Jewish tradition is that Mishnaic Judaism wished to emphasize that the Jewish tradition was able to survive even the destruction of the temple. Hence, the connection between the Pharisaic movement—which was *not* temple centered; instead, they sought to take the temple practices to everyone—and subsequent Judaism was heightened.

On the other hand, the conventional *Christian* understanding has been to present the Pharisees as part of the Jewish elite at the time of Jesus, almost as if they were akin to the chief priests in Jerusalem, although the Pharisees' emphasis on *laïcité* placed them on the other end of the spectrum of Jewish groups at that time.

Bad Pharisees are virtually omnipresent in Christian teaching and preaching. Although impossible to establish with any certainty, is it not at least plausible that it was in the sermons of her father Patrick Brontë, the Anglican priest, that Emily Brontë had heard the anti-Pharisaic discourse that surfaces in *Wuthering Heights*? In her book, the servant Joseph is likened to a Pharisee:

> He was, and is yet, most likely, the wearisomest self-righteous pharisee that ever ransacked a Bible to rake the promises to himself and fling the curses on his neighbors. By his knack of sermonizing and pious discoursing, he contrived to make a great impression on Mr. Earnshaw; and the more feeble the master became, the more influence he gained.[34]

In short, previous generations of scholars, teachers, and preachers have espoused a *maximalist* approach to the Pharisees—that is, overrepresenting their significance and influence: while Jews have often asserted that Judaism is the legitimate heir to the pious Pharisees, Christians have frequently claimed that contemporary Judaism is the heir of the hypocritical Pharisees in antiquity.

Introduction

A collection of essays published in 2021 that is quickly becoming the standard work in the field, *The Pharisees*, edited by Joseph Sievers and Amy-Jill Levine, takes a *minimalist* approach.[35] Rather than asking when the Pharisees became rabbis (as if there were a genetic connection between the two groups), many scholars now follow Annette Yoshiko Reed's tack and ask when the rabbis became Pharisees; to wit, at what time were the rabbis *perceived* to be the heirs of the Pharisees? It is quite likely that we can trace that line of thought all the way back to antiquity.[36]

In addition to the misleading maximalism, which has overstated the importance of the Pharisees, various etymological endeavors have also been misleading. An introduction to the Pharisees typically begins with an etymological *exposé* of the background of the term *Pharisees*. But Craig E. Morrison, who penned the prelude in the collection of essays *The Pharisees*, requests that we stop defining the Pharisees (Hebrew: *perushim*) as a group that wished to be "separate" (from the Hebrew root *p-r-sh*), because we cannot be sure of what they sought to separate themselves from and for what purpose: from *ordinary people* (probably not good, if one consults a mainstream Christian sermon on the Pharisees) or *from sin and evil* (much better, according to most sermons), *for the purpose of holiness* (also commendable), or perhaps *for a special assignment*, akin to Paul's understanding of himself as an apostle to the Gentiles (quite good, according to most preachers). Morrison's sobering assessment of various etymological definitions ends with the conclusion that etymological guesses serve as a shaky foundation for our understanding of the historical Pharisees.[37] His chapter ought to be mandatory reading for all those with an urge to describe the Pharisees primarily on the basis of the group's name. We do not acquire a better picture of Gustav Mahler's music by stating that his name means "painter" in German; nor do we appreciate the meticulous scholarship of the textual critic Bruce M. Metzger better by knowing that his name means "butcher" in German. So why should we expect to understand the Pharisaic movement better simply by expounding the etymology of *perushim*?

In addition to, firstly, the tendency to overemphasize the historical connection between the Pharisees and subsequent forms of Judaism and, secondly, the etymological fallacy, there is also a third wide-spread phenomenon—that is, that readers of the New Testament tend not to think of "good" Pharisees as "typical" Pharisees.[38] Two illuminating examples are how Nicodemus (possibly the historical figure Naqdimon ben Gorion) and Joseph of Arimathea are depicted in Christian teaching and preaching. Does the Johannine character Nicodemus approach Jesus *because* he was a

Pharisee and "a leader of the Jews" (3:1)? Or does he do so *in spite of* this fact? Or does he do so *regardless* of it? Harold W. Attridge casts him negatively, concluding that, according to John, "anyone, *even* a Pharisee, can have eyes opened and learn, however reluctantly, to see and react appropriately."[39] And when he brings myrrh and aloes, weighing about a hundred pounds (19:39), to the grave where Joseph of Arimathea has put the dead body of Jesus, and the two men follow "the burial customs of the Jews," is this a sign of *piety and respect*, whether of the Jewish, Pharisaic, or Christian sort? Or is it instead a sign of *disbelief*—be it Jewish, Pharisaic, or Christian—in the impending resurrection of Jesus? Church father John Chrysostom argues that the costly burial reveals their disposition to regard Jesus as a mere human; hence, he *criticizes* them for their actions.[40] However, when Mary of Bethany takes a pound of costly perfume and anoints Jesus's feet, thereby drawing criticism from Judas Iscariot, she is *defended* by Jesus: "Leave her alone. She bought it so that she might keep it for the day of my burial" (12:7). Attridge points out that, although the amount of perfume in this narrative is much smaller, it is still very valuable: "Thus both Mary and Nicodemus engage in extravagant acts that focus on Jesus's death."[41] The deceased Jesus was unable in the narrative to defend Nicodemus and Joseph of Arimathea against John Chrysostom's invective. Are present-day readers as condemning as John Chrysostom?

The most well-known Pharisee in the New Testament is Paul, the Apostle. We will shortly discuss his texts and theology (see the third challenge below); suffice it now merely to point out that in history he has almost never been perceived or presented as a Pharisee, only a *former* Pharisee. But what evidence do we have in the Pauline epistles that he considered himself to be an *ex*-Pharisee? (As a matter of fact, in Acts, Paul is not an apostle as much as he is a Pharisee; see, e.g., 23:6.) Indeed, as Paula Fredriksen points out in her article "Paul, the Perfectly Righteous Pharisee," Paul is the only self-identified Pharisee whose writings have been preserved to posterity, and the picture that emerges in these writings is that, "Paul had thought of himself as a flawless Pharisee. Now that he was 'in' Christ and Christ 'in' him, his opinion of himself never diminished....Paul could only be an even *better* Pharisee."[42]

These three New Testament examples—Nicodemus, Joseph of Arimathea, and Paul of Tarsus—illustrate that teachers and preachers alike must carefully choose how to present these characters from the lectern and pulpit. In one word, it is not only a matter of interpreting the information we have in the texts (*exegesis* literally means bringing information *out from a text*), but also what we bring when we start reading these texts about the Pharisees (*eisêgêsis* means bringing something *into the text*). If we want to find "bad" Pharisees in the New Testament, we will easily find them there. If we want to find some "good" Pharisees, we will find them too—but only if we insist on labelling them as Pharisees.[43] In short, it is not a uniform picture of the Pharisees that emerges in the New Testament texts.

All this encourages us to seek to rediscover the *historical* Pharisees. The fact that "Pharisee" in Christian discourse has become a theological insult for various inadequacies—that is, hypocrisy, unbearable strictness in terms of *halakhah*, ethnocentric chauvinism, political correctness, just to mention a few faults with which they habitually are identified—makes this an even more urgent theological duty. What, then, do we know about the *historical* Pharisees?[44]

Josephus famously lists three philosophical schools: Pharisees, Essenes, and Sadducees, and then adds a "Fourth Philosophy" (of which Judas the Galilean set himself up as a leader); Josephus estimates that there were approximately six thousand Pharisees.[45] If we, with Fredriksen, accept historians' lowest population estimation that there were some five hundred thousand Jews within King Herod's borders, the Pharisees would not amount to more than 1.2 percent of the population.[46] In other words, the extraordinary impact of the Pharisees in Christian teaching and preaching is inversely proportional to the factual size of the group.

Firstly, in theological handbooks it is often registered that the Pharisees believed in an afterlife: souls have power to survive death. Hence, this Pharisaic belief was in contradistinction to the Sadducees' rejection of a hereafter, as seen in the synoptic passage about resurrection, in which Jesus—as did the Pharisees—argued in favor of the belief that there is a world to come (Matt 22:23–33, Mark 12:18–27, and Luke 20:27–40); the Markan Jesus succinctly tells the Sadducees: "You are quite wrong" (*poly planasthe*).

Secondly, it has already been mentioned that the Pharisaic movement wanted to take the temple practices to the entire people. Josephus mentions that they were "extremely influential among the general public [*tois te dêmois*]." Again, compared to the Sadducees, who were relatively few and mainly located in Jerusalem, the Pharisees were quite popular. Josephus even states that whenever Sadducees assume some office, they submit to the principles of the Pharisees, since otherwise the masses would not tolerate them. This is reminiscent of the ending of one of the synoptic parables (Mark 12:12; cf. Matt 21:45f., and Luke 20:19): "When they realized that he had told the parable against them, they wanted to arrest him, but they feared the crowd. So they left him and went away" (see chapter 10 in this book).

Thirdly, the Pharisees were trailblazers in terms of the scriptural hermeneutics now known as the Dual Torah—that is, that alongside the Written Torah (Scripture) there is also an Oral Torah that was eventually written down and is now known as the earliest layers of the rabbinic literature (Mishnah, Tosefta, Talmud, and Midrashim). In the New Testament, this early form of Oral Torah is known as "the traditions of the elders" (*hê paradosis tôn presbyterôn*; cf. Matt 15:2 and Mark 7:5). The Sadducees, in contradistinction, had a narrow definition of Scripture: probably only the Pentateuch. Given that Jesus, according to the New Testament Gospels, frequently *quotes* scriptural verses also outside of the Pentateuch, and that he insists on *interpreting* Scripture, he is undoubtedly closer to the Pharisaic movement than to, for example, the Sadducees.

Fourthly, whereas the Pharisees in numerous Christian sermons have been presented as exceptionally *harsh* in their applications of the commandments in Scripture, a growing number of scholars are now inclined to argue that the Pharisees were known for their hermeneutical *leniency*, especially compared to the Qumran community (from which the Dead Sea Scrolls stem). It is likely that the Pharisees were considered by the Qumran sectarians to be "seekers of smooth things" (*dorshei ha-chalaqot*): they were accused of interpreting the commandments too *lightly*.[47] One is reminded of the saying attributed to Jesus that his yoke is easy, and his burden is light (Matt 11:30).

Fifthly and finally, given that both the Jesus movement and the Pharisaic philosophy (1) believed in an afterlife; (2) sought to bring the spiritual treasures of the temple to the people, also in faraway Galilee; and (3) articulated a scriptural hermeneutics that expanded beyond the texts of the Pentateuch—is it remarkable that Jesus so often engaged precisely with the Pharisees? After all, of all the philosophical and theological fractions of his time, *the one closest to the Jesus movement seems to have been the Pharisaic school*. And is not this affinity also, at least partly, a reason for the many harsh and bitter accusations in the gospel tradition against the Pharisees? Now, if this line of thought is correct, then the starting point for the increasing denigration of the Pharisees in both the texts and in Christian tradition is quite simply *that the two groups had exceptionally much in common, not that they were outstandingly different*. Here one is reminded of the Freudian concept *Narzissmus der kleinen Differenzen* (narcissism of

Introduction

small differences), which suggests that the more two individuals or groups have in common, the more likely it is that their small differences are emphasized.[48]

Thus far, we have seen that the predominantly negative portrayal of Pharisaism in Christian teaching and preaching is built on a quite devastating misrepresentation of the *historical* Pharisees. Interestingly enough, it has been suggested that this misrepresentation can be detected not only in the *reception history* of the New Testament but also in its *prehistory*. Probably the most illuminating example is Luke 16:14f.:

> The Pharisees, who were lovers of money [*philargyroi*], heard all this [i.e., the teachings of Jesus], and they ridiculed him [i.e., Jesus]. So he said to them, "You are those who justify yourselves [*hoi dikaiountes heautous*] in the sight of others; but God knows your hearts; for what is prized by human beings is an abomination in the sight of God."

Many years ago, T. W. Manson suggested that this saying originally referred to the Sadducees rather than the Pharisees, since the Sadducees "held the great vested interests."[49] Furthermore, there may be a wordplay here: the three letters *tzadeh*, *dalet*, and *qoph* form the root of both "Sadducees" and "justified" (Hebrew: *tzaddiqim*). Hence, it is possible that we can detect a Semitic wordplay under the surface of the Greek text. This saying of the Lukan Jesus is preceded by the parable of the unjust steward who swindles his master, the conclusion of which is that one should use the mammon in this world in such a way that one will be welcomed into the dwellings that are everlasting (see chapter 13). Now, since the Sadducees did not believe in the world to come, this comment would have been particularly provocative for them.[50] Manson reconstructs the message in this saying in the following way:

> "You are the people, who by taking the name 'Sadducee,' make public claim to be the party of righteousness." But God looks deeper than party labels, and knows that the name does not correspond to any real righteousness within.[51]

Manson's conjecture may not convince everyone. If he is correct, however, then this Lukan text is an example of the shift of focus *already in the Synoptic Gospels* from several Jewish groups in late second-temple Judaism to only one: the Pharisees. If so, then this would also strengthen the quite obvious deduction that, in the New Testament, not all the blameworthy were Pharisees and not all Pharisees were blameworthy.

We have pointed out that the depiction of Pharisees seldom has been detached from the way Jews in general have been described, which takes us to the next challenge. It is time to turn to the Fourth Gospel, the Gospel of John, and its most particular and peculiar way of using a term that is often translated precisely as "Jews."

The Second Challenge: "Jews" in the Gospel of John

The Gospel of John is known for its many ambiguities: it speaks of both what is revealed and what is concealed; Clement of Alexandria called it "a spiritual gospel" (Greek: *pneumatikon...euangelion*), and it simultaneously articulates incarnational theology (i.e., that "the Word became *flesh*") more than the other Gospels (see chapter 20); it solemnly declares that God loves the world, but the disciples are encouraged not to do the same; and whereas for numerous readers the Gospel of John is genuinely comforting, quite a few find it disturbing, one major reason being the way *hoi Ioudaioi*—habitually translated as "the Jews"—are depicted.[52] This list could certainly be longer, but hopefully these examples illuminate that there are numerous ambiguities in this text, and it is likely that the author *deliberately* wrote the text in this way. Hence, ambiguities form an important part of the author's pedagogical strategy. In other words, the author's wish to nurture the disciples who read the text cannot be separated from the ambiguities in the text. One is reminded of Carl Gustav Jung's statement that we become more mature as human beings when we acknowledge the ambiguities in life.[53] Misunderstandings in this Gospel are part of the learning process, and they help the readers reach higher levels of understanding and gain new insights. We should not expect epistemological consistency to be a Johannine trademark.

With this in mind we pursue the peculiar usage of the expression *hoi Ioudaioi* in this Gospel. In his article "New Testament" in the *Jewish Encyclopedia*, Kaufmann Kohler famously described the Gospel of John as "a gospel of Christian love and of Jew hatred"—and the Gospel's usage of *hoi Ioudaioi* is undoubtedly part of the problem.[54] As Adele Reinhartz writes in one of her books on the Gospel of John: "Each of the seventy references to 'the Jews' in the Gospel of John felt like a slap in the face."[55]

There are as many as seventy occurrences of the term *hoi Ioudaioi* (in various inflected forms) in the Gospel of John. Given that the expression

Introduction

only occurs sixteen times in the three Synoptic Gospels all together (and—noteworthy—never from the lips of Jesus), its ubiquity in the Fourth Gospel calls out for an interpretation.[56] Hence, every introduction to the Gospel of John must address this issue: how are we to understand this Gospel's particular and peculiar usage of *hoi Ioudaioi*? There are several ways to interpret this term, five of which will be presented and discussed briefly.

(a) **Racism:** It may strike us as offensive to use this word when describing the first interpretation, but it is a matter of fact that modern racial-biological discourse, when referring to Christian sources, has frequently quoted the Gospel of John, especially 8:44, where, to our astonishment, we read that the father of the Jews is the devil (see chapter 22). However, we must also stress that such an understanding of *hoi Ioudaioi* is anachronistic (i.e., a chronological misplacing). Racial classifications of Jews belong to later ages—probably first discernable in Spain after the rise to power in 1492 of Ferdinand II of Aragon and Isabella I of Castile, when Jews had to choose between baptism, exile, or death.[57] And, as is well known, the racialized discourse gained territory in the nineteenth and twentieth centuries, especially during the Third Reich era. To read this kind of programmatic racism into the New Testament texts is simply anachronistic.

However, ethnicity was one of the dimensions of Judaism in antiquity. Jews worshiped the God of Israel; they had their own Scriptures and their own languages: Hebrew and also Aramaic (even though some other ethnic groups spoke this language). But these characteristics did not separate Jesus and his disciples *from* Judaism—instead, they made clear that it was an intra-Jewish phenomenon. All the first members of the Jesus movement, obviously, were Jews. So why would this group of Jews lock the doors "for fear of the Jews" (20:19)? D. Moody Smith correctly concludes when analyzing the Johannine usage of *hoi Ioudaioi*, "Jesus and his disciples are not among 'the Jews,' although they are plainly Jewish."[58] Furthermore, the message in 4:22 is that "salvation is from the Jews," but five chapters later it is stated that the parents of the blind man are afraid of "the Jews" (9:22), although nothing in the text suggests that they themselves are not Jews. In short, the first approach is inadequate as it does not help us understand the Johannine usage of the word.

(b) **Religious affiliation:** We may be tempted to take for granted that the term simply refers to their theological provenance: today we habitually speak of people who identify themselves with, for example, the Jewish, Christian, or Muslim religious traditions. However, this, too, is an anachronistic approach. Although we see signs in the Gospel of John of the gradual separation between what we *now* know as Judaism and Christianity, the text was written far too early to allow us to think of them as two separate religious systems. It is hardly convincing to state that a first-century audience would be inclined to think of Christ-believing Jews as less "Jewish" than other Jews. It was scarcely their understanding of Jesus of Nazareth that defined their Jewishness.

(c) **Region:** Malcolm Lowe has suggested that the expression be understood in terms of the regional antagonism between people stemming from Galilee in the north and those from Judea in the South.[59] Hence, Lowe argues that *hoi Ioudaioi* be translated as "the Judeans." This is an interesting proposition, and it seems to be applicable in many of the seventy cases in the Gospel of John, although not in all of them, the most famous being the question of the Samaritan woman in 4:9, upon hearing the dialect of Jesus, *the Galilean*: "How is it that you, a Jew, ask a drink of me, a woman of Samaria?" That people in Jerusalem could detect a Galilean dialect is indicated in the Gospels (Matt 26:73, Mark 14:70, and Luke 22:59) as well as in Acts (2:7).

(d) **Ruling class:** It has also been suggested that the term refers primarily to the religious establishment in Jerusalem. Franz Mussner writes, "In the expression 'the Jews,' so often weighted in the Gospel of John with a negative accent, it is the opponents of Jesus from the leading class, especially the chief priests, who are thought of."[60] Similarly, D. Moody Smith concludes, "'The Jews' is, then, a term used of a group of *Jewish leaders* who exercise great authority among their compatriots and are especially hostile to Jesus and his disciples."[61] If so, then it is quite clearly inadequate to mechanically interpret *hoi Ioudaioi* as "the Jews," since the leaders were not more "Jewish" than the people in general. At the same time, it is also quite clear that the expression does not always refer to members of the leading class; if so, why would the Samaritan woman use this very expression in 4:9 in her interlocution with Jesus, who was not of the leading class?

Introduction

(e) **Rhetoric of rejection:** The last interpretation presented here thinks of it as primarily a *rhetorical term of rejection*: that is, *hoi Ioudaioi* are those who, by definition, are wrong. They are no more or less "Jewish" (in the parlance of our time) than the other characters in the narrative. What makes them different is simply that they do not agree with the core convictions of John's Christ-believing movement in the true identity of Jesus of Nazareth. Robert Kysar, calling it a "stereotype of rejection," writes, *"Any person who refuses to accept the human identity proposed by Christ in the Gospel is for the evangelist a 'Jew.'"*[62] Arguably, in this view, the opposite of *hoi Ioudaioi* are "Israelites," as in 1:47 in which it is stated: "When Jesus saw Nathanael coming toward him, he said of him, 'Here is truly an Israelite in whom there is no deceit!'"[63]

Whereas the first two interpretations are inadequate explanations, the last three mentioned are more helpful when seeking to understand the Gospel of John. It is perhaps most likely to conclude that *hoi Ioudaioi* in John is a combination of the three remaining explanations: firstly, given that the Jesus movement started in Galilee and that the Master was executed by the Romans in Jerusalem in Judaea, the text may give vent to certain frictions between Galileans and Judeans; secondly, all Gospels suggest that the Romans collaborated with the ruling class in Jerusalem in various issues, including the series of events that led to the crucifixion of Jesus, although, of course, it was the Romans who executed him; and, thirdly, *hoi Ioudaioi* in the Fourth Gospel represent, undoubtedly, theological adversaries. Indeed, if only one explanation were to be promoted, it would probably be the fifth: any person who does not believe in the Christ in the way the Johannine Christ-followers did was a "Jew."

Given that *hoi Ioudaioi* does not mean "Jews" as we understand and use that word today, how, then, are we to translate this Greek word? Indeed, almost the only thing that we can establish with some certainty is that to translate the term as "Jews" would be wrong. Not only would it be *incorrect*, quite simply because it is a bad translation, but, furthermore, it would also be an incorrect translation that is *iniquitous* because it adds fuel to an antisemitic discourse—both within and outside of Christian milieux.

Most New Testament *scholars* are aware of the shortcomings of simplistically choosing the translation "the Jews," but this insight is not as well known outside of the scholarly ivory tower. For this reason, *priests*, *preachers, and religious educators* have an enormous responsibility in their teaching: they need to find ways to talk about their Jewish Master without blaming his own people. And *all readers* of the New Testament need to be vigilant when referring to and quoting Johannine texts about *hoi Ioudaioi*. They need to learn to listen to their Master's voice without denouncing his people, without whom there would be no Torah, no Psalms, no prophetic writings, indeed no Holy Scriptures at all.

There are no easy answers here, but it is nevertheless imperative to keep posing the crucial question: how are we to translate *hoi Ioudaioi*— and how are we to talk about them when lecturing and preaching on the Gospel of John? Three suggestions may be of some assistance here: firstly, *incarnational theology*—based on the Gospel of John, particularly the Prologue—stresses that "the Word became flesh" (1:14). It is sometimes suggested that this be paraphrased "And the Word became a Jew," emphasizing, as Dorothy Savage states, that "Jesus was shaped by and deeply valued his Judaic religious heritage."[64] The Jewish tradition cherishes the expression *Dibberah Torah ki-leshon benei adam* (The Torah spoke in the language of humans).[65] In a parallel way, Christians need to state more clearly that the Word of God spoke in the language *of the Jewish tradition*. Second-temple Judaism was the historical context of Jesus of Nazareth, not his theological contrast. The persistent endeavor to present Jesus solely in opposition to Judaism smacks of Docetism, to use the terminology for attempts in late antiquity to describe Jesus as only *seemingly* having a human body (cf. Greek: *dokei*, "it seems"). And this takes us to the second suggestion: *biblical scholars* cannot understand his teaching without sufficient knowledge about the Jewish tradition, as D. Moody Smith writes: "The revival of scholarly historical interest in Jesus of Nazareth has for good reason centered upon his Jewishness, that is, upon his rootedness in the traditions of Israel. Apart from that rootedness he cannot be understood."[66]

Finally, the third suggestion takes us back to where we started: the observation that *ambiguities* seem to be part and parcel of John's pedagogy. The text wants its readers to be more mature by learning from numerous ambiguities in the gospel, in its message, and also in our world. We have every reason to believe that readers of the New Testament will become more mature when they start speaking responsibly about the Jewish people.

Introduction

The Third Challenge: The Law in Pauline Theology

On the very first page of his book *The Beginning of the Gospel*, Joshua D. Garroway poses an interesting question: Having disembarked in Neapolis—now known as Cavalla—and walked the Via Egnatia to Philippi, what did Paul preach?[67] To be sure, he was a tentmaker, but it was not primarily to repair and sew tents that he had traveled the long way to Europe. What message did he deliver to Gentile Europeans in response to the vision that Acts reports that he had had that night? "There stood a man of Macedonia, pleading with him and saying, 'Come over to Macedonia and help us'" (16:9). Here the text switches to the first person: "We immediately tried to cross over to Macedonia, being convinced that God had called us to proclaim the good news [*euangelisasthai*] to them" (v. 10). But what was "the good news" (*to euangelion*)?

Now, had Paul been familiar with and were he inspired by Christian preaching throughout history, he would probably have started by informing them that the Jewish tradition had misunderstood God in crucial respects, that *shabbat* (the Jewish day of rest) should not be understood literally, that food regulations (*kashrut*; cf. Yiddish: *kosher*) were to be ignored, that the "Law" is the opposite of the Gospel, that the Jewish Scriptures can only be read Christologically, and that the covenant with the Jewish people had been replaced by a new—and significantly better—covenant with the church. However, Paul was ignorant of all this. Yet, when he wrote the eleventh chapter of the Epistle to the Romans, he seems to have anticipated that Gentile Christ followers gradually would begin to exalt themselves over those who for a much longer time had been engaged in worshiping the God of Israel. But he had neither read Christian books, nor seen church art, nor listened to Christian sermons. His message was different, completely different. His mission was not to teach Europeans that Judaism was so bad that Jesus "had to come" (as the matter is so often expressed); instead, he wanted to announce that the God of Israel at the end of times was reaching out to the Gentiles. They were invited—indeed, encouraged—*as non-Jews* to worship the God of Israel. This is what he calls *to euangelion*—"the good news." If we do not realize this, we completely misunderstand the mission of the earliest Christ followers. But if we begin to grasp what Paul meant, we have far better chances to understand the core not only of the Pauline message but also of the other New Testament writings.

Pauline scholarship is enormous; the modest purpose in this introductory chapter is to highlight three traits of particular importance to the issues that are discussed in the present book: thinking of the Torah, firstly, as a *burden*; secondly, as a set of *boundaries*; or, thirdly, using the Hebrew word for "covenant," as *berit*.[68]

(a) **The Torah as a burden:** This first line of thought presents an apostle who is weighed down with guilt. To previous generations of scholars—not least among those who identified themselves with the Lutheran tradition—it was a given that the pre-Christian Paul was burdened with guilt.[69] With this assumption, Christian faith turns into the very opposite of keeping the *mitzwot* (Hebrew: "commandments") because Christian faith removes the veritable yoke that the Torah constitutes for those who try to keep the commandments.[70] As Fredriksen writes, it has been "a long-standing gentile Christian theological position [that]…'observing the Law'—that is, living according to Jewish ancestral practices—is *intrinsically* incompatible with Christian 'belief.'"[71] According to this line of thought, halakhic Judaism becomes the prototype for the kind of Christian faith that is *undeveloped* (as it is "still" too concerned with the Law), *ungrateful* (because it does not realize what Christ has achieved and has to proffer those who believe in him), and *uncomprehending* (because it, quite frankly, rejects the most important part of the Christian gospel: the alleged deliverance from the unbearable demands of the Jewish Law).[72] In short, Judaism after Jesus is a manifestation of theological insubordination; it is the epitome of religious rebelliousness. In Pamela Eisenbaum's words, Judaism is often presented as "the ultimate paradigm of bad religion."[73]

Krister Stendahl's influential essay, published in English in 1963 (in Swedish already in 1960), on Paul and the introspective conscience of the West was groundbreaking and is still a must read for all who wish to acquaint themselves with Pauline theology.[74] In this article Stendahl famously stated that Paul had "a rather 'robust' conscience."[75] What role, then, does the Torah play in Pauline theology? It is time to focus on the new perspective on Paul.

(b) **The Torah as boundaries:** A growing number of scholars seek to do justice to first-century Judaism by not presenting it as the rhetorical and gloomy background to early Christianity. The article

Introduction

on "the new perspective" by James D. G. Dunn, published in 1983, was therefore due to come and was a most welcome correction of much of what previously had been written in Pauline scholarship.[76] It is a great advantage that the Torah nowadays is less often described as some sort of juggernaut that crushes people beneath its unbearable weight. Today most Pauline scholars are aware of the apologetic concerns that characterized and constrained earlier scholarship. The supporters of the new perspective focus on the Torah as a set of identity markers, which thereby become a theological obstacle because they lead to exclusivism. *Berit milah* (the covenant of [male] circumcision), *shabbat*, *kashrut*, and others—these commandments are excluding because they set up a wall of separation between Jews and non-Jews. In short, according to the new perspective, Jewish *halakhah* is insufficient not so much because it constitutes a *burden* but because it creates unnecessary *boundaries* between people and peoples. Hence, according to this second line of thought, by breaking down barriers and crossing boundaries, Paul establishes a religious movement characterized by boundlessness.

Now, understanding Torah as primarily a set of identity markers, which provides Israel with social boundaries, is certainly not *incorrect*, but it is *incomplete* when seeking to do justice to Jewish self-understanding and to comprehend the mission of Paul. If it were true that Paul wanted to break down barriers between Jews and Gentiles and, therefore, went into a theological battle against Jewish *halakhah* (which will be contested in the present study), we have to keep in mind that he most certainly reinstated exclusiveness, albeit in a new form: were not Christ belief and baptism new criteria when separating insiders from outsiders?[77]

All this is to say that we need a third perspective, which sometimes is called "the radical new perspective" on Paul—as it is grateful to the promoters of the new perspective, but, nevertheless, seeks to formulate Pauline theology in an alternative way that furthers our understanding of first-century Judaism and earliest Christianity.[78] The Torah to Paul is not a *burden*, nor is it primarily a *boundary*, but something else; it is an expression of covenantal particularity and a sign of the covenant: *berit*.

(c) The Torah as "berit": In his groundbreaking scholarship on Paul, Stendahl stressed that Paul's self-understanding must be

the cornerstone of modern attempts to reconstruct his theology. How did Paul understand himself? An important component of Stendahl's reconstruction is, firstly, that Paul describes himself in his letters as "an apostle of the Gentiles" (*ethnôn apostolos*; Rom 11:13), who was sent specifically "to the nations" (*eis ta ethnê*; Gal 2:8). Secondly, Stendahl emphasizes that Paul, when describing his experience on the way to Damascus, uses a terminology from the prophetic texts in the Scriptures. Hence, his experience should be classified as a *calling* rather than a *conversion*. As Fredriksen writes, "Paul held these convictions as a committed Jew, and he *enacted* them as a committed Jew. In brief,…Paul lived his life entirely within his native Judaism."[79] Someone who converts exchanges one religious system for another, but the person who is called receives a special assignment—and Paul was convinced that his mission was to bring Christ, with an emphasis on the meaning of his life and death, to the nations. This means that the relationship between people and peoples—between the people of Israel and the nations of the world—is of utmost importance.

Stendahl states that if we are looking for a hermeneutical focal point in his epistle to the Romans, it is not to be found in the first chapters as so often has been assumed but rather in chapters 9—11. In his book *Final Account*, Stendahl writes, "I am convinced that Pauline theology has its organizing center in Paul's apostolic perception of his mission to the Gentiles."[80] In other words, according to Stendahl, Paul is first and foremost a theologian who reflects on the relations between the people and the peoples: If the Torah is given to Israel and to Israel only, and if the Torah constitutes and defines Jewish life with its commands and prohibitions, what then is the meaning of Christ offering the nations a covenantal relationship with the God of Israel? The Pauline discourse of justification by faith—which is extraordinarily influential in church history—cannot be isolated from his mission and work. Pagans are offered a relationship with God, not defined by the Jewish Law but through faith in Christ—or perhaps, better expressed, *through the faithfulness of Christ* (Greek: *pistis Christou*).[81] Stendahl quite correctly points out that the Law is not associated with a discourse of conscience and guilt but with covenantal theology. According to this third

Introduction

line of thought, the Torah is not to be described as a *burden* to the halakhic person, nor primarily as a set of *boundaries* (even if this is a more relevant description), but rather, once again using the Hebrew word for "covenant": *berit*. In short, observing the commandments is not a desperate attempt to please God; it is a way to respond to a gracious God who is active in this world and who reaches out to people. When reading the Pauline epistles, one must remember that the word *Torah* in the Jewish tradition does not stand for a problem to be solved, but a life to be lived. Torah is an inherently positive concept.

Historically, New Testament scholars, especially within a Protestant context, have tended to argue that the Law fosters an attitude of egotism and arrogance. But the vast majority of religious Jews throughout history take for granted that it is quite the opposite: studying and adhering to the Torah cultivate people to become better persons. One need only consult how the Jewish tradition usually describes Moses, and how Jewish commentaries elaborate verses such as Numbers 12:3: "Now the man Moses was very humble [*'anaw meod*], more so than anyone else on the face of the earth."[82]

The consequences of the third line of thought are far-reaching, primarily because it reveals that the distinction in Pauline theology between Jews and Gentiles remains intact, in spite of Paul's belief in Christ. Hence, according to this understanding, *the only thing more obvious than the belief that the covenantal commandments in the Torah address Israel is the notion that these commandments are not addressing Gentiles*. If readers of the New Testament fail to acknowledge this, then their conclusions will no longer be convincing. To repeat, Paul consequently and coherently argued in favor of the assertion that Gentiles remain Gentiles. It is imperative, as Fredriksen writes, to keep in mind that all of Paul's extant letters are addressed to Gentiles: "All of this supposed *Jewish* Law-freeness...rests on inferences drawn from *gentile* Christ-followers' 'Law-freeness'"; "This means that, whatever Paul says about the Law, he says it first of all with reference to gentiles."[83] Paul's theology of the Law actually *upholds* the distinction between Jews and Gentiles by emphasizing the particularity of the commandments in the Torah (because they only apply to Jews), as it is stated in Rom 3:31: "Do we then overthrow [*katargoumen*] the Law by this faith? By no means! On the contrary, we uphold [*histanomen*] the Law."[84]

Returning to our initial question, what did Paul proclaim those first days in Philippi? Of course, we cannot know this, but it is far more likely that he taught non-Jews about faith in the God of Israel: how this God of Israel had revealed Godself throughout history, and covenantally embraced the people of Israel in both the Land and the Diaspora, through ups and downs. Although found in the writings of another New Testament author, the conclusion of Simeon's hymn "Nunc Dimittis"—which millions and millions of Christians pray every evening—expresses this Pauline perspective: Paul's eyes had seen the salvation that God has prepared for all peoples, a light for revelation to the nations and glory to the Jewish people (cf. Luke 2:30–32). The third interpretation argues that this complementarity—that Christ conveys both a light to the nations and glory to the people Israel—was a theological given not only for Luke but also for Paul. After all, that is far more likely than the tentmaker doing the opposite: teaching non-Jews about alleged shortcomings of Jews and the Jewish tradition. In short, Paul did not cross sea and land to proclaim that God had relinquished Israel—and nor would he want his followers to teach this.[85]

The Fourth Challenge: The "New Covenant" in the Epistle to the Hebrews

One of the biblical texts most often referred to in discussions about how Christians ought to think of Christianity in relation to Judaism is the Epistle to the Hebrews.[86] There is no single text in the New Testament that to a greater degree than Hebrews has cemented the notion that Judaism and Christianity can and should be described as two covenants, and that the new covenant is *better* than the previous one.[87] It is perhaps not surprising: after all, the Greek word *diathêkê* (covenant) occurs thirty-three times in the New Testament, fourteen of which are in Hebrews: in other words, almost half of all occurrences are found in this single book. And the word *kreittôn* (better) occurs nineteen times in the New Testament, of which thirteen are in Hebrews. If the main purpose of the text is to compare Christianity to Judaism, is it then so far-fetched to draw the conclusion that Christianity is a better religion than Judaism? Indeed, does it not explicitly state in 8:13 that "in speaking of 'a new covenant,' he [i.e., God] has made the first one obsolete. And what is obsolete and growing old will soon disappear"?[88] At a first glance, this may seem to be a comparison between

Introduction

Judaism and Christianity.[89] And indeed, in the scholarly and ecclesiastical endeavor to uncover an early Christian hermeneutics that is non-supersessionist, the interpretation of Hebrews seems to be one of few exceptions: Jews, Christians, scholars, people in the pulpit and in the pew—they all seem to agree that Hebrews is a supersessionist text. But would it not be strange if such an early text—probably written around the fall of the second temple in 70 CE—expressed the programmatic and problematic supersessionist theology that came to be developed only later, when it was possible to consider and describe Judaism and Christianity as two sharply defined religions? Have we sufficiently considered that this is a text written *before* they were perceived as two different religious systems?

A circumstance that has contributed to this text being read timelessly—by which we mean anachronistically—is that we know so little about its historical context. Probably, Hebrews was originally a sermon, noteworthy for its elegant Greek and rhetoric, eventually edited in order to fit the format of an epistle, but that is far from the only suggestion.[90] Hence, we can only conjecture by whom, to whom, when, where, and why it was written. Origen famously stated that "who wrote the epistle, truly only God knows."[91] Introductory essays to Hebrews tend to suggest that it was probably written between 60 and 90 CE and that it has something to do with Italy (see 13:24)—but that is all![92] This lack of even a minimum of historical knowledge has probably contributed to the mainstream interpretation: that Hebrews is the first example of the Christian supersessionism that later would determine so much of Jewish-Christian relations. In other words, it is more often presented as a lucid first volume in Christian dogmatics than as an enigmatic New Testament text.

So what to make of the word *covenant* in Hebrews? Christians are so used to referring to the Jewish Bible as "the Old Testament" and Judaism as "the old covenant" that they might not be able to see what the author here actually has in view. But at the time of the composition of Hebrews, "the old covenant" could not be a technical term for second-temple Judaism.

As we shall see, it is crucial to note that the "new covenant" for the anonymous author of Hebrews belongs to the future because Hebrews is far more *eschatological* than most biblical scholars and numerous readers of the Bible have realized and taken into consideration. This is not a farfetched proposition: if both the oldest *letters* (written by Paul) and the oldest *gospels* (the synoptic tradition) are eschatological—then why should not the oldest preserved Christian *sermon* (Hebrews) also be eschatological? As Marie E. Isaacs writes, "Like Deuteronomy (Deut 12:9), its author addresses his readers as those who stand on the very brink of entry into that promised land (Heb 3:12–4:14)."[93] In short, they are very close to the destination of their journey, but they are not yet there.

Hebrews presupposes the dialectics between the present and the future: we now live in "the time that is" ([*parabolēn*] *eis ton kairon ton enestēkota*; Heb 9:9), and the author longs for "[until] the time for a better order" (*mechri kairou diorthōseōs epikeimena*; Heb 9:10). The heavenly service, in which Jesus Christ serves as high priest, is already in progress, which is invisible to human eyes, inaudible to human ears, and incomprehensible to human thoughts. But the time of the new era has not yet completely broken. In the words of Peter J. Tomson: "The 'new covenant,' if we may thus accentuate it, is valid only in heaven, not yet upon earth. The 'good things,' of which Christ is the direct image, are yet to come."[94]

It is also crucial to note how the verb *palaioun* ("to grow old") is used. The verb occurs three times in the New Testament: once in the Gospel of Luke and twice in Hebrews. (1) The Lukan Jesus encourages his disciples in 12:33 to sell what they have and give alms, so that they provide themselves with money bags that "do not grow old" (*mē palaioumena*), a treasure in the heavens, that does not fail as do earthly goods. Hence, in Luke this verb is set in a comparison between earthly possessions (that are perishable) and the heavenly treasure (that never grows old). (2) Hebrews 1:10–12 quotes Psalm 102:26–28, where God is praised for the creation, which, although breathtakingly splendid, will one day perish: it will "wear out" (*palaiōthēsontai*) like clothing.[95] The verb is used to describe the frangibility and limitations of this world. (3) Finally, in Hebrews 8:13 it is anticipated that the old covenant "will soon disappear" (*engys aphanismou*). Is not the most plausible interpretation that the author here, too, articulates the belief that one day this world will "grow old"—only God will remain? If yes, then this verse is an expression of an intense eschatological longing for the future, for a complete and perfected world. And if yes, is it not a tragic irony that so many Christians have inverted the meaning in these two passages in Hebrews, to wit, that God actually changes, since God is understood as someone who prefers newer religion to older religion, wishing that the latter would soon disappear? This is, as a matter of fact, the opposite message from the book's own assertion: "But you [God] are the same, and your years will never end" (Heb 1:11).

It has already been accentuated that it would thus be anachronistic to assume that what is compared in Hebrews is Christianity and Judaism (at a time when they were not yet regarded as differentiated religions). Instead,

Introduction

the future and the perfect are compared to the earthly and the fragmentary. In short, what is being compared is heaven and earth—and the author of Hebrews states, not surprisingly, that the heavenly is perfect and that the earthly is deficient. *The new is better than the old because the Kingdom of Heaven is better than earthly life.*

Hence, it is not plausible that Hebrews 8:13 seeks to predict the fall of the temple (if written before 70 CE). Nor is it likely that it gives vent to theological *Schadenfreude* (if written post–70 CE). But it is all the more likely that it articulates a profoundly eschatological expectation. The message in Hebrews is hardly that Christian services are "better" than those that take place in synagogues, but that the celestial service is heavenly compared to earthly—more or less mundane—services.

This line of thought is presented in more detail in my chapter in the collection of essays *Christ Jesus and the Jewish People Today*.[96] As a matter of fact, this interpretation of Hebrews has become relatively influential, as shown by the eighteenth paragraph in a Roman Catholic document from 2015 called "The Gifts and the Calling of God Are Irrevocable," which is a quotation from Romans 11:29 and also the cornerstone in the fourth paragraph of *Nostra Aetate*:

> At issue in the Epistle to the Hebrews is not the contrast of the Old and New Covenants as we understand them today, nor a contrast between the church and Judaism. Rather, the contrast is between the eternal heavenly priesthood of Christ and the transitory earthly priesthood.[97]

In other words, the *comparative ("new" and "better") paradigm* that has governed so much of Jewish-Christian relations is based on a flawed reading of Hebrews, failing to take into consideration the role of the early Christian apocalypticism when interpreting this text. All of the above leads to three recommendations that hopefully will help us read Hebrews responsibly and well.

(a) *The need to rediscover the pilgrimage motif in the Bible in general, and in Hebrews, in particular*: Christians who look upon themselves as pilgrims are reminded that they have not yet reached their destination, that they are still on their way, and that they do not have all the answers. One famous example of a theological peregrination is *Pilgrim's Progress* by John Bunyan (1628–88). Another example is Ernst Käsemann's *Das wandernde*

Gottesvolk, written while he was in prison in 1937 for insubordination (having given a sermon on Isaiah 26:13: "O Lord, our God, other lords besides you have ruled over us, but we acknowledge your name alone"). He argues that the wandering of the people of God is the principal motif in Hebrews: "*the form of existence in time appropriate to the recipient of the revelation can only be that of wandering,*" and he ends his book with the statement that "*all the utterances in Hebrews…take their basis… from the motif of the wandering people of God.*"[98] A third example is an article by William G. Johnsson on the pilgrimage motif in Hebrews.[99] Fourthly and finally, Richard B. Hays describes the "remarkably open-ended eschatology" in Hebrews:

> …those who know that they have no lasting city are likely to recognize that they themselves stand under impending judgment. Perhaps they are also more likely to recognize the provisional character of their own understanding and to acknowledge that God's ultimate redemptive grace may yet hold surprises.[100]

(b) *The importance of reading Hebrews holistically*: it seems reasonable to argue that the author of Hebrews is no less eschatological in chapters 8 and 9 than in chapters 11—13. We often read the concluding chapters of Hebrews eschatologically, forward-oriented. One particularly forward-looking verse is 13:14: "Here we have no lasting city, but we are looking for the city that is to come" (*tēn mellousan* [i.e., *polin*]).

This is also the perspective in, for example, 11:16: "But as it is, they desire a better country, that is, a heavenly one….God… has prepared a city for them." Whereas chapter 8 is often read with a polemical agenda, other chapters are read in a parenetical context, say, at funerals.[101] This observation should give us pause.

(c) *Noting what is being compared in Hebrews*: There is certainly a comparison in this sermonic epistle, and something is "better" (*kreittōn*) than something else—*but it is not Judaism and Christianity that the author compares*. As has been underlined repeatedly in this chapter, it is simply anachronistic to require that first-century Christ followers were able to discern two distinct religious traditions. Instead, the comparison is between

Introduction

what is now and what shall one day be, and between what is visible and what is invisible—and not only a staunch Platonist, such as the author of Hebrews, would state that the heavenly service must be better (*kreittôn*) than the ones on earth. As Clark M. Williamson and Ronald J. Allen write:

> Heaven is a place of perfection, which in this sermon [i.e., Hebrews] refers to immediate access to God. To be perfected is to be in the full, immediate presence of God. The earth is a realm of imperfection in which access to God is partial and available only through intermediaries.[102]

Needless to say, an eschatological reading of Hebrews does not answer all questions. Rather, it adds a new question: *how on earth are we to read the text*? The answer is that *on earth* we should read it as we read eschatological statements in the Pauline epistles. Paul, too, thought that the end of the world was imminent; he, too, thought that he belonged to the last generation. He, too, longed to depart and to be with Christ, as he writes: "for that is far better" (*pollô[i] gar mallon kreisson*; Phil 1:23).

Indeed, when listening to the voice of the Hebrews—without presupposing supersessionism belonging to later generations of Christ followers—we hear in the oldest Christian sermon that has been preserved for posterity what we are already familiar with when listening to Paul and other voices in the New Testament: a yearning for a world that is better (*kreittôn*) than this world. In one word, this is how we should read Hebrews on earth.

These, we are inclined to argue, are the four fundamental challenges: problematic presuppositions about *Pharisees*, *Jews*, *the Law*, and *the new covenant*. They will reappear several times in the following thirty chapters. Hopefully this introduction may serve as a sea chart because now is the time to set sail, and to set out on the seven seas—with the sea chart in hand: bon voyage!

1
WHO IS HEEDING THE TEACHING OF JOHN THE BAPTIST?

Matt 3:1–10, Mark 1:2–6, and Luke 3:1–9
(cf. John 1:19–23; see chapter 22)

All four New Testament evangelists begin their narratives about the adult Jesus with him encountering John the Baptist in the Jordan Valley.[1] All three Synoptics—Matthew, Mark, and Luke—recount that many went into the desert in order to be baptized, but it is only in the Matthean and Lukan versions that John the Baptist exclaims, "You brood of vipers!…and do not presume to say to yourselves, we have Abraham as our father."[2] As a matter of fact, the passage to which this outburst belongs is almost identical in Matthew and Luke: out of sixty-three words in Matthew and sixty-four in Luke, sixty are in common.[3]

What is the reason for the infamous words of John the Baptist in the Matthean and Lukan narratives? There are several lines of thought in the interpretations of this particular passage, four of which will be presented here, ranging from *contrast and conflict* to *context and continuity*:

(a) Harsh words are necessary: The chilling image "brood of vipers" is used two additional times in Matthew, uttered by the Matthean Jesus with reference to either Pharisees (12:34) or both scribes and Pharisees (23:33). It has been suggested that the expression refers to a popular belief that newborn vipers ate through their mother's stomach, thereby killing her.[4]

Characteristic for the first interpretation is the assumption not only that John the Baptist and Jesus of Nazareth in the Gospels have an identical understanding of the Pharisees and the Sadducees but also that the words are justified. Quite simply, they are harsh because there is a reason to be harsh. An example is a website called gotquestions.org, which provides an answer to the question "Why did John the Baptist refer to the Pharisees as a brood of vipers?"

> The Pharisees and Sadducees were the religious leaders in Israel during the time of John the Baptist and Jesus. The Pharisees were the Law-keepers and promoters of tradition, and the Sadducees comprised the wealthier ruling class. Over the centuries, these well-meaning groups had become corrupt, legalistic, and hypocritical and would eventually be responsible for crucifying the Son of God. They earned their label "brood of vipers," a sobriquet with deeper meaning than is obvious at first glance. The viper was seen to be an evil creature. Its venom was deadly, and it was also devious—the viper that bit Paul was hiding in the firewood (Acts 28:3). The Hebrew Scriptures, which the Pharisees knew well, associate the serpent with Satan in Genesis 3. For John to call the Pharisees a "brood of vipers" implies that they bore satanic qualities. This idea is clearly stated by Jesus in John 8:44, where He says the unbelieving Jews "belong to [their] father, the devil."[5]

This sweeping and far-reaching quotation prompts three comments. Firstly, we note that the Sadducees are gradually marginalized. Although Sadducees and scribes are also called "brood of vipers" in the Gospel of Matthew, here the Pharisees become the *summa summarum* of various Jewish groups at the time of Jesus. They are perceived as *the* typical Jewish group. Secondly, John the Baptist and Jesus of Nazareth speak with one voice when it comes to the deficiencies of the Jewish leadership at that time. No distinctions are made between them in this respect. Thirdly, the website does not hesitate to claim that the Pharisees bore "satanic qualities," adding John 8:44—where it is stated that the father of "the Jews" is the devil—as proof for this allegation. But as a matter of fact, the Pharisees are not mentioned at all in John 8:31–59 (see chapter 22 in this book). In short, the website takes for granted that Jesus not only seconds the teaching of John the Baptist but also extends it to refer to "the Jews" (see introduction, second challenge).

This first line of thought often seems to take an apologetic stance, by defending the harsh words uttered by John the Baptist, and taking for granted that they are necessary not only because of alleged shortcomings of a few individuals but also due to a much more fundamental religious dilemma in the Jewish tradition. Some readers of these texts seem to operate on various levels, oscillating between the teachings of John the Baptist and Christian teaching about Jesus of Nazareth, so that the discussion is less about John's baptism but all the more about *Christian* teaching on *Christian* baptism and a confession to Jesus as the *Christ*. Blurring this distinction invites anachronistic approaches to the texts, an error that all historians should seek to avoid. Indeed, at times one may even discern a shift of emphasis that takes us away from the original intra-Jewish context, perhaps because John's words are fused with Christian teaching on original sin and redemption—that is, the necessity for everyone to recognize the need to repent from a non-*Christian* worldview, convert to *Christianity*, and undergo a *Christian* baptism. And at the same time, paradoxically, Christianity can be portrayed as a phenomenon outside of the religious world: "All religion attempts to constrain God by means of magic, ritual, amulets, as well as by sacrifice, prayers, and sacraments, or, as here, by scrupulous fulfillment of the Law."[6] In this quotation, Eduard Schweizer seems to imply that even if those who went into the desert actually lived in accordance with the commandments in the Torah, it would not have been considered virtuous. This prompts the question: are harsh words necessary merely because the characters in the narrative were not Christians?

(b) The Pharisees and the Sadducees were not willing to be baptized: When analyzing the Matthean text, some commentators ask why a number of Pharisees and Sadducees went out into the desert to the river Jordan where John the Baptist was baptizing.[7]

In Greek it says that they went there *epi to baptisma*. It is not quite clear what the preposition *epi* followed by the accusative case means here. It could simply imply that they went there "because of the baptism," but it is also possible to discern some form of hesitance: maybe they merely went there "in order to inspect the baptism," or perhaps they even went there "against the baptism."[8] In other words, it is quite possible that Matthew wants to emphasize that they had no intention to undergo baptism, and that is what spurred the harsh words. However, W. D. Davies and Dale C. Allison correctly point out that "the Baptist's words would not then hit their mark so well since they seem to be aimed at those seeking some benefit from baptism; but this inconcinnity could be the outcome of imperfect editing."[9]

As mentioned above, there are several ways to translate the Greek preposition *epi* into English. An illuminating example can be found in Revelation 7:1. (Although the Greek in Revelation is not always consistent with other parts of the New Testament, this example may nevertheless be illustrative of how the Greek preposition *epi* is translated into English.)

> After this I saw four angels standing *at* [*epi* + accusative] the four corners of the earth, holding back the four winds of the earth so that no wind could blow *on* [*epi* + genitive] earth or *at* [*epi* + genitive] sea or *against* [*epi* + accusative] any tree.

In other words, the interpretation that some of the Pharisees and the Sadducees sought out John the Baptist only because they were hostile to him and his baptism cannot be based on the preposition *epi* alone. Matthew *may* have wanted to emphasize that some of the Pharisees and the Sadducees merely approached John the Baptist in order to inspect and survey, not in order to be baptized by him—and that it was this attitude that sparked John the Baptist's criticism and his harsh words. But it is also possible that Matthew meant that they went there because they wanted to be granted some form of benefit from his baptism.

(c) Evolving anti-Jewish hermeneutics: A recurring theme in the present book is that there was a trajectory of accumulating anti-Judaism during the first centuries of the Christian tradition, and that this development can be detected already within the New Testament. The depiction of John the Baptist's teaching in the Gospels is an illuminating example of this trajectory.

In the Markan version the people that went into the desert came from "the whole Judean countryside" (*pasa hê Ioudaia chôra*), and "all the Jerusalemites" (*hoi Hierosolymitai pantes*) were going out to him, and were baptized by him in the river Jordan, confessing their sins. Nothing suggests that the words *pasa* ([the] whole) and *pantes* (all) are used in order to emphasize an excessive depravity; rather, these terms are an expression of the people's belief in and their willingness to take part in the eschatological drama that unfolded at that time. Those who only read Mark do not encounter the harsh expression "brood of vipers."

In contrast, the Matthean version articulates an explicit criticism of many of the Pharisees and Sadducees who went into the desert: the image "you brood of vipers" refers to them. Finally, the Lukan version goes one step further. When comparing Matthew 3:7 and Luke 3:7, we note that whereas the Matthean version criticizes only "many Pharisees and Sadducees," the Lukan version directs this accusation against the crowd (*hoi ochloi*)—that is, it is no longer a matter of the religious leadership or certain religious factions but "people" in general. When comparing the depictions of this story in the Synoptic Gospels chronologically, we detect more generalizations and gradually a harsher language when describing Jews and Jewish tradition.

Who Is Heeding the Teaching of John the Baptist?

The phenomenon of an evolving anti-Jewish *Tendenz* is quite striking in this particular passage in the Gospels. For the purpose of this book—namely, reading the New Testament differently—this story in the Synoptic Gospels is something of a textbook example of the trajectory of evolving anti-Jewish descriptions and attitudes. It seems quite clear that the development in the direction of evolving anti-Judaism can already be detected in the New Testament.

This third interpretation studied the Gospels diachronically (through time) and discovered a trajectory of expanding anti-Jewish expressions and formulae. Now what if we went in the opposite direction? What if we went back in time in order to find a theological context that is not anti-Jewish but intra-Jewish? That takes us to the next interpretation.

(d) An intra-Jewish discussion: The fourth interpretation situates John the Baptist's teaching in a Jewish context and suggests that this is a story about the requirements of a Jewish life. It is a matter of one *Jew* urging other *Jews* to live a more authentic *Jewish* life.[10]

E. P. Sanders has coined the expression *covenantal nomism*, which describes the Jewish belief that a Jew is brought into the covenant by God's grace and remains in the covenant through works.[11] God first brought the people out of slavery in Egypt and only then gave them the Torah at Mount Sinai. Living an observant life is a response to God's initial redeeming acts. It is not, as it so often has been portrayed in New Testament scholarship, a futile effort to please a grim God. Such a portrayal of Judaism has more to do with an intra-Christian discourse, especially in the wake of the Reformation.

Quite simply, in this passage John the Baptist does not insist on Jews becoming something else than what they are; rather, they ought to live in accordance with what they already are: Jews called by God to live a Jewish life. The Greek word *metanoia* (and the Hebrew equivalent *teshuvah*), often translated as "repentance," does not imply that John the Baptist propagated an entirely new *Weltanschauung* but rather a return to an authentic life *within* one's own tradition. It is certainly not a matter of converting to a new religion.

A relevant parallel in the rabbinic literature is found in *Mishnah Yoma* 8.9, a tractate that discusses various aspects of forgiveness and reconciliation. (*Yoma* is the Aramaic word for "The Day"—that is, the Day of Atonement, *Yom Kippur* or *Yom ha-Kippurim*):

> [If] a person says: "I will sin and repent, I will sin and repent," it will not be given him an opportunity to repent [*ha-omer echeta wa-ashuv, echeta wa-ashuv, ein maspiqin be-yado la-'asot teshuvah*].

The emphasis here may be on the *repetition*: if a person says the same thing *twice* (on two different occasions?), he will not be forgiven. Or is it the point rather that the person *intentionally* sins, taking for granted that repentance is a possibility? In any case, this statement in the Mishnah provides us with a relevant parallel to the New Testament texts.

Another Jewish notion that may help us situate this story within a Jewish frame of reference is *zekhut avot* (merits of the fathers). This concept refers to the belief that the great deeds of the Hebrew patriarchs—and matriarchs, as many are inclined to add today—influence God's judgment favorably upon the Jewish people.[12]

The apostle Paul takes *zekhut avot* for granted in Romans 9:5 and 11:28 when he lists the grace and gifts that have been entrusted to the Jewish people. W. D. Davies states that while the doctrine perhaps did not play a dominating part in first-century Judaism, it did form a well-defined element in the religious thought of the milieu into which Paul came. He also points out that criticisms were made of the doctrine, and are not the Matthean and Lukan versions of the teaching of John the Baptist examples of this?[13] His teaching is not a rejection of Judaism but a critique of what he believes to be an overemphasis of one particular notion.

Scholarship has recognized the motif of *zekhut avot* in Matthew 3 and Luke 3 but has often tended to draw the conclusion that John the Baptist dismisses it completely, to the extent that being born into the covenant becomes completely meaningless.[14] That certainly takes it too far. In an *intra muros* perspective (i.e., understanding the text within the boundaries of Judaism, not as an outsider), it is more plausible that the debate is really about the necessity to live according to one's beliefs.[15] It is not a matter of rejecting *zekhut avot* but critically relating to it and discussing its implications. One tendency among New Testament scholars is to overemphasize haggadic concepts so that they almost become comparable to the centrality and unquestionability of Christian doctrines. There is a certain playfulness in *Aggadah* that is easily misunderstood. John the Baptist as an Aggadist could be understood not as *rejecting* the concept, but *relating* to it, *reflecting* on it, and possibly *reinterpreting* it.

It is not surprising to find that the figure Abraham is referred to in these texts. After all, he is the most important figure from the Hebrew Bible in the New Testament writings—especially in the Pauline epistles—and there are two reasons for this. Firstly, Abraham is quite obviously exceptionally important to Paul, who in his search for a hermeneutics that included the Gentiles *qua* Gentiles in God's plan, often referred to Abraham. To Paul he was the prime example of a person who, although outside of the covenant, was covenantally embraced by the God of Israel; indeed, the very first and, in addition, the paradigmatic person. Gentile mission required a renewed reflection on the role and importance of Abraham. Secondly, Abraham is of profound importance in a Jewish context because he is the ancestor of the entire Jewish people. He is the foundation stone, as Solomon Schechter writes: "Abraham is the very *petra* [rock] on which the Holy One, blessed be he, established the world, as it is said, 'For the foundations of the earth are the Lord's'" (1 Sam 2:8).[16]

Speaking of Abraham as "the rock," commentators often point out the resemblance between the words for "stones" (Hebrew: *avanim*; Aramaic: *avnayya*) and "children" (Hebrew: *banim*; Aramaic: *benayya*), which is a pun that does not survive when translated into Greek (*lithoi* and *tekna*). Hence, these Hebraisms or Aramaisms point in the direction of a pre-Synoptic source in a Semitic language.[17]

In short, Abraham is, firstly, the paradigmatic figure in Pauline theological thinking on the inclusion of the Gentiles. Secondly, he is the first patriarch and the origin of the Jewish people, "the rock from which you were hewn....Look to Abraham your father" (Isa 51:1f.). There are haggadic statements that go as far as to claim that God created humanity and, indeed, the world for the sake of Abraham.[18]

To sum up, the fourth interpretation understands the text about John the Baptist within Judaism with the help of the two expressions *covenantal nomism* and *zekhut avot*. These motifs seem to provide a plausible intra-Jewish context for this text.

A quite relevant parallel in an intra-Christian context would be the discussions about the extent to which baptism alone makes a person Christian or whether, in addition to baptism, a certain lifestyle is required. In such a situation, a Christian peer to John the Baptist would probably emphasize that it is not enough to merely be baptized "to Christ" (Greek: *eis ton Christon*); one has to seek to live a Christian life as well. And who would claim that such a position amounts to a total refutation of Christian faith?

2
"AN EYE FOR AN EYE?... WE ARE NOT BARBARIANS!"

Matt 5:38–48 and Luke 6:29f.
(cf. Didache 1.3–5, Exod 21:23–25,
Lev 24:19f., and Deut 19:21)

The quotation above is from the mafia movie *Lady Mobster*, uttered by Father Paul, a Catholic priest. The words are directed to the protagonist, Lauren Castle, when she wants to punish the man who killed her parents.[1] And this is far from the only film, book, newspaper article, or TV program in which this biblical expression "an eye for an eye" occurs, usually with the assumption that this is a compendium of "Old Testament ethics," thus an alleged *Jewish* ethics. What is noteworthy about the film quotation above is that it is a *Christian* priest who distances himself from a verse in the *Christian* canon, with the supposition that it is *not Christian* but something else.

Another example of this discourse is the fact that the cruel villain Shylock in Shakespeare's play *The Merchant of Venice* is often perceived as "a typical Jew," for example when demanding a "quarter pound of flesh," while other characters plead for him to have a more lenient—allegedly *Christian*—attitude. A consequence of this distinct focus on Shylock is the fact that people tend to assume that he, not Antonio, is the protagonist of the play.

Many assume that the expression "an eye for an eye"—and somehow, they often seem to know that it is found in the Old Testament—can only be interpreted as a call for retaliation. This has spurred assertions about Shylock and "an eye for an eye" as prime examples of an alleged *Jewish* ethics. Hence, many people conclude that Judaism is a religion of vengeance and retaliation, exemplified by Shakespeare's character Shylock and the biblical expression "an eye for an eye." Benno Jacob argues that no part of biblical law has been "as maliciously or ominously misinterpreted."[2]

In short, the expression "an eye for an eye" is exceedingly well known.[3] Bernard S. Jackson is most probably correct when he writes that it is "the most widely known principle of Biblical law,…represent[ing], in the popular mind, the whole tenor of Old Testament legislation."[4] Similarly, Raymond Westbrook and Bruce Wells state that this is "perhaps the most notorious phrase in biblical law."[5] This understanding of the expression "an eye for an eye" has been fueled by the way the concluding eleven verses in the fifth chapter of Matthew (part of the Sermon on the Mount) have been interpreted.

Simultaneously, the call to love one's enemies is one of the most cited and influential sayings attributed to Jesus in early Christian literature. Many would agree with, for example, W. D. Davies and Dale C. Allison that it is a "succinct, arresting imperative…[that] stands out as fresh and unforgettable."[6] Indeed, it has been asserted that these verses constitute a compendium of New Testament ethics, and, consequently, a *Christian* ethics.

In one word, the most famous—indeed, infamous—statement in the Hebrew Scriptures is "an eye for an eye," and arguably the most well-known statement in the Greek New Testament is the demand that love not stop short of one's enemies. This antithetical dichotomy between the alleged nuclei of the two parts of the Christian Bible spur us to survey the so-called antitheses in the Sermon on the Mount.

The twenty-eight verses in Matt 5:21–48 form a unit in which the Matthean Jesus explains a series of commandments in the Scriptures, concerning anger (vv. 21–26), marriage and divorce (vv. 27–30 and 31f.), oaths (vv. 33–37), "an eye for an eye and a tooth for a tooth" (vv. 38–42), and loving one's neighbor (vv. 43–48). The structure in each passage is generally similar: initially there is a standardized formulation with only minor differences (typically "You have heard that it was said"), and then a commandment from the Scriptures is quoted, followed by the interpretation of the Matthean Jesus of the commandment with the wording, "But I tell you:…" These sections are often called antitheses due to the fact that it is assumed that the Matthean Jesus here contrasts his own teaching with the commandments in the Scriptures, thereby abolishing these scriptural commandments. But such an assumption does not do justice to Matthean theology. A central passage is Matthew 5:17–19:

Do not think that I have come to abolish the law or the prophets; I have come not to abolish but to fulfill [*ouk êlthon katalysai alla plêrôsai*]. For truly I tell you, until heaven and earth pass away, not one letter [*iôta hen*], not one stroke of a letter [*mia keraia*], will pass from the law until all is accomplished. Therefore, whoever breaks one of the least of these commandments, and teaches others to do the same, will be called least in the kingdom of heaven; but whoever does them and teaches them will be called great in the kingdom of heaven.[7]

The *iôta* is a reference to the smallest letter in the Hebrew alphabet, the *yud*.[8] The meaning of *keraia* is more elusive. This word, a diminutive of *keras* (hence "little horn"), is often interpreted as a reference to the *keter* (also known as *tag* or *taga*; plural: *ketarim* and *tagin*), which is an ornament atop some of the Hebrew letters in a Torah scroll. It should be pointed out that the *keter* does not change the pronunciation or the meaning of the text.[9] Hence, the words *iôta* and *keraia* in this passage serve as examples of the Matthean Jesus's insistence on the validity even of the details in the Scriptures.

Although they are traditionally called *antitheses*, it would, as a matter of fact, be more fitting to rename them *hypertheses*, since the Matthean protagonist does not go against the commandments but wants to go further and higher (cf. Greek: *hyper*, "over," "above").[10] Consequently, the quotations from the Scriptures and the scriptural interpretations in Matthew 5:21–48 are not each other's opposites. The rabbinic expression for this genre of interpretations is "to place a fence around the Scriptures" (Hebrew: *la-'asot seyag la-Torah*; see, e.g., *Mishnah Pirqei Avot* 1.1), which means that, in order to make sure that the biblical commandments are not violated, they are applied in such a way that their application is extended. One example of this practice is the welcoming of *shabbat* on Friday evening somewhat earlier than is required in order to be on the safe side of not violating the *shabbat* laws.

One clear example that they are indeed *hypertheses* is the passage on how to interpret "you shall not murder." This hardly means that the Sermon on the Mount teaches that the biblical commandment no longer applies, indeed, that it is repealed, and that Christian ethics welcomes bloodshed. Instead, quite obviously, it means that the Matthean Jesus argues that when someone gets angry at another person it is, in a certain sense, *as if* murder were committed. Hence, it is not enough to merely desist from committing murder; one must also be careful with what one says. (For this thought—that, so to speak, one can commit murder with words—see chapter 9.)

It has already been mentioned that one of these hypertheses has had a particularly harmful influence, precisely because it has been interpreted as an antithesis. In Matthew 5:38, "an eye for an eye and a tooth for a tooth" is quoted.[11] Annika Wenemark lists nine interpretations of this particular verse, four of which are presented here.[12]

(a) Jesus abolishes retaliation: The English word *retaliation* comes from the expression *lex talionis*, which is the principle that a punishment should correspond precisely to the injuries and damages that have been inflicted upon the victim, hence "an eye for an eye, a tooth for a tooth."

It has already been mentioned that the default setting in movies, books, articles, and TV programs often appears to be that Jesus was born into a culture of revenge and vengeance, and without his words people would continue until this day to act in accordance with this "Old Testament ethics."[13] This first line of thought is an example of what could be called a *paradigmatic* interpretation because it emphasizes that an alleged *uniqueness* of the teaching of the historical Jesus constitutes a radically new perspective on these matters. A biblical scholar who gives vent to this paradigmatic understanding is John Piper, who writes that "Jesus was in some sense abolishing the *lex talionis*."[14] In a similar way, Eduard Schweizer claims that Jesus "abrogate[s] the Old Testament regulations" that we are now discussing, that he "demolishes all the fences into which men would *confine* love of neighbor," and that he overthrows "legalistic thinking."[15] Ironically, the Matthean hermeneutics is actually the opposite: as we have seen, the protagonist places a fence around the Scriptures in order to *expand* the application.

However, as Jonathan Klawans points out, "ancient Jewish law is not defined by the plain, literal sense of any given passage from the Torah."[16] It is therefore crucial to explore the ways in which "an eye for an eye" was interpreted in the Jewish tradition at the time of Jesus. But before doing that, we need to survey a second and influential understanding of "an eye for an eye."

(b) The Torah is an improvement: It is often suggested that the commandment in the Torah—in comparison to endless vendettas in pre-biblical times—represented a moral advance. A comparison with pre-biblical texts indicates that the demand was previously more than one eye, more than one tooth, more than one life, and so on, as in this Hittite law (c. 1650–1500 BCE):

[If] anyone kills [a man] or a woman in a [quarr]el, he shall [bring him] for burial and shall give four persons, male or female respectively. He shall look [to his house for it].[17]

Hence, as Hans Jochen Boecker writes, the intention of the Torah text may be "not, therefore, to *inflict* injury—as it might sound to us today—but to *limit* injury."[18] In other words, the Torah restricts the penalty: *no more than* an eye, *no more than* a tooth, *no more than* a life is to be taken. Another comparison, it is often claimed, is that the commandments in the Torah represent justice. This, too, is something of a paradigmatic interpretation—that is, that the Torah ends excessive bloodshed by emphasizing proportionality. Christians have sometimes described a hermeneutics with several successive steps taken: first endless vendettas, then regulated punishment followed by the proportionality of "an eye for an eye" in the Torah, and, finally, the abolishment of punishments altogether by the teaching of Jesus. But is this a plausible historical reconstruction? What do we know about how "an eye for an eye" was interpreted at the time of Jesus? We must thus consult the rabbinic texts.

(c) Jewish tradition eventually interpreted "an eye for an eye" as monetary compensation: The most relevant rabbinic parallel is *Mishnah Bava Qamma* 8.1, which establishes what one should do if one "hurts one's fellow [human being]" (Hebrew: *ha-chovel be-chavero*). Now, had the antithetical interpretation been historically plausible, this rabbinic text—belonging to the earliest stratum of rabbinic texts—would describe how retaliation should be executed (pun intended) by the wounded or offended person, but nothing of the kind is described in the text. The Mishnaic text is not directed to the person who has been injured but to the person who has caused the damage, and this person is obliged to compensate the injured party. Hence, it is crystal clear that the rabbinic interpretation is a call not for *revenge* but for *recompence*, and more precisely a description of how to estimate the amount to be paid to the person that has been injured. It is not a carte blanche for vendettas but a manual in claims' settlements.

Many commentaries acknowledge the importance of this Mishnaic parallel, but since some readers may not look it up, it may be worthwhile to give a brief summary of the Mishnaic discussion. What criteria should be applied in the event of bodily injury? The Mishnah states that damages be based on five factors: (1) One should try to estimate how the *injury* itself (e.g., the loss of an arm) should be compensated by going to the slave market and comparing the price of a two-armed slave with the price of a single-armed slave so that the difference could be paid to the person that has recently lost one arm. (2) Another aspect is *pain*, which is assessed by asking how small an amount a person agrees to be paid for accepting to be exposed to this pain. Pain, by definition, does not leave any marks (since the damage itself is regulated under the previous point). (3) The one who injured a fellow human being is obliged to cover all *health care costs* until the patient has recovered completely. (4) The person who has been injured shall also be compensated for *lost earnings*. The Mishnah states that everyone should be compensated with at least the same amount (since damage has already been considered in the first paragraph and reputation is taken into account in the next paragraph), namely, with the salary paid to someone "watching over a cucumber field" (Hebrew: *shomer qishuin*), perhaps because it was a task that was remunerated with what we would call the minimum wage. It suggests that even a person who has a comparatively low-skilled employment should be compensated. (5) Finally, what the text calls *reputation* (lit. "shame," Hebrew: *boshet*) refers to injuries that may be even more catastrophic to some people than others. (Modern examples include, e.g., disfigurement or a pronounced limp.) The Mishnah therefore states that one should also take into consideration the injured party's "reputation."[19]

Jewish tort law thus stipulates that damages are to be based on these five criteria. Nothing at all in the text suggests that the emerging rabbinic Judaism meant that "an eye for an eye and a tooth for a tooth" was a carte blanche for revenge. This is even said explicitly in the Talmudic text, which is based on the Mishnaic text:

Why [should the damage be settled financially]? The merciful One says [in the Torah]: "An eye for an eye"? Why not a real eye [i.e., why should we not interpret this literally: that one should destroy the eye of the perpetrator]? Let this not even enter your mind [Aramaic: *lo salqa da'takh*]![20]

Nothing in the Mishnah indicates that the biblical text was interpreted literally at that time; in the Talmud, the literal interpretation is even explicitly rejected. This survey of the halakhic discussion in *Bava Qamma* shows that Matthew 5:38 cannot be intended to refute the interpretation of contemporary Judaism of "an eye for an eye." In the words of Samuel Tobias Lachs:

By the time of Jesus the *lex talionis* was no longer practiced and the biblical text was interpreted to mean that a money payment was to be paid to the injured party, as prescribed by the then current law.[21]

It is often stated that the Gospel of Matthew is the New Testament Gospel that is most familiar with the theology and hermeneutics of the emerging rabbinic Judaism that shaped the tannaitic texts (the oldest corpus of rabbinic texts, from the first two centuries CE). It is argued here that the Sermon on the Mount—where the Matthean Jesus places "a fence around the Torah"—is the prime example for the veracity of that assertion. Why then would it be ignorant of the Jewish interpretation of "an eye for an eye" that does not conform to the theological and historical reconstruction provided in many of the Christian handbooks on Judaism in the time of Jesus? Why would Matthew's account of the teaching of Jesus in the Sermon on the Mount contrast it with a false picture of then contemporary Jewish teaching, as so many commentators are inclined to take for granted?

But to what extent can the Mishnah—written down around 200 CE—illuminate the halakhic discussion at the time of the historical Jesus (c. 30 CE) and the evangelist Matthew (possibly fifty to sixty years later)? When addressing this issue, David Daube argues that it is likely that

> by the time of Jesus, retaliation in the case of damages to a person had been superseded by monetary penalties. Not a single instance of the practice of retaliation is mentioned in the sources. Both Mishnah and Mekhilta reject any literal interpretation of "Eye for eye" and lay down that the wrongdoer has to pay damages....*The system of damages of Mishnah and Mekhilta is of so elaborate and subtle a nature... that we must allow a long time for its growth*. In other words, talion must have been ousted by a pecuniary settlement long before the detailed provisions concerning the latter which we find in Mishnah and Mekhilta were established....We...arrive at the conclusion that talion can no longer have formed part of the law in the age of Jesus. Had he attacked this principle, he would have been guilty of a strange anachronism.[22]

When taking pains to focus on the *intra*-Jewish context (and not solely thinking of it as an *anti*-Pharisaic text) of the Gospel of Matthew, we realize that not only can it be read in the light of Jewish sources but, furthermore, the New Testament itself may shed light on the evolution of the rabbinic traditions, as Daube states: "This utterance is the earliest positive testimony preserved to us of that stage of Jewish law where the principle 'Eye for eye' had only the refined meaning of restitution by means of money."[23]

In other words, Daube argues that Jesus was in agreement with the then prevailing rabbinic law: "the New Testament has preserved to us a pre-Talmudic stage of Jewish private law, a stage far removed from the law of the Bible…but less advanced than that of Mishnah and Mekhilta."[24] Indeed, is it not far more judicious to interpret the Matthean text in light of the Mishnah, compiled around 200 CE, than with the help of Hittite laws from the sixteenth century BCE? In short, the Matthean Jesus does not *eradicate* Jewish law; quite the contrary, he helps us *reconstruct* the hermeneutical trajectory from the text in the Torah to the rabbinic interpretations.

(d) "An eye for an eye" in the Torah was always—also originally—discussing monetary compensation: The fourth interpretation goes even further—it, so to speak, walks the second mile—when claiming that the rabbis' reading was the *original* meaning of the text. The expression "an eye for an eye" related only to proportionality. Benno Jacob presents twelve arguments in favor of this interpretation.[25] The difference between Jacob's interpretation and the previous one is that whereas Jacob's reading may be debatable, the aforementioned is unquestionable. We will probably never be able to ascertain whether the monetary interpretation of "an eye for an eye" is as old as Jacob suggests, but we have good reasons to assume that it was applied in the first century.[26] Hence, rather than seeking to establish first-century *halakhah* based upon more or less sweeping generalizations and anti-halakhic interpretations, we should seek to read the New Testament in the light of the earliest rabbinic stratum—that is, the Mishnah. Whereas there is a consensus among Jewish scholars that in tannaitic times "an eye for an eye" was interpreted as a text about monetary compensation, New Testament commentaries ever so often present the teaching of Jesus as terminating retaliation. This observation should give us pause. In short, we should not take the Matthean hyphertheses in the Sermon on the Mount to be an *abrogation* of the commandments in the Torah but instead see them as an expanded and cautionary *application* of them.

An additional question ought to be addressed: Even if there are similarities between Matthew's Gospel and the Mishnah—both resist the vengeful interpretation—why are they so different? If, as has been argued here, Matthew was familiar with the evolving rabbinic reading of the texts in the Torah, which interpreted them as referring to monetary compensation, why is this not Matthew's chief concern? The answer, most likely, is the different genres of the two texts. There is a difference between Matthew's Gospel and the Mishnah in terms of whom the text addresses. Whereas the Mishnah focuses on what the *offender* is liable to do, the New Testament texts focus on what the *offended* should do or avoid doing. More specifically, it addresses what they as disciples of Jesus of Nazareth should avoid doing when treated badly by the Romans. The fact that this is not part of a judiciary process or an assessment of monetary compensation is even clearer in the Lukan parallel, in which the order of the two garments mentioned in Jesus's teaching is reversed (6:29). Whereas Matthew's context is the court scene, when he proscribes that one should be willing to yield up not only the inner garment but the outer as well, the Lukan parallel (as well as *Didache* 1.4) mentions them in the reverse order. This suggests that it describes a scene in which a disciple is robbed of the outer garment and is nevertheless willing to yield up the inner garment as well.[27] The texts in the Torah belong to *the judiciary process in an intra-Jewish context*. This is not the sphere of application in the Gospel of Matthew, which discusses *Christ-believing discipleship* when being offended living under Roman occupation.[28] Matthew's Gospel and the Mishnah stem from two different contexts; this is yet another example of how the *Wirkungsgeschichte* of the text is rich, and does not go only in one direction. In other words, the teaching of Jesus, on the one hand, is intended for the Jewish victim living under Roman occupation. His instruction is how to act—or rather how *not* to react—when being threatened and humiliated by the Romans. The other person—the opponent—is a representative of the Roman Empire. The teaching of the Mishnah, on the other hand, is intended for Jews who have hurt another person, and the texts give detailed instructions about what they have to do in order to compensate the other person *monetarily*. In this case the other person is the victim—and this is the main reason for the Torah being applied in different ways in Matthew's Gospel and in the Mishnah.

Another important observation is that revenge is not ruled out altogether; rather, it is postponed. Davies and Allison point out that several affirmative statements about *lex talionis* can be found in the New Testament (see, e.g., 1 Cor 3:17 and Mark 8:38).[29] Hence, the principle is not wholly rejected, but it will be applied by God at the end of time. Is, then, the reason to desist from revenge that the revenge is God's? In Romans 12:19–21 Paul writes:

Beloved, never avenge yourselves, but leave room for the wrath of God; for it is written, "Vengeance is mine, I will repay, says the

Lord." No, "if your enemies are hungry, feed them; if they are thirsty, give them something to drink; for by doing this you will heap burning coals on their heads." Do not be overcome by evil, but overcome evil with good.[30]

Certainly, we always ought to remember that all these texts by the first Christ followers were written with the eschatological horizon in sight. The authors were convinced that the end of the world was near, and so was the final judgment, to which Paul is referring in this passage.

Now, after this quite extensive discussion of *lex talionis*, we also need to briefly address interpretations of the Hebrew word *rea'*, which plays an important part in the command in Leviticus 19:18, in the Gospel tradition about "the greatest commandment," and in Matthew 5:43: "You shall love your [*rea'*] and hate your enemies." Although often translated as "neighbor," it does not refer to someone living next door to you. The Septuagint chose *plêsion*, which actually means someone close, but not necessarily a neighbor; the Vulgate has *amicus* (friend). In comparison, in the texts that discuss the greatest commandment (see chapter 11), the Greek word is *plêsion*; the Vulgata has *proximus/proximum*, and in the Peshitta the root is *q-r-v*; all three words have to do with proximity. Etymologically, as Lenn E. Goodman notes, the Hebrew word *rea'* bears connotations of care, as in the opening words of the twenty-third psalm: *ADONAI ro'i* ("The Lord is my shepherd"); "perhaps [it was] taken up from the pastoral life of its first users."[31]

In the Jewish tradition there are texts that promote either a universalistic or a particularistic perspective. Raphael Jospe demonstrates that this only partly has to do with the interpretation of the word *rea'*.[32] Even if *rea'* is interpreted as referring to a fellow Jew only, one can still argue in favor of a universalistic ethics, that takes into consideration all human beings, not only fellow Jews. Some commentators argue for universalism with references to Leviticus 19:18, but it can be based also on other biblical texts. To use an image, it can be likened to two overlapping circles, one of which describes the usage of *rea'*, and the other universalism. In other words, it is detrimental to contrast an alleged "tribalistic" Jewish understanding of *rea'* and a Christian universalistic interpretation of *plêsion*.

Generally speaking, Leviticus 19:18 does not have a universal meaning.[33] This does not mean, however, that the Jewish tradition at the time of Jesus encouraged loving "only" fellow Jews. There are other passages, indeed even in the same chapter, that command that one love the stranger, with the motivation that they are what you *are* (or, to be more precise, what you *have been*): you, too, have been strangers. Lachs reminds us that in *Aggadah* the universal application prevails, whereas in halakhic exegesis the neighbor in general refers to fellow Jews.[34]

Also in the New Testament we have examples of both maximalist and minimalist interpretations of the word *rea'*. The issue thus comes down to a discussion about how to define the word *rea'*. This word can be narrowly or broadly defined, also by Christ followers. In the Johannine literature we have examples of a quite narrow definition of whom to love: the expression *hoi adelphoi* (the brethren) most probably refers solely to those Christ followers who belonged to the Johannine community; not to Christ followers of other then contemporary theological schools. And even in the Gospel of Matthew, with this apparent critique of a narrow definition of *rea'*, the constant and vitriolic attacks on the Jewish leadership makes one wonder just how universal Matthew's ethics is.[35]

Another issue is the striking phrase "You have heard that it was said,… hate your enemy" (Matt 5:43), a commandment nowhere to be found in the Scriptures![36] On the contrary, in Proverbs 24:17 it is even stated, "Do not rejoice when your enemies fall, and do not let your heart be glad when they stumble."[37] To be sure, in *The Community Rule*, one of the Dead Sea Scrolls, it is stated that "they may love all the Sons of Light, each according to his lot in God's design, and hate all the Sons of Darkness, each according to his guilt in God's vengeance.[38] Hence, it is possible that the teaching in this part of the Sermon on the Mount is aimed at the miniscule Qumran community in the Judean desert. But there is no exhortation to hate one's enemy in the Scriptures, and such a line of thought is not pursued in the rabbinic literature.

In conclusion, this passage in the Sermon on the Mount is often referred to as the center of *Christian* ethics, and at times as the opposite of *Jewish* ethics, that allegedly, firstly, is based on the retributive notion of "an eye for an eye," and, secondly, only takes into consideration the well-being of one's fellow Jews. Therefore, it is assumed that Jesus of Nazareth in the Sermon on the Mount refutes such a "tribalistic" teaching of revenge, replacing it with a distinctly Christian ethics. What is particularly disturbing with this line of thought is that Judaism is presented as being completely unable to develop a hermeneutics that copes with challenging texts; it is portrayed as a religious tradition that is at the mercy of a love-centered Christian religion, without which it is doomed forever to indulge in revenge and vendettas. But, as a matter of fact, reading ancient and authoritative—and every so often ambiguous—texts is one of the very hallmarks of the

Jewish tradition. "We are not barbarians," the priest said in *Lady Mobster*. Is the unspoken message that other readers of the Bible are?[39]

As this discussion has shown, such assertions are incorrect. The *Matthean* Jesus certainly did not abolish the Law. He is teaching that he has "not come to abolish but to fulfil" (5:17). And it is argued in the present survey that neither did the *historical* Jesus see as his mission the abolition of the Torah. His at times radical interpretation of the commandments is a way to honor the Torah. In the words of Davies and Allison, the ethics of Jesus did not begin with a *tabula rasa* but a *tabula Torah*. Indeed, he "upheld tradition, even when surpassing it."[40]

3

THE GOLDEN RULE IN THE ROYAL LAW

Matt 7:12 and Luke 6:31
(cf. Jas 2:8; see chapter 11)

In various forms, the Golden Rule can be found all over the world in most of the religious traditions, as well as in philosophical writings, such as Immanuel Kant's categorical imperative: "Act only according to that maxim whereby you can at the same time will that it should become a universal law."[1] As W. D. Davies and Dale C. Allison write, "The idea of doing to others as one wishes to be done to is, it should be remembered, almost a universal sentiment."[2] Not unexpectedly, there is also an abundance of parallels in Jewish sources.[3]

Given the centrality of the Golden Rule in Jewish and Christian texts, it is not surprising that it can be found in various literary contexts and also in various versions. Two motifs tend to overlap: On the one hand, there are texts that present the Golden Rule either as a specific *commandment* ("In everything do to others as you would have them do to you") or as a *prohibition* ("Do not do what is hateful to you").[4] On the other hand, there are texts that discuss whether there is a hermeneutical center in the Scriptures: "a great rule in the Torah" (Hebrew: *kelal gadol ba-Torah*)—and the answer is often Leviticus 19:18: "You shall love your neighbor as yourself."[5] Hence, our current discussion and the chapter on the greatest commandment (see chapter 11) will partially overlap.

The contexts in the Gospels differ somewhat from each other: The Matthean Jesus has previously stated that even those who are evil know how to give good gifts to their children (7:11). The Lukan Jesus has just commanded his disciples to love their enemies (6:27). Hence, in Matthew's Gospel evil people are the *subjects*, who are the ones that act; in Luke's

Gospel evil people are the *objects*, whom one should love. The Lukan version does not include the Matthean conclusion: "for this is the law and the prophets." Davies and Allison quite correctly see the concluding words as an expression of the distinctly Matthean scriptural hermeneutics that the teaching of Jesus does not abolish the Torah (see chapter 2).

> [It brings] to a climax the entire central core of the sermon on the mount, 5.17–7.11....Mention of "the law and the prophets" takes the reader back to 5.17...[Matt 7.12 is] a general rule which is not only the quintessence of the law and the prophets but also the quintessence of the sermon on the mount and thus the quintessence of Jesus' teaching in general.[6]

After these initial observations and reflections about the Golden Rule as an ethical touchstone, four lines of thought will now be presented.

(a) A positive commandment is superior to a negative prohibition: Whereas the Golden Rule in Matthew 7:12 and Luke 6:31 is a commandment (declaring *positively* everything one ought to do), the most famous Jewish parallel is a prohibition (asserting *negatively* from what one should refrain). Hillel famously stated in a conversation with a Gentile—whom he had made a proselyte—that the Golden Rule (in its *negative* version) was the center of Judaism: "What is hateful to you, do not do to your neighbor. That is the whole Torah. The rest is commentary. Go and study!"[7]

Much ink has been spilled over the difference between the commandments in the New Testament Gospels and the prohibition attributed to Hillel, such as W. A. Spooner's article on "Golden Rule" in the *Encyclopaedia of Religion and Ethics*:

> It would appear, then, that as a negative or limiting principle, a principle of justice, the maxim obtained a wide acceptance among the best and most enlightened intellects of the ancient world; but it was for them a restraining principle, a guide of what they ought not to do rather than of what they ought. With our Lord, however, it has a wider sweep than this: with Him it is a rule of universal application, a rule of benevolence embracing all our relations to our fellow-men.[8]

We find similar statements in commentaries to the New Testament Gospels, here exemplified by George Bradford Caird and Eduard Schweizer:

But an ethical programme which consists in not-doing, especially when it has to be expounded in a vast commentary of rules and ceremonies, can hardly be compared with one which calls for positive and unlimited benevolence. Most people—even sinners—have a rough-and-ready ethic based on common sense, enlightened self-interest, give-and-take; and they can claim to be as good as their neighbours. But the followers of Jesus must go further....Other systems distinguish what is right from what is wrong: Jesus distinguishes what is good from what is merely right, and urges his disciples not to be content with the lower standard. Duty is not enough. Duty obeys the rules, but love grasps opportunities. Duty acts under constraint, love is spontaneous and therefore gracious. Duty expects to be recompensed or at least recognized, love expects nothing in return. To love like that is to be sons of the Most High; for likeness is proof of parentage.[9]

Other instances [of the negative form] are admittedly nothing more than worldly wisdom to the effect that anyone who wants to live in peace should not attack others. From this source the saying first infiltrated Greek-speaking Judaism....Presumably, then, Jesus himself gave the saying its present terse and universal form. It can *no longer* be understood as self-centered advice, for what a man desires for himself is usually limitless, and the requirement of doing that for others represents the most radical of summons to love one's neighbor. In this form the saying states that it does not take scholarly expertise to know what we should do for our neighbors. A man usually knowns what he himself would like.[10]

Whereas Schweizer calls the Golden Rule in its negative form "nothing more than worldly wisdom," George Foot Moore, in his *Judaism in the First Centuries*, does not find this point even "worth while to argue":

Jewish teaching about the treatment of others, countrymen or aliens, friends or enemies, was not deduced from an aphorism, but based upon the positive general rule in Lev. 19, 18...and the many specific injunctions and exhortations, both positive and negative, in which the Scriptures abound in all parts; and these virtues are exemplified by instances in the familiar narratives of the Bible and by the character and conduct of eminent rabbis.[11]

Indeed, the Achilles' heel of the somewhat triumphalistic comparisons between the Jewish *prohibition*—which people quite effortlessly can keep—and the Christian *commandment*—which is all the more demanding—is, quite obviously, that Christian texts, too, quote the Golden Rule in its negative form, seemingly without its allegedly and distinctly *Christian* message being lost.[12] This observation immediately takes us to our next point.

(b) *Christian texts quote both the positive and the negative versions of the Golden Rule:* Davies and Allison state that "the negative formulation does not always presuppose a calculating attitude with its own selfish ends in view: it can be rooted in a genuine concern for one's fellows."[13] We have no indication that Paul ever differentiated between negative and positive versions of the instructions on how to relate to others. In Romans 13:8–10 he first quotes Leviticus 19:18 (which is a *positive* commandment), and then, immediately after, he adds a *negative* form of the Golden Rule: "Love does no wrong to a neighbor."[14] As a matter of fact, Davies and Allison argue that this passage reveals how deeply rooted Paul is in the Jewish hermeneutics of his time: "These words must reflect either Paul's 'rabbinic' training or, what could be true at the same time, his knowledge of the Jesus tradition."[15] Menahem Kister, too, argues that the Matthean version is typical of the wording of rabbinic "rules" or "principles."[16] Another example from the early Christ-believing movement is *Didache*. When describing the Two Ways, one of Life and one of Death, the text specifies that (1.2) "the Way of Life is this: first, you shall love the God who made you; secondly, your neighbor as yourself, and whatever you would not have done to yourself, do not do to another." Given the closeness in terms of theology and vocabulary between Matthew and *Didache*, this parallel is particularly relevant.

Interestingly, Kister has suggested that the hermeneutical bridge between Leviticus 19:18 (which is the basis for various *positive* versions of the commandment) and the *negative* forms may well be Leviticus 19:33f.:

> When an alien [*ger*] resides with you in your land, you shall not oppress the alien. The alien who resides with you shall be to you as the citizen [*ezrach*] among you; you shall love the alien as yourself, for you were aliens [*gerim*] in the land of Egypt.

In this passage it is evident both how the stranger (*ger*) is to be treated as a citizen (*ezrach*)—because the people of Israel, too, have been strangers—

and that the positive commandment to love the alien as oneself is demonstrated with a negative prohibition: "you shall not oppress the alien."[17]

All this illustrates that the conclusion by Davies and Allison holds water: "The claim to find in the synoptic logion profound originality seems ill-conceived and probably stems more from Christian apologetics than from an objective examination of the texts….the truth of his [i.e., Matthew's] Lord's teaching did not necessarily hinge upon its novelty."[18]

(c) Jewish texts, too, contain both positive and negative versions: It has already been mentioned that in the Talmud the negative version of the Golden Rule is attributed to Hillel (in a conversation with a Gentile whom he had made a proselyte): "What is hateful to you, do not do to your neighbor [*chaver*]." But in another text, *Pirqei de-Rabbi Nathan*, it is attributed to Rabbi 'Aqiva (in a dialogue with a Jewish donkey driver):

> [The donkey driver] said to him: "Rabbi, teach me the whole Torah at once [*be-achat*]." He answered him: "My son, our master Moses spent forty days and forty nights on Mount [Sinai] before he learned it, and you ask me to teach you the whole Torah all at once [*ke-achat*]! But, my son, this is the rule [*kelal*] of the Torah: 'What is hateful to you, do not do to your neighbor [*chaver*].' If you do not want one to cause you damage, then you too should not cause him damage. If you do not want one to take what is yours, then you should not take what belongs to your neighbor [*chaver*]."[19]

Hence, in both these texts we find the negative version. But a positive version is also attributed to Rabbi 'Aqiva: "Love your neighbor [*rea'*] as yourself," which, of course, is the biblical version—both in terms of the verb ("to love") and the object (*rea'*).[20] In short, it is neither correct that Jewish texts only cite *negative* versions nor that Christian texts have a monopoly on *positive* versions of the commandment. Kister states that there is no "neat and linear explanation of the development of the rabbinic passages," and he describes the phenomenon as a "pluriformity of a tradition."[21]

(d) The entire Torah is royal because it is magnificent and is to be obeyed: One more text remains to be discussed in this chapter: James 2:8. When quoting Leviticus 19:18, the author uses a striking term: "You do well if you really fulfill the royal law [*nomos basilikos*] according to the scripture, 'You shall love your neighbor as yourself.'"

Now, the question is what the term *royal law* may mean. Is it royal because *Jesus Christ* is the royal king? Or is it royal because *the kingdom of God* has arrived? Or is this a reference to the texts that state that the commandment to love God and to love one's neighbor together are the greatest of all commandments? In other words, is it royal because it is *a hermeneutical focus* in the Scriptures?[22] And if so—if it does refer to the hermeneutical center—does that mean that other parts of the Scriptures are *not* royal? In other words, does the term *nomos basilikos* indicate that, according to this epistle, some parts of the Torah are not considered to be binding? In 1:25 another expression is used: "the perfect law of freedom" (*nomon teleion, ton tês eleutherias*). How are we to understand the combination of "Law" and "freedom" in this epistle? After all, it does not describe a freedom *from* the Law; instead, it states that the Law is a liberating Law.

None of these three suggestions convince Martin Dibelius and Heinrich Greeven. Comparing this passage in James to relevant parallels in, for example, the writings of Philo of Alexandria and Clement (also of Alexandria), they conclude that *basilikos nomos* can mean "the law with royal authority" as well as "the law which is set for kings." James's purpose is "to applaud obedience to the Law," "what he wants to do is to represent the law as important and unconditionally binding."[23] They also state that:

> The commandment of love is not considered in our passage to be the chief commandment, in the sense of the famous saying of Jesus (Mk 12:31 par); instead, it is one commandment alongside others, for otherwise the argument in vv 10f would make no sense. Therefore, the dominical saying just mentioned does not seem to be on the author's mind at all, and if that is true, then there is no reason to take "royal law"…as a reference to the commandment of love.[24]

In other words, they argue that the expression *nomos basilikos* is not a reference to the commandment of love. Hence, "The predicate 'royal' befits the whole law."[25] In this particular epistle it is not a matter of reducing the Torah to one principle, certainly not by ignoring the other commandments, but, quite the opposite, of reinforcing the validity of all the commandments in the Scriptures. In short, this is not a discussion of the greatest commandment but an appeal to the reader to obey *all* the commandments in the royal Torah.[26] And it is in this interpretative framework that we should understand the expression "the perfect law of freedom"—it is not a law in contradistinction to the Torah but a descriptive paraphrase. The people, once slaves in Egypt, are now free and have the privilege to keep the Law. In that sense it is "the perfect law of freedom."

Regrettably, the way the Epistle of James describes the Torah as "the royal law" and "the perfect law of freedom" is not typical of how Christians in general have approached the Scriptures. Hence, it may be appropriate to consider what Krister Stendahl and Emilie T. Sander once wrote in *Encyclopaedia Britannica*:

> The Letter of James, though often criticized of having nothing specifically Christian in its content apart from its use of the phrase the "Lord Jesus Christ" and its salutation to a general audience depicted as the twelve tribes in the dispersion (the Diaspora), is actually a letter most representative of early Christian piety. It depicts the teachings of the early church not in a missionary vein but to a church living dispersed in the world knowing the essentials of the faith but needing instruction in everyday ethical and communal matters with traditional critiques on wealth and status.[27]

In conclusion, when studying the Golden Rule, we have encountered a problematic approach to Jewish and Christian ethics in antiquity: the differences between the negative and the positive versions of the Golden Rule have been overemphasized far beyond what is reasonable—and this could only be explained as the outcome of an apologetic endeavor that seeks to exalt one—to wit, one's own—tradition over against another.[28] As a matter of fact, we see that both Jewish and Christian texts refer to and base their theological arguments on both negative and positive versions of the Golden Rule. Perchance it is time to start reading others' texts as you would like them to read your texts. Or, to put it differently, do not read your neighbor's texts in a hateful way.

4
SHOULD AULD ACQUAINTANCE BE FORGOT, AND NEVER BROUGHT TO MIND?

Matt 9:16f., Mark 2:21f., and Luke 5:36–39
(cf. Gospel of Thomas 47)

This passage actually consists of two parables: one on sewing a piece of new cloth on an old coat, and one on pouring new wine into old wineskins.[1] In the New Testament Gospels these dual parables are preceded by a question on the topic of fasting.

David Flusser has suggested that the hermeneutical starting point when interpreting these parables is "the simple truth that old wine is better than new wine."[2] Why, Flusser asks, would Jesus not know the value of an old wine? Indeed, who would know this better than someone who was accused of being a "glutton and drinker" (*phagos kai oinopotês*; Matt 11:19)? It is indeed quite remarkable that these parables more often than not are referred to as proof for the new covenant's superiority in comparison to the old one, when, as a matter of fact, the message is quite the opposite: in the Lukan version—and also in the Gospel of Thomas—it is stated that old wine is better than new wine: "and no one after drinking old wine desires new wine."

When acquainting ourselves with the long trajectory of supersessionist readings of biblical texts, we soon realize that the words "old" and "new" are exceptionally loaded. Indeed, the entire collection of texts is called the *New* Testament. Alistair Kee has suggested that we rename this passage "the parable of the Patch and the Wine," and it is quite possible that such a terminology would help us discern aspects that we often tend to ignore.[3] In the following paragraphs, we will discuss four interpretations of the two parables. These four readings are interrelated, in the sense that one leads to another.

(a) Judaism versus Christianity: Kee has noted that what unites many commentaries is the word *incompatibility*.[4] Some commentators limit the incompatibility to the new and old in the text per se, but some speak of the incompatibility of the two religions, Judaism and Christianity; for example, Samuel MacLean Gilmour argues for an incompatibility of "the new Christian message and the old ceremonial forms of Judaism," and D. E. Nineham concludes that the new age is "incompatible with the practices of Judaism."[5] Similarly, Eduard Schweizer asserts that "in Jesus something fundamentally new has dawned, something that revolutionizes all earlier forms of religiosity…fasting is no longer a meritorious exercise."[6] Furthermore, he also asserts that Christian fasting is different from Jewish fasting since it is a matter of "something totally new, not comparable in any way to the old fasting of John's disciples and the Pharisees."[7] However, in *Didache* 8.1–3 (cf. Luke 18:12) it is only the fasting days that differ (on Wednesdays and Fridays, instead of on Mondays and Thursdays, i.e., the chronology), not its features (i.e., its alleged Jewish or Christian "essence").[8] Given the proximity in context and chronology between the Synoptic Gospels and *Didache*, is this not worth considering? Should not a general rule be that whenever we discover that our interpretation has more to do with contemporary anti-halakhic Christian teaching than with the Christ-believing movement in the first century, this should give us pause? W. D. Davies and Dale C. Allison correctly state that "Jesus has explicitly endorsed fasting in the post-Easter period, so the old has hardly been cancelled."[9] Furthermore, they also underline that "for Matthew Judaism is Christianity's inheritance, and it would be unthinkable to abandon the legacy. Judaism is for him not a past phenomenon external to Christianity, but a continuing presence carried on within it."[10]

Hence, this first interpretation, which asserts that it is possible to distinguish in first-century texts between two incompatible religious systems, is both supersessionist and anachronistic, and does not further our understanding of the two parables.[11]

(b) Old era versus new era: This second line of thought is related to the previous one, but here it is possible to detect a more distinct emphasis on apocalypticism rather than an alleged anti-halakhic piety. Joachim Jeremias argues that tents, sheets, and garments are common symbols of the cosmos, and that the conclusion therefore is that "the old world's age has run out; it is compared to the old garment which is no longer worth patching with new

cloth; the New Age has arrived."[12] Kee rightly objects that the message of the parables is that the old actually is worth patching because the old skins indeed are worth preserving.[13] Davies and Allison pose the question "whether our two parables do not show some concern for the old. Are not the old wineskin and the old garment worth saving…?"[14] Once again we see that the two words *old* and *new* tend to lead our attention in the wrong direction.

(c) The message is repentance: Kee argues that the double parable is an example of free-floating sayings of Jesus that have been included in different narratives by the gospel writers: it is not in its immediate—to wit, current—context but in the general teaching of Jesus that one should look for its meaning.[15] We have already seen that Kee underlines that the message is that the old coat is still worth patching. The message, according to him, is *the danger of loss*; it is a text about the danger of losing something that, if not perfect, is still useful. Hence, the coat in the parable refers to human beings, and what they ought to do and not do in moments of crisis, because through ill-considered action, through being unprepared, we may suffer loss: "It deals with inappropriate action and thoughtlessness. It speaks of people not prepared for what they undertake."[16] Hence, Kee argues that this passage belongs to a group of parables about the imminent coming of the kingdom. According to this third line of thought, the context is eschatology, and its message is repentance (Hebrew: *teshuvah*; Greek: *metanoia*). Within the eschatological context, Kee takes the previous interpretation one step further by relocating the focus from the two words *old* and *new* to *patch* and *coat*. He rejects both interpretations above, (a) and (b); it is neither about two incompatible religious systems nor simply giving vent to an apocalyptic cosmology. Instead, it is an exhortation within such an apocalyptic worldview. In other words, it may be a reminder of the possibility to start anew in times of crisis.

(d) The Torah is compared to old wine: Whereas Kee focused on the old coat, David Flusser concentrates on the old wine. We have noted his observation that everyone knows that old wine is better than new wine and that this is also Luke's conclusion in 5:39: "And no one after drinking old wine desires new; for he says, 'The old is good,'" or, according to some manuscripts "'The old is better [*chrêstoteros*].'"

Logion 47 in the Gospel of Thomas consists of several originally independent traditions: firstly, three examples of the impossibility to mount two horses, to stretch two bows, and to serve two masters, followed by a series of statements about old and new wine.[17] What is interesting is that the

Gospel of Thomas *commences* with the Lukan *conclusion*—that is, that the connoisseur of old wine does not want to drink new wine. We have no clear indications that the Thomas version is dependent on the Synoptic Gospels; rather, it is a question of sayings that circulated in isolation, and the statement about old being better than new is attested in two out of four texts: we find it in *both Gospels of Luke and Thomas, but not in the Gospels of Matthew and Mark*. It is a fact that commentators seldom know what to do with the Lukan-Thomas conclusion: according to Kee it "destroys the meaning of the parable on any interpretation."[18] And although Kee does not interpret the text as a stern verdict on Judaism and/or a prediction about the end of the world, most commentators do. One can easily understand why this statement is regarded as a textual maverick and a theological misunderstanding since it is completely contrary to the conventional conclusion that the new covenant or the new religion is far better than the previous one.

Now, we need to pose a question: have readers of the New Testament taken into consideration the fact that wine—and especially old wine—is a stock symbol in the Jewish tradition for the Torah? In *Sifrei Devarim* 48 it is stated:

> Just as you cannot relish the taste of the wine when it is still new, and the longer it ages in the vessel, the better it tastes, so too words of the Torah: the longer they age within a person, the more they improve, as it is said: *Wisdom [is] with the aged* (Job 12:12).[19]

And the fact that old wine is better than new is actually *taken for granted* in Sirach 9:10, when an old acquaintance is compared to matured wine: "Do not abandon an old friend, for new ones cannot equal him. A new friend is like new wine; when it has aged, you can drink it with pleasure [*met' euphrosynês piesai auton*]." One cannot reach this conclusion without the rhetorical starting point: since, quite obviously, one should not "abandon" (*egkataleipein*) old wine, why *should auld acquaintance* (with the Torah) *be forgot and never brought to mind*?

There are other passages of interest. Occasionally commentators refer to *Mishnah Pirqei Avot* 4.20 (*Siddur* 4.25–27), but often without drawing any comprehensive conclusions:

> Elishah ben Abuyah said, if one learns as a child, what is it like? Like ink written on new paper. He that learns as an old person, what is it like? To ink written on blotted paper. Rabbi Jose ben Rabbi

Yehudah of Kephar ha-Bavli said, if one learns from the young [*min ha-qetannim*], to what is that person like? To one that eats unripe grapes, or drinks wine from his winepress. And one who learns from the aged, to what is that person like? To one that eats ripe grapes and drinks old wine [*yayin yashan*]. Rabbi [Meir] said, look not at the flask [*qanqan*] but at what is therein; there may be a new flask full of old [wine], and an old flask wherein is not even new [*chadash*] [wine].

We see that the Mishnah discusses the dialectics between old and new: on the one hand, people are encouraged to study the Torah when it is easier for them to learn, because the mind is fresh and receptive when one is young: learning is like ink written on fresh paper.[20] But, on the other hand, one should not judge the wine from the bottle. A new vessel could still contain old wine. Once again, the unquestionable starting point is that old wine is better than new wine—and wine is a metaphor for the Torah.

In short, Flusser emphasizes the Lukan conclusion—which is also the introduction in the Gospel of Thomas—when interpreting this text, and he argues that, by recognizing the Jewish context, in which wine is often a metaphor for the Torah, we can easily conclude that this is yet another text that expresses the idea that Jesus wanted to rediscover "the original meaning of Judaism."[21] In other words, if Flusser is correct, then this text would be a parallel to Matthew 5:17, in which the Matthean Jesus states that he has "come not to abolish, but to fulfill." Flusser's conclusion is that "in contrast to their experience as drinkers, the interpreters and theologians were inclined, in their theological reflections, to prefer new wine to old."[22]

Four lines of thought have been presented in this chapter, and they form a chain, not only in the sense that one interpretation is related to other interpretations but also in the sense that they illustrate the variation of interpretations that go from what is *impossible* to *improbable* to *possible*, and finally to *plausible*.

5
WHAT YOKE GIVES REST FOR THE HEAVY-BURDENED?

Matt 11:28–30
(cf. Gospel of Thomas 90)

This passage encourages the Matthean listeners and readers to live a life that is described as taking upon themselves the yoke of Jesus. The key question, of course, regards the concrete referent of this material image. The word *yoke* (*zygos*) is never used for a literal yoke in the New Testament, but always in a figurative sense. Likewise, the Hebrew word for *yoke* (*'ol*) is a frequently used metaphor in rabbinic literature for important aspects of a Jewish life. In *Mishnah Berakhot* 2.2 it is stated that one should first take upon oneself "the yoke of the Kingdom of Heaven" (*'ol malkhut shamayim*; i.e., the willingness to serve God), and only then "the yoke of the commandments" (*'ol mitzwot*; i.e., the practical consequences of this decision).[1] Matthew 11:28–30 has been interpreted in various ways, four of which will be discussed here.[2]

(a) Judaism is too heavy a burden: Needless to say, this is a central topic for those who think of the Torah as a heavy millstone from which Christians are liberated.[3] Generations of theology students have been taught that it is impossible to observe all 613 commandments in the Torah; see, for example, Rudolf Bultmann: "To take them seriously meant making life an intolerable burden. It was almost impossible to *know* the rules, let alone put them into practice."[4] It is noteworthy that Bultmann's book, published in German in the late 1940s, refers to halakhic Judaism in the *past* tense, as if observant Jews did not exist at his time. And in the *Theological Dictionary of the New Testament*, Otto Bauernfeind boldly states that those invited in Matthew 11:28–30 are people "who in truth have found in Judaism only a burden...and no rest."[5] Eduard Schweizer asserts that the Matthean Jesus

What Yoke Gives Rest for the Heavy-Burdened?

"is speaking of discipleship, which gives men freedom from the Law and the criteria by which the world judges, thus placing them in the service of the world."[6] Such a statement assumes that living a Torah-observant life is incompatible with a "service of the world."

Against this first interpretation, one could object (as we have previously) that a majority of New Testament scholars recognize that a key issue for the Matthean Jesus is the remaining *validity* of the Torah, as is stated in Matthew's hermeneutical key verse (5:17): "I have come not to abolish but to fulfill." Furthermore, if Judaism were such an oppressing burden, and if Jesus wanted to convey the message that he terminated Judaism, why should his teaching be illustrated with a *yoke*, the very symbol of the alleged "Jewish" oppression?

(b) The Pharisaic interpretations of the Torah are too strict: In the same discussion in his commentary, Schweizer also articulates a narrower understanding of what this passage targets. He asserts that the Matthean Jesus has in mind specifically "the individual commandments of Pharisaic legalism, which were impossible to fulfill."[7] Apart from the fact that the Pharisees certainly would disagree with such a statement and that there were groups that expected an even stricter observance (e.g., the Qumran community), is it, nevertheless, possible that the Matthean Jesus here proposes simply a more lenient interpretation of the Torah? A similar debate wholly within the Jewish community framed Hillel and Shammai as the respective advocates. *Beit Shammai* (the School of Shammai), in general, was more stringent than *Beit Hillel*. In *Avot de-Rabbi Natan* 2.9 it is stated that Shammai only allowed worthy candidates to study the Torah, whereas Hillel accepted everyone.[8] But *Beit Shammai* was not considered beyond the pale of Judaism, even though it was decided that *halakhah* was according to Hillel: a heavenly voice (Hebrew: *bat qol*) declared *eilu we-eilu divrei Elohim chayim* (These and those are the words of the living God).[9]

The interpretation that the *halakhah* according to Jesus was more lenient than other contemporary interpretations appears to conflict with our observation that the Matthean Jesus actually requires his disciples to *exceed* the scribes and the Pharisees in terms of righteousness (5:20). What we have called the "hypertheses" in the Sermon on the Mount certainly are far-reaching, such as loving one's enemies and praying for one's persecutors (5:44; see chapter 2). No less demanding is his teaching on self-denial (16:24f.): "If any want to become my followers, let them deny themselves and take up their cross and follow me. For those who want to save their life will lose it, and those who lose their life for my sake will find it."

These references to the teaching of the *Matthean* Jesus seem to indicate that his teaching was not one of leniency. If, however, the emphasis is on the group that is addressed here ("all you who are weary and carrying heavy burdens"), then this second interpretation gains strength. His message to those who suffered and were marginalized was seldom one of high demands. But from everyone to whom much has been given, much was required; and from the one to whom much has been entrusted, even more was demanded (cf. Luke 12:48).

But is not the Matthean Jesus referring to the yoke of the Pharisees in the twenty-third chapter when denouncing them and the scribes? Matthew 23:4 does criticize those who weigh down other people: "They tie up heavy burdens, hard to bear, and lay them on the shoulders of others [*epititheasin epi tous ômous tôn anthrôpôn*], but they themselves are unwilling to lift a finger to move them." But we also have to pay attention to the previous verse: "do whatever they teach you and follow it, but do not do as they do, for they practice not what they teach." Clearly the point here is not that the *teaching* of the scribes and the Pharisees is wrongheaded and unbearable. Why else should the disciples *do* what they *teach*? It is the incongruity between what they *say* and what they *do* that is decried.

(c) However difficult a Christ follower's life may be, it is richly rewarded with repose: "There is no discipleship without a task," Floyd V. Filson writes, and continues: "Those who come to him [i.e., Jesus] must by their own decision accept the yoke he places on them."[10] The third interpretation argues that what Matthew has in mind when writing this passage is the travail from the demands of discipleship: the yoke is a metaphor for Christ followers' suffering. Hence, the burdens, so to speak, are not specifically *Jewish* burdens but refer to various trials and tribulations that a *Christ follower* has to endure.[11]

When the Matthean and Lukan Jesus conditions that "whoever does not take up the cross and follow me is not worthy of me" (Matt 10:38; cf. Luke 14:27)—is he referring to persecutions? Before the crucifixion of Jesus, the cross cannot have been understood as a distinctly *Christian* sign. In short, it was not a symbol of a Christian confession but of Roman oppression, since it was the Romans who executed Jews by crucifixion.[12] This provokes the question: Is the cross to be understood as the Christ followers' yoke?

However difficult the life of the Christ follower may be, it is rewarded with *anapausis* (rest). What is striking is that the word *anapausis* occurs only four other times in the entire New Testament, twice with reference to the restless roving of an unclean spirit and twice in Revelation.[13] Hence, it is far from a central theme in the teaching of Jesus. Certainly, in the Gnostic writings *anapausis* became an important goal for those who had obtained *gnôsis*, but the church fathers (including the writings of the apostolic fathers) also used the word *anapausis*.[14] One example is 2 Clement 5.5:

> And be well assured, kindred, that our sojourning in this world in the flesh is a little thing and lasts a short time, but the promise of Christ is great and wonderful, and brings us rest [*anapausis*], in the kingdom which is to come and in everlasting life.

The related word *katapausis* (also "rest") occurs seven times in the New Testament, with six in one single text, the Epistle to the Hebrews (Acts 7:49; Heb 3:11, 3:18, 4:1, 4:3, 4:5, and 4:10), but never in the Gospels. In short, in order to understand what is referred to by *anapausis*, we will have to look outside of the New Testament Gospels.

The two most relevant occurrences of *rest* elsewhere in the Scriptures are (1) Exodus 33:14, in which God says, "My presence will go with you, and I will give you rest [Hebrew: *we-hanichoti lakh*; LXX: *kai katapausô se*]," and (2) Jeremiah 6:16, in which, however, *rest* does not translate *anapausis* but *hagnismos*, which has more to do with cleansing. In short, if *anapausis* is the central word, there are few relevant parallels in the Septuagint or New Testament, which takes us back to the word for *yoke* (*zygos*) in combination with *anapausis*.

(d) Studying the Torah is the way to wisdom: The most striking parallels—and consequently often pointed out by commentators—are found in Sirach 6:23–28 and 51:23–27:

> Listen, my child, and accept my judgement; do not reject my counsel. Put your feet into her fetters, and your neck into her collar. Bend your shoulders and carry her, and do not fret under her bonds. Come to her with all your soul, and keep her ways with all your might. Search out and seek, and she will become known to you; and when you get hold of her, do not let her go. For at last you will find the rest [*anapausin*] she gives, and she will be changed into joy for you.
>
> Draw near to me, you who are uneducated, and lodge in the house of instruction [*en oikô(i) paideias*].[15] Why do you say you are lacking in these things, and why do you endure such great thirst? I opened my mouth and said, Acquire wisdom for yourselves without money. Put

your neck under her yoke [*zygon*], and let your souls receive instruction [*paideian*]; it is to be found close by. See with your own eyes that I have labored but little and found for myself much serenity [*anapausin*].

Hence, it is likely that the image of the yoke is not exclusively referring to hardships in general in the Matthean community. In an intra-Jewish context at the time of Jesus, walking the way to wisdom is not always easy, but the yoke, despite being a yoke, will prove to be easy to carry for those who realize how precious it is. The yoke may be a reference to wisdom's yoke or to the yoke of the Torah, because although learning and faithfulness may be laborious, they are always rewarding.[16]

Hence, it is plausible that the Matthean Jesus wanted to convey the message that his interpretations of the Torah, although at times strict and demanding (as in the Sermon on the Mount), were nevertheless—ultimately—liberating and refreshing. *Didache*, which is theologically and chronologically close to the Matthean text, states in 6.2: "If you can bear the whole yoke of the Lord [*holon ton zygon tou Kyriou*], you will be perfect, but if you cannot, do what you can."

By way of conclusion, within a couple of generations, a theology would evolve that identified Jesus of Nazareth not only with Wisdom but also with the Torah, as seen in the Gospel of John (e.g., 1:14; see chapter 20). The Wisdom motif in the entire passage of Matthew 11:25–30 provides a theological background and perhaps even the momentum for that influential development.[17] Not only does Jesus of Nazareth convey wisdom, but he also embodies Wisdom. Not only does he teach Torah, but he also incarnates Torah. The Parabler became the principal Parable of God.

6

A SNOWBALL ROLLING DOWN A HILL IN GALILEE

Matt 12:1–8, Mark 2:23–28, and Luke 6:1–5

Leonhard Goppelt is best known for his reconstruction of early church history, with an emphasis on the tensions between Hebrews and Hellenists, out of which grew the two parts of the early Christian movement that he called "two very different brothers": the Palestinian Church and the Gentile Church.[1] He stated that, when seeking to reconstruct the teaching of the Palestinian Church, the sources are only the New Testament writings, and among these, first and foremost, the Synoptic tradition, especially the Gospel of Matthew.

One would have thought that a historical reconstruction based primarily on the Gospel of Matthew—the narrative text that most explicitly emphasizes that the protagonist always remained within the framework of Judaism—would reach the conclusion that, to use John P. Meier's poignant expression, "The historical Jesus is the halak[h]ic Jesus."[2] But Goppelt apparently managed to perceive what Meier could not: he argues that Jesus's teaching and that of the scribes were "mutually exclusive," that Jesus "exploded the idea of the Sabbath law as an absolutely binding regulation," and that his attitude "meant the end of Judaism."[3] As a consequence,

> the synagogue remained isolated and robbed of its religious value.... Here begins the great turning point in the history of Judaism. From the Israel who had brought witness to the Gentile world of God's salvation now develops the post-Christian Judaism which closed itself off from those outside.[4]

E. P. Sanders calls Goppelt "an extreme case of a fairly widespread tendency," which neatly sums up what is at stake here.[5] Hence, no one can deny that Goppelt's conclusions are far-reaching, and many scholars nowadays would say that they are too far-reaching, but in one certain respect he is correct: if these gospel traditions mean that the historical Jesus abrogated, terminated, and "exploded" *shabbat*, this would indeed have had tremendous implications for Judaism. *Shabbat* is one of the cornerstones of Judaism, upon which a vibrant Jewish spirituality in all ages has been built.

Goppelt states what other scholars merely imply, because to state that a religious first-century Jew "exploded" the *shabbat* is not only historically implausible but also an explicit attack on Judaism as a religion—and one would have wished for a more nuanced theological *Fingerspitzengefühl* of a Jewish self-understanding from a German theologian who defended his doctoral thesis in 1939 and his *Habilitationsschrift* (postdoctoral monograph) in 1946.

(a) The shabbat abrogated: One of the texts Goppelt uses is the passage about plucking grains on *shabbat*. He argued that "Jesus did not propound an alternate interpretation of the sabbath as a topic of discussion. He suspended the sabbath commandment as such and by doing so suspended the Law, the very foundation of Judaism."[6] *Hence, the disciples merely plucked the ears of grain, but the implication of this act, at least according to Goppelt, is that the foundation of Judaism falters.* Now, it is difficult to escape the sense that Goppelt's conclusions are too sweeping. There are certainly other—and more convincing—interpretations of this text. W. D. Davies and Dale C. Allison list eight interpretations, some of which are presented here, in elaborated form.[7]

(b) Historicity questioned: It is often pointed out that this text smacks of an artificial flavor; for example, Francis White Beare asks, "Are we to suppose that they [i.e., the Pharisees] kept company with the disciples on their sabbath afternoon strolls, as a regular practice; or that some of them just happened to be passing by the very fields in which the disciples were plucking the grain?"[8] And E. P. Sanders laconically ascertains that "Pharisees did not actually spend their sabbaths patrolling fields."[9] Indeed, one can only hope that the field was not situated more than two thousand cubits (approximately one thousand meters) from the town, which was the length that they were allowed to walk outside of a town on *shabbat* (Hebrew: *techum shabbat*, "shabbat limit").[10] Similarly, Beare, calling it an "anecdote," ascertains that the setting is artificial.[11]

Given that Jesus and his disciples were observant Jews, why would they not have prepared for *shabbat*? The day before *shabbat*—as well as before a religious feast—is called *paraskeuê* in the New Testament (Matt 27:62, Mark 15:42, Luke 23:54, John 19:14, 31, and 42), which literally means "preparation"—and that is how we should imagine that Jesus and his disciples looked upon Fridays in general: they were days when they prepared for *shabbat* to be a day of genuine rest and utmost joy.

Those who disagree with Sanders and colleagues (that the setting of the story is artificial) have to admit that it is extremely difficult to reconstruct an alleged historical nucleus, and even more difficult to draw far-reaching theological conclusions based on the resulting flimsy reconstruction. Davies and Allison compare the complex tradition-history of this passage to "a snowball rolling down a hill," akin to what the rabbis called "a mountain hanging by a hair," and this should give us pause.[12]

(c) An evolving oral tradition defining "work": However, the *qal wa-chomer* argument (Hebrew: "[from] light...[to] heavy"; cf. Latin: *a minore ad maius*, "from a minor [example] to a major") in this text suggests that it developed in a historical and theological context, in which *shabbat* was valid: it seems quite clear that it was originally a matter of the *application* of the *shabbat*, not of its *abrogation*.

It has been suggested by David Flusser that in this pericope one can detect a Galilean halakhic interpretation of *shabbat*. Rabbi Yehudah, who was from Galilee, argued that one was allowed to rub grains with one's hand, whereas the general opinion was that it was only allowed to be done with one's fingers.[13] Hence, the conclusion would be that the disciples are ridiculed for following the regional Galilean *halakhah* instead of the one that was dominating in Judea.[14] Another interesting part of this text is the addition in manuscript *Codex Bezae Cantabrigiensis* (Luke 6:4): "On the same day he saw a man working on the sabbath and said to him, 'Man, if indeed you know what you are doing, you are blessed, but if you do not know, you are cursed and a transgressor of the Law.'"

This statement is obscure and difficult to interpret; the most reasonable intra-Jewish interpretation is that one should always have a halakhic motive for one's behavior, as in Romans 14:23, where Paul states that everything that one does should be "out of faith," or perhaps better translated as "out of conviction" (*ek pisteos*).[15]

Hence, the third line of thought emphasizes that the story contains evidence of an intra-Jewish halakhic discussion on the *application* of the *shabbat* restriction, not the *abrogation* of everything that has to do with *shabbat*. As theologians often state, *abusus non tollit usum* (abuse does not cancel the use), meaning, in this case, that general conclusions cannot be drawn from an exception. At the time of Jesus the oral tradition was evolving; *halakhah* was not yet established.

(d) A matter of life and death? The concept *piquach nephesh* in Jewish *halakhah* refers to the principle that the preservation of human life outweighs all other commandments, except for three: idolatry, illicit sexual relations, and murder. The motivation is that one should *live* by the Torah, and not *die* because of the Torah, since it is stated, "You shall keep my statutes and my ordinances; by doing so one shall live: I am the LORD" (Lev 18:5), and also, "I gave them my statutes and showed them my ordinances, by whose observance everyone shall live" (Ezek 20:11).[16]

Hence, if it were a matter of life and death in this story, the disciples would have been allowed—indeed, even mandated—to honor *shabbat* by preserving life, even when it meant superseding observance of any lesser commandment. The reference to what King David did when he and his men were hungry seems to point in this direction, and in Matthew 12:1 it is actually explicitly mentioned that the disciples were hungry (*hoi de mathêtai autou epeinasan*) when this happened. But this seems to be an unlikely explanation. Nothing in the text suggests that the disciples of Jesus were starving and that they ate in order to save their lives.[17] Many commentators argue that the connection to 1 Samuel 21:1–6 does not belong to the oldest stratum of this passage.[18] Hence, it seems likely to assume that it was added at a later stage, perhaps even to bring the story into halakhic conformity; but the original teaching probably does not invoke a matter of *piquach nephesh*.

(e) Fasting on shabbat? It has already been mentioned that Matthew adds the information that the disciples were hungry, and we have many examples in this particular gospel of emendations that highlight such inner-halakhic parameters, such as criteria for divorce (5:32), handwashing (15:20), and not having to flee on *shabbat* (24:20). Hence, in the final Matthean stratum—that is, in the text as we now have it—the information that the disciples were hungry is stated as the halakhic reason for being allowed to desecrate *shabbat*. If it is not a matter of *piquach nephesh* (see [d] above), then could it be a question of fasting? Since fasting is generally not allowed on *shabbat* (*shabbat* overrules fasting) because it is a day of joy, the question may be that the disciples, for one reason or another, did not have enough food. Was it, then, *not a matter of surviving starvation but of avoiding fasting*? Were there, perhaps, different opinions on fasting on *shabbat*, and is this the rationale for

their behavior? We know, for example, that there was an ancient practice in Babylonia to fast on *Rosh ha-Shanah* (the Jewish New Year) and on *Shabbat Shuvah* (the *shabbat* between *Rosh ha-Shanah* and *Yom Kippur*) that eventually disappeared.[19] Is this perhaps the halakhic context for the text?

(f) Christology: Finally, we must explore the text in relation to Christology since the story also discloses Christological features. Nothing suggests that the scholarly world will agree anytime soon on how to understand the title "Son of Man" (Aramaic: *bar enosh*). Interpretations range all the way from understanding it merely as an emphatic synonym for the personal pronoun "I" to an established messianic title in first-century Judaism, which would be understood by everyone in the audience of Jesus and by all Jewish readers of the Gospels.[20] As so often is the case, it seems safest to stay on the middle ground. Hence, on the one hand, even if the historical Jesus may have used it as a synonym for himself, we have every reason to believe that it has additional connotations in the Gospels. But, on the other hand, Beare is certainly correct when stating the following about high-christological interpretations of "the Son of Man":

> There is, however, a long leap from this figure of apocalyptic vision, this symbolic figure which comes "with the clouds of heaven," and the modest terrestrial company of itinerant Galileans headed by Jesus…[and it is] utterly inconceivable that Jesus should have used the term in any such sense, so that anyone should have understood him if he had done so.[21]

The starting point for our discussion, then, should be to seek to establish the connotations not of the term *ho hyios tou anthrôpou* (the Son of Man) in Mark 2:28 but of the expression in the previous verse: *to sabbaton dia ton anthrôpon egeneto kai ouch ho anthropos dia to sabbaton* (The sabbath was made for humankind, and not humankind for the sabbath). It is often pointed out that there are parallels to this statement in the rabbinic literature, not only in the Talmud but also in the older *Mekhilta de-Rabbi Yishma'el*.[22] Hence, we have parallels both in Aramaic and in Hebrew. In Hebrew it says: *la-khem shabbat mesurah we-ein atem mesurin la-shabbat* (The sabbath is given to you, but you are not given to the sabbath). The context is a discussion of the implications of *piquach nephesh* (see [d] above). Hence, it is interpreted as a permission to disregard one sabbath (*shabbat achat*) in order to keep many sabbaths (*shabbatot harbeh*). Hence, two conclusions can be drawn here: firstly, there is nothing distinctly—and certainly not uniquely—Christian about this statement. On the contrary, it can be found both in an early Hebrew commentary to Exodus and in the later and authoritative Talmud. Secondly, it does not require a Christological rationale, in the sense that only a messianic figure could utter these words, and to do so in order to abrogate and terminate *shabbat*. In short, Mark 2:27 need not be understood in a messianic way.

Now, both Matthew and Luke exclude the statement in Mark 2:27, probably not because it was seen as erroneous but rather because it was superfluous, given the Christological implications of the following verse. In other words, Mark 2:27 makes perfect sense in an intra-Jewish context of honoring *shabbat* in such a way that one is able to honor *shabbat* also in the future. The *Mekhilta*, quoting Rabbi Jose the Galilean, even states that *yesh shabbatot she-attah shovet we-yesh shabbatot she-ein attah shovet* (there are sabbaths on which you should rest and there are sabbaths on which you should not rest).[23] The Matthean and Lukan omission of such an assertion constitutes a shift from the general and proverbial statement about *piquach nephesh* to a specific and Christological one. This is how Davies and Allison summarize their understanding of the Matthean line of thought: "Jesus' authority is illustrated by David's authority; and if David could act as he did, surely Jesus, in a manner of uncertain infringement..., could act similarly."[24]

To conclude, the tradition history of this text is undoubtedly overly complex. It has already been mentioned that Davies and Allison compare it to "a snowball rolling down a hill," and, we might add, this snowball has often been interpreted as an avalanche moving in the direction of Jewish *shabbat* observance: it is not uncommon that scholars mount remarkably far-reaching criticisms, based on this and similar texts, about the validity of halakhic *shabbat* observance.

Our previous discussion gives rise to four observations. Firstly, given the highly unlikely historical setting of this story, which portrays Pharisees spending the *shabbat* in the field, *the burden of proof is on the side of those who argue for the historicity of the story*. To be clear, it is not a matter of a negligible detail. Quite the contrary, the statement that, for some reason, the Pharisees chose to spend *shabbat* in the field is the very prerequisite for the story—and it is precisely this information about their whereabouts that makes the text incongruous and raises suspicion about its historicity.

Secondly, nothing in the story suggests that the disciples were starving (although Matthew adds the note that they were "hungry"), and therefore the *piquach nephesh* argument (the mandate that saving life is weightier than other *shabbat* observances) hardly helps us detect a possible original theological context. Most scholars believe that the reference to what King David did has been added to the story at a later stage; for example, Beare: "The saying about David and the shewbread is a secondary accretion."[25] Hence: the older layer is the saying about the Son of Man, and the reference to King David was added only later.

Thirdly, the statement that *shabbat* is made for humans, and not vice versa, can be found in non-Christian sources, which proves that it is quite possible to interpret it in an intra-Jewish, halakhic way. The theological context both in the *Mekhilta* and the Talmud is a halakhic discussion of *piquach nephesh*.

Fourthly, it is far from clear what the *halakhic* implications of this story are. By his followers Jesus of Nazareth was believed to be the Christ, and it is stated that "something greater that the Temple is here," but that does not necessarily equate to "Christ is above the Temple," certainly not in the sense that his disciples, *too*, would be above the temple.[26] What, *precisely*, are the halakhic consequences for *his followers*?

In other words, whereas the Christ event is larger than the temple, the implication is hardly that the text is a carte blanche for neglecting *shabbat*, and certainly not for ridiculing it.[27] In short, numerous questions remain unanswered after this survey of interpretations. The text can definitely not be used as proof for the assertion that the historical Jesus was anti-halakhic in his teaching. One simply cannot build a historical reconstruction on such a flimsy foundation. A better foundation stone for what Jesus habitually did on *shabbat* is Luke 4:16: "When he came to Nazareth, where he had been brought up, he went to the synagogue on the sabbath day, *as was his custom*."[28]

7

MUSTARD: TREE, WEED, OR SEED?
Matt 13:31f., Mark 4:30–32, and Luke 13:18f.
(cf. Gospel of Thomas 20)

Most interpretations of this parable emphasize the dialectics between, on the one hand, what once was small and, on the other hand, what eventually grew large. It is followed by a similar parable of the yeast (see chapter 8). Four interpretations of the parable of the mustard seed will be presented in the following discussion.

(a) The importance of transgressing the Jewish Law? Many commentators take as their starting point the Mishnaic statement that mustard (Hebrew: *chardal*) is only allowed to be sown in a "field" (Hebrew: *sadeh*).[1] Since the Lukan version narrates that the mustard seed is not planted in a field but in a "garden" (Greek: *kêpos*), is the parable, then, relating something that is explicitly forbidden in Jewish *halakhah*? One of those who believe this to be the case is Bernard Brandon Scott. He discusses the fact that none of the other versions of the parable states that it took place in a garden (Matthew: "field" [*agros*]; Mark: "land" [*gê*]; Thomas: "tilled soil" [Coptic: *kah*; probably *gê* in Greek]), and argues in favor of the Lukan wording, since it is the more difficult reading, quite simply because it was forbidden to do so: he asserts that it is "a metaphor of impurity."[2] For Scott this is a parable about the imperative to mix what should not be mixed: since the planting of the mustard seed is in violation of the halakhic laws of diverse kinds, then "the planting and growth are a scandal—illegitimate, tainted, unclean."[3] Hence, according to Scott, this is a story that illustrates that "God's mighty works are among the unclean and insignificant."[4]

Whereas this line of thought certainly resonates both with the Augustinian concept of the church as *corpus permixtum* ("a mixed body [of good and evil]") and the yearning of many Christians today that their congregations be more hospitable communities welcoming various groups of people, this interpretation could and should be questioned exegetically, for several reasons. Firstly, as has already been mentioned, it is only one of four versions that explicitly states that the mustard seed is planted in a garden, and we cannot even be sure that the Lukan "garden" corresponds to the Mishnaic concept *'arugah* (garden bed). Furthermore, the Mishnaic regulations about prohibited mixing of certain seeds and plants is not a matter of impurity; it is quite similar to the halakhic prohibitions against mixing meat and milk—that does not imply that either meat or milk is impure (see chapter 9). Hence, this interpretation is a rather rickety reconstruction based on one single word in the Gospel of Luke: *garden*.

Secondly, there are other instances where Matthew, the gospel author most well-versed in *halakhah*, takes pains to narrate the stories within the boundaries of *halakhah*, for example, 15:20 ("...but to eat *with unwashed hands* does not defile") and 26:59 ("Now the chief priests and the whole council were looking for *false* testimony against Jesus..."), parameters that are not known to the other gospel authors. Should not as much emphasis be put on the Matthean text since this Gospel in other instances is closer to the original theological context? Matthew knew that mustard seeds are not planted in a garden.[5] Hence, if he had in front of him a text with the word for *garden*, he is not *concealing* what is shocking, he is *correcting* what is incorrect.

Thirdly, as Ryan S. Schellenberg has pointed out, the evidence for the mustard seed as a stock image in the early first century is surprisingly sparse: there are no references to mustard in the Hebrew Bible (nor, unsurprisingly, in the Septuagint), and when mentioned in antiquity, it is most often for its *positive* effects in medicine, not for its *negative* connotations.[6] Hence, it could be argued that the parable is about what is beneficial and curative, not the opposite (see below, interpretation [d]). Only one other pair of texts in the New Testament mention the mustard seed. The Matthean and Lukan Jesus states that if the faith of the disciples were "as" (Greek: *hôs*) a mustard seed, it would be possible for them to move a mountain (Matt 17:20) or uproot a mulberry tree (Luke 17:6).[7] Here the mustard grain is an ideal to strive for, not a symbol of pariah. To sum up, it seems safe to side with Klyne R. Snodgrass: "Halakhic regulations have no relevance for this parable."[8] Or as Amy-Jill Levine phrases it, the chief purpose of the parables of Jesus is not to show "how bad Jewish Law is."[9] Quite clearly, the first interpretation is deficient: we cannot base such far-reaching conclusions on one particular word in the Lukan version.

(b) What was once small will one day be large: This is, by far, the most common line of thought, although interpreters do not agree on what the mustard seed symbolizes. It is quite common that it is understood as a symbol of *faith* (as in Matt 17:20 and Luke 17:6, see above). Another suggestion is that it refers to the *church*, the spread of Christendom for two thousand years to billions of people all over the world. However, the parable itself compares the mustard seed to the *kingdom of heaven*, which is not identical with people's faith, and quite a few readers hasten to emphasize that the kingdom of God is not identical with the earthly church. W. D. Davies and Dale C. Allison argue that the parable seeks to convey "a vital truth about God's kingdom: a humble beginning and a secret presence are not inconsistent with great and glorious destiny."[10] Hence, interpreters emphasize either the contrast or the continuity between what was small and then became such a large "tree." If the focus is on contrast, then the conclusion is that one should always keep in mind the fact that what is miniscule may have an almost miraculous effect. If the focus is on continuity, then the emphasis is on the inherent potential in the small seed (cf. John 12:24: "if [the wheat grain] dies, it bears much fruit" and 1 Cor 15:36–40 on earthly and heavenly bodies).

Biblical scholars have taken a considerable amount of interest in horticulture and arboriculture when interpreting this parable: does it refer to *Brassica nigra, Salvadora persica*, or perhaps something else? Some readers have been concerned about whether the mustard seed really is the smallest of all seeds. But that part of the parable should be understood colloquially rather than as a factual statement. As Snodgrass states, "Since we are dealing with a proverbial use, anxiety about issues of accuracy are [*sic*] out of bounds."[11]

It is more rewarding to reflect theologically on how the grown-up mustard shrub is described in the four versions. In the Gospel of Mark it is "the greatest of all shrubs" (*meizon pantôn tôn lachanôn*), in the Gospel of Matthew it is "the greatest of all shrubs and becomes a tree" (*meizon pantôn tôn lachanôn estin kai ginetai dendron*), in the Gospel of Luke it "becomes a tree" (*egeneto eis dentron*). In the Gospel of Thomas it is merely stated that the seed falls on the ground; hence, it is the *soil*, rather than the mustard seed, that "puts forth a great branch" (Coptic: *shaphteuo ebol ennounotsh entar*).[12]

Why is it called a "tree" (*dendron*) in Matthew and Luke? Although it was well-known to grow quickly into a several-foot-high herb in one season, it is hardly a tree comparable to, for example, the impressive cedars.[13]

The most common answer is that the tree was a traditional symbol for a great kingdom (Dan 4:10–27, Ezek 17:23 and 31:10f., possibly also Ps 104:12).

It has been suggested that the birds nesting in the tree may be a reference to the righteous Gentiles who have not participated in the oppression of Israel. T. W. Manson refers to *Midrash Tehillim* 104.13 where the expression *'oph ha-shamayim* (the bird[s] of the heavens) is decoded as *umot ha-'olam* (the nations of the world). Hence, Manson writes, "Jesus thought of the Kingdom as increasing by addition until even the Gentile nations should be brought within its scope."[14]

However, some scholars claim that the tree motif is not original, that it is an addition that goes against the grain (!) of the parable itself, since the text emphasizes the importance of the smallness of the seed, not the grandeur of the impressive tree. Scott argues that the "distinctive voice" of the parables often plays against the expectations of "common wisdom," and that this "voice is in jeopardy because, even though these parables come out of and play against common wisdom, in the end common wisdom frequently wins."[15] This takes us to the third interpretation.

(c) A subversive parable against current notions of pride and power: If indeed the tree and the birds nesting in this tree are well-known references to mighty empires, they are also references to *fallen* empires in the past, especially in the Book of Daniel, in which King Nebuchadnezzar describes his dream (4:10f. and 14):

> Upon my bed this is what I saw; there was a tree at the center of the earth, and its height was great. The tree grew strong, its top reached to heaven, and it was visible to the ends of the whole earth....The birds of the air nested in its branches, and from it all living beings were fed....[A holy watcher] cried aloud and said: "Cut down the tree and chop off its branches, strip off its foliage and scatter its fruit. Let the animals flee from beneath it and the birds from its branches."

Daniel, who is asked to interpret the king's dream, says (4:20, 22, and 24f.):

> The tree that you saw...it is you, O king! You have grown great and strong. Your greatness has increased and reaches to heaven, and your sovereignty to the ends of the earth....This is the interpretation, O king, and it is a decree of the Most High that has come upon my lord the king. You shall be driven away from human society, and your dwelling shall

be with the wild animals....Until you have learned that the Most High has sovereignty over the kingdom of mortals, and gives it to whom he will.[16]

The parallels between this passage in Daniel and the New Testament parable are quite apparent. The tree reaching to heaven was a stock metaphor that would have led a first-century audience's thought to an earthly empire that is haughty and eventually will be destroyed. With this frame of reference, is it not likely that the parable about the mustard "tree" may be understood as a warning that God's kingdom, which the disciples are proclaiming, could deteriorate and become similar to the Roman Empire: magnificent and celebrated, yet with all its flaws and failures hardly a fitting image of the kingdom of God?

However, some commentators take this established critique of *foreign* empires and turn it against Jesus's own people, so that it is transformed into a condemnation of Israel. Is it possible that Jesus in this parable is, as Robert W. Funk writes, "poking fun in a deadly serious vein"?[17] Funk describes the mustard weed as short-lived and "a pain in anyone's garden."[18] He calls it "a parody of symbols," since the parable "parodies the mighty cedars of Lebanon as the symbols of Israel's Davidic hopes."[19] In other words, is he turning the traditional messianic hopes into a weed?[20] Postcolonial perspectives and knowledge about the sheer brutality of Roman occupation may draw us to interpretations that shun worldly power. It is a fact that the previous interpretation, with its emphasis on growth, size, and strength, seldom has been questioned. But one should be cautious, of course, if the Jewish parabolist is presented as going against a particularly *Jewish* notion of pride and power. There are numerous Jewish texts that praise the virtues of meekness, for example, Numbers 12:3: "Now the man Moses was very humble, more so than anyone else on the face of the earth." Cannot chauvinism be found in all cultures? Furthermore, when scrutinizing this interpretation, one may want to refer, once again, to Schellenberg's article, in which it was pointed out that there is a paucity of evidence for an alleged proverbial status of the mustard seed in the ancient world.[21] In other words, it is the word *tree*—not that it is a *mustard* plant—that triggers the interpretation that understands the parable as a critique of what is haughty and arrogant.

(d) Mustard was considered beneficial and curative: The fourth and final interpretation focuses neither on the alleged proverbial smallness of the mustard seed nor on the connotations of great trees and Gentile birds. It

takes as its starting point the statements of Pliny the Elder in his *Natural History* about the mustard being extremely beneficial, and even curative for patients suffering from a variety of illnesses, for example, serpent and scorpion bites, toothache, indigestion, asthma, epilepsy, constipation, dimness of vision, dropsy, lethargy, tetanus, and leprous sores.[22] This is what triggers Levine's own interpretation:

> To speak of the parable as demonstrating that great outcomes arrive from small beginnings is correct, but it is banal. To note *what* outcomes might occur provides better provocation. Mustard is a curative, and one available to anyone. It is part of the good world God gives us; like the sun, which insists on shining, the seed insists on growing, to be used by anyone who finds the plants....[T]he mustard plant offers more than a single person can use. The invitation to partake is a universal one, as the birds so neatly demonstrate. Instead of looking at the plant as a noxious weed, we might be better off seeing it as part of the gifts of nature; something so small, allowed to do what it naturally does, produces prodigious effects.[23]

Levine also notes that the Gospel of Thomas surrounds the parable with comments on discipleship.[24] This suggests that we may develop yet another line of thought, when rereading the parable in the light of the teaching in the Sermon on the Mount on the far-reaching consequences of the Christ followers' way of life (Matt 5:16): "Let your light shine before others, so that they may see your good works and give glory to your Father in heaven."

In conclusion, four interpretations have been presented in this chapter: Is it an anti-halakhic parable? Or is the emphasis on the smallness of the seed and the largeness of the mustard "tree" an indication of the growth of the kingdom of God? Or is it a reminder of the significance of smallness and a warning against theological arrogance? Or, finally, is it a parable about the beneficial qualities of mustard?

As often pointed out in this book, the unswervingly anti-halakhic—and therefore anti-Jewish—readings of the New Testament are more often than not anachronistic. Scholars who ascribe to the first interpretation seem to take for granted that the *main* purpose of the teaching of Jesus is to highlight over and over, to quote Levine again, "how bad Jewish Law is."[25] Her understanding of the parable—the fourth interpretation above—focuses on the many beneficial effects of mustard. This is quite the opposite of the first interpretation that described it as a noxious weed and hastened to compare it to *halakhah* and, consequently, to Jewish life at the time of Jesus. In short, the four readings of the parable of the mustard seed constitute yet another example of how differently biblical scholars interpret the New Testament texts. Indeed, one may even wonder if at times scholars happen to plant their own preconceptions in their field of studies and are surprised to see their own favorite ideas blossom in the texts.

8
BREAD (UNFIT) FOR PASSOVER OR HEAVENLY HOSPITALITY?

Matt 13:33 and Luke 13:20f.
(cf. Gospel of Thomas 96)

This succinct parable, consisting of merely one sentence in the New Testament Gospels (and only marginally more extensive in the Gospel of Thomas), has two notable features: the protagonist is a woman (*gynê*), and the keyword is *leaven* (*zymê*). It is preceded by a similar parable about the mustard seed (see chapter 7). Four interpretations will be presented and discussed briefly.

(a) God's Kingdom is not like Jewish sourdough: A number of interpreters take as their starting point the fact that leaven is a negative image in Judaism.[1] When preparing for Passover, observant Jews remove everything that is *chametz* (everything that is leavened), namely, foods that contain any of the five sorts of grain—wheat, oats, rye, barley, and spelt—that has been in contact with water for more than eighteen minutes. Hence, not only is bread included in this definition but also beer, whisky, and other such beverages. The term *seor* specifically refers to yeast—see, for example, Exodus 12:15: "You shall remove leaven [*seor*] from your houses."

That leaven was a negative metaphor at the time of Jesus can be seen elsewhere in the New Testament, for example, Matthew 16:6 and Luke 12:1 ("Watch out and beware of the yeast of the Pharisees and Sadducees"; "Beware of the yeast of the Pharisees, that is, their hypocrisy"). This fact—that leaven is a negative image in Judaism—sometimes serves as a trampoline for exegetical *salti mortali* that seek to prove that the teaching of Jesus, here and elsewhere, is the exact opposite of Judaism—for example, Robert W. Funk:

In the span of a single sentence Jesus combines a new symbol, yeast, with mystery and an epiphany to signal God's domain. By doing so he creates a burlesque of the old standard—the unleavened—that used to be associated with the sacred. Now it is what is leavened that is connected with the sacred. To invert the images of the sacred in a society is to subvert its sacred institutions. *His word-act was thus understood as an attack on the temple and the temple cult in place in his day.*[2]

One has to admit that this is quite an achievement: in one sentence, consisting of either nineteen (according to Matthew) or twenty-one (according to Luke) words, the protagonist in the Gospels manages to subvert the entire Jewish temple cult! Amy-Jill Levine gives numerous examples of this line of thought and concludes that "as soon as 'purity' gets on the menu of certain forms of New Testament exegesis, the taste is predictably a bad one, and the food is again spoiled."[3] One more quotation may suffice to illustrate this Jesus-versus-Judaism approach: C. H. Dodd writes in his classical *The Parables of the Kingdom* that leaven is "in general" a symbol of evil influences carrying infection, and then immediately continues by describing what characterized the Jesus movement: growth. And this inherent power was, he argues, in contradistinction to "religious Judaism." Hence, whereas the Jewish sourdough is dead, the Christian sourdough is alive. At first, it may seem that nothing happened with the Kingdom of God that was heralded by Jesus:

But soon the whole mass swells and bubbles, as fermentation rapidly advances. The picture, I think, is true to history. The ministry of Jesus was like that. There was no element of external coercion, but in it the power of God's Kingdom worked from within, mightily permeating the dead lump of religious Judaism in His time.[4]

While he is more explicit in his portrayal of second-temple Judaism than scholarship in general, he is, as we have seen, not alone in using the fermentation discourse of this parable in order to foment against the religious context out of which the Christian movement grew.

(b) The growth of the kingdom: Dodd's quotation leads into the second approach, which argues that the parable's emphasis is on the inherent power, the irresistible spreading, and the theological universalism of the kingdom of God that Jesus preached and inaugurated. Eduard Schweizer writes: "God's Kingdom permeates the world, where it has a fructifying and stimulating effect." He adds, however, that the parable "must not be debased by being made to refer to a church that gradually wins over the majority of a Christianity silently transforming the world."[5] Similarly, Floyd V. Filson concludes that the message is not "that all men will accept the gospel, but the Kingdom will show an amazing growth from modest beginnings."[6]

In favor of the second interpretation is the narrative context. Immediately after this parable, the Matthean Jesus states that he "will proclaim what has been hidden from the foundation of the world" (13:35). And both the previous parable about a small mustard seed that is sowed in the field and this parable about the yeast in the flour could be summarized as something that is hidden, and yet gradually grows.

(c) Beware lest you make the kingdom a sour dough: In addition to the two instances in the parable about the bread-baking woman (Matt 13:3 and Luke 13:21), the word *zymê* occurs eleven times in the New Testament, and consistently in a negative way, as a metaphor for arrogance, hypocrisy, and evil (Matt 16:6–12, Mark 8:15, Luke 12:1, 1 Cor 5:6–8, and Gal 5:9).[7] And if we want to situate the Gospels firmly in a Jewish context, why should we not explore the possibility that the word is used for something negative in Matthew 13:33 and Luke 13:21 as well?

Hence, it has been suggested that the parable may be read as a warning. The meaning, then, would be: be cautious, lest arrogance and hypocrisy destroy the conditions for the kingdom to be visible among us![8] Once again, if leaven is used as a warning of hypocrisy among other Jewish factions—why not within an equally Jewish group, the Nazarenes, as well? As a matter of fact, Paul actually did warn the Christ followers in Rome that there was a risk that Gentile Christians would become haughty vis-à-vis Jews who did not believe in Jesus as the Christ (Rom 11:18–20, esp. v. 20: "So do not become proud, but stand in awe").

W. D. Davies and Dale C. Allison recognize that "some earlier exegetes" understood the parable to predict the corruption of the church in the world. However, while dismissing this view, they assert that it is somewhat more likely that Jesus "intended it to reflect the disreputable character of many of the members of the kingdom."[9]

(d) The hyperbolic dimension—heavenly hospitality: The fourth interpretation focuses on the excessive amount of flour that the woman uses in this parable: three measures equals some forty liters of flour (approx. ten US gallons).[10] Referring to *Mishnah Peah* 8.7, Joachim Jeremias asserts that it would suffice for a meal for over a hundred people.[11] Even if that

may be an exaggeration, it is still quite a substantial amount of flour for the woman to use when baking.

In Ruth 2:17 we are told that in one day she gleaned one *ephah* of barley, and this is translated into three *sata* in the targum (a paraphrasing translation into Aramaic). In Exodus 16:36 it is stated that one *'omer* is one-tenth of an *ephah*, and in Exodus 16:16 we are told that one *'omer* of manna was sufficient for one person per day. If the numbers in Exodus and Ruth are relevant for these calculations, this would imply that the woman in the parable baked bread for ten people (i.e., enough for Ruth and Naomi for five days). But more important than seeking to establish the exact amount of flour is the observation that it is stated in the targum that Ruth used three *sata* of flour— that is, the exact same amount as in the New Testament parable.

Genesis 18:6 is more often referenced than Ruth 2:17 when discussing this parable. There it is stated that Abraham, having invited three guests into his family's abode, asks Sarah to bake bread for their guests using three *seah* of flour.[12] It is a story about hospitality, table fellowship, and also an unexpected and miraculous pregnancy.[13] Against all odds, Sarah will bear a child, and "all the nations of the earth shall be blessed in him [i.e., Abraham, who is about to become a great and mighty nation]" (Gen 18:18). Levine suggests: "Perhaps the parable tells us that, like dough that has been carefully prepared with sourdough starter or a child growing in the womb, the kingdom will come if we nurture it."[14]

The motif of food and beverage in abundance is mentioned repeatedly in the New Testament, for example, at the wedding at Cana (John 2:1–12) and in the miracles that take place by the Sea of Galilee, when bread and fish miraculously suffice for thousands of people (Mark 6:30–44 and 8:1–10 par.). And, as Davies and Allison note, "Jesus often spoke of the kingdom as a great banquet."[15] If indeed the three measures of flour are of such a great importance when interpreting the parable, because they indicate that the woman is preparing bread for a feast with many guests, then perhaps messianic overtones are not implausible? The Lord's Prayer reminds Christians daily about the intrinsic relationship between the kingdom, earth, heaven, and bread: "Your kingdom come. Your will be done, on earth as it is in heaven. Give us this day our daily bread" (Matt 6:10). Or in the words of Levine:

Perhaps the parable tells us that despite all our images of golden slippers and harps and halos, the kingdom is present at the communal oven of a Galilean village when everyone has enough to eat.[16]

9

IS NOSHING SACRED ANYMORE?
*Matt 15:1–20 and Mark 7:1–23
(cf. Gospel of Thomas 14)*

This text has often served as a cornerstone in the theology of those who have presented Jesus of Nazareth as not only critical toward some contemporary interpretations of the Scriptures but also fundamentally anti-Jewish in his teaching.[1] Indeed, it is not difficult to find numerous commentaries, articles, and monographs that present his entire mission as an exodus away from enslaving Jewish interpretations of the Scriptures, as if Jewish life were the problem that Christianity claims to have solved.

The evangelists called the central statement of this passage a *parabolê*, often translated simply as "parable." More likely what is meant, however, is an enigmatic statement:

There is nothing outside a person that by going in can defile, but the things that come out are what defile. (Mark 7:15)

It is not what goes into the mouth that defiles a person, but it is what comes out of the mouth that defiles. (Matt 15:11)

The most obvious difference between the two Gospels is that the Matthean version emphasizes that it is what comes "out of the mouth" (*ek tou stomatos*) that defiles a person. This difference in wordings—Matthew's explicit mentioning of "the mouth"—will prove to be highly significant.

How, then, has this enigmatic statement been interpreted? Before presenting five interpretations, we should address the issue of various forms of purity and impurity. We will focus on three categories that overlap in terms of terminology but nevertheless must be distinguished from one another.

Firstly, a few characteristics of *ritual purity* in first-century Judaism: It was no sin to become ritually impure. On the contrary, being ritually impure at certain times was one of the basic conditions of life. It is unfortunate that the words *impure* and *unclean* have become so negatively charged, because some of the most important events in a person's life caused her to become ritually impure. Impurity arose, for example, at the conception, birth, and death of a human being. Many would probably argue that few things are more important than honoring one's parents by burying them. Since burying a person meant that one became impure, this is an example that illustrates that there were times when it was honorable and even a duty (*met mitzwah*) to become ritually impure. There are additional examples that overturn common misconceptions of impurity: for example, the fact that sacred objects, such as prayer capsules (*tefillin*) and a Torah scroll, make a person impure proves that "impurity" is not inherently negative. Now, if the Scriptures "defile," how could it be an altogether negative concept? As a matter of fact, the rabbinical question "Does this text defile the hands?" can therefore in a free, but faithful, translation be reformulated into: "Will this text still be holy even if translated into another language?"[2] Or, "Is this text canonical?" See, for example, *Mishnah Yadayim* 3.5:

Rabbi 'Aqiva said:…No one in Israel disputed about the Song of Songs, [saying] that it does not defile the hands. For the whole world is not as worthy as the day on which the Song of Songs was given to Israel; for all the writings are holy but the Song of Songs [*Shir ha-Shirim*] is the Holy of Holies [*Qodesh Qodashim*].

In short, ritual impurity in antiquity, firstly, was *unavoidable* (every person was impure for certain periods of life); secondly, it was *not sinful* (as Daniel Boyarin writes, it carries "no moral opprobrium"); and, thirdly, it was *impermanent* (there were rituals that made the impure person or object pure).

The second category is *moral impurity*, which was (1) *the result of grave sin*, (2) *not contagious*, (3) *long-lasting, sometimes permanent*, (4) *removed by punishment or atonement*, not a purification ritual that involved immersion in water, and finally, (5) *described as an "abomination"* (Hebrew: *to'evah*; in plural *to'evot*). In short, moral impurity should always be avoided. Ritual impurity—which, as has already been stated, was not sinful—was of a transient nature, but moral impurity accumulated, and its ultimate consequence was that the gap between the people and God became so great that the Divine "Presence" (Hebrew: *ha-shekhinah*) might ultimately leave the people.

The third category is *permitted and forbidden foods*. Jewish food laws (Hebrew: *kashrut*) are based on the lists in Leviticus 11 and Deuteronomy 14. How do food rules relate to ritual and moral impurity? Food laws are not to be mixed up with ritual impurity since ritual impurity occurs during a limited period of time: immersion in water and waiting are the two criteria for leaving the state of impurity in order to become pure. Food laws are always to be observed. In addition, ritual impurity was associated with the temple services. When the temple was destroyed in 70 CE, many of the purity rules lost their significance. An indication of this is that there is no *Gemara* (Talmudic commentary) to most of the Mishnah tractates that deal with temple-related impurity. The food laws, on the other hand, are of great importance to Jews all over the world, even today.

But not observing *kashrut* is not to be confused with the grave sins that cause moral impurity. This means that the food rules are *tertium genus*—they form a third group. All three groups are related to one another through the common terminology ("impure" and "impurity"), but they are still so different that they must be kept apart. The food laws should be understood primarily as signs of the covenant, a reminder of the covenant between the God of Israel and the people of Israel. As it is stated in Leviticus 20:24–26 (emphases added):

> I am the Lord your God: I have *separated* you from the peoples. You shall therefore make a *distinction* between the clean and the unclean animals and between the unclean bird and the clean; you shall not bring abomination on yourselves by animal or by bird or by anything with which the ground teems, which I have *set apart* for you to hold unclean. You shall be holy to me; for I the Lord am holy, and I have *separated* you from the other peoples to be mine.

Several times in this text it is emphasized that God has separated Israel to be a people with a specific vocation—and that Israel therefore must distinguish between permitted ("pure") and forbidden ("impure") food. Thus, the rationale for *kashrut* is expressed in terms of covenantal theology. The people of Israel should refrain from certain foods neither because it is *dirty* (in a sanitary sense) nor because it is *dangerous* (in terms of healthfulness), but because the food laws serve as a *divine reminder* of Israel's vocation. It is important to understand the difference between the adjective *impure* (about unlawful food) and the verb *to make impure* (about the laws of purity). In short, *not everything that one is forbidden to eat is impure, nor is everything that is impure always forbidden*. It is crucial to distinguish between biblical *purity* laws and biblical *dietary* laws.

Since the three categories—ritual impurity, moral impurity, and food laws—overlap, we also need to pose the question of whether forbidden foods actually defile ritually. A few examples may suffice: Jewish tradition says that a person who eats forbidden vegetarian food does something that is incorrect, but the person does not become ritually impure. Boyarin states that the only food, according to the Torah, that renders a body impure is carrion—certainly not the eating of permitted food that has become impure, or of forbidden foods in general.[3] The person who mixes meat and milk fails to observe a central part of the laws of *kashrut*, but the person does not become ritually impure by doing so. Someone who eats forbidden seafood acts wrongly but does not become ritually impure. In other words, in most cases it is not to avoid ritual impurity that "impure" foods are forbidden, and transgression of the food laws does not impart moral impurity.

To sum up, we are thus operating with three concepts here: *ritual purity and impurity*, *moral impurity*, and *permitted and forbidden food*, and although these three categories overlap, primarily because of nomenclature (the words *pure* and *impure*; in Hebrew *tahor* and *tame*), we need to distinguish between them in order not to misunderstand them. It is now time to present five interpretations of this text.

(a) An anti-Jewish proclamation: Important parts of Jewish life in antiquity—both in the Land of Israel and in the Diaspora—were sabbath observance (*shabbat*), circumcision of male children on the eighth day (*berit milah*), and *kashrut*. Would a person in antiquity who was consistently indifferent or even blatantly negative in all these three respects even be considered Jewish? If Jesus of Nazareth consistently, in both teaching and in daily life, disregarded *kashrut*, he would probably by most people be understood as going beyond the pale of Judaism. On the other hand, as Boyarin states in an essay called "Jesus Kept Kosher," "if the earliest of Christians believed that Jesus kept kosher, then we have good reason to view that Christianity as another contending branch of Judaism."[4] In short, the *Jewishness* of Jesus is put to the test when interpreting Matthew 15:1–20 and Mark 7:1–23.[5]

A tendency is clearly detectable among commentators to sharpen their pens before writing about this particular passage. Eduard Schweizer, for one, uses the following drastic words when describing the purpose of Mark 7:1–23: "What is primarily important to Mark is this *absurd* Jewish legalism and Jesus' *victory* over it—a *victory* which is evident to everyone."⁶ A similar belligerent discourse can be found in Ezra Palmer Gould's commentary: "In *attacking* this [i.e., tradition], Jesus was *assailing* the very citadel of the Judaism of his time."⁷ Similarly, Ernst Käsemann writes,

> When Jesus in Mark 7,15 refuses to agree that man contracts defilement from external sources, he is abandoning the foundation principle on which the whole Jewish cultus was based....This word of Jesus strikes not merely at rabbinic exegesis and practice but at the very heart of the legislation governing ceremonial and ritual purity; on this occasion Jesus did not scruple to attack and abrogate [*anzugreifen und außer Kraft zu setzen*] what for Judaism had the force of, indeed, according to the literal sense of the Old Testament, actually was, a divine commandment.⁸

Robert W. Funk describes the implications of the statement as a destabilization of Judaism: "If Jesus taught that there is nothing taken into the mouth that can defile, he was *undermining* a whole way of life. That... sounds like Jesus."⁹ Richard McConnell understands this as a paradigm shift from cultic religion to an ethical one: "In reality Jesus is laying down a new ethical principle to *replace* a cultic one....Jesus finds it necessary to *abolish* the purity laws in order to propound the ethical command of God for the present age."¹⁰ Charles E. B. Cranfield uses a Pauline concept from Romans 10:4—usually translated as "the end of the Law"—when commenting on Jesus's statement: "Jesus speaks as the one who is, and knows himself to be, *telos nomou*."¹¹ Hence, Cranfield sees a deep connection between the teaching of Jesus—here understood as the abrogation of the Torah—and an anti-nomistic interpretation of the Pauline message. And, finally, Herbert Braun asserts that it is the very *un*-Jewishness of the Galilean's teaching that ensures the authenticity of this statement: "Das *extrem Unjüdische* dieser Position sichert die Echtheit eines Jesuswortes wie Markus 7,15."¹²

In short, these scholars see this text not merely as a critique of then emerging Jewish interpretations of the Law, what Jewish tradition subsequently called "the Oral Torah" (Hebrew: *Torah she-be-'al peh*), probably referred to in Mark 7:3, 5 and Matthew 15:2 as "the tradition of the elders" (Greek: *hê paradosis tôn presbyterôn*), but as evidence that Jesus in his teaching opposed all the biblical laws of *kashrut* in Leviticus 11 and Deuteronomy 14.¹³ However, if one takes pains to understand the text in an intra-Jewish context, it is quite unlikely that what is questioned is the entire concept of *kashrut*: The animals prohibited in the Torah were not part of the normative diet.[14] To be blunt, why would shellfish, eel, and scorpions be offered in the marketplace in Galilee? It is time to explore alternative interpretations.

(b) A statement not reflecting the teaching of the historical Jesus: The Markan comment in Mark 7:19—"thus cleansing all foods"—is not a statement attributed to the Markan Jesus (since *katharizôn* is a present participle). Thus, it is an interpretation of the teaching of Jesus, but one that need not necessarily reflect his actual teaching (similar to the explicit authorial comment to the readers in Mark 13:14, which addresses the reader in the Gospel's day rather than the crown in Jesus's day). Some scholars go one step farther, questioning whether the statement in Matthew 15:11 and Mark 7:15 per se echoes the teaching of the historical Jesus. Heikki Räisänen is one of those who have argued against the authenticity of the statement, one of his arguments being the missing *Wirkungsgeschichte*—that is, the fact that no one refers to this statement in the earliest Christian sources, although *kashrut* was a crucial issue when Gentiles became Christ followers.[15] Indeed, when Christian texts that are not polemical but parenetical started to refer to this statement, they tended to emphasize the second part of the statement: that one should be careful not to bad-mouth people because it is what goes out of the mouth that makes a person impure. We will return to this observation below.

However, those who question the authenticity constitute a minority; most scholars argue in favor of authenticity. The words of Claude G. Montefiore are famous: he stated that a calling into question of the authenticity "seems scepticism run wild"[16] Indeed, as we saw above, when presenting the previous interpretation, it is the alleged *un*-Jewishness of the statement that has triggered scholars to argue for authenticity. The criterion of dissimilarity, which asserts that lacking Jewish and early Christian parallels are arguments for authenticity, would, taken to the extremes, present a totally un-Jewish Jesus, or at least one who is most himself when he is extreme, as Norman Perrin suggests:

> Mark 7.15 is, therefore, completely without parallel in either rabbinic or sectarian Judaism and more than this, it completely denies a fundamental presupposition of Jewish religion: The distinction between the sacred and the secular....This is perhaps the most radical statement in the whole of the Jesus tradition, and, as such, it is certainly authentic.[17]

(c) A comparison between two valid parts of Jewish life: Jewish tradition has specified 613 commandments in the Torah, of which 365 are positive commandments ("thou shalt") and 248 prohibitions ("thou shalt not"). Of these 613 commandments, three are considered particularly important: the prohibitions against (1) shedding of innocent blood (*shephikhut damim*); (2) illicit sexual relations (*giluy 'arayot*), for example, incest; and (3) idolatry (*'avodah zarah*). These three are sometimes called "the cardinal sins" or in Hebrew *[mitzwot shel] yehareg we-al ya'avor* ([Commandments for which] one should allow oneself to be killed in order not to transgress [these three prohibitions]). Hence, while all commandments are valid, some are even more important than others. It has been suggested that the parabolic statement ought to be understood not in an absolute sense ("there is nothing…") but in a relative sense ("not as much as"). Hence, it is not a matter of abolishing *kashrut* and/or laws of purity but of comparing two valid categories: what goes into a person does not make a person impure *as much as* what goes out of the person.[18] A contemporary parallel is what Rabbi Joseph Telushkin said some years ago in an interview:

> "A major concern of mine is that somehow the term 'religious' became exclusively connected with ritual," he says. "If someone eats nonkosher, no one would call him a religious Jew. But if he speaks *lashon ha'ra* [gossip] or is otherwise unethical, yet performs all the rituals, we do. This gives the impression that ethics are an extracurricular activity. I want to restore ethics to its central place in Judaism.[19]

In short, the third interpretation argues that what the statement seeks to convey is that ritual purity, while still in force, is not as important as the avoidance of immorality. It is a comparison between two valid parts of second-temple Judaism. An example from a Christian context that may illuminate this line of thought is a priest or minister who says that *even more* important than receiving the Eucharist ("going into the mouth") is not to bad-mouth others after the service ("what goes out of the mouth"). That would certainly not amount to a critique of the Eucharist; instead it emphasizes the importance of not separating Christian liturgy from Christian life, at the expense of the latter.

(d) Focusing on "what goes into"—that is, handwashing: The enigmatic statement of Jesus consists of two parts, and we will analyze these in turn. What did the Jewish tradition at the time of Jesus think of what goes into the mouth of a person? How were the biblical texts on *kashrut* and

impurity interpreted? It has already been mentioned that when Jewish dietary rules define what is permitted and what is forbidden, permitted food is called "pure" (*tahor*) and forbidden food "impure" (*tame*). However, generally speaking, forbidden food—although it is called "impure"—does not render a person ritually impure. In that sense, it is quite correct that "it is not what goes into the mouth that makes a person impure," even if it is non-*kosher* food that this person is eating. Hence, for this reason, too, this is not a text that questions the laws of *kashrut*.

What, then, is the key issue if we scrutinize the first limb of the saying in Matthew 15:11 and Mark 7:15 ("going into…")? One answer assumes that those who come to Jesus and his disciples thought that everyone, without exception—even those who did not have to do so according to the traditional interpretation of the Scriptures—should treat ordinary food as sacred food, that is, as if it were food eaten in the temple. They wanted to turn every Jew's every meal into a sacred meal; they wanted everyone to live as if they were priests in the temple. The discussion in this case is thus not about food laws in general but about the very specific question whether rules that previously were applicable only for priests in the temple should now be obligatory for everyone. Indeed, the conclusion of the Matthean version supports the interpretation that the focus is on *handwashing* (15:20): "But to eat without washing your hands, that does not defile man." It is also important to note that this conclusion responds to the text's initial question: Why do Jesus's disciples eat bread without washing their hands (Mark 7:2 and Matt 15:2)? The question therefore concerns a self-imposed purity regulation, not food laws in general. Gedalyahu Alon called this *the expansionist inclination*.[20]

However, this assumption has been questioned by Yair Furstenberg. He sides with those who reject the idea that it is food laws per se that are discussed in this text, since *kashrut* was a given in the first-century Galilean context. Instead, it was a particular approach to ritual purity that was questioned.[21] He claims that the handwashing custom was not a component of the priestly purity system, and, consequently, the issue cannot be an expansion of it.[22] Furstenberg's thesis is that the Pharisees had changed the rules of *halakhah*, and that this is what is reflected in Mark 7 and Matthew 15. The Pharisees had introduced a Greco-Roman practice of handwashing. What is being discussed in the text is not an expansion of priestly practices but an innovative approach to ritual impurity. The Pharisees promoted this new (!) approach, and Jesus rejected it. Jesus, arguing that there was no need to wash one's hands before eating, challenged the very purpose of the

Pharisaic approach to ritual purity. Hence, the dispute over handwashing contrasts two understandings of ritual defilement: one concerned with "that which enters the body," and another concerned with "that which comes out of it."[23] In other words, Furstenberg suggests that the laws of hand purity developed in the opposite direction from the one usually suggested.[24]

Two different systems of purity are compared in this text: on the one hand, the *levitical* system, described in the biblical texts and defended by Jesus, which understands impurity as flowing from people and vessels to food. The implication is that if holy food is contaminated, then its consumption is prohibited. On the other hand, we have the *rabbinic* system, which claims that a vessel can be defiled by foods and liquids. The biblical law—that is, the levitical system favored by Jesus—posits the person as a source of contamination of foods and vessels, whereas the Pharisees are concerned with the effects of contamination on the person.[25] This is how Furstenberg paraphrases Jesus's critique of the handwashing rituals of the Pharisees: "Contrary to your *halakhah*, which is unknown in the bible, the body is not defiled by eating contaminated food. Rather, it is defiled by what comes out of it."[26]

It is interesting that Furstenberg's interpretation actually also provides us with a plausible context for the comment in Mark 7:19 ("declaring all foods clean"). Jesus claims that there is no need for handwashings because food cannot make a person impure. Hence, he is declaring all foods clean (*katharizôn panta to brômata*). What Jesus rejected was the laws of defiled foods that were imposed by the Pharisees. Jesus was permitting the eating of bread without ritual washing of the hands.[27]

In his book *The Jewish Gospels: The Story of the Jewish Christ*, Boyarin supports Furstenberg's thesis that the Pharisees had instituted a new practice of ritual purification by pouring water over the hands before eating bread, so that the hands would not make the bread impure.[28] The Gospels describe a Jesus who rejects the Pharisaic extension of these purity laws beyond their original specific biblical foundations. In short, he is not *rejecting* the Torah's rules and practices but *upholding* them.[29] It was thus against those Pharisaic innovations, which they are trying to foist on his disciples, that Jesus railed, and not against *kashrut* at all.[30] Interestingly, Boyarin suggests that the text reflects regional tensions between Galilee and Judea. The Galileans were antipathetic to the urban Judaean Pharisaic innovations by those "who had come down from Jerusalem" (Mark 7:1, cf. Matt 15:1).[31]

To sum up, when focusing on the first limb of the saying—on "what goes into a person"—we have seen that the traditional understanding has been that Jesus objected to the *expansionist* interpretations of the Pharisees who sought to convince others to live in a state of priestly purity. However, Furstenberg has argued that the question is that some had introduced a whole new system of purity, one that did not trace impurity from people to foods but the other way around: from foods to people. The Furstenberg-Boyarin position neatly explains why Jesus criticized the Pharisees for making void "the word of God" (Matt 15:6) or "the commandment of God" (Mark 7:8) for the sake of their own tradition. When Jesus defends the biblical system of purity, he is actually claiming what Mark concludes in his comment in 7:19 and what Matthew writes in his conclusion in 15:11: eating foods with unwashed hands does not defile a person.

(e) Focusing on "what goes out"—that is, evil speech: E. P. Sanders has argued that the saying in Mark 7:15 appears to be "too revolutionary to have been said by Jesus himself....If, of course, we provide a new context for the saying, it can be saved as an authentic logion."[32] The remainder of this chapter seeks to provide us with such a plausible *intra*-Jewish context for the latter half of the saying. This is not only a fascinating endeavor but also a necessary one. Boyarin points out that a recurrent problem in New Testament scholarship is that interpreters and scholars have been "reading the text backward from later Christian practices and beliefs about the written Torah and its abrogation."[33] In order to avoid such an approach, which is necessarily anachronistic and often also apologetic, we need to take pains to rediscover plausible intra-Jewish contexts. The focus now is *how then-contemporary Jewish tradition looked upon what comes out of the mouth.* In the interview cited above, Rabbi Telushkin used the expression *lashon ha-raʻ* ("the evil tongue"; cf. *ʻayin ha-raʻ*, "the evil eye"). In the rabbinic texts, we see that amoraic rabbis (c. 200–500 CE) took *lashon ha-raʻ* literally—that is, what comes out of the mouth. In order to persuade people not to commit *lashon ha-raʻ* there was a tradition that stated that the evil speech is not only as serious as the three cardinal sins described above, but even as serious "all of them together" (*ke-neged kulam*).[34]

This statement is combined with a list of the alleged three most important positive commandments: (1) *to honor one's parents*, (2) *to show generosity*, and (3) *to seek peace between people*. Then comes the conclusion: studying the Torah is as important as all these three together (*ke-neged kulam*). The two lists thus become mirror images of each other. The opposites of the three cardinal sins are the three greatest commandments—and the opposite of evil speech is the study of the Scriptures. It seems reasonable to assume that the underlying idea is that those who study the Scriptures allow the words to *go in* through eyes and ears (listening and not only reading was important in antiquity), and that those who commit *lashon ha-ra'* abuse what *goes out* through their mouths. In short, evil speech is the very opposite of studying the Torah.

Perhaps it needs to be pointed out that the purpose of such statements is not to diminish the seriousness of shedding innocent blood (cf. Matt 5:21–26). Instead, it is about treating evil words "as if" (Hebrew: *ke-ilu*) they were as serious as murder. One should thus regard them as murder with words. In rabbinic literature there is a notion that making someone blush in public is "as if" it were murder; and in the Sermon of the Mount, it is stated that if one insults another person, it is as if one has murdered that person.[35]

Since the expression *lashon ha-ra'* cannot be found in the Torah, the rabbis had to reach this conclusion indirectly. A biblical text that turned out to be especially important in this endeavor is Numbers 12, in which it is stated that Miriam—arguably with Aaron's help (but the verb is in feminine, singular, so her role is emphasized)—blamed Moses for marrying a Cushite woman. However, this seems to be a pretext for something else. It is stated in the second verse: "[Miriam and Aaron] said: 'Has the LORD spoken only through Moses? Has he not spoken through us also?'" Hence, the real reason seems to be that there was a power struggle between the siblings, which is a motif that occurs frequently both in Genesis and elsewhere: Miriam and Aaron also wanted to lead the people. The text states that Miriam, because she slandered Moses, suffered from something called *tzara'at* in Hebrew, a term we traditionally translate with the word *leprosy*. However, there is no indication that it really was leprosy (Hansen's disease).

It seems that it was the statement in Deuteronomy 24:9 that helped the rabbis see how to apply Numbers 12. The readers of the Torah are urged to "remember what the Lord your God did to Miriam on your way out of Egypt." Since *tzara'at* made a person ritually impure, the rabbis could—by combining all these texts—thus create a chain of thought that urged people to be aware of the destructive powers of the evil tongue:

- Evil speech is associated with *tzara'at*.
- *Tzara'at* renders a person impure.
- Evil speech makes a person impure.

In order to avoid misunderstanding, we may need to clarify one thing here. Rabbinic Judaism did not maintain that evil speech made a person ritually impure de facto. If that were the case, there would have been actual purification rituals in the rabbinic texts for those who are guilty of *lashon ha-ra'*. Since there is not a single such ritual, we can say with certainty that it is *another* form of impurity that is meant: it is not a halakhic impurity, but a haggadic one, which means that it is an anecdote or a parable that seeks to illustrate something. The purpose of the rabbis was to persuade their communities to use the tongue in a cautious way: they wanted to dissuade them from using it in a destructive way.

It is now time to summarize what has been said so far. Firstly, in the rabbinic texts there is a technical term for evil speech: *lashon ha-ra'*. Secondly, the rabbis considered the abuse of the tongue to be a very serious violation. There are even texts that go so far that evil speech is considered as serious as all three cardinal sins *combined*. Thirdly, the rabbinical interpretation of Numbers 12 about Miriam's accusations of Moses makes it clear that they saw a connection between *lashon ha-ra'* and *tzara'at*, which makes a person impure. Fourthly, it may be significant that evil speech takes place in a situation where there is a power struggle. (After all, is not that one of the most plausible contexts for evil speech?)

We have already mentioned that *lashon ha-ra'* is a concept that we find fully developed in amoraic sources. In other words, it is likely that the texts in the New Testament constitute the oldest evidence of this haggadic idea.[36] There are other instances when the New Testament indicates that traditions have a long prehistory. Two examples may suffice: firstly, the very oldest evidence for the tradition of reading a text from the Prophets in the synagogue service (the *haphtarah* reading) is found in Luke 4:17, and, secondly, a parallel to the statement in *Mishnah Sanhedrin* 10.1 ("All Israel have a share in the world to come") is found already in Romans 11:26, thus predating the tradition at least 150 years.

All this makes it possible to draw the important conclusion that evil speech—what comes out of the mouth—in a certain sense (i.e., in *Aggadah*) makes a person impure. All this suggests that this is a context in which the parabolic statement in Matthew 15 and Mark 7 could be interpreted. Imaginatively, we could suggest that the following words were written between the lines:

> Why do you slander my disciples, and thus also me? Why do you insinuate that I do not keep the Law? Remember that it is an even greater sin to speak ill of others than not to keep your additional interpretations of the rules of purity. Yea, I say unto you, it is not so much the things which enter into the mouth, that defile a person; it is much more what goes out of the mouth that makes a person unclean.

Is Noshing Sacred Anymore?

Remember what the Lord our God did to Miriam on our way out of Egypt.

In this chapter it has been argued that (1) it is likely a matter of comparison between what goes into and out of a person, in a relative sense (i.e., A is *even more* important than B), not in an absolute and abrogating sense (i.e., A is important, whereas B is *not at all* important); (2) that the underlying issue possibly is the innovations of the Pharisees, and certainly not *kashrut* per se; and (3) that the haggadic expression *lashon ha-ra'* is helpful when interpreting the statement.

Many years ago, when the internet was a rather new phenomenon, this story was found on a Jewish Orthodox website about a group of *chasidim* [pious men] who are on a journey:

> They reached a small wayside inn run by a Jew. Here they stopped. Not knowing the owner, the chasidim asked for a dairy supper. "I am terribly sorry," the innkeeper apologized, "but I have nothing dairy to serve you. I can only offer meat." The chasidim began cross-examining him. "Who is your shochet [butcher]?" "Who certified him to slaughter?" "Does anyone inspect his knives periodically?" "Who kashered the meat?"…Suddenly, a voice was heard from the corner. Everyone looked and saw a shabbily dressed man sitting behind the stove. "Chasidim" he said. "You have no end to your questions. You wish to make sure that every single particular is perfectly kosher. *You are so careful and meticulous about what goes into your mouths. Tell me, are you also as careful about what comes out of your mouths?*"[37]

In other words, at this website, belonging to a Jewish Orthodox congregation, a phrase similar to Matthew 15:11 is used and makes perfect sense! Numerous commentators have argued that the statement attributed to Jesus proves that he weighed anchor and departed from the shores of the Jewish tradition. However, when locating this statement *within* a Jewish context, one is inclined rather to ask whether there is *any* statement attributed to Jesus that to the same extent anchors him in the halakhic sea of then-contemporary Judaism.

10
THE TEXT ABOUT THE TENANTS IN THE VINEYARD: PARABLE PROPER OR YET ANOTHER ALLEGORY?

Matt 21:33–46, Mark 12:1–12, and Luke 20:9–19
(cf. Gospel of Thomas 65f.)

For centuries, this story—found in all the three Synoptic Gospels, as well as in the Gospel of Thomas—has been the proof text par excellence when Christians have sought to substantiate, with the help of biblical texts, the deicide charge against the Jewish people. The story about how the mismanagement and abusive behavior of wicked Jewish tenants resulted in the vineyard being handed over from Israel to the church was simply too good to be ignored by advocates of punitive supersessionism. But is this really the only way to interpret the text? As a matter of fact, it has been understood in several different ways, here summarized in four lines of thought.

(a) An allegory about the crucifixion of "the Son": Remarkably early it was taken for granted that it was an allegory in which Jesus speaks of himself as "the son," in accordance with the embryonic Trinitarian theology that would eventually describe and address him first and foremost as "the Son," as in the Nicene Creed: "Jesus Christ, the only Son of God, eternally begotten of the Father, God from God, Light from Light, true God from true God."

According to this view, the tenants in the vineyard were the Jewish people, who not only mishandled the vineyard but also abused the Lord's messengers to the Jewish people (i.e., the prophets), and finally also murdered the Son of God. Aaron A. Milavec summarizes this interpretation in the following chilling words: "According to the terms of the parable, the Jews had finally gone too far. Murdering 'the Son,' Jesus Christ, was the last straw, God's patience was strained to the breaking point."[1] This line of thought gives vent to the idea that the Jewish people refused to listen to the message of both the prophets and Jesus. Firstly, they persecuted and killed the prophets, and when God finally sent his own Son into the world, they killed him also (cf. Acts 7:51f.). Therefore, consequently, God must reject the Jewish people—because the Jews have now actually gone one step too far.[2] In his commentary to the Gospel of Matthew, Eduard Schweizer summarizes the message of the Matthean version as "The Parable of Israel's Rejection of Jesus": "The message of the parable is stated explicitly: God's Kingdom will be taken from Israel and given to a people that 'produces the proper fruits.'…The new people comprises all nations, as 28:19 will show."[3] In his commentary to the Markan version Schweizer states that "Israel's rejection of the gospel is the reason why the gospel passed from Israel to the other nations."[4] "Taken by itself the parable explains that Jesus' Passion is a result of Israel's disbelief just as was the fate of the prophets."[5]

This interpretation has been exceedingly influential in church history, and no one can doubt that it has been detrimental to Jews living under Christians: it has forged Christians' understanding of the Jewish people at the time of Jesus—and in their own times. From an exegetical point of view, a problem with this interpretation is that the text genre-wise no longer is a proper parable but rather an allegory—that is, a story that both with its many details and in its entirety refers to something else. In short, does the text refer to the death of Jesus? Is Jesus, as Crossan says, "rather awkwardly allegorizing his own death"?[6] If yes, then it is an allegory. A parable, on the other hand, is in the classical definition of C. H. Dodd "a metaphor or simile drawn from nature or common life, arresting a hearer by its vividness or strangeness, and leaving the mind in sufficient doubt about its precise application to tease it into active thought."[7]

Ever since the time of Adolf Jülicher, however, biblical scholars have questioned that this text originally was an allegory about Jesus's own person and role. If it were, it would, as a matter of fact, be an allegory without parallels in the synoptic tradition. We do not have another example of an allegory in the New Testament in which Jesus would be talking about himself in a similar way. It is true, of course, that the Gospel of John contains numerous sayings about Jesus as the Son, who has a unique relationship with the Father, but this story is found in the synoptic tradition (and also in the Gospel of Thomas). However, if it did refer to the death of Jesus, would it not end with at least a hint of the resurrection (cf., e.g., Matt 16:21, Mark

8:31, and Luke 9:22)? These ambiguities have motivated scholars to seek an alternative interpretation.

(b) A parable about the political situation in Galilee: In several books and articles, John Dominic Crossan has sought to unveil how a first-century Galilean audience would have understood the parable.[8] Crossan situates the original version of the parable in a precarious political context at the time of Jesus in Galilee with absentee landlords and rebellious—but not-so-wicked—peasantry. In his view this is *not* a theocentric allegory, but a parable proper about historical actualities in Galilee at that time. In other words, he argues that the owner of the vineyard is not an overt reference to God but quite simply a landowner of flesh and blood, who wants his tenants to reimburse him for his investment in the vineyard, perhaps even before there was a reasonable chance for the vineyard to have produced a crop, which would take some four or five years (cf. Lev 19:23–25).[9] The parable originally told the story of a son, "with absolutely no self-reference to Jesus whatsoever."[10] In short, the parable reflects the historical actualities in the region of Galilee rather than a theological idealism of the kingdom of God. Crossan also argues that the Coptic version of the parable is a very early and quite independent version of it, which takes us to the Gospel of Thomas.

One of the most remarkable achievements by scholars who have studied this particular text is Dodd's reconstruction of the original parable, which turned out to be almost identical with the version in logion 65 in the Gospel of Thomas, a text that had not yet been discovered when Dodd published his book in 1935. The Nag Hammadi texts were not found until ten years later, and made accessible to the scholarly world only when it was first published in 1956, and in a subsequent English translation published in 1959.[11]

Despite this, Dodd maintained that in this parable Jesus foretells his own death and "the disaster to fall upon the Jews."[12] Hence, toward the end of the day, Dodd did interpret it as an allegory by Jesus *about Jesus*, a conclusion that gave Matthew Black reason to write the famous statement: "While thus showing allegory firmly to the door, one cannot but wonder if Dr. Dodd has not surreptitiously smuggled it in again by the window."[13]

When discussing the allegorization of the parable, Richard Valantasis's observation is relevant: the word *slave* (Coptic: *hmhal*) in logion 65 has been provided a superlinear stroke, which is an indication that somewhere along the line of the evolving manuscript tradition someone understood the two servants as divine figures and, consequently, wrote the word *slave* as a *nomen sacrum* (Latin for "holy name").[14]

It is stated in the Gospel of Thomas that the landlord is "good" (Coptic and Greek: *chrêstos*)—or is he? As a matter of fact, the Thomas manuscript is severely damaged, and we can only guess what was once written at the top of page 45. We can only detect the first two letters and the last letter: *Ch R...S*. After the first two initial consonants the conjecture for the third letter is unquestionably an *E*, but what about the penultimate letter? It is quite possible that it was not an *O* but an *E*, thus describing the owner as a "creditor" (Coptic and Greek: *chrêstês*). Moreover, no one in the Gospel of Thomas is described as "good" (*chrêstos*). The only instance where the word occurs is in a description of the leniency of the halakhic interpretations of Jesus, the "yoke" of Jesus (logion 90; see chapter 5).

In other words, we have no textual evidence that proves that the owner of the vineyard in the Gospel of Thomas is good. And when we seek to reconstruct the text, we need to take into consideration that in logion 64 it is stated that "tradesmen and merchants [shall] not [enter] the places of my Father," which does not provide the reader with a positive understanding of landowners. The version of this story in the Gospel of Thomas need not be a theocentric parable, in which the owner necessarily represents the good God of Israel.

Compared to the synoptic tradition, what are the distinctive features of logion 65? The owner is not the planter of the vineyard, he is simply its owner who wants to collect the *karpos*, the "fruit" (i.e., the profits); there are no allusions to Isaiah 5:1–7, no servant is killed before the murder of the son, there is no mention of the son being thrown outside the vineyard (cf. John 19:17 and Heb 13:12f.), it does not say that he is the owner's *beloved* son (as in Mark 12:6 and Luke 20:13), and there is no concluding question with an answer or any punishment of the tenants.[15] In short, the version of the Gospel of Thomas does not show any equivalent allegorizing tendencies.

Jane E. and Raymond R. Newell have suggested quite a specific context for the original parable. Galilee in the first century was a stronghold for the Zealot movement, which was discontented with foreign landowners: "To kill the foreign son of a foreign landowner in order to regain a vineyard for Israel would not be an atrocity, but a hero's accomplishment."[16] But Jesus does not ask his listeners whether they think that the tenants' behavior was justifiable or not; instead, he asks what they thought the owner of the vineyard would do to those tenants—and the answer is that he would put them to death for insurrection. Hence, the outcome of their actions is utter self-destruction. According to the Newellean reading, it is neither a Christological allegory nor a story about the fate of those who oppose Jesus and his work but "an authentic parable that speaks to a particular audience in a particular situation that was common in Jesus' own day."[17]

In sum, this second line of thought interprets the parable not as theological but sociological: it does not depict the God of Israel, but an absentee landlord who demands his profits from the tenants in an actual vineyard. As Amy-Jill Levine wittingly phrases it, according to this interpretation the owner in the parables is more a Don Corleonesque "godfather" than "God the Father."[18] Not everyone is convinced by the supporters of this reconstruction of an original Galilean parable, but even those who reject it have to reflect on the identity of "the son" in the parable. If Jesus is not referring to himself, to whom does he refer? This takes us to the next interpretation.

(c) A conflict about "authority" in Jerusalem? Malcolm Lowe and David Stern both argue that the parable was originally perceived as a critique of the mistreatment of John the Baptist, and that he is "the son" in the parable.[19] As a matter of fact, there are a number of indications that speak to the benefit of this interpretation. Previously in the Gospels, Jesus discusses with the religious leadership of Jerusalem precisely what happened to John the Baptist and the question of religious authority (Matt 21:23–27, Mark 11:27–33, and Luke 20:1–8). Indeed, the Markan commentary on the impact of the parable is not comprehensible without the previous text (Mark 12:12; cf. Matt 21:46 and Luke 20:19): "When they realized that he had told this parable against them, they wanted to arrest him, but they feared the crowd. So they left him and went away."

It is only when reading this verse in the light of the concluding verses in the eleventh chapter that the reader understands to whom the word "they" refers. An advantage of this interpretation is also that it was understandable in the days of Jesus. The historical Jesus may very well have discussed with the religious and political leadership the fate of the recently executed John the Baptist.

(d) Is the son necessarily a historical person? Milavec proposes that "the son" does not refer to any particular person but quite simply is the culmination of the story: the owner sends not only servants but also his own son.[20] Milavec belongs to those who argue that the focus in the parable is the critique of the religious leadership, who are to be identified with the bad tenants in the vineyard; it is their fault that the vineyard of Israel does not bear as much fruit as it could with better leaders.

The Text about the Tenants in the Vineyard

Although allegorized early on, we have good reasons to claim that the parable was *not* originally an allegory, and, consequently, it was *not* originally a story by Jesus about Jesus. According to Milavec, this is not *a Jewish-Gentile allegory* (i.e., Gentile Christians replacing Jews as "the people of God") but a veiled description of *a Jewish-Jewish rift* (i.e., an intra-Jewish critique).[21]

Now, three additional issues need to be addressed before we can draw our conclusions: (1) Given that the parable is often understood as a stern critique of the people, we need to reflect on *how the disciples—who are part of the people—are portrayed in the Gospels*. (2) Furthermore, we ought to ponder *to whom the kingdom of God is given*. (3) Finally, we need to explore *how we are to understand the saying about the cornerstone*.

Firstly, a few reflections on the portrayal of the disciples, especially in the Gospel of Mark: Theodore J. Weeden is well known for his proposal, first presented in an article as early as 1968 and subsequently in a book in 1971, that the Gospel of Mark deliberately portrays the disciples in a starkly negative way, characterized by, firstly, *imperceptivity* (1:16—8:26), successively by *misconception* (8:27—14:9), and, finally, by *rejection* (14:10–72). He argues that this is "a carefully formulated polemical device created by the evangelist to disgrace and debunk the disciples."[22] Arguably the strongest statement of his is that

> Mark is assiduously involved in a vendetta against the disciples. He is intent on totally discrediting them. He paints them as obtuse, obdurate, recalcitrant men who at first are unperceptive of Jesus' messiahship, then oppose its style and character, and finally totally reject it. As the coup de grace, Mark closes his Gospel without rehabilitating the disciples.[23]

The reason is, Weeden argues, that there were conflicting Christologies at the time of Mark, and that "authentic messiahship is suffering messiahship which leads inevitably to crucifixion."[24] Since the disciples do not understand this, they misunderstand the person and passion of Christ. Hence, the disciples are in no way role models for the readers of the earliest narrative account of Jesus of Nazareth. Weeden's suggestion has convinced most New Testament scholars—but the question we need to pose here is: to what extent have we allowed this to influence our interpretations of the parable of the wicked tenants? Given that the disciples are not a positive example, how probable is it that the vineyard will be handed over to them? Are they really "the others" (Greek: *allois*) to whom the vineyard will be handed over? According to Mark, the disciples are, first and foremost, fallible followers of Jesus. They, too, are imperfect tenants, unable to harvest the fruits of the vineyard. It is unlikely that Mark would consider the fallible followers worthy of such a great assignment.[25]

Secondly, to whom is the kingdom of God given? In the Matthean conclusion in verse 43 it is stated that "the Kingdom of God" will be taken away from "you" and given to an *ethnos* producing the fruits of it.[26] The word *ethnos* has more often than not been understood as a reference to the nations of the world, but, as W. D. Davies and Dale C. Allison correctly ask, if the Gentiles were in view, would we not expect the plural, as in the concluding words about making disciples among all the nations (*panta ta ethnē*)?[27] Matthew uses the singular form elsewhere (24:7; cf. Mark 13:8), where it clearly means "one group of people." The fact that the word is used in the singular, and not the plural, may seem to be a miniscule observation, but it is nevertheless an important one, and with far-reaching implications. The handover of the kingdom from "you" to "a nation" is lacking in both the Markan and Lukan versions, and in Matthew it is unlikely that it is a reference to the nations of the world. Hence, nothing in the synoptic tradition points in the direction of a transfer of the kingdom from Israel to the Gentiles, from the people to the peoples, from, using the traditional Hebrew expressions, *'am Yisrael* (the people of Israel) to *ummot ha-'olam* (the nations of the world).

Thirdly, who is the stone that the builders rejected? The short standard answer in the commentaries to the New Testament is that the stone is Jesus Christ—and there is certainly an undeniable connection between the metaphor "stone" and the person Jesus of Nazareth (Acts 4:11, Eph 2:20, and 1 Pet 2:6). However, that statement must be nuanced, when we seek to do justice to all the biblical texts in which this metaphor occurs. There are at least three texts in the Old Testament of particular relevance when discussing the usage of the word *stone*, not used in the concrete—pun intended—sense, but metaphorically: Exodus 28:12, Isaiah 28:16, and Psalm 118:22.

(i) A good starting point when reflecting on the metaphorical interrelationship in the Scriptures between "stones" and "the people of Israel" is Exodus 28, a chapter that describes how Aaron is to be dressed for his holy service. The text states that they shall write on two stones the names of the twelve tribes of Israel in the order of their birth—that is, Reuben, Simeon, Levi, Judah, Dan, and Naphtali on one of them, and Gad, Asher, Issachar, Zebulun, Joseph, and Benjamin on the other, which actually amounts to exactly twenty-five letters on each stone (if Benjamin is spelled with dou-

ble *yud* as in Gen 35:18). In the twelfth verse it says that these shall be *avnei zikkaron li-vnei Yisrael* (stones of memorial for the children of Israel). Hence, these two stones are to be carried on the shoulders as a remembrance for the children of Israel. The fact that the two words *avnei* (stones of) and *li-vnei* (to the children of) rhyme has triggered a line of thought that is sensitive to the phonetic connection between "stone(s)" and "the people of Israel" (cf. Matt 3:9 and Luke 3:8).

In verse 21 it says that there should also be twelve separate stones with the names of the twelve tribes. Hence, when Aaron comes before God in the Sanctuary, he shall be wearing a set of stones that will be a remembrance for the people of Israel. There is thus an interrelationship among remembrance, stones, and the people of Israel. It is interesting to note that when commenting on Psalm 118, medieval Jewish philosophers David Kimchi (=*Radaq*; 1160–1235) and Abarbanel (1437–1508) argue that Israel is the foundation block of the nations: as Avrohom Chaim Feuer writes, "When the dawn of redemption arrives, all nations will realize that Israel is the cornerstone of the world."[28]

Additionally, there is also a connection between "children" (*banim*) and "builders" (*bonim*). For example, in *Talmud Bavli Berakhot* 64a, a revocalization is suggested of a word in Isaiah 54:13: "And all your children shall be taught of the Lord, and great shall be the peace of your children." Then it states *al tiqrei banayikh ella bonayikh* (do not read "your children" but "your builders"), thus widening the mission: one is also to teach one's students (*talmidim*), so that they may be builders of increased peace in the world. Hence, this brief study of the text and reception history of Exodus 28 and related texts revealed that there is a fascinating set of associations among the notions of "stone," "people of Israel," and "builders."

(ii) The second relevant text to study is Isaiah 28:16: "See, I am laying in Zion a foundation stone, a tested stone, a precious cornerstone, a sure foundation" (*hinneni yissad be-Tziyyon aven even bochan pinnat yiqrat musad mussad*). This probably refers to the temple, in which the liturgy takes place. And in another text in the same book, Isaiah 8:14, it says that God will be "a stumbling block and a rock of offence" (*even negeph u-letzur mikhshol*). In Genesis 49:24 God is called "the Stone of Israel" (*even Yisrael*). Hence, God, too, can be likened to the Rock, as in the famous prayer *Adon 'Olam: Tzur chevli be-'eit tzarah* (Rock of my affliction in time of trouble).[29]

(iii) Thirdly and finally, Psalm 118:22 states that the stone that the builders rejected has become the cornerstone. It has been suggested that the

implied author of this psalm is the king, but that is only a qualified guess. What we do know is that this psalm is part of the *Hallel* (Ps 113—118), to be recited at major festivals, for example, Passover. It is most certainly this set of psalms that is referred to in Matthew 26:30 and Mark 14:26: "When they had sung [the psalms], they went to the Mount of Olives." It is not difficult to understand that Psalm 118 became such an important hermeneutical key for the first Christ followers to see a reoccurring pattern in the death and resurrection of Jesus Christ (v. 17): "I shall not die, but I shall live and recount the deeds of the Lord."

To sum up, the keywords that we are discussing do not refer to one single object or one single person. However, what they all have in common is *the people of Israel*: the people are described with the help of *stones* (Exod 28:12), as a *child* (e.g., Exod 4:22: "my son"), and as *builders* (*Berakhot* 64a). The idea in Christian thought that Jesus embodies his crucified and resurrected people helps us to understand the connection between the traditional explanations of the metaphors and the new dimensions they gain in the New Testament. A relevant parallel is the cluster of texts about the suffering servant in Deutero-Isaiah. Chronologically speaking, the fifty-third chapter was originally a description of the people of Israel; in Christian thought it is *also* a text that has relevance when seeking to understand who Jesus of Nazareth was and what he accomplished.[30] However, the Christological interpretations of the passages do not void the original context and relevance. Similarly, the young woman in Isaiah 7:14, who is to give birth to a child, who shall be called *Immanuel*, has already in the New Testament Gospels been understood *also* to be relevant for Christology, but that need not mean that the Christian reception of the image is the *only* one.

What we are looking for here is a way to seek to understand the hermeneutics of the first Christ followers, and an important aspect seems to be that the Scriptures were read and reread in order to understand what God was currently doing, not to undo what God had previously done. In the words of Krister Stendahl, "There is a distinct shape to God's way of doing things, a shape that the Scripture reinforces and helps us to recognize."[31]

Going back to Psalm 118:22, and given the context in the Gospels, it is reasonable to assume that the builders are the political and religious leaders ("chief priests and Pharisees" in Matt 21:45; "scribes and chief priests" in Luke 20:19; in Mark 12:12 simply "they"). But who is "the cornerstone" (*kephalē gōnias*)? It has already been pointed out that the traditional answer by commentators has been that it is Jesus himself. Needless to say, in an allegorized interpretation of the *mashal* (Hebrew for "parable") both the son in the parable and the stone in the *nimshal* (Hebrew for "moral" or "application") refer to Jesus, the parabolist. But if the *mashal* is not an allegory, then why should we insist on allegorizing the *nimshal*?

Given that we can detect a pre-allegorized version of the parable, is it not more likely that the stone actually refers to same thing as the vineyard—that is, Israel? As mentioned above, in Exodus 4:22f., God calls the people of Israel "my son" (*beni*). The builders—the members of the establishment—have not been good tenants, but God is able to transform a stone into children of Abraham (see chapter 1). "God is able from stones to raise up children to Abraham." Hence, there is a connection among "stone" (*even*), "son" (*ben*), and "the people of Israel" (*benei Yisrael*).[32]

It is certainly true that the-rejected-stone-becoming-the-cornerstone was popular among the first generations of Christ followers who believed that the Scriptures foresaw and foretold the resurrection of Jesus. But before the parable became an allegory about Jesus himself, did Psalm 118 play an independent role? Or was it only added to the original parable when it was allegorized? If it is a parable proper in Mark (as we have argued in this chapter), should we then not seek for a parabolic understanding also of the quotation from the Psalms? The most plausible interpretation ought to be that the stone refers to the vineyard—that is, God's Israel.

By way of conclusion, when studying this particular text, one is struck by the extent to which it turns out to be a textbook example of how a *parable* (in pre–New Testament times) is transformed into an *allegory* (in post–New Testament times). Three strata and, indeed, also three contexts (two *intra*-Jewish and one *anti*-Jewish) have been suggested: it is plausible that we can reconstruct a *Galilean* context, we can undoubtedly detect a *Judean* context, and we cannot avoid seeing a *Christian* context, which regrettably gives vent to an anti-Jewish approach to the parable.

- (i) ***Pre–New Testament times (a parable proper in a Galilean context):*** Crossan *et alii* have sought to reconstruct an original version of the parable that reflects the political situation in Galilee at the time of Jesus. While not all scholars are convinced by his suggestion, no one can deny that the version of the story in the Gospel of Thomas lacks all the allegorizing features that accompany most interpretations of the parable.
- (ii) ***The New Testament (still a parable, now in a Judean context):*** We have seen that in the Synoptic Gospels this parable is still placed within an *intra*-Jewish context. It is quite plausible that it is a matter of *intra*-Jewish critique of the then-contemporary

religious and political leadership in Jerusalem. Bearing in mind that the movement of the Nazarene began in Galilee, we may ask whether this is a clash between the Galilean movement and the religious establishment in Jerusalem in Judea. The conclusions of the three synoptic accounts make it clear that it is the religious and political authorities *themselves* that identify with the wicked tenants in the parable, and that they choose not to interact because they fear the crowd, which, quite logically, is to be identified with the vineyard in the parable. Davies and Allison state that "it is therefore misguided to interpret the parable as though it concerns ethnic relations."[33] No critique whatsoever against the vineyard is asserted in the story. On the contrary, it is because the owner of the vineyard takes for granted that the vineyard bore fruit that he sent his servants to the tenants. However, what the vineyard needs is good tenants, especially in difficult times. Indeed, the people of Israel are entitled to a good leadership.

(iii) ***Post–New Testament times (an anti-Jewish allegory in a Christian context):*** Only in postbiblical times can we detect a full-blown supersessionist reading of the parable. It then became a *Christian* allegory about the fate of the Jewish people; an allegory that proclaims that the Jews have been replaced by the church. The parable was transmuted into an allegory about the transfer of the promises and the covenant from the Jewish people to the Christian church. However, such a sweeping supersessionism is preposterously anachronistic. And an anachronistic Jesus is incomprehensible, quite simply because he is positioned outside of his own historical context.

Nevertheless, it is quite clear that supersessionism is what many Christian readers have read *into* this text. They have understood it to be a text that mandates them to point a finger at the Jewish people and say: "This is the heir, come, let us kill him, and the inheritance will be ours," thus disinheriting the Jewish people. But, as Milavec states, the parable "stands much more to caution and to judge the Church than to assure her of her superiority over the Jews."[34] Hence, the supersessionist reading is not the original perspective, nor should it be our approach today, as Milavec also writes:

I would say that the late Fathers of the Church discovered within the parable of Jesus *a passionate resonance with their own historically*

The Text about the Tenants in the Vineyard

conditioned antagonism toward Jews. The contemporary Church, having abandoned its teaching of contempt, is now once again in a favorable situation for rediscovering some lost meanings and even for pioneering new understandings which harmonize with the recently recovered sense that there exists a common heritage which unites Christians and Jews.[35]

Indeed, we can in this parable discover "a passionate resonance" with our own historical context today. When read in a *non*-supersessionist way—or should we say a *pre*-supersessionist way?—it may encourage Jews and Christians together to harvest the fruits that grow abundantly in God's vineyard.

11
A COMMANDMENT IN COMMON?
Matt 22:34–40 and Mark 12:28–34
(cf. Luke 10:25–28; see chapter 12)

This story narrates a discussion between the Synoptic Jesus and an anonymous scribe about the very center of the Scriptures. Especially in the Markan version it is quite obvious that they agree that loving God and loving one's fellow human being are the two fundamental commandments in Jewish tradition. Hence, one would assume that this text has been a stepping stone for improved Jewish-Christian relations, but, au contraire, it has often been something of a stumbling block, as we will see, especially in the first of the four interpretations that will be discussed here.

(a) Only Christianity is a religion of true love: Some Christians state that we ought to make a distinction between ethical and ritual commandments in the Torah: the former are valid also for Christians, but the latter have ceased to be valid after the advent of Christianity, when there no longer is a need for Jewish legalism. Eduard Schweizer argues that, at the time of the Gospel of Matthew, the *only* commandments that needed to be obeyed were loving God and loving one's neighbor, which is quite a radical description of a Jewish-Christian community at that time.[1]

> [Matthew] sets Jesus clearly apart from Pharisaic pettifogging....The whole point is the contrast between Pharisaic legalism and the ethics of love for God and one's neighbor. Jesus not only limits the necessary commandments to two, but by fusing those two he also prescribes how to perform the first:...one can love God only by loving one's neighbor. Thus Matthew un[d]erlines the fundamental difference between Pharisaic observance of the Law and Jesus' call to love one's neighbor. Not through legalistic observance of particular com-

mandments but through a sense of love for one's neighbor, expressed in concrete actions and embracing all of life, is the Law fulfilled.[2]

As a matter of fact he [i.e., Jesus] was comparing love which comes from the whole heart and can no longer be measured quantitatively with the legalism which allows one to ascertain how many commandments he has kept and how many he has violated.[3]

These quotations are part of the long and influential legacy that seeks to present Judaism at the time of Jesus as a religion that only focuses on trivial issues and thereby overlooks the most important commandments.

But, as a matter of fact, the combination of the commandments to love both God and one's neighbor was not unique to Jesus in the Jewish world. It occurs several times in the collection of texts known as *Testaments of the Twelve Patriarchs*, the most palpable parallel of which is found in *Testament of Issachar* 5.2: "You [plural] shall love the Lord and the neighbor" (Greek: *agapêsate ton Kyrion kai ton plêsion*). Lachs concludes that the combination of these two commandments was "commonplace in rabbinic teachings."[4] Philo of Alexandria called those who obey the commandments of the first table *philotheoi* (lovers of God), and those who obey the commandments of the second table *philanthrôpoi* (lovers of people; cf. philanthropists).[5] All these examples make it clear that the combination of these two commandments is not found only in the Christian tradition.

(b) A gradual hostility in the Synoptic texts: Commentators often remark that there are differences between the three synoptic versions of this narrative. Is Jesus's interlocutor a scribe or a lawyer? Is he a Pharisee? And why are various words used when describing how to love God (three in Hebrew: *lev, nephesh,* and *meod*; but three or four in Greek of the following nouns in various combinations: *kardia, psychê, synesis, dianoia,* and *ischys*)? But an even more important observation is to notice the gradual alienation in the introduction of the narrative:

Mark 12:28: seeing that [Jesus] answered them well, [the scribe] *asked* him.
Matt 22:35: one of them [the Pharisees] asked him *a question to test* him.
Luke 10:25: a lawyer stood up to *test* Jesus.[6]

It seems quite clear from this comparison that Matthew and Luke edited the Markan narrative, so that two of the features of the Markan account disappear: firstly, that the scribe hears how "well" (Greek: *kalôs*; twice in the text) Jesus answers, and, secondly, that they agree on the importance of loving both God and one's neighbor. These features disappear in the Matthean and Lukan versions.[7] In the Markan version, he poses a question not in order to trap Jesus but because he was earnestly interested in the answer. Schweizer observes that there is no other instance in the Gospels where a teacher of the Law is found agreeing with Jesus.[8] Since the Markan version is the oldest, it is possible to detect a trajectory of growing hostility between the Jesus movement and the group that is represented by Jesus's interlocutor.

Whereas Christians have far more often than not emphasized the radical difference between second-temple Judaism and the teaching of Jesus, the Markan version actually says that when they discuss what is most central to them—indeed, the greatest commandments in their tradition—they agree.

(c) The quotations are references to two entire passages in the Torah: The way of referring to the Scriptures before there were chapters and verses was often to quote a verse or a key phrase, and, as a matter of fact, this is still very often the case in the Jewish tradition: hence, *Noach* (Noah) refers to Genesis 6:9—11:32 and *Lekh Lekha* (go) to Genesis 12:1—17:27. *Bereshit* (in the beginning) refers to either Genesis 1:1—6:8 or the entire book of Genesis. J. B. Stern suggested that the two quotations in this synoptic pericope are references to the *Shemaʿ Yisrael* (Hear, Israel) and the weekly portion that today is known as *qedushim* (Lev 19:1—20:27). Since Deuteronomy 6 and Leviticus 19 (and adjacent chapters) contain both so-called ethical and ritual commandments (the distinction often upheld by Christians, as noted above under *[a]*), Stern argues that the implication of these two quotations is that "Jesus was in effect saying that he recognized the organic unity of the whole law, both ritual and ethical, as one indivisible unit."[9]

The *parashiyot* (the divisions into sections that are read each *shabbat*) are from a later date: in the Land there was a system of reading the Torah in three years, and in Babylonia in one year—and it was the Babylonian one-year cycle that won the day. Hence, we cannot know what chapters and verses the synoptic Jesus was referring to, but it is, nevertheless, intriguing to consider that it may not be references to specific verses but to larger passages.

In passing, Stern's case would have been stronger had he discussed the fact that we actually do have at least one New Testament example of the custom to quote a key phrase: Jesus referring to "the passage about the bush" (Mark 12:26 and Luke 20:37).[10] And, as a matter of fact, this occurs in the passage immediately before the discussion about the greatest commandment in the Torah.

Stern suggests a distinction that would make more sense in a Jewish context than an alleged dichotomy between ethics and rituals. This is the Jewish division of the commandments into *mitzwot she-ben adam la-Maqom* (commandments between a person and God [lit. the Place]) and *mitzwot she-ben adam le-chavero* (commandments between a person and a fellow person). Hence, the two quotations may be a reference to the division of the commandments between oneself and God (Deut 6:5) and between oneself and one's neighbor (Lev 19:18).[11] According to Stern, we misunderstand the discussion about the greatest commandment if we conclude that Jesus makes a distinction between ethical and ritual commandments, as if only the former were important. In any case, we find in Jewish texts a millennia-long discussion about the heart of the tradition, which takes us to the next point.

(d) The Jewish endeavor to find a major principle in the Torah: As early as the book of Micah we have an example of an attempt to establish an epitome in the Scriptures. (The prophet Micah lived in the eighth century BCE; the book that bears his name may have been completed in the fifth century BCE.) Micah 6:8 famously states that God requires Israel to do justice, to love kindness, and to walk humbly with God. The most famous discussion of an alleged center in the Scriptures is found in *Talmud Bavli Makkot* 23b, where Rabbi Simlai states that 613 commandments were given to Moses, and that David reduced them to eleven (Ps 11), Isaiah reduced them to six (33:15f.), Micah to three (6:8), Isaiah, given a new chance, this time reduced them to two (66:1), and Amos reduced them to one (5:4), as did Habakkuk (2:4): "The righteous person shall live by faith." That verse also happens to be the central verse in Pauline hermeneutics in Romans 1:17, as well as in much of Lutheran theology (cf. Latin: *sola fide*, "by faith alone").[12] Needless to say, Rabbi Simlai's endeavor to find a center in the Torah is not at the expense of the other commandments. Nor are Rabbi 'Aqiva and Ben 'Azzai demeaning the validity of the Torah when discussing the greatest commandment (lit. "a great rule"; *kelal gadol*). While 'Aqiva argued that it was Leviticus 19:18 ("You shall love your neighbor as yourself"), Ben 'Azzai claimed that, as a matter of fact, it was Genesis 5:1 ("This is the book of the generations of humanity," which continues with the statement that all humans are created in the image of God).[13] Hence, for him it was important to find a center in the Scriptures that included every person without exception—and perhaps he also wanted to avoid relying on "love" for one's neighbors, although love to previous generations most probably was understood more in terms of *action* than of *emotions*. As George Foot Moore states, "*Reverence* for the divine image in man is of wider scope than *love* to our fellow-man."[14] In addition, as Michael Fagenblat writes, it is possible that Ben 'Azzai wanted to avoid the possibility of mistreating one's neighbor as one mistreats oneself or has been mistreated.[15] Similarly, Lenn E. Goodman concludes, "Our creation in God's image [as Ben 'Azzai stressed] teaches us not to retaliate, even when another shames us. Simple reciprocity [as 'Aqiva accentuated] does not say that. It might even seem to invite us to answer in kind!"[16] Quite clearly, these discussions about a hermeneutical center do not take place as an alternative to Judaism *outside* of the Jewish tradition but precisely *within* it.

David Daube, seeking an answer to the question why Matthew dispensed with the words, "Hear, O Israel, the Lord our God, the Lord is one," does not believe that the reason is that the Christian concept of the nature of God—that is, high Christology and emerging Trinitarian theology—prompted this redaction. Instead he argues that the words *Shema' Yisrael...*, strictly speaking, are not a *mitzwah* (Greek: *entolê*): the creed is not a commandment.[17] It may be called a *kelal* (a comprehensive maxim) or a *guph* (an essential part), but it did not fall under the category of a *mitzwah* in its strictest sense. Hence, the quotation was abbreviated by Matthew (or someone prior to him) "in order to suit meticulous Rabbinic scholarship."[18] If Daube is correct here, this is another example of the intra-Jewish character of the earliest narrative accounts of the Jesus movement.

Menahem Kister argues that the historical background of the double love commandment probably was that the theocentric verse Deuteronomy 6:5 was added to an original reference to Leviticus 19:18 "due to an innate Jewish sensitivity."[19] If this is correct, then it is *not* a matter of a religious tradition that eventually had to realize that one's fellow human being *also* is important, not only an exclusive love for God but the other way around: when loving one's neighbor, the sacred words recited daily gain new meanings: "You shall love the Lord your God with all your heart, and with all your soul, and with all your might."[20]

To sum up, in the Gospel of Mark, the oldest narrative account of Jesus of Nazareth, the discussion between him and a scribe about the greatest commandment in the Torah emphasizes commonality. There are times when people emphasize contrasts to such an extent that they forget what they have in common. Indeed, Jews and Christians have far more in common than what separates them. What the two scribes—the anonymous one and Jesus of Nazareth, who was also a scribe in the sense that he knew and taught the Scriptures—have in common is the belief in the God of Israel, the reverence for the Scriptures, and the importance of keeping the commandments. Many Christians are so accustomed to a teaching that presents second-temple Judaism as Jesus's *theological contrast* that they forget that, as a matter of fact, it was his *historical context*.

It is disquieting that discussions about the greatest commandment often have an apologetic leaning: "My tradition is better than yours!" "Our love commandment is superior to yours!" Reflections on the hermeneutical center in the Scriptures and in one's religious tradition should be able to provide space for the Other's integrity and self-understanding. This reminds one of what Franz Rosenzweig wrote in his diary on July 23, 1914:

> Jews and Christians both deny that the ethical and religious principle of "Love God and thy neighbor" is their common possession. Each tries to impute paganism to the other: the Christians by disallowing our love of neighbor, we by disallowing their love of God.[21]

12

THE GOOD SAMARITAN AND BAD JEWS

Luke 10:25–37

Two Samaritans in the New Testament stand out: the Samaritan woman by the well in John 4:1–42, and the Samaritan man in this Lukan parable. Whereas the Samaritan *woman* is often portrayed as acting in a manner unbecoming, the Samaritan *man* has a solid and good reputation, to such an extent that the original connotations may not be evident to all readers of the Lukan parable. One is reminded of the positive reception history of the Samaritan man when pondering the number of hospitals that are named after him. Four interpretations of the parable will be presented in this chapter.

(a) An allegory about salvation history: Early in church history, this parable was understood to be an allegory, which meant, in C. H. Dodd's words, that "each term stood as a cryptogram for an idea, so that the whole had to be de-coded term by term."[1] He exemplifies this with Augustine's interpretation, in which the man is Adam who left the heavenly city Jerusalem, signifying Paradise (its name is sometimes understood to mean "city of Peace"; *'ir shalom*), and traveled "down" to Jericho, representing the Fall. Since the name Jericho in Hebrew is related to the word for "moon" (*yareach*), Augustine thinks of it as a symbol of our mortality; the moon is new(born), waxes, wanes, and, so to speak, dies. When the thieves, who are the devil and his angels, strip him, this refers to him losing his immortality. The priest and the Levite passing by the half-dead man in the ditch next to the road signify the priesthood and ministry of the Hebrew Scriptures. The Samaritan (in Hebrew related to the word for "guardian": *shomer*) represents the Lord, who takes the wounded man to the inn, which signifies the church, where the man meets the innkeeper, who is Paul.[2] (Interestingly, in

Augustine's allegory, Christ takes [the] man to Paul, not the other way around; in church history, generally speaking, the purpose of the message of Paul has been to bring his readers to Christ.)

This allegorizing method of interpreting the parables of Jesus has been quite common and influential in history, and it was only with the rise of modern biblical scholarship that it was questioned. Starting with Adolf Jülicher's book *Die Gleichnisreden Jesu*, scholars now refrain from explicating the minor details, but instead focus on the overall message of the parables. And what might that be? That takes us to the second line of thought.

(b) Judaism hinders the priest and the Levite from doing good: It is noteworthy that in Augustine's reading the two men who ignored the wounded man represented the old covenant. Ultimately, they were unwilling or unable to assist the person who needed their help. Although contemporary scholarship takes pains to distance itself from such allegorizing interpretations, it still often claims that Jewish purity regulations made it impossible for them to reach out to their compatriot who was lying "half-dead" (*hemithanê*) in the ditch. The Augustinian reading prevails in this aspect: Judaism cannot "save" a person. As George Bradford Caird writes:

> It is essential to the point of the story that the traveller was left half-dead. The priest and the Levite could not tell without touching him whether he was dead or alive; and it weighted more with them that he might be dead and defiling to the touch of those whose business was with holy things than that he might be alive and in need of care. Jesus deliberately shocks the lawyer by forcing him to consider the possibility that a semi-pagan foreigner might know more about the love of God than a devout Jew blinded by preoccupation with pettifogging rules.[3]

In other words, Caird even goes as far as to state that it is *the Jewish religion* that provides the rationale for the unmerciful behavior of the priest and the Levite. Had they not been restricted by their Jewish way of life, perhaps they would have acted more compassionately. Although this is a quite popular interpretation, both among scholars and preachers, it is open to criticism. Ritual purity is one of the most misunderstood topics in second-temple Judaism (see chapter 9). Many readers of the New Testament seem to be more interested in *condemning* purity regulations altogether than in seeking to *comprehend* them. A few comments are therefore required.

Most of the purity regulations had to do with the temple service in Jerusalem. Since it is explicitly stated in the parable that the priest is going *down* (v. 31: *katebainen*), he is not on his way to the temple in Jerusalem. He has already been there, and ritual impurity was primarily a question for those who were going *to* the temple in Jerusalem. (In terms of Jewish religious topography, all roads lead *up* to Jerusalem, and all roads lead *down* from Jerusalem. But in this case, it is also geographically true. The road from Jerusalem to Jericho—from 800 meters above sea level to 275 meters below the sea level in just 25 miles—inevitably goes down steeply.)

Furthermore, Jewish *halakhah* states that saving life overrules virtually all other rules, for example, the *shabbat* restrictions. The technical term for this is *piquach nephesh* (watching over a life), and the verse referred to in the Torah is Leviticus 18:5: "You shall keep my statutes and my ordinances; by doing so one shall live: I am the LORD" (see also Ezek 20:11). Consequently, one shall live by the Torah, and not die because of the Torah. If *piquach nephesh* is applied in the context of the parable, no purity regulations would hinder them from assisting the man. Furthermore, even if it could not be ascertained that the situation was indeed life-threatening, they should consider him to be so ill that it was a life-threatening situation. In *Talmud Bavli Yoma* 85b the *piquach nephesh* principle is ascribed to Shmuel bar Abba (165–245 CE). We cannot, of course, ascertain that it had developed at the time of Jesus, but to ignore this fundamental halakhic principle completely when interpreting the Lukan parable seems somewhat eccentric.

And if he were already dead? Then another concept is relevant: the *met mitzwah* (commandment about a corpse), which is the importance of honoring the dead by providing the body with a burial, in the case that there is no next of kin. And in the Lukan parable there was no one there who could take care of the dead body. Hence, anyone passing by—especially a religious person, for whom *halakhah* was important—was required to bury the dead body.[4] Once again, it could be argued that it is difficult to ascertain that the *met mitzwah* was in force at the time of Jesus, but why should we take for granted that it was not? An early example of the *met mitzwah* is Tobit 1:16–20, in which Tobit, who is described as "walk[ing] in the ways of truth and righteousness all the days of [his] life" (1:3), attended to unburied bodies.[5] This text, showing the importance of burying the dead, is several hundred years older than the Gospel of Luke. In the rabbinic texts, the motif is described in detail already in the *Mishnah*, and subsequently developed in the Talmud:

Mishnah Nazir 7.1: a High Priest and a nazirite may not become unclean because of their kindred, but they may contract uncleanness because of a dead body according to the Law (*le-met mitzwah*, i.e., a neglected corpse).

Talmud Bavli Nazir 43b: Who is a *met mitzwah* [for whom a priest must become impure]? [It is] anyone who does not have [people] to bury him [apart from this priest].

The trajectory from Tobit to the Mishnah and the Talmud implies that the Lukan parable be read with the assertion that *met mitzwah* was a familiar halakhic category. As Amy-Jill Levine writes: "Jewish Law requires that a dead body be treated with utmost respect."[6] In short, either the man's life could perhaps have been saved or the man was dead. In both cases, the halakhic answer is not to ignore him. In short, *if he is not dead, he is not impure. And if he is dead, he must be buried.*[7]

By way of conclusion, we agree with Levine that "Samaritans were also bound by laws concerning corpse contamination; just as the Samaritan found the question irrelevant, so should we in our attempt to understand the parable."[8]

(c) An alleged (one-sided) Jewish contempt for Samaritans is criticized: The third line of thought is focusing on the factual and centuries-old *mutual* enmity between Jews and Samaritans, in a way that Jewish animosity against Samaritans is isolated from what Samaritans certainly must have felt vis-à-vis Jews.

It is strange and unexpected that a Samaritan is the third person traveling between Jerusalem and Jericho. Given that the two first were a priest and a Levite, a first-century audience would certainly have expected an Israelite to be the third person.[9] Did Luke, for the sake of his Gentile audience, change the person's identity from a "regular" Israelite to a Samaritan, as several scholars have suggested?[10] Or was the third person, as Manson suggests, originally an *'am ha-aretz* (lit. "people of the Land"), which in the Talmud is a term for an uneducated Jew, but in earlier texts probably referred to those who were not deported to Babylonia (see, e.g., Ezra 4:4).[11] It is difficult to evaluate these suggestions about the identity of the third person; we only know that in the Lukan text as we now have it he is a Samaritan. We also know that interpreters have tended to decontextualize the Samaritan, in order to make him more of a role model for Christians today than a representative of first-century Samaritans. And, of course, the priest and the Levite, as we saw above, have often been portrayed as if they were acting according to the regulations of Judaism.[12] Ironically, because of this, Augustine's allegorical reading has resurfaced in these latter days: whereas the two first persons represent Judaism, a religion that fails to help someone in need, the third person in the parable represents Christianity, a religion that can and will comfort the afflicted. However, we have to take into account that, at the time of Jesus, Jews did not regard Samaritans as Gentiles; rather, as Fagenblat writes, "The Samaritans were Israelites with entrenched opposition to the Jewish ways of understanding their shared tradition."[13]

Levine emphasizes that she does not believe that this is a parable about prejudice, because it is not a prejudice that Jews and Samaritans loathed one another: They did—and *both* groups did![14] The Samaritan was most probably not an outcast in the eyes of Jews any more or any less than Jews were in the eyes of Samaritans.[15] And the Samaritan is a role model because he managed to overcome traditional Samaritan disdain for Jews, not because he was able to be less "Jewish" than the priest and the Levite. According to this line of thought, the priest and the Levite were *bad Jews*—and he was a *good Samaritan*.

(d) The key question is: "And who is my neighbor?" The last line of thought focuses on the question that is posed to Jesus in Luke 10:29, immediately before the parable: "And who is my neighbor?" Is this, ultimately, a parable about how to define the Hebrew word *rea'* in Leviticus 19:18: "You shall love your neighbor as yourself"? (See chapters 3 and 11.) In order to keep this commandment, the word *rea'* has to be defined.[16] Originally, the term most probably referred to fellow Israelites. This should not surprise us: to reflect on legal codes in other societies was beyond the scope of this intra-Israelite text. But eventually such questions arise: how is one to relate to members of other communities? One example is the way the Tosefta adds a new perspective to the Mishnah. In *Mishnah Sanhedrin* 10.1 it is famously stated that "all Israel have a share in the world to come." The Tosefta—which incidentally means "addition"—adds that righteous Gentiles, too, have a share in the world to come (*Tosefta Sanhedrin* 13.2).

In the New Testament there is a tension among various authors about the scope of the ethical perspective: whereas the Johannine community seemingly had a narrow definition of whom to hold dear (cf. John 13:34f., 15:12f.; 1 John 3:23; and 2 John 5), the Jewish-Christian school of Matthew extended the neighborliness far beyond the limits of the own group—"With malice toward none, with charity for all," as Abraham Lincoln famously phrased it in his Second Inaugural Address. If one greets only those who belong to one's own group, what merit does one have? "Do not even the gentiles do the same?" (Matt 5:47). Hence, we see here how *non*-Jews in the Matthean community are *not* exemplary. And it is to this discussion the Lukan parable is probably directed. Rhetorically, Luke goes in another direction: he uses a *non*-Jew as an example of someone who did *not* have a narrow definition of "neighbor."

Hence, there were *narrow* definitions of the Hebrew word *rea'* (often translated as "neighbor"). One of the most extreme examples is probably the Community Scroll of the Dead Sea Community, which states that one should "hate all the Sons of Darkness" (*The Community Rule* [1QS] 1.9–11); most probably this refers to all those who did not belong to their own community. And there were *wide* definitions of *rea'*—the most well-known is found in the Sermon on the Mount of the Jewish-Christian community of Matthew. Most likely the commandment to love one's enemies goes all the way back to the teaching of the historical Jesus.[17] Hence, according to this interpretation, the key question in the Lukan parable is "Who is my neighbor?" And, yet, ultimately it is perhaps not primarily a matter of *finding* a definition of neighbor but of *seeing* one's neighbor. As T. W. Manson once wrote, "For love does not begin by *defining* its objects: it *discovers* them."[18]

How, then, can the Lukan parable be transposed to our times? Levine suggests that the setting remains the same: an Israeli Jew travels on her way from Jerusalem to Jericho, what today is called the West Bank, Occupied Palestine, or Greater Israel. She is attacked by thieves and left half dead in a ditch. A Jewish medic from the Israel Defense Force passes by without assisting her; likewise, a member of the Israel/Palestine Mission Network of the Presbyterian Church USA passes by without assisting her. Finally, a Palestinian Muslim, whose sympathies lie with Hamas, "a political party whose charter not only anticipates Israel's destruction, but also depicts Jews as subhuman demons responsible for all the world's problems," comes along and takes compassion on her.[19]

> "Which of these three, do you think, was a neighbor to the [wo]man who fell into the hands of the robbers?" He said, "The one who showed [her]...mercy." Jesus said to him, "Go and do likewise." (Luke 10:36f.)

13

WHY COMMEND A DISHONEST STEWARD?

Luke 16:1–13

This Lukan parable is probably one of the most intriguing texts in the entire New Testament. Jonathan Knight calls it "one of the most extraordinary parables in the Gospels," and Paul Trudinger sees it as "one of the most difficult to interpret of all Jesus' parables."[1] Is Jesus really commending a person who is embezzling another person's economical means?

The steward is an *oikonomos* (cf. "economist").[2] Joseph A. Fitzmyer describes him as "not merely a head-servant placed in charge of the household staff…but a trained, trusted, and duly empowered agent of the master. He was able to act in the name of the master in transactions with third parties," and he "was especially trained and tested in the supervision of a farm-estate."[3]

C. H. Dodd noted that Luke added a whole series of "morals" to the parable proper. These homiletic conclusions go in various directions: "The children of this age are more shrewd in dealing with their own generation than are the children of light," "Make friends for yourselves by means of dishonest wealth," and "If then you have not been faithful with the dishonest wealth, who will entrust to you the true riches?" Therefore, Dodd famously concluded that "we can almost see here notes for the three separate sermons on the parable as text."[4]

Hence, the questions that readers of the parable ask are many—and many are also the answers that scholars give. Klyne R. Snodgrass offers an overview with as many as sixteen interpretations and adds in a footnote that "Many other interpretations could be listed."[5]

Before presenting a series of interpretations, two preliminary observations should be mentioned. Firstly, we do not actually know who is meant by "the lord" (*ho kyrios*) in the eighth verse: is it Jesus (the parabolist) or is it the rich man (in the parable)? The way various Bible translations spell the word indicates how the editors interpret the word: if spelled with an initial capital *L* ("the Lord"), the underlying idea is that it is Jesus who praises the steward; if spelled without a capital *L*, it refers to the master in the parable. In that case, the praise is part of the parable itself rather than Jesus's conclusion.[6]

A second observation is that the narrative context of this parable in the Gospel of Luke is important. The text begins with the remark that Jesus "also" (*kai*) gave them this parable. It thus constitutes a continuation of the fifteenth chapter—often called "the chapter of the lost"—with the three well-known parables of the lost sheep, the lost coin, and the lost son (known as the "prodigal" son). It is not certain that everyone thinks that the shepherd in the first parable acts judiciously when leaving the ninety-nine sheep in the desert to search for the hundredth sheep—but they are perhaps still glad that God seeks and finds the sheep and people that are lost. Calculations in the kingdom of God are not always like the conventional four arithmetical operations. As a matter of fact, the verb *diaskorpizein* (to scatter) occurs in both the previous parable about the prodigal son and in the one we are now analyzing (cf. 15:13 and 16:1); this constitutes another link between the two parables. Indeed, the protagonist in the parable could be called *the prodigal steward*. As the prodigal son in the previous chapter returned to his father's home, and is received by his father, the master in the sixteenth chapter praised the steward for acting shrewdly.

The subsequent passage is also important. In the fourteenth verse it says that the Pharisees heard "all this" (*tauta panta*), and in the next verse it says that Jesus tells them that they "want to appear righteous before men." T. W. Manson argued that this verse bears traces of how the antagonists are described: from various religious groups of the time to Pharisees only.[7] Manson suggested that these words were originally addressed to the Sadducees, who on average were more affluent than the Pharisees. In addition, the name Sadducees means "the righteous ones" (Hebrew: *tzaddiqim*). Hence, it is quite possible that there is a Semitic pun below the surface of the Greek text, a pun that serves to remind us that not all reprehensible people were Pharisees—and not all Pharisees were reprehensible (see introduction, first challenge).[8] Given the purpose of the focus and aim of the present study, three interpretations will be discussed below.

(a) An eschatological warning to Israel. N. T. Wright identifies the dishonest steward with Israel.[9] He argues that the people, having mismanaged the task, must realize how perilous the situation is—and repent. Hence, it is understood as a salvation-historical allegory about the faith and fate of the people of Israel. Wright is, of course, not the first to read the parable allegorically. According to Tertullian, the parable is aimed not just at the Pharisees but at the whole Jewish nation.[10]

> But how we are to understand, *Make to yourselves friends of mammon*, let the previous parable teach you. The saying was addressed to the Jewish people [*ad populum Iudaicum dictum*]; inasmuch as, having managed ill the business of the Lord [*commissam sibi rationem domini cum male administrasset*] which had been entrusted to them, they ought to have provided for themselves out of the men of mammon, which we then were, friends rather than enemies, and to have delivered us from the dues of sins which kept us from God, if they bestowed the blessing upon us, for the reason given by the Lord, that when grace began to depart from them [*cum coepisset ab his deficere gratia*], they, betaking themselves to our faith, might be admitted into everlasting habitations.[11]

Asserting that the master in the parable is God and the steward is the entire people of Israel, N. T. Wright writes that "Israel—as we've seen in so much of this gospel [i.e., the Gospel of Luke]—has failed in the task, and is under threat of imminent dismissal. What then ought Israel to do?"[12] The answer to that question, Wright states, is to do not what the Pharisees once did: "to pull the regulations of the law even tighter, to try to make Israel more holy. This, as we've seen, had the effect that they were excluding the very people that Jesus was reaching out to."[13] Wright's homiletical recommendation for Christians today is to avoid such a "Pharisaic" supererogatory approach. Hence, the parable "advises us to sit light to the extra regulations which we impose on one another, not least in the church, which are over and above the gospel itself."[14]

Now, it is certainly true that in rabbinic parables Israel is often likened to a steward (and there are also numerous parables about a son or a daughter, or a prince or a princess). But against this allegorical interpretation, one could adduce that this observation does not imply that every steward in every parable always refers to the entire people of Israel.[15] Secondly, if interpreted as a salvation-historical allegory, it would be different from most (if not all) of the parables in the New Testament gospels. Snodgrass states that N. T. Wright is painting "with too broad a brush" and Trudinger is quite unwavering in his analysis: "The parable is *not* an allegory.

Whatever its meanings are, they must be found within the narrative structure of the story itself."[16] He states that the parable should be read *synchronically*, not *diachronically* (i.e., allegorically), which takes us to the next interpretation.

(b) It is not the steward's dishonesty but his ingenuity that is commended: The majority view, however, steers away from allegorizing interpretations, and focuses on the reason for praising the dishonest steward. Manson's brief conclusion is often quoted:

> Whether it is the employer or Jesus that speaks, we must take the purport of the speech to be: "This is a fraud, but it is a most ingenious fraud. The steward is a rascal; but he is a wonderfully clever rascal."[17]

Hence, the disciples are to imitate him in ingenuity, for acting prudently in a critical situation. As Caird writes, he is "commended not for his dishonesty, but for his realism and determination in dealing with a sudden emergency."[18] The way the sons and daughters of this age act could prove to be an example for Christ followers.

But when analyzing the steward's behavior, one also has to ask whether he is truly unjust. In the eighth verse it is stated that he is acting "wisely" (*phronimôs*), and he is described as *ho oikonomos tês adikias*.[19] Although often translated as "the unjust steward," it could also mean "a steward in an unjust situation"—that is, that he is "a steward of the unjust." Therefore, Hans Kosmala has argued that the steward is not unjust; he belongs to this world, as opposed to the children of light. And it is this world that is *tês adikias*—that is, he is a man "who is completely bound up with this world in which *adikia* is the ruling principle." Read this way, according to Kosmala, "the text (including its additional comments) becomes perfectly clear and presents no difficulties whatsoever."[20] Similarly, Trudinger argues that the parable depicts

> a typical confrontation between landlords and tenants/merchants, with the steward as a go-between. The situation is one in which the weak and oppressed are royally shafted in a system that is maintained by greed and exploitation through and through....Jesus tells the story *in anger* to expose the depth of oppression inflicted on the poor. The steward's plan to make friends by his manipulation of the material assets at his disposal again only underscores the depth of the injustice: it cannot bring any real, lasting hope to those oppressed.

...Jesus, instead, is working for a fully egalitarian society...where expendables and acts of oppression and injustice no longer exist. This is Jesus' vision of the kingdom of God.[21]

We see how the second interpretation seeks—and indeed also finds—ways to understand the words of praise for the steward. Is he, as Manson described him, "a wonderfully clever rascal"? Is he just seeking to act wisely in an unjust world? Is he, so to speak, a cultural progenitor of the kibbutz movement, in the sense that he is "working for a fully egalitarian" system? These questions about his behavior take us to our third reading.

*(c) **The steward renounces profits:*** The most ingenious interpretation takes as its starting point the fact that an absentee landlord could entrust the transaction of all usual business in the management of his estate to an *oikonomos*.[22] Hence, the steward was working quite independently, and may even have added quite a substantial interest to the loans, an interest that was his own commission.

As early as 1902, Margaret D. Gibson suggested that the steward may simply have renounced *his own profits* without defrauding the master.[23] This line of thought has been developed by J. Duncan M. Derrett. The background is the biblical prohibition of interest (see Exod 22:25–27, Lev 25:37, and Deut 23:19f.). In order to circumvent these provisions, there was a practice at that time that promissory notes were written for an amount higher than the actual loan amount, hence with no interest being explicitly stated in the bond.[24] The technical term for this practice is *atokos* (without interest), which does not imply that interest was not demanded but only that no interest was explicitly stated in the written contract. An example of this practice is found in Josephus's *Jewish Antiquities*: Herod Agrippa I, when in need of money, had to write a bond of 20,000 Attic drachmas, even though he only received 17,500 drachmas.[25] Hence, the actual interest paid was 2,500 drachmas (approx. 14.3 percent).

Given that what is described in the parable is the *atokos* system, the first debtor had thus not borrowed an amount corresponding to one hundred jars of oil (but rather fifty), and the second had not borrowed the equivalent of one hundred barrels of wheat (but instead eighty). What the steward does in this parable is to refrain from a usury rate of between 25 and 100 percent in order to win the trust and gratitude of people around him. Thus, no matter how strange this may seem at first glance, he can become a role model for a good steward. In short, the portion of the debt that is taken away is the steward's interest. When the steward acted wisely in this way, the master "would get an undeserved reputation for piety."[26]

To sum up, three interpretations have been presented here. In a sense, the second and the third are each other's mirror images. Both portray him as shrewd, but the second interpretation praises him for his *ingenuity*, and the third for his *generosity*. There was nothing dishonest about the *atokos* system; it was also ingenious. But to forego its benefits in a dire situation could be understood as generous, in addition to being prudently self-serving. Whereas the first interpretation—the salvation-historical reading—certainly is in accordance with the conventional understanding in church history that the people of Israel are assessed *solely* in terms of whether they believe in Jesus as the Christ, it fails to do justice to Lukan theology, as articulated in, for example, Nunc Dimittis (Luke 2:29–32), that speaks of the "glory to your people Israel."

14
LAZARUS—"WHAT'S IN A NAME?"
Luke 16:19–31

To paraphrase the famous words of the Jewish Passover Haggadah: *How is this parable different from all the other parables?* The answer is that the poor man has a name. Indeed, the only person in the parables of Jesus who has a name—is Lazarus. His name means "God has helped." As Joseph A. Fitzmyer writes, "It is a fitting name for the beggar in this parable, who was not helped by a human being, but in his afterlife is consoled by God."[1]

It is probably no coincidence that he has this particular name, or that the rich man is anonymous in the parable. We have indications that the namelessness of the rich man was noteworthy. The manuscript p[75], the oldest Greek text of the Gospel of Luke, adds *onomati Neuês* (by the name Neues), an obvious parallel to *onomati Lazaros* in verse 20. The name *Neuês*, however, is unknown; it is probably a shortened form of *Nineuês* (which, incidentally, is found in the Sahidic version of Luke), hence, related to the notorious city Nineveh. There, the inhabitants actually did repent (to the great dismay of Jonah; see 3:1—4:1), in contradistinction to the rich man, who cared for neither God nor fellow human beings. Whereas the inhabitants of Nineveh were covered in sackcloth and fasted, the rich man was always dressed in purple and fine linen, feasting sumptuously every day (Luke 16:19). Later in church history, he was given the sobriquet *Dives*, which is Latin for "a rich person." Quite obviously this comes from the Latin text: *homo quidam erat dives* (there was a certain rich man), which was understood as: "there was a certain man [and his name was] Dives."[2] Hence, strictly speaking, he is still nameless.

Five interpretations of the parable will be presented in this chapter, starting with the most contrastive, and then going in the direction of more contextual readings that seek to do justice to the worldview of a first-century audience.[3]

Lazarus—"What's in a Name?"

(a) Jewish law prevented the rich man from assisting Lazarus: Some scholars assert that Lazarus was ritually impure, that this was the reason for the rich man's behavior. Hence, the anonymous man was not *allowed* to reach out to Lazarus. The supposedly oppressive religion at that time was so distinctly on the rich man's side that it resulted in an apathy for Lazarus. But in the text, it is mentioned neither that Lazarus was ritually impure nor that the rich man was excessively interested in purity regulations.[4] Given that Luke is the evangelist who more than the others warns his audience against the perils of wealth, why should we assume, without any indications in the text, that the rich man's behavior was governed by religious zeal for halakhic observance rather than the indolence of some affluent people when encountering a person in need? We simply do not have any good arguments for this hypothesis. Rather than seeing Lazarus as "a leprous poster child for the evils of Jewish purity laws," as Amy-Jill Levine writes, we may want to think of him as "a first-century Job—covered in sores and mistreated by those who should have befriended him, including not a few New Testament interpreters."[5]

(b) Jewish refusal to believe in the resurrection of Jesus despite the testimony in the Scriptures: Whereas the previous interpretation portrayed the rich man as someone who was overzealous in terms of religion, the second suggestion depicts him as indolent and religiously disobedient. Is the parable, as C. H. Cave has proposed, actually a salvation-historical allegory about "the severity of the judgment of Israel if she persists in her unrepentant state," in which the rich man represents Israel, refusing to accept the witnesses of Moses and the prophets about resurrection—and, therefore, not believing in the resurrection of Jesus?[6] Cave argues that Lazarus in the parable is related to Abraham's servant Eli'ezer of Damascus (Gen 15:2), who, according to Jewish tradition, was a Gentile. Hence, the Lukan parable describes the outcome for the rich man (representing Israel) and Lazarus (representing the Gentiles), and whereas the Gentile Lazarus is carried away by angels to be with Abraham, the rich Jew is tormented in Hades. In short, according to this interpretation, it is an allegory about how the Jews will be disinherited if they do not repent.

Arguments against this interpretation include, firstly, the fact that scholarship in general now seeks to *de*-allegorize the parables in order to go beyond the salvation-historical readings of the church fathers, not to *re*-allegorize them. Secondly, the name of Abraham's servant in Genesis 15:3 in the Septuagint is Eli'ezer, not Lazarus. Hence, the suggested intertextuality would not be obvious to *Greek*-speaking first-century listeners and readers (although, admittedly, Eli'ezer *in Hebrew* means "Help of my God").

Bernard Brandon Scott argues that the conclusion of the parable comes from Jewish Christianity, and that it aims at those Jews who refuse to believe in Jesus as raised from the dead and therefore stand convicted by Moses and the prophets.[7]

Is the context of the parable—especially the concluding verses about scriptural hermeneutics—an early Jewish-Christian group, in which the members reflected on how to regard and relate to Jewish sisters and brothers who were not Christ followers? In short, this interpretation emphasizes verse 31: Those who do not pay attention to the message of "Moses and the Prophets" will not believe in the One who has been resurrected by God.[8] However, the premise for this interpretation is that the parable is a salvation-historical allegory about the fate of the Jewish people.

(c) Judaism at the time of Jesus promoted a prosperity gospel: Levine quotes several scholars who state that a first-century audience would believe that while rich people are blessed, the poor deserve their lot. Klyne R. Snodgrass asserts that "many Jews would assume that the rich man was blessed by God and that the poor man was cursed (cf. John 9:2 and Job)";[9] Arland Hultgren suggests that Lazarus was an outcast: "He is the type of person about whom it would have been socially acceptable for the rich man to be indifferent";[10] and Joachim Jeremias stated that beggars were believed to have sinned previously, thus having deserved their helplessness and hopelessness.[11]

All these assertions point in the direction of a pervasive sin-and-punishment paradigm at the time of Jesus. It is true that one can find such a model in the Hebrew Bible (known as the Deuteronomistic understanding of history), and, indeed, in most religious traditions. However, the Book of Job and many of the Psalms point in another direction. In Job 22:21 we find the advice to "agree with God, and be at peace; in this way good will come to you" (perhaps more well-known to some in the words of King James Version: "Acquaint now thyself with God; thereby good shall come unto thee"). These are, however, the words of Eliphaz—and his simplistic advice is rebuked by Job, and by the Book of Job, and also by the God of the Book of Job, as we see in the concluding chapter: "the LORD said to Eliphaz the Temanite: My wrath is kindled against you and against your two friends; for you have not spoken of me what is right, as my servant Job has."[12] In short, the Book of Job defies the sin-and-punishment paradigm. It constitutes a strong argument against a simplistic model of the interrelationship of faith, health, and wealth.

But, to be honest, in Jewish and Christian texts throughout the centuries (not to speak of Muslim texts, which to an even higher extent emphasize the correspondence between the will of God and what happens in the world), the Book of Job is a lonely voice crying in the desert. On the whole, the sin-and-punishment model has been far more influential, as Crossan states:

> But sadly, the book of Job was but a speed bump on the Deuteronomic superhighway. The delusion of divine punishments still prevails inside and outside religion over the clear evidence of human consequences, random accidents, and natural disasters. This does not simply distort theology; it defames the very character of God.[13]

Nevertheless, the Lukan parable should not be contrasted with a monolithic portrayal of Judaism at the time of Jesus.[14] There are quite a few commandments in the Torah that would have spoken directly to the rich man—and that would have had consequences for Lazarus, for example, Deuteronomy 15:11 and 17: "Open your hand to the poor and needy neighbor in your land....If there is among you anyone in need, a member of your community in any of your towns...do not be hard-hearted or tight-fisted toward your needy neighbor."

Likewise, in the Book of Isaiah the prophet defines true worship as hospitality when asking rhetorically (58:7): "Is it not to share your bread with the hungry, and bring homeless poor into your house; when you see the naked, to cover them, and not to hide yourself from your own kin?" As Levine states, the Lukan Jesus is "not being religiously innovative here; he is reflecting his Jewish culture."[15] Furthermore, she states that "the scriptures of Israel repeatedly express God's concern for the poor, the widow, the orphan, and the stranger—if they deserved their states, the divine concern makes no sense."[16]

To sum up, while the sin-and-punishment paradigm certainly can be found in the Scriptures and in the rabbinic writings, this is not the only theological option in Jewish thought. Indeed, as Outi Lehtipuu writes, the motif of the reversal of fate of rich and poor was "a well-known folkloric motif that circulated all over the Hellenistic world."[17] There are numerous parallels that would have been known to either the parabolist or his listeners—or, most probably, both to him and his audience. In other words, when a first-century audience heard or read the Lukan text, how would they imagine the outcome of the parable? Levine states that any time a parable begins with a presentation of a rich man, the audience knows that this person is a particularly *poor* role model: "They would not have been on the side of the rich man, they would not have regarded his wealth as a sign of righteousness, and they would not have been surprised at his fate."[18] "Jews glorified wealth and worshipped Mammon, while Jesus invented social conscience and liberation theology. The message from the pulpit is, once again, thank God Jesus came to restructure the value system."[19] That is Levine's concise summary of this misguided interpretation—which takes us to the next line of thought.

(d) A Jewish preferential option for the poor: The expression "[God's] preferential option for the poor" stems from Latin American liberation theology.[20] Interestingly, this theological school bases much of its teaching on the Hebrew Bible; indeed, at times it has been criticized for not anchoring its message enough in the New Testament.[21] Be that as it may, what is of concern to us now is that there is no shortage of texts in the Hebrew Bible helping readers to see and care for the poor.

In contrast to the previous interpretation, this reading portrays a God who has a special concern for the disadvantaged, the deprived, and the destitute. As has already been pointed out, it is the *poor* man in this parable who has a name; the *rich* man is anonymous, despite various textual critical emendations. Indeed, in all the parables in all the Gospels in the New Testament, it is only Lazarus who has a name—and his name means "God helps." Indeed, as Levine writes, "the only help Lazarus will get will come from God, since the rich man is not doing what God had commanded."[22] The rich man is anonymous. His riches did not help him. It is difficult to imagine that this would be a sheer coincidence.[23] Lazarus's name encourages the reader to see him and to care for him. An interesting parallel is Hagar, who is the first person to give God a name: *El roi* (Gen 16:13; "the God of my seeing," which could be interpreted either as "the God who sees me" or "the God that I see"). God and Hagar see each other—the question is whether the readers see the destitute and vulnerable in the texts.

(e) A belief in the resurrection from the dead not at the expense of the message of Moses and the prophets: The fifth and final interpretation that is presented here highlights the interrelationship of Scripture and supernatural signs. Now in Hades, the rich man's only hope is for his brothers; if someone were resurrected from the dead and returned to them, they would repent. But Abraham responds that if his brothers do not listen to Moses

and the prophets, they will not be convinced if someone rose from the dead (16:30f.). Fitzmyer concludes from this that

> the essential message in the Hebrew Scriptures is still a valid guide for the conduct of his offspring. Those who will not submit themselves to God's word will not be convinced by a sign, even the miraculous return of one from the realm of death.…Those who reject or care not about God's word in "Moses and the prophets" will not be moved by the testimony of such a messenger even from death's realm.[24]

In other words, nothing suggests that Christ followers ought to disregard the teaching of the Torah and the prophets, texts which certainly emphasize the importance of taking care of the poor and vulnerable. This is also in accordance with the overall message in the Gospel of Luke, which constantly underlines that key figures observed the teaching of the Torah—for example, Elizabeth and Zechariah, who were the parents of John the Baptist (1:6): "Both of them living blamelessly according to all the commandments and regulations of the Lord." And as the Gospel begins in the temple, it also ends there: "and [the disciples of Jesus]…were continually in the temple blessing God."

Similarly, Levine points out that "the parable tells us that we do not need supernatural revelation to tell us that we have poor with us.…Ironically, what the rich man asked Lazarus to do…the parable does for readers."[25] Hence, the Lukan narrative may give us, the readers today, a renewed interest in reading and reflecting on the teaching of the Torah and the prophets.

One is reminded of the famous story in the Talmud (*Talmud Bavli Bava Metzia* 59b) about Rabbi Eli'ezer, who argued against the majority of the rabbis with the help of supernatural events: a tree was uprooted, the water in a stream changed its course, the walls of a synagogue started to fall, and finally even a heavenly voice was heard that proclaimed that Eli'ezer was right. But then one of the rabbis said *lo va-shamayim hi* ([The commandment] is not in heaven; Deut 30:12).

The underlying hermeneutics that surfaces in this Talmudic story is that God has not only given the Torah to the Jewish community but also entrusted them with the hermeneutical keys to interpret it. The Word is not in heaven, it is not on the other side of the sea. It is near and it is here; hence, hear what it says—and do what it demands!

15

A PARABLE ABOUT PRAYER OR POLITICS?

Luke 18:1–8

Prayer is one of Luke's favorite themes (see, e.g., Luke 3:21, 5:16, 6:12, 22:32, and 23:34), and by framing this parable with an introduction (v. 1) and a conclusion (vv. 6f. or 6–8), Luke portrays this as a parable about (v. 1): "the need to pray them [i.e., the prayers?] always and not to lose heart" (*to dein pantote proseuchesthai autous kai mê egkakein*). But whereas it is quite obvious that the parable in its current form and context underlines the importance of perseverance in prayer, many scholars argue that the message of the pre-Lukan version was somewhat different. In the following paragraphs, five interpretations are presented, in which the keywords are *(a) pious, (b) poor and pitiful, (c) powerful, (d) protagonist,* and *(e) problematic*.

(a) The perseverance of a pious person's prayers: This is certainly the most well-known interpretation. The widow is understood to be a role model in praying to God who hears prayers, because even an unjust judge (the opposite of God, who is just) reacts to incessant requests. Hence the contrast is stark between, on the one hand, the earthly and deficient judge and, on the other hand, the heavenly and flawless Judge. The only thing the two judges have in common is that both of them "give in" because of the pleading person's persistence. An interesting parallel is found in Plutarch's *Moralia*; it is a story about Philip, the father of Alexander the Great:

When a poor old woman insisted that her case be heard before him, and often caused him annoyance [*pollakis enochlousês*], he said he had no time to spare, whereupon she burst out, "Then give up being

A Parable about Prayer or Politics?

king [*kai mê basileue*]." Amazed at her words, he proceeded at once to hear not only her case but those of the others.¹

In a parable in *Talmud Yerushalmi* the message is the opposite—that is, whereas a human being will ultimately ignore a person that is bothersome, the person who turns to the heavenly Patron will not be ignored:

[A person of] flesh and blood has a protector [*patron*]. If the person bothers him too much, he [the patron] says, "I will forget him, he bothers me." But the Holy One, blessed be He, is not like that [*aval ha-Qadosh barukh Hu einu khen*]. He receives you with all that you burden him. As it is written [Ps 55:23]: "Cast your burden on the LORD, and he will sustain you."²

What the Lukan and Talmudic parables have in common is that both compare God with human beings, saying something about who God is and what God is like. William Barclay argues that the point is less the importance of persistent prayer but rather the manifest contrast between God and people.³ Sirach 35:15–17 constitutes an illuminating parallel to the interpretation of the Lukan parable that portrays God as a heavenly judge:

For the Lord is the judge, and with him there is no partiality. He will not show partiality to the poor; but he will listen to the prayer of one who is wronged. He will not ignore the supplication of the orphan, or the widow [Greek: *chêran*] when she pours out her complaint.

It has already been mentioned that this is the most common interpretation, that if even an unjust judge would give in to the relentless pleas of a widow, how much more will God, who is upright?⁴

In a Jewish context it would not be far-fetched to think of the pious and persistent widow as an image of the people of Israel, especially as the terminology in verse 7 is God's "chosen one" (*tôn eklektôn autou*). In Psalm 68:6 (=English trans. v. 5) it says that God is "Father of orphans and protector of widows."

This first interpretation could be called *vertical* in the sense that it understands it to be a theocentric parable about the nature and acts of God, compared with the nature and acts of human beings. But many readers remain unsatisfied with the way God is portrayed in this parable. Can we really learn anything about God by comparing God with an unjust judge? This takes us to the second interpretation.

(b) The vulnerability of a poor and pitiful person in an unjust society: The starting point for this interpretation is that the judge is so wicked that he cannot be a representative of God. Hence, there is a shift of focus. It is not a *vertical* parable (about the interrelationship between God and humans) but a *horizontal* one: no longer is it a parable of the persistence of a *widow* (who serves as a role model for the pious person's prayer); instead it serves as a *window* to interpersonal relationships in first-century Judaism (what were Jewish judges like at the time of Jesus?).[5] What most of these interpreters have in common is that they assume that the widow was destitute and that the judge is not primarily a character in the Lukan narrative; rather, he exemplifies the behavior of actual judges at the time of Jesus (see chapter 10). Amy-Jill Levine gives several examples of how the widow has been described as an "enraged bag lady," an "outcast" in a society that looked upon women and widows as "weak, foolish, silly, impotent, chattering, useless." She was "probably illiterate and [she] clearly lacks political influence," and she is "the victim of a man who undermined the economic foundation of her life." And "the majority of the population was poor, and the majority of widows were extremely exploited and oppressed on account of their class *and* gender."[6]

All these statements assume that the Lukan parable is a window to the conditions for poor people—especially widows—in the land at the time of Jesus, which one commentator describes as the "ugly and oppressive socio-legal world of first-century Palestine." It seems that this emphasis has to do with the shift from the vertical to the horizontal interpretational mode. Can we detect a certain discomfort among interpreters of the parable? Is the historical context at the time of Jesus described in this way, at least partly, because one wants to avoid describing a just God with the help of the unjust judge in the parable? This line of thought not only emphasizes that the widow is destitute but also suggests that the judge is portrayed as a representative of all judges at that time. Is this interpretation an example of how anti-Judaism serves as a hermeneutical tool for redeeming the characters in the text—even God?

Before we continue exploring this interpretation, a personal reflection may not be out of place: not to ignore the living conditions of the poorest of the poor when reading texts from antiquity is, generally speaking, laudable. Far too many history books have focused solely on the political leaders and not on ordinary people. Hence, it is often good hermeneutics to pay attention to the fate of the poor and marginalized and powerless. But the persistent question remains to what extent this parable can be understood as evidence for the conditions of widows in general in the Jewish community at the time of Jesus.

Levine points out that Jewish tradition mandates that God has particular concern for the poor, the widow, the orphan, and the stranger. Whereas these commandments certainly are more proscriptive than descriptive, they are not irrelevant when we seek to describe the society at the time of Jesus.[7] According to these normative religious texts, widows are in God's special care. (We have already quoted Ps 68:6: "Father of orphans and protector of widows is God in his holy habitation.")

But what are the consequences of this shift of perspective? When it is no longer a *vertical* parable (in which the judge is compared with God) but a *horizontal* one, the unrighteous judge represents an officeholder in an utterly unjust (Jewish) society. A theology that presents the society at that time as particularly cruel seems to save the interpreters from the line of thought that God may be compared with an unjust judge. We see here, once again, how an anti-Jewish hermeneutics serves an apologetic purpose.

What unites those who subscribe to this second interpretation is that the widow must be poor and powerless—but can we really assume this? It is time for the third interpretation.

(c) Powerful widows in the Bible: Levine points out that "biblical widows are the most unconventional of conventional figures…[that] defy the convention of the poor and dependent woman," and she gives several examples to prove this statement: for example, Tamar, Naomi, Ruth, Orpah, Abigail, and Judith.[8] As a matter of fact, nothing in the Lukan text suggests that the widow is poor.[9] Indeed, it is stated that she is from "a certain city" (*en tê[i] polei*), which seems to be an indication that she is not from rural Galilee, where the inhabitants, arguably, were poorer than in the cities. We simply do not have enough information to conclude that Luke has a *poor* widow in mind when writing down this parable. Levine calls some of the characterizations of the widow "completely pathetic."[10] There seems to be another motivating force for taking for granted that she is poor, apart from the narrative setting and characters. It has already been suggested that one may detect a connection between, on the one hand, the inclination to emphasize her alleged poverty and, on the other hand, the excessively negative descriptions of the asserted "ugly and oppressive" conditions in first-century Judaism.[11]

In short, the widow in the Lukan parable may be much more powerful and autonomous than is usually assumed. The question is whether she is even more than that. This question takes us to the next interpretation.

(d) The widow is the true protagonist when revealing something about God: Barbara Reid poses the interesting question: Who in this text reveals something about God? She argues that it is not the unjust judge who represents God. The judge does not reflect what most readers believe about God's response to the cries of the poor; he remains utterly unmoved by the widow's persistent pleas.

Hence, Reid argues that one does not have to assume that this is a parable about praying people who boldly face God, who can be likened to an impervious judge. If this were the case, then the message would be that if one only badgers God persistently enough, one can eventually wear God down and get a positive response. Reid states that such a notion for her is "theologically abhorrent and is flatly contradicted by texts such as Luke 11:9–13 and Sirach 35:14–19, which insist that God is eager to give all good things to those who ask, particularly to those who are poorest."[12]

According to Reid, there is a far simpler way to understand the parable. She proposes that it is the widow who is an icon of godliness, not the unjust judge. It is the widow who is cast in "the image of God," presented as a figure to emulate. She represents "godly power revealed in seeming weakness."[13]

As a matter of fact, Luke is certainly no stranger to allowing women to be protagonists in his parables: the most striking example is the woman who has lost one coin, and searches until she has found it (15:8–10). Not only does that parable immediately follow the parable of the male shepherd with a hundred sheep (15:3–7), but it is also a perfect parallel. Hence, Luke does not hesitate to liken God to a woman as well as to a man.

Reid sees the widow as the Godlike figure, and the message of the parable is that "when one doggedly resists injustice, faces it, names it, and denounces it until justice is achieved, then one is acting as God does."[14] In other words, her perseverance is commendable, but not because she is a role model for the praying person; it is because she represents God. Or is the widow perhaps a role model for the praying person simply because she is "an icon of godliness?"

(e) The widow is a morally ambiguous and problematic character: Levine's own interpretation is that Luke does not paint a flattering portrait of the widow in this parable. Hence, not only is the unjust judge, whose actions are not based on justice, a dubious character, but so is the widow, who keeps coming to pester him. In that sense, the text points beyond itself. All interpreters agree that he clearly is not a good judge, but Levine goes one step further and argues that the widow seeks revenge, based on her

A Parable about Prayer or Politics?

interpretation of the verbs *ekdikein* (to help get justice, to avenge) and *hypopiazein* (to hit under the eye). Levine argues that the widow is not only interested in justice but also in revenge, and that she is threatening to go as far as physically hitting the judge if he does not give her what she wants. The verb *hypopiazein* is a boxing term (once used by Paul in 1 Cor 9:27: "I punish [*hypopiazō*] my body"), and it indicates that it is not only a matter of the judge being tired of the widow's persistence but also his being scared of a physical blow—which is quite a striking (!) image. Hence, what pushed him to arrive at his decision is that he is threatened.[15]

The widow does not love her enemies, nor does the judge, as one is requested to do (Matt 5:44 and Luke 6:27). The parable raises a critical question about the difference between justice and vengeance. Is it the desire for *vengeance* that motivates the widow?

In other words, according to Levine, both the widow and the judge are problematic characters in a parable that is ambiguous and therefore difficult to interpret. Klyne R. Snodgrass confesses that he considers this to be one of the more difficult parables. It is brief, and without the explanation in the concluding verses, there is little indication of its intent.[16]

Levine suggests that the parable deconstructs itself because it points beyond itself. Luke understands it as a parable about the power of prayer, but—according to Levine—he has not adapted it enough. We still see its pre-Lukan traits. Levine argues that there is no easy closure to the widow's story: indeed, "there is no closure at all."[17] Since the readers cannot find justice in the setting, we have to look elsewhere. And we also have to cross-examine ourselves in regard to stereotypes of, for example, widows and judges. Levine wishes the parable to remain problematic, not to be domesticated. Levine states that Jesus was invested in fairness, reconciliation, and compassion. But in this parable, there is no fairness, no reconciliation, and no compassion. With this story, Jesus forces us to find a moral compass *outside* of the parable. We must go *beyond* the parable in order to find what we are seeking.

In short, five interpretations have been presented here: the widow has been portrayed as a *pious* praying person, a *pitiful* victim, a *powerful* woman, the actual *protagonist* in the parable, and a highly *problematic* character, whose behavior provokes a reaction from the reader. Some readers will continue to think of the parable as one about the importance of fervent prayer. However, having been acquainted with the fifth interpretation, we will perhaps be more aware of the ambiguity of the characters in the parable. Ultimately, all characters in all parables are insufficient when seeking to portray God: "But the Holy One, blessed be he, is not like that," as it says in the quoted passage from *Talmud Yerushalmi*. Or in the words of the Second Isaiah, who seeks to comfort the people with references to the strong bonds between parents and children but eventually admits that not even such a strong image suffices when describing God's covenantal steadfastness (Isa 49:14–16):

> Zion said, "The LORD has forsaken me, my Lord has forgotten me."
> Can a woman forget her nursing child, or show no compassion for the child of her womb? *Even these may forget*, yet I will not forget you. See, I have inscribed you on the palms of my hands.[18]

It is the perils of the second interpretation—especially the tendency to think of the unjust judge vis-à-vis an exploited widow in the narrative as a credible source of information when reconstructing the historical setting of first-century Judaism—that are of particular importance to the topic of the present book.[19] We cannot transfer the judge's behavior in the narrative directly to the historical world outside of the parable any more than we can crime statistics from the books and movies about Kurt Wallander's Ystad or Tom and John Barnaby's Midsomer.

16

JUSTICE IN THE TEMPLE COURT?
Luke 18:9–14

When reading this parable, one runs an obvious risk of interpreting it anachronistically. An example is the act of beating one's chest, which many modern readers think of as a sign of triumphalism and arrogance. Since their biased presumption is that the Pharisee is an arrogant hypocrite, they assume that it is he who is beating his chest—but it is not! As a matter of fact, it is the tax collector who is doing it, since in his culture this was a sign of mourning and even despair.[1]

This, however, is just a minor detail. A more frequent anachronistic error is to identify and present the tax collector as the ideal Protestant, who is justified *sola fide* (by faith alone). As a consequence, Christian teaching and preaching present the Pharisee in such a way that the conclusion is that the congregation would like to exclaim: "Thank God, that I am not like the Pharisees!"[2] It is somewhat ironic that such a condescending conclusion is, as a matter of fact, precisely the raison d'être for the parable, because in the Lukan introduction it is stated that the parable was intended for those who "trusted in themselves that they were righteous and regarded others with contempt" (18:9). The Greek for "regarded others with contempt" is even stronger: *exouthenein* literally means "to reduce to nothing," "to bring to naught." Hence, perhaps this parable today more than anything else is directed to those Christians who regard first-century Pharisees with contempt. The three keywords for the interpretations presented in this chapter are *contrast*, *comparison*, and *complementarity*.

(a) Contrast—an anti-Jewish parable on the perils of having too "Jewish" an approach to the interplay of faith and deeds: The concepts of righteousness and righteous play an important role in Christian discourse, especially for those who identify with the Reformation traditions. When all is said and done, as it is often stated in these Protestant quarters,

it is not what a person does or does not do that makes that person righteous—but who God *is*.³ But whereas the tax collector in the parable undoubtedly seems to be sincerely humble, there is nothing in his confession that is distinctly "Christian," nor are there any indications that he will change his way of life. It says that he went home righteous, yes, but did he start living a righteous life? As Levine asks, "Will he keep his day job and continue to sin, or will he make restitution for his sins and find another line of work?"⁴ We simply do not know. In comparison, we do know that his colleague Zacchaeus promised to change his way of life: "Look, half of the possessions, Lord, I will give to the poor; and if I have defrauded anyone or anything [which is quite likely, given that he worked for the Romans], I will pay back four times as much" (Luke 19:8). And it is after this solemn declaration that Jesus states, "Today salvation has come to this house, because he too is a son of Abraham. For the Son of Man came to seek out and to save the lost" (v. 9). Whereas it is explicitly stated that Zacchaeus changed his mind and behavior, we have no similar information in the parable we are now discussing. Hence, we cannot take for granted that he made any reparations or that he changed his lifestyle.

Because of some ambiguity in the eleventh verse in the Greek manuscripts, it has been suggested that the Pharisee was not *standing* by himself but *praying* to himself, which has promoted the portrayal of him as being an egocentric hypocrite, who is not even God-centered in his prayer. If this were the case, it was not even a prayer. However, the most likely reading is that the evangelist wishes to convey that the Pharisee was *standing by himself* when praying to God, not that he was *talking to himself* when standing next to others.⁵

Levine points out that as early as Augustine the Pharisee was made into the paradigmatic Jew, and the tax collector into the model Gentile Christian, the conclusion being that it is better to be a Christian saved by God's grace than a Jew who despises others and teaches salvation by works.⁶ But this is not a parable contrasting two distinctly different religious systems; it takes place *within* the Jewish tradition, which takes us to the second interpretation.

(b) Comparison—an intra-Jewish parable on the importance of humility: Both the Pharisee and the tax collector are *Jews*, the parable is situated in the *Jewish* temple in Jerusalem, and it is to the God of *Israel* that they are praying. The parable is critiquing neither the temple nor prayers in the temple, and every interpretation that de-emphasizes the Jewishness of one of the characters (the tax collector)—and at the same time stresses the

Jewishness of the other (the Pharisee)—will inevitably be anachronistic. Indeed, it is quite striking how *biblical*—that is, *Jewish*—the tax-collector's prayer is. When he prays to the God of Israel for mercy (v. 13), the verb is *hilaskesthai* (to appease, to be gracious), which occurs only twice in the New Testament (here and Heb 2:17, with reference to Jesus Christ as the chief priest) and a dozen times in prayers in the Septuagint.[7] The synonym *exilaskesthai* is far more common. The Hebrew behind the two Greek verbs is usually *kipper* (as in *Yom Kippur*, "the Day of Atonement"), which is a central concept in both the Jewish and the Christian traditions.

In short, the humility of the tax collector in the parable does not make him less Jewish. The conventional critique that his contemporaries would have articulated would be based on his *work* for the Roman administration, not his *words* in the temple. Correspondingly, the theological arrogance of the Pharisee is not what makes him Jewish. It is quite remarkable that Rudolf Bultmann understood his prayer in the Lukan parable to be an actual prayer by an actual Pharisee to which scholars can refer when seeking to depict the Pharisees' prayer life:

> It is a remarkable fact that side by side with this sense of sin and urge to repentance we find the "righteous" proud and self-conscious. They look down on the publican and sinner and preen themselves on their own good works. "I thank thee, that I am not as other men are, extortioners, unjust, adulterers, or even as this publican. I fast twice in the week, I give tithes of all that I possess" (Luke 18.11f.). And, strangely enough, this self-praise can be combined with a sense of sin.[8]

Indeed, it is quite "remarkable," to use his own word, that Bultmann chooses to combine the fictious prayer of what seems to be a caricature of a Pharisee in a Lukan parable with a quotation from 4 Ezra 8.47–49 that underscores the importance of humility, as if these two texts could be read in the light of each other in order to describe the piety of actual Pharisees at the time of Jesus.[9]

But we could also pose the question whether this really is a caricature. Michael Farris states that "it *was* appropriate to thank God for a righteous life. Taken in its own terms, the Pharisee's prayer is not self-righteous or arrogant; it properly thanked God, as the true author of righteousness. Jesus' hearers would have respected the prayer and surely would emulate it if they could."[10] Similarly, Timothy A. Friedrichsen compares it to traditional Christian discourse about divine grace and suggests that what the Pharisee says is no more arrogant than the Christian declaration that "There but for the grace of God, go I."[11] If it is not a Lukan caricature, then the Pharisee clearly goes above and beyond what is halakhically required.[12] When doing more than he is expected to do, are his acts meritorious or even vicarious?[13] This takes us to the third interpretation.

(c) Complementarity—does it perhaps even allude to **zekhut** *avot?* A key question when comparing various readings of this parable is how we are to interpret the Greek preposition *para* followed by the accusative in the fourteenth verse. In the first interpretation above it is understood as a *contrast* (person A is righteous *instead of* person B), implying that the Pharisee, when leaving the temple, was no longer in right relationship with God (if that ever had been the case): he is outright unrighteous. In the second interpretation it is a matter of *comparison* (person A is *more* righteous *than* B): humility is even more important than *halakhah*, but without overturning the latter.[14]

But *para* and accusative can also refer to *complementarity* (cf. "parallel," "parable," and "parapsychology"). Hence, the meaning could be that person A is righteous *as well as* person B. Is, then, the conclusion to be drawn here, that the tax collector went to his home justified *alongside* the Pharisee?[15]

In an excursus to an article on this parable, Friedrichsen suggests that the message is that the tax collector went down from the temple *because* of the Pharisee (or *on account of* the Pharisee). He asks whether the tax collector left the temple justified "because he had benefitted from the vicarious virtue of the Pharisee's fasting and tithing."[16] This line of thought is developed by Levine, who refers to the Jewish notion of *zekhut avot* (the merits of the fathers). This concept refers to the belief that the great deeds of the Hebrew patriarchs and matriarchs influence God's judgment favorably upon the Jewish people.[17] Friedrichsen points out that since this divine justification was effected in the temple area, the parable confirms the significance of the temple.[18] This resonates with Lukan theology and the narrative flow of the gospel that begins and ends in the sanctuary: in the first chapter an angel appeared in the temple to John the Baptist's father Zechariah (in Hebrew his name means "The LORD remembers"), and the Gospel ends with the statement that the disciples "were continually in the temple blessing God" (24:53). As Levine writes, "It is in the Temple that the tax collector believes he can find atonement, and he is correct."[19]

Now, strictly speaking, the suggestion that the Pharisee's lifestyle is meritorious constitutes a *fourth* interpretation. The third interpretation simply argued that both men left the temple justified. Although references to the concept of *zekhut avot* may be unexpected for numerous readers (especially Protestants), it does make sense in a first-century Jewish context.[20]

A relevant parallel is the current discussion in Pauline scholarship about the expression *pistis Christou*, which is to be understood either as "faith in Christ" or as "faithfulness of Christ." The latter interpretation suggests that it is Christ's faithfulness in life, death, and resurrection—not Christ followers' belief it him—that is the stepping stone for Paul's theology of the inclusion of the Gentiles.

The first of the interpretations presented above has often been exploited by Protestants who wish to validate their own theology by presenting a tax collector who is justified by faith in divine grace (*sola fide*) in contrast to the Pharisee who *solely* believes in his own self-righteousness. The last interpretation—that *zekhut avot* may be relevant when studying this text—is quite "Catholic," in the sense that it resembles the intercession of saints. An illuminating example that may help us appreciate *zekhut avot* better is presented by Levine. She vividly describes the group dynamic in a school project: there are a couple of motivated pupils who do all the work, and there is the pupil that perhaps shows up late and contributes nothing to the group work but who, nevertheless, receives the same grade as all the others in the group. Is it not worth pondering that some of us may take divine grace for granted but find the "injustice" in the school example somewhat disturbing? (One is reminded of the parable about the laborers in the vineyard [Matt 20:1–16]. Although some of them only start working in the eleventh hour, all laborers receive the very same payment: one *denarius*.)

By way of conclusion, three interpretations of the Lukan parable have been presented in this chapter: the first one *contrasting* the two characters in the parable, the second interpretation *comparing* them, and the third interpretation suggests a *complementarity*. This parable addresses several important issues, one of which is the prayer life of people then and now.

Luke shows us that negatively judging others is not a trait that signals "Jewish" values; it is, rather, a *human* trait, and one to which the followers of Jesus themselves may fall prey. Or as Israel Abrahams once wrote,

> The real point...is not against Pharisaic prayer, but against ostentatious prayer, and ostentation is neither a vice from which Pharisees were free, nor a vice of which they had a monopoly.[21]

17

JUDAS ISCARIOT: "I KNOW WHO EVERYBODY'S GONNA BLAME"[1]

Matt 10:1–4, 26:14–16, 26:21–25, 27:3–10;
Mark 3:13–19, 14:10f., 14:18–21, 14:43–45;
Luke 6:12–16, 22:3–6, 22:21–33, 22:47f.;
John 6:70f., 12:1–7, 13:2, 13:21–30, 17:12;
and Acts 1:15–26
(cf. 1 Cor 11:23–26 and 15:5)

The word *Quisling* is not only the surname of the Norwegian pro-Nazi leader Vidkun Quisling, who ruled Norway during the Second World War, but also a synonym for a traitor. An early example of this phenomenon is a cartoon by Ragnvald Blix (alias Stig Höök) published in a Swedish newspaper in 1944, in which Quisling, saluting an adjutant in Berlin, proudly states, "I am [a] Quisling," whereupon the adjutant dispassionately asks him: "And what is your name, sir?"[2]

Similarly, in Christian imagination, Judas is much more than the name of one of the twelve disciples of Jesus. For most people he is the archetype of a traitor, the embodiment of betrayal, or, as Anthony Cane writes, "Judas is *the* sinner of the New Testament."[3]

However, he was not the only one who was called Judas. As a matter of fact, Judas (Hebrew: *Yehudah*) was—and it still is—a common Jewish name. And Judith, the heroine of the apocryphal book, bears the feminine version of this name: *Yehudit*. The name Judas derives from the Greek form of the name of one of Jacob's sons, *Yehudah* (often abbreviated to Judah), who was the progenitor of the powerful tribe that gave its name to the Southern Kingdom after Solomon's kingdom was divided after his death. It remained the name of the country throughout Jesus's lifetime and until the second century CE, when the Romans renamed it *Syria Palaestina* to erase the identity of this province that had twice unsuccessfully rebelled against them.

Now, why was Judas called "Iscariot?" There are several suggestions, three of which are presented here.[4] (1) It may be a reference to the Greek word *sicarios* (cf. Latin: *sicarius*). Is this an indication that he was one of the *sicarii*, a militant anti-Roman group of assassins, known for carrying daggers? (A *sica* was a curved dagger or sword; cf. Acts 21:38). Does this imply that he may have been more *politically* motivated than the other disciples? (2) In Hebrew *Ish Qeriot* means "the man from Qeriot." Although its location is uncertain, it was most likely situated in Judah (cf. Joshua 15:25). Does this imply that he may not have been from Galilee, unlike all the other disciples? (3) The root *sh-q-r* is behind words such as *a liar* (Hebrew: *shaqrai* or *shaqran*; Aramaic: *sheqarya*), *to lie*, and *a lie*. This is the most likely explanation, and if this is the background for his name, it means that it was given to him after the death of Jesus.[5] Hence, it does not help us if we want to find a motif for his behavior. Furthermore, Gustaf Dalman argued that it is "a very plausible conjecture that 'Iskariôt' was already unintelligible to the evangelist."[6] In other words, the only safe conclusion we can draw is that the surname was added because *Yehudah* (transliterated as "Judas") was such a common name. There was a need to distinguish him from other people with the same name.

While Judas has almost always been portrayed in a distinctly negative way, there have been several different interpretations of what made his behavior negative.[7] On the following pages, four interpretations of the figure of Judas will be discussed.

(a) The archetypical Jew: Quite early in church history, Judas was thought of and presented as substantially more *Jewish* than the rest of the disciples, and certainly more Jewish than the protagonist, Jesus of Nazareth. It is often pointed out that even his name literally means "Jew," as in this quotation from a text by Oscar Quensel, published in Swedish in 1914:

> He appears to me to be *the typical Jew*, at once *a religious fanatic* and—*a money man!* For his faith in the promises of the prophecy and his hope that these found their fulfillment in Jesus, he could out of religious devotion sacrifice *everything*, home, reputation, well-being; and yet, in the end—his love of money unbroken! It was not without reason that he bore the name *Judas* [*Icke utan skäl bar han namnet Judas*].[8]

It may suffice with one more example of the influential trajectory in Christian texts that connects Judas to the people of Israel in a particular and, indeed, peculiar way: a couple of notorious chapters in the section on "The Election of God" in Karl Barth's *Church Dogmatics*, written in the early 1940s.[9] In Barth's text, Judas is the archetypical Jew, and a representative of Judaism. Undoubtedly, it surprises many a reader that he chose such a typological exegesis in a text written during the Shoah when antisemites in raging fury persecuted, tormented, and murdered Jews not far from Barth's safe haven in Basel.

Barth's line of thought will be quoted quite extensively in the following paragraphs, with the aim of highlighting an influential trait of the Christian discourse about Jews and Judaism. Is Barth actually suggesting a correlation between, on the one hand, the *faith* of Jews and, on the other hand, his quite disengaged attitude to the *fate* of the same Jews? It is quite clear that Barth, the main author of the Barmen Declaration, sternly opposed the influence of Nazi leaders over the Christian churches, but this courageous—and often costly—commitment cannot serve as a carte blanche for latent anti-Jewish theology that surfaces in numerous Christian texts written at that momentous time in history. Because of his influence, the writings of such a prominent scholar have to be scrutinized all the more. Barth argues that Israel can best be likened to the rootless existence of a severed branch, whose unavoidable and immediate prospect is to wither away:

> This is the existence of all those in Israel who, from Ishmael up to the present-day Synagogue, although they were and are Israelites, have proved unserviceable in relation to what God willed with Israel and finally brought forth from it, so that in their totality they can only form that dark and monstrous side of Israel's history. This is the disobedient, idolatrous Israel of every age [*Das ist das ungehorsame, götzendienerische Israel aller Zeiten*]: its false prophets and godless kings; the scribes and Pharisees; the high-priest Caiaphas at the time of Jesus; Judas Iscariot among the apostles....[10]
>
> For the time of the temple itself, of Jerusalem itself, of the special worship of this city and of the existence of Israel as the special people of God, had passed. When Judas handed Jesus over, this era drew to its close [*Indem Judas Jesus auslieferte, begann diese Zeit abzulaufen*]....Nothing more could be made of the Judaism that Judas had chosen as his portion in place of the promised and manifested Messiah of Israel. After the rejection of this Messiah as initiated by Judas, no more could be done for the continuance of the temple and Jerusa-

lem and Israel as the special people of God [*für den Fortbestand des Tempels und Jerusalems und Israels als des besonderen Volkes Gottes* [*war*] *nichts mehr zu machen*]....[11]

With the killing of its Messiah, Israel has entered a road on which not only is God's judgment upon its whole existence inevitable, but in sheer self-consistency it must end by committing suicide. That is what Israel finally did in the revolt against the Romans and particularly in the defence of Jerusalem against Titus in A.D. 70. Unable to live any longer, it gave itself up willingly and wittingly—we have only to think of the account of the end of the last high-priests—to the death which in itself could not be an expiation for its sins, but only their consummation [*keine Sühne für seine Sünder, sondern nur deren letzte Vollendung*]....[12]

Judas, the *paradidous* ["the betrayer"] in his concentrated attack upon Israel's Messiah, does only what the elect people of Israel had always done toward its God, thus finally showing itself in its totality to be the nation rejected by God [*das von Gott verworfene Volk*]. In Judas there live again (as it were in compendium) all the great rejected of the Old Testament who had already had to testify that this elect people is in truth rejected, that it is elect in and from its rejection, that it is elect only in the form of the divine promise given to it in the beginning and never taken away, that it is elect finally only in the person of the One for whose sake this people could and must have its special existence. In view of the act of Judas there can be no further doubt about the rejection of this people and the seriousness of the typical rejection of all these individuals within it. For it has delivered up to the Gentiles for death the very One in whom it is elect. This Judas must die, as he did die; and this Jerusalem must be destroyed, as it was destroyed. Israel's right to existence is extinguished, and therefore its existence can only be extinguished [*Israels Existenzrecht ist dahin, so kann seine Existenz nur noch ausgelöscht werden*].[13]

Derek Alan Woodard-Lehman states, quite correctly, that what is implied in these texts by Barth is "what for Judas ends in the potter's field, for Israel ends at Masada."[14] (The Roman conquest of the fortification Masada in 74 CE is often described as the end of the first Jewish revolt against Rome.) Hence, not only is Judas described as the archetypical Jew and his behavior as representative for Israel throughout history, but, in addition, every Jew who is not a Christ follower assumes the guilt of Judas's betrayal.

Once again, when considering that Barth wrote this during the Shoah, his insensitivity is stunning, and we may want to ascribe it to the anti-Jewish Zeitgeist of that era, even among those who sternly opposed Nazism. But, as a matter of fact, long after the end of the war, Barth openly confessed his deep-seated discomfort with Jews and Judaism. In a letter to Friedrich-Wilhelm Marquardt, written in 1967, in which Barth thanked him for sending his book about Barth's theology on Judaism (German: *Israellehre*), Barth wrote quite honestly about his discomfort when meeting with Jews:

> I am decidedly not a philosemite, in that in personal encounters with living Jews (even Jewish Christians) I have always, so long as I can remember, had to suppress a totally irrational aversion [*eine völlig irrationale Aversion*], naturally suppressing it at once on the basis of all my presuppositions, and concealing it totally in my statements, yet still having to suppress and conceal it. Pfui! is all that I can say to this in some sense allergic reaction of mine [*zu diesem meinem gewissermaßen allergischen Reagieren*]. But this is how it was and is. A good thing that this reprehensible instinct is totally alien to my sons and other better people than myself (including you). But it could have had a retrogressive effect on my doctrine of Israel [*es möchte sein, daß auch er sich in meiner Israellehre retardierend ausgewirkt hat*].[15]

One cannot but be impressed by the honest self-reflection that Barth gives vent to in this letter to Marquardt. However, at the same time we also should credit his suspicion that this allergic reaction of his to *Jews* may have had a negative effect on his portrayal of *Judaism*. So, too, it would have shaped his portrait of Judas as a representative of Judaism, indeed, as the embodiment of Judaism, a religion that, according to Barth, ceased when Jesus was handed over to the Romans, or at least lost its raison d'être.

We must bear in mind that an important feature in the Gospels is that *the people were on the side of Jesus*. It is often stated that those who wanted to seize him feared the people (e.g., Matt 21:46f., Mark 12:12, and Luke 20:19). Hence, Judas is necessary or at least useful only because the political and religious leaders were looking for an opportunity to seize him *when the Jewish crowds were not there with him*. Yet those Jewish crowds were no less Jewish than Judas. To describe Judas as the quintessence of Judaism is bizarre for historical reasons and offensive for theological reasons.

(b) A trajectory of betrayal and treason: When comparing the earliest accounts of the figure of Judas, it is quite noticeable that, over time, he is presented as increasingly more evil. This is a trajectory that *commences* but is not *concluded* in the New Testament. Thus, already within the New Testament, there is a clear evolution of Judas's character, from being one of the twelve apostles to being possessed by the devil. Judas was an integral part of the Twelve. He was the treasurer of Jesus and his disciples, which makes him a member of the inner circle.[16] And when the Gospels narrate what happened at the Last Supper, they specifically mention that Judas dips his bread in the bowl together with Jesus, which may be an indication that he was particularly favored among the Twelve, because only those who had been assigned one of the most prestigious places at the *triclinium* could do so (see Matt 26:23, Mark 14:20, Luke 22:21, and John 13:26).[17] Those who, so to speak, were highest in rank lay closest to the Master—and the texts inform us that Judas is positioned close enough to both Peter and Jesus for Peter to overhear their conversation.

Before the Gospels were written down, Paul referred to what happened on the night when the Last Supper took place. It is quite remarkable—and worth pondering—that if we only had Paul's version, we would not even know Judas's name or fate! As William Klassen writes, "Paul has no interest in the person of Judas or the role that he played."[18]

In the oldest account of the Last Supper, Paul describes "the night that he was handed over" (1 Cor 11:23)—in the passive. The agent obviously is not important here. A few chapters later, he points to "our sins," not the actions of one particular person. As a matter of fact, Paul does not seem to know anything about the fate of Judas as reported in the Gospels but rather writes about the risen Jesus appearing to an intact *Twelve* (1 Cor 15:5).

Returning to the New Testament Gospels, we see the negative image of Judas emerge. Here, Judas seeks out a bribe to betray Jesus, betrays him with a kiss in Gethsemane, and then, according to Matthew, commits suicide in despair. This evolution can be detected and analyzed step by step.

(i) Mark describes Judas as "one of the Twelve" (*heis tôn dôdeka*; 14:43, cf. Matt 26:47, and Luke 22:47) who are appointed to proclaim the message and cast out demons. However, when Mark lists these apostles by name, he identifies Judas as "Judas Iscariot, who handed him over" (3:19). In Mark, Judas went to the chief priests in order to betray him. When hearing this, the priests were greatly pleased (*echarêsan*, from *chairein*, "to rejoice") and offered him silver (14:11). There is no connection between his behavior and the demonic.[19]

(ii) Matthew elaborates on the amount of silver. Judas solicits the bribe, and the chief priests offer him thirty silver coins. This draws on a prophetic tradition of Zechariah's being insulted when offered this amount, known to be the worth of a slave (Matt 26:14–16; cf. Zech 11:12).[20] But, in fact, silver coins had not been in circulation for several hundred years.[21] Hence, this piece of information is probably similar to Matthew's changing the identity of the "Syrophoenician woman" (Mark 7:24–30) into a "Canaanite woman" (Matt 15:21–28)—although there were no Canaanites at the time of Jesus. References to the Scriptures are typical for the Gospel of Matthew: "Then was fulfilled what had been spoken...." In short, we have reason to believe that Matthew deliberately chooses an archaic terminology. However, thirty silver coins was not a large sum of money, approximately the minimum wage for a few months' work.

(iii) Luke mentions that Satan enters into Judas at this particular moment when money is involved (22:3). As is often pointed out, Luke, more than the other gospel authors, repeatedly warns his readers of the perils of *mammon*: money and wealth are treacherous.

(iv) The association with Satan and the negative portrayal of Judas goes even further in the Gospel of John, the latest of the four. John accuses Judas of stealing from the funds that Jesus and the disciples held in common (12:6). Like Luke, John understands Judas as being possessed by the devil, but he places the devil's entering into him at the Last Supper. He reports that, before the meal, "The devil had already put it into the heart of Judas son of Simon Iscariot to betray him" (13:2).[22] After receiving bread from Jesus, John reports that "Satan entered into him" (13:27). However, as early as in John 6:70, Judas is identified as a *diabolos* (lit. "destroyer," "divider"; cf. "diabolic"): "one of you is a devil" (*ex hymôn heis diabolos estin*). In short, in the Gospel of Mark, Judas is "one of the Twelve," Matthew adds the information about the thirty silver coins with its scriptural resonances, Luke interprets this as greed (a typically Lukan motif), and in the Gospel of John, Judas is a thief and even a *diabolos*.

Judas Iscariot: "I Know Who Everbody's Gonna Blame"

We have three accounts of what eventually happened to Judas. According to Matthew, Judas, out of despair, committed suicide by hanging when he realized what he had done (Matt 27:1–10). Thought-provokingly, Klassen writes that

> Judas was the first and the strongest witness to Jesus' innocence.... He could well have been the first to die with Jesus. Thus, in solidarity with Jesus, he would have died for what he believed: that Jesus was a good man, innocent of death, deserving no evil.[23]

According to Luke (Acts 1:16–20), Judas died when he fell and burst open in the middle: now, was this an accident or divine intervention? Did he die because he had an evil spirit inside?[24] The third account was written by Papias, in his fourth book of *Exposition of the Sayings of the Lord*. (Papias was a bishop in Hierapolis, today in Turkey.)[25]

> Judas lived his career in this world as an enormous example of impiety. He was so swollen in the flesh that where a wagon could pass easily, he could not pass. Indeed not even his oversized head alone could do so. His eyelids were so puffed, they say, that he could no longer see the light at all; nor could his eyes be detected even by an optician's instrument, so far had they sunk below the outer surface.

Papias continues describing the fate of Judas, but this quotation may suffice. It is not difficult to imagine that one of the chief questions for the early Jesus movement, when pondering the passion narrative, must have been how Jesus could have chosen a traitor to be one of his disciples.[26] Can the trajectory in the New Testament be understood as a response to that query? However we answer that question, it is quite clear that the *older* the sources are, the *less* focus there is on Judas. As has already been pointed out, in the writings of Paul, Judas is not even mentioned. And the *later* they are, the *more* focus there is on his alleged greed. Candida Moss has examined the way Papias depicts the physical condition and the manner of death of Judas in light of ancient medical, biographical, and physiognomic literature. She concludes that Papias's depictions use images associated in antiquity with greedy people. His physical condition is "an outward manifestation of an internal corruption."[27] Hence, Papias's focus on financial gain fits the trajectory from Judas—one of the Twelve—to the timeless, archetypal traitor who out of greed betrayed his Master for thirty pieces of silver.

Due to his betrayal of Jesus, Judas became a particularly evil figure in Christian imagination. But if the death and resurrection of Jesus resulted in the dawn of the new era, why would anyone still blame Judas? This takes us to the next interpretation.

(c) An instrument of salvation: The third hermeneutical strategy takes as its starting point discussions on how to translate the Greek word *paradidonai*. The most common translation in connection to Judas's behavior is "to betray," but that is hardly the only possible translation of *paradidonai* (and the Latin equivalent, *tradere*). Klassen, referring to Liddell and Scott's lexicon for classical Greek, gives four fundamental meanings for *paradidonai*: (1) *To give, hand over to another, transmit*, such as virtues from teacher to students, documents, give up an argument, among others. (2) *To give a city or a person into another's hands*, especially, a hostage or an enemy with the collateral notice of "treachery, betray," (3) *To give up to justice*, and (4) *To hand down legends, opinions, and the like.*[28] Arguing that none of the three references in the dictionary to the second meaning above supports the translation "to betray," Klassen concludes that no Greek classical texts have so far surfaced in which *paradidonai* has the connotation of treachery:

> Any lexicon that suggests otherwise is guilty of theologizing rather than assisting us to find the meaning of Greek words through usage. Nor is the word found with that meaning in the papyri.[29]

The verb occurs in the well-known Words of Institution, recited when Christian celebrate the Eucharist:

> Our Lord Jesus Christ, on the night *when he was betrayed*, took the bread, and when he had given thanks, he broke it and gave it to his disciples and said: Take; eat; this is my body which is given for you. Do this in remembrance of me.[30]

However, previously in this verse Paul uses *the very same verb* in order to describe how he is faithfully handing over the traditions that he has received (11:23):

> For I have received from the Lord what I also delivered [*paredôka*] to you, that the Lord on the night when he was betrayed [*paredideto*]....

Judas Iscariot: "I Know Who Everbody's Gonna Blame"

Hence, Paul could be using the verb in this sentence to describe both how he is faithfully transmitting the liturgical traditions and how Jesus was handed over to the Romans. The Latin word *tradere* brought about both "traitor" (negative connotations) and "tradition" (positive connotations). (It is of some relevance here that "to betray" once meant "to hand over" [cf. Latin: *tradere*]. Therefore, the English noun "tray" refers to a utensil used for "handing over" something, and not necessarily in a negative way.[31])

Now, if we translate the verb not as "betrayed" but as "handed over"—by whom, then, was he handed over? One answer is that the grammatical agent is *Judas*, who is not so much betraying Jesus as handing him over (possibly according to a divine plan). But it is also possible—especially given the fact that grammatical passive voice often is chosen when God is the agent—that it is *God* who is handing over Jesus to the Romans. This is clearly the perspective in Romans 8:32: "He [i.e., God] who did not withhold [*epheisato*] his own Son, but gave [*paredôken*] him up for all of us, will he not with him also give us everything else?" It is quite plausible that Paul has the ʽ*aqedah* motif in Genesis 22 in mind when writing this, especially the twelfth verse, in which the angel says to Abraham: "Now I know that you fear God, since you have not withheld your son, your only Son, from me." The word for "withheld" in the Septuagint, the translation into Greek, is *pheidesthai*, the same verb as Paul uses in Romans 8:32.

Raymond E. Brown, in his monumental treatment of the Passion Narratives, *The Death of the Messiah*, discusses *paradidonai*. He argues that to translate the verb as "to betray" actually "blurs the parallelism to the agency of others expressed by this verb."[32] By this he means that there is a spectrum of interpretations: Jesus could be given over by God, by human beings, or by himself, and he points out that a prominent theme in the Gospel of John is that the Son gives himself over to death (e.g., 10:17f.).

In short, in the Words of Institution, is it eventually *Judas, human beings, Jesus* himself or *God* who is the agent? If the answer is that God is the grammatical agent, then the Pauline epistle here gives vent to what Orthodox theology calls the divine "economy" (*oikonomia*) of salvation, the divine plan according to which God interacts with the world. In the words of Klassen:

> The task of "giving over" is seen by the early church as fundamentally God-centered, initiated and carried out under the direction of God. It is, we would say, today, a theological task. So both the devil (in Luke and John) and God get involved in this "handing over."[33]

The fact that Paul does not even mention Judas's name points in the direction of a divine passive—that is, that Paul states that Jesus is *handed over by God*, this being the reason for not even mentioning the role of Judas, and even less so the role of "the Jews" (see chapter 29).

This takes us to the interminable discussion of horizontal and vertical theologies of the cross. *Horizontal* theologies emphasize the role of humans in the passion narrative: according to this understanding, ultimately, the Cross event is a failure; it is what happens when God withdraws (Hebrew: *tzimtzum*; "[divine] contraction") and the forces of evil triumph.[34] Whereas the resurrection is an Act of God, the crucifixion is not. The day that Jesus died was a *bad* Friday.

In contrast, *vertical* theologies accentuate that what happened on Good Friday was according to a divine plan, as in Acts 2:23: it happened because of "the definite plan" (*hē hōrismenē boulē*) and "foreknowledge" (*prognōsis*) of God. Similarly, the last book in the New Testament states that the Only Begotten son is as "a Lamb slain before the foundation of time" (Rev 13:8).[35] Hence, according to this understanding, it was not a bad Friday, but a *Good* Friday.

It would border on the indefensible to end the discussion of this interpretation without quoting the renowned poem by John Donne, "Upon the Annunciation and the Passion." The circumstance for the poem was the fact that in 1608, the Feast of the Annunciation (celebrating the Mystery of Incarnation, when the angels greeted the mother of Jesus with the words "Ave Maria") and Good Friday (when the last words of the Johannine Jesus are "it is finished": *consummatum est*) occurred simultaneously on March 25:

All this, and all betweene, this day hath showne,
Th'Abridgement of Christs story, which makes one
(As in plaine Maps, the furthest West is East)
Of the "Angels *Ave*" and *Consummatum est*.[36]

(d) A fallible follower of Jesus: Whereas the previous interpretation went as far as portraying Judas as a *divine* agent for salvation, the fourth and final line of thought presents him as utterly *human*, as one of the many fallible followers of Jesus of Nazareth.[37] An early supporter of this view was Friedrich Gottlieb Klopstock, who published his poem *Messias* in 1773. He presented a Judas who was jealous because he felt that his Master preferred John. This line of thought describes Judas as a person who was treated unfairly, who is a symbol of skepticism—or even disbelief—or,

quite simply, a representative of a fragile human being: a fallible follower of Jesus.

And as a matter of fact, among the Twelve, Judas is not the only one who is found wanting in one respect or another: Thomas famously *doubts* the resurrection of Jesus, and it is only when he can put his fingers into the wounds in Jesus's hands that he finally believes; and Simon Peter *denies* his Master—when asked whether he is one of those who were with Jesus the Galilean, he solemnly declares, "I do not know the man!" (Matt 26:72 and 74).

It is probably not a coincidence that the note with the highest musical pitch that the voice of the Evangelist reaches in the entire "St. Matthew's Passion" by Johann Sebastian Bach is when singing the word *heraus* in 26:75: *Und ging heraus und weinete bitterlich* (And he [i.e., Peter] went out and wept bitterly). This is followed by the aria, *Erbarme dich, mein Gott* (Have mercy, my God), and this, in turn, is followed by the choral, *Bin ich gleich von dir gewichen, stell ich mir doch wieder ein* (Although I have strayed from you, yet I turn back once again). In short, arguably, Peter's denial also plays a more central role than Judas's betrayal in Bach's magnificent piece of music.

Hence, one disciple is *disbelieving*, another disciple flatly *denies* his Master, and a third *discloses* him.[38] Even the Rock upon which the church will be built—Simon Peter—will eventually fail.[39] The supporters of the fourth interpretation ask whether there is such a vast difference between the behavior of Judas and Peter. And if not—what are the consequences?

The Gospel of John emphasizes the deficiency of Simon Peter's behavior in a particular way. It is often pointed out that the word *anthrakia* (charcoal fire) occurs only twice in the New Testament: first in John 18:18, when Peter, warming himself next to the charcoal fire because it was cold, denies his Master three times; the second time, in John 21:9, when the risen Lord is waiting for the disciples to return after having been fishing in the Sea of Galilee, Jesus asks Simon Peter three times if he loves him. The three denials have often been associated to the three questions; it is as if the Johannine Jesus restores Peter after his failure so that he may tend the Christ followers, who are likened to a flock of sheep (21:15–17).

Without exception, Judas is listed among the Twelve (*heis tôn dôdeka*; "one of the Twelve"). To be sure, he is listed last, but he is nevertheless a follower of Jesus, a disciple of Christ. The readers of the New Testament learn that he, as treasurer, had charge of the disciples' money. And, as Klassen writes, "as such must have enjoyed the sustained trust."[40]

We have seen that the Gospel of John—the latest of the Gospels in the New Testament—emphasizes the flaws of Simon Peter, the leader of the Twelve. Already in the Gospel of Mark—the oldest narrative account—it is quite clear that *all* the disciples are fallible followers of Jesus. Theodore Weeden famously argued that there is a "vendetta" against the disciples in the Gospel of Mark—it is not only Judas who is sternly criticized, but all of them. Indeed, the real villain is actually Simon Peter![41] In this perspective, Judas is not so much an *exception* from the behavior of the loyal disciples as an *example* of what fallible followers do when they doubt, when disbelieving, when in despair. Once again, we must ask ourselves whether there is any great difference between Judas's *betrayal* and Peter's *denial*.

We have already seen that Barth's typological reading of the Judas figure presented him as representing an entire group. According to Barth, Judas is the distinctly *Jewish* element among the Twelve. As Woodard-Lehman writes about Barth's theology:

> [Judas is] that negative determination of Israel amidst the positive determination of Church. His betrayal is Israel's final, yet original and prototypical, rejection of its election. After this there can be only judgment, the divine rejection of the paradigmatic human rejection of the divine....Judas's act is described [by Barth] as the act of all Israel, of each and every Jew who ever lives.[42]

Indeed, the fourth interpretation of Judas also sees him as a representative, but not of a particularly *Jewish* behavior (in contrast to loyal, confessing, and right-minded Christians); rather, he exemplifies disloyal, doubting, and erring *Christ* followers. He is not an individual who acts on his own in a way different from everyone else; instead, he is one of the Twelve, an imperfect disciple among other imperfect disciples. In one word, he is a *fallible* follower of Jesus.[43]

When comparing how Peter and Judas have been presented in history, it is quite clear, on the one hand, that Peter is revered as the leader of the early church, and, on the other hand, that Judas is always remembered as the one who betrayed Jesus and died in ignominy. In other words, Judas became the archvillain whose name can be translated as "Jew." True, Judas's name *Yehudah* means "Jew" (or "Judean"), but it is also stated in the New Testament that "Our Lord [i.e., Jesus] was descended from Judah" (Heb 7:14; cf. Matt 1:2f. and Luke 3:33). Hence, the *Judaization* of Judas, which has been going on for almost two millennia, is part of the larger question of the *de-Judaization* of Jesus. If the latter had not occurred, it would not have triggered the former. Is not the best way to oppose the exclusive connection between Judas and Judaism to underline the inherent *Jewishness* of Jesus? Indeed, they were all Jews: Jesus, the Twelve, the other disciples, the crowd. If occasionally there are non-Jews in the narratives, this fact is always pointed out, quite simply because they are exceptions to the rule: all the others were Jews. To seek to portray Judas as more "Jewish" is both historically and theologically nonsensical.

As we have seen, Simon Peter is always mentioned first and Judas Iscariot last—but Judas is always one of the Twelve. Is it not quite astonishing that not only the latter but also the former fails, especially given that his sobriquet means "the Rock?" Indeed, why should Judas's behavior become a source of eternal blame while Peter's is quickly *condoned* and soon not only *commended* but even *celebrated*? In one of his poems, Edgar Lee Masters links Judas to Peter, emphasizing the similarity between them: "And none except Judas and you broke the faith":

> How did you, Peter, when ne'er on His breast
> You leaned and were blest—
> *And none except Judas and you broke the faith*
> To the day of His death,—
> You, Peter, the fisherman, worthy of blame,
> Arise to this fame?[44]

The answer to Masters's question may show us a way to new horizons when seeking to understand the fate of the figure of Judas in the history of New Testament interpretation.

18

WHO ARE SHOUTING: "HIS BLOOD BE ON US AND ON OUR CHILDREN"?

Matt 27:25

The statement "His blood be on us and our children" plays a central role in the anti-Jewish discourse that alludes, refers to, or even quotes New Testament texts in order to strengthen its case. When commenting on the cry "Crucify him!," Claude G. Montefiore writes that "oceans of human blood and...endless human misery" have streamed from these words.[1]

Previously, the Matthean narrator has described how Pontius Pilate, well-known in antiquity for his cruelty, had washed his hands, declaring that he did not take any responsibility for the death of Jesus. And the gospel narrative continues with a description of how "responding, all the people said" (*apokritheis pas ho laos eipen*) that the blood of Jesus should come over them and their children.[2] The washing of hands and "the blood curse" occur only in the Matthean version. Various interpretations of the notorious statement have been offered, six of which will be discussed here.

(a) All Jews are cursed for all time: The statement "His blood be on us and our children" belongs to the bedrock of punitive supersessionism and the deicide charge (Latin: *Deus*, "God"; *caedere*, "to murder") against the Jewish people in toto—that is, that all Jews in all times are accused of murdering God—and have to bear the consequences of this act.[3] One example of this line of thought is Richard C. H. Lenski's commentary. He died in 1936, but the commentary was published posthumously in 1943:

> As far as the blood with which Pilate dreads to stain his hands is concerned—these Jews make light of it. They offer to take it completely off the governor's hands and to load it upon themselves. That implies that they assume all the guilt, that they make themselves lia-

Who Are Shouting: "His Blood Be on Us and on Our Children?"

ble for any punishment that may follow, that they may face God's justice and will suffer his wrath. And to this sacrilegious declaration they add even their children, all future generations of Jews. Why did these Jews have to challenge God's justice in so horrible a way? Why did they not keep still and let Pilate indulge in his little performance with the water? Was the devil riding them so completely that they cared not what damnation they called down on themselves? This prophetic word has been confirmed. The curse the Jews so gayly and so unanimously (note *pas ho laos*) took upon themselves that morning has turned out to be a curse indeed. They are now a separate people, are scattered over the whole earth, they have no country, no government, no entity and are a disturbing element among the nations. Even this fact shows that Jesus' blood is still upon them.[4]

Another example of a collective interpretation of this verse is found in the book *Le jugement dans l'Évangile de Matthieu*, in which Daniel Marguerat argues that the Matthean conclusion of this *terrible exclamation* is that Israel is repudiated (*Israël est renié*), that the polemics is not against merely a fraction of the people but *Judaism in its entirety*, as a theological and historical reality (*la polémique n'est pas tournée contre une fraction du peuple mais contre le judaïsme tout entier, considéré comme une entité théologique et historique*), and that by this cry, Israel has wiped itself out of the history of salvation (*Par ce cri, Israël s'est effacé lui-même de l'histoire du salut*).[5]

In favor of a collective interpretation is the peculiar expression *pas ho laos* (all the people). In the Gospels, other words are used for various groups of people—for example, *ochlos* (crowd), *plêthos* (crowd), *dêmos* (crowd—four times in Acts; cf. "democracy"), and *ethnê* ([non-Jewish] nations; cf. "ethnography"). In general, the group referred to by the word *ochlos* (occasionally in the plural: *ochloi*) is interested in the teaching of Jesus, and Paul's mission is to reach out to the Gentiles (*ta ethnê*). On the other hand, the word *laos* classically refers to the people of Israel (Hebrew: *'am Yisrael*), as in the conclusion of Nunc Dimittis in Luke 2:29–32: "… [the] salvation, which you have prepared in the presence of all peoples [*pantôn tôn laôn*], a light for revelation to the Gentiles [*ethnôn*] and for glory to your people Israel [*laou sou Israêl*]."

Hence, Israel is typically described as *ho laos* and the Gentiles as *ta ethnê*—but, in addition, all peoples, too, are *hoi laoi* (i.e., in the plural). In other words, it is not used exclusively about the people of Israel. And in the paradigmatic text for covenantal theology in Exodus 19:6, Israel is called to be a priestly kingdom and "a holy nation (LXX: *ethnos hagion*), which in Hebrew is *goy qadosh*. And Abraham in Genesis 12:2 is promised to become the father of a *goy gadol* (which in modern Hebrew would be "a big Gentile," not "a great nation"; LXX: *ethnos mega*). In short, the words *'am* and *laos* are not used exclusively for Israel. Nevertheless, readers and interpreters of the New Testament will have to explain why the expression *pas ho laos* is chosen in Matthew 27:25. The crowd in Mark 15:15 is consistently the *ochlos*, and Luke 23:18 uses an expression that occurs only once in the New Testament: they "altogether" (*pamplêthei*; cf. *pan*, "all," *plêthos*, "crowd") shouted that Barabbas be freed instead of Jesus of Nazareth.[6]

The collective accusation is so widespread that readers of the New Testament may not even have reflected on its inherent weaknesses, not counting its destructive *Wirkungsgeschichte*. Firstly, parallels in Scripture take pains to make a distinction between, on the one hand, those who have committed wrong (and their descendants) and, on the other hand, the people in its entirety, for example, 1 Kings 2:33 (cf. 2 Sam 3:28):

> So shall their blood come back on the heads of Joab and on the head of his descendants forever; but to David, and to his descendants and to his house, and to this throne, there shall be peace from the Lord forevermore.

Secondly, given the eschatological framework of the New Testament writers, it is unlikely that a several-millennia-long perspective was intended. The Christ-following readers of the text took for granted that the end of the world was imminent. The idea, centuries and centuries later, and, in addition, in other parts of the world, that all Jews are accused of murdering Jesus is quite an eccentric exegesis of this passage.

(b) An intra-Jewish etiology: W. D. Davies and Dale C. Allison classify the statement as an etiological "legend" that seeks to explain the tribulations during the first revolt against Rome, which culminated in the destruction of the temple in 70 CE. The fact that Matthew presumably writes his Gospel within a couple of decades after this event underscores that this statement is part of a Jewish reflection on theodicy—that is, as an answer to the question why God allowed the temple to be destroyed. And the reason is the same as when the first temple fell: *mi-pnei chataeinu* (because of our sins). However, the theological alternative to suffering is rejection. When interpreting the fall of the temple within the framework of sin and suffering, they are eliminating the alternative that the God of Israel has

abandoned the Israel of God. Hence, punishment within this frame of interpretation is a token of divine *election*, not of divine *rejection*.[7]

This would be neither the first nor the last time in Jewish history that destruction is associated with sin. Davies and Allison assert that "the text nurtures the feeling of tragedy, not self-satisfaction that the Jewish nation got what it deserved."[8] (It is possible that the expression "on us and on our children" should be understood as a limitation to two generations only—that is, to approximately the fall of the temple in the year of 70 CE.)

Davies and Allison also write that the expression "His blood be on us and our children" is a common idiom that signifies responsibility for someone's death. Hence, it is not a self-curse but rather a declaration of responsibility. Those who uttered these words acknowledge their involvement in what happened—even if Pontius Pilate chose not to by washing his hands.[9] Similarly, Hans Kosmala argued that the blood cry refers only to the issue of responsibility, not to that of blood-guilt: "The cry was not a solemn declaration of the whole people of Israel....That crowd did not represent the whole Jewish people nor could it speak in its name. The cry of that crowd means: We will bear the responsibility for the execution, and you will be innocent—no more and no less."[10]

Aaron M. Gale claims that the blood cry more likely should be understood as a prophetic fulfillment than a universal condemnation of Jews, and that "Matthew's first readers likely related the verse to the Jerusalem population killed or enslaved by the Romans as a result of the First Revolt against Rome in 66–70 CE."[11]

In general, when non-Jews read such Jewish reflections, the self-critical *mea culpa* (my sin) is easily transmuted to *tua culpa* (your sin), which is characteristic of how Christian supersessionism has interpreted the destruction of the temple in 70 CE. (Typically, "the temple was destroyed because *they* did not believe in Jesus as the Messiah.") In order to appreciate the consistently Jewish character of the second interpretation, one has to think of it as a statement that some of *us* Jews sinned—and there are consequences to sinful behavior.[12] But, as Davies and Allison conclude, the text does not nurture a Christian self-congratulatory understanding that the Jewish nation finally got what it deserved.[13]

(c) The blood of Jesus covers the sins of the wrongdoers: It has been argued that this statement must not be separated from the role of blood as a means for atonement in general, and in the Matthean text specifically. Timothy B. Cargal suggests that the verse be interpreted ironically: the solemn statement uttered by "all the people" invokes salvation for the people. That is why he calls it a *double entendre*: the verse is open to two interpretations.[14] In order for the promise in the beginning of the Gospel—"he will save his people [*laos*] from their sins" (1:21)—to make sense, and not be made void, the people's utterance should be understood not as condemnatory, but salvific.

Although Davies and Allison argue that this interpretation goes against the context, they go on to pose a similar question in a footnote: "One can ask but not answer how Matthew related 27.25 to the promise of 26.28 (blood poured out for the many)."[15]

Arguably the most extensive survey of the theme of innocent blood is Catherine Sider Hamilton's book *The Death of Jesus in Matthew*.[16] Focusing on the traditions about the innocent blood of Abel and Zechariah, she points out how central this theme is both in the Gospel of Matthew and in then-contemporary Judaism. The Matthean version of the Words of Institution, referred to by Davies and Allison above (26:28: "for this is my blood of the covenant, which is poured out for many for the forgiveness of sins"), should be interpreted within this context. The shedding of his innocent blood is not only what caused the destruction of the temple; it is poured out also for the forgiveness of sins. Hamilton argues that Matthew's perspective is "thoroughly Jewish"; he is not setting the good news of Jesus Christ over against Israel.[17]

In this context it may be worth pointing out that the Ten Points of Seelisberg, issued in 1947 by the International Council of Christians and Jews, and whose purpose was to urge the Christian world to denounce antisemitism, counsels that Matthew 27:25 always be interpreted in the light of Luke 23:34:

> Avoid referring to the scriptural curses, or the cry of a raging mob: *His blood be upon us and upon our children*, without remembering that this cry should not count against the infinitely more weighty words of our Lord: *Father, forgive them for they know not what they do*.[18]

A matter outside the scope of New Testament studies in a narrow sense is the implication of this issue for those who identify as Jews today and who do not see any reason to ask for forgiveness for shedding the innocent blood of Jesus, *quite simply because there is no reason to blame them for the death of Jesus*. This is an issue of vital importance to address because they and their ancestors may have been accused, harassed, and perhaps even persecuted because of that allegation.

(d) A solemn commitment to the covenant: Desmond Sullivan argues that Matthew's purpose is to emphasize that Christ-believing Judaism is the authentic form of Judaism, and that his Gospel was written while "the struggle for the soul of Judaism was as yet unresolved."[19] He suggests that the Matthean narrative about what happened at the time of Passover reminds the readers about Exodus 24:3, where the covenant was presented to "the entire people," who, responding "with one voice" (*kol ha-'am qol echad*), solemnly accepted the covenant. In other words, Matthew 27:25 narrates that "the people in a prophetic way acclaimed their commitment to this covenant."[20] Sullivan suggests that 27:25 is a reminder to the Jewish people that they have committed themselves and their children to the covenant in Jesus and that it is impossible to go back on such a commitment. In short, what is described is that the people in a prophetic way acclaimed their allegiance to the Christ-centered Judaism. According to Sullivan, the phrase *pas ho laos* does indeed refer to the entire nation, but it is in no way a curse, rather a solemn obligation that reenacts the Sinai event.[21]

(e) Not all Jews were there: Although quite obvious, it is regrettably still imperative for interpreters to underline that all Jews in antiquity evidently were not present in that courtyard on that day. If we want to reconstruct a plausible historical situation behind the Matthean text, we realize that neither all Jews in Jerusalem, nor all Jews in the land, nor all Jews in the entire Diaspora were there. Since Jews lived all the way from modern Iraq to Spain, the majority of Jews in antiquity never heard of Jesus of Nazareth, and even fewer chose to distance themselves from him and his teaching. The only generalization for which one finds some support in the Gospels is that *the religious authorities were more negative to him than people in general.*[22] In addition, is it plausible that the Jewish members of the Matthean community included themselves in the category "the whole people?" If the answer to that question is negative, we are reminded of the scholarly discussion of *hoi Ioudaioi* in John, which is a term that cannot not refer to all Jews (see introduction, second challenge).

(f) Not only Jews were there: Why would Pontius Pilate have allowed only Jews to enter the courtyard? Is it possible, probable, or plausible that some of those present were *non*-Jews: Roman soldiers and Roman citizens working in Jerusalem? It is worth noting in this context that the Greek word *laos* is the origin of the English word *laity* and the French *laïcité*, which both are understood as the opposite of *clergy*. If *pas ho laos* refers to those who actually were there, is it not also likely that non-Jews shouted the infamous words in 27:25? And Pontius Pilate, without whom no one would

be crucified—what responsibility does he have?[23] Floyd V. Filson describes him as a person "without moral courage," who "tries the last desperate measure of a guilty man who knows he is doing wrong; he tries to put the blame on others....Pilate by pretence of innocence cannot evade his responsibility."[24] In approximately 41 CE, Philo of Alexandria wrote that during Pilate's administration "executions without trial were constantly repeated" (Greek: *tous akritous kai epallêlous phonous*).[25] Joseph B. Tyson concludes an article on the historical causes for the death of Jesus, stating that "[it] was not brought about by *Jewish opposition* but rather by *Roman political oppression*."[26] In what ways can and must Christian theology incorporate these reflections?

To sum up, whereas the Markan text states that Pontius Pilate released Barabbas in order to satisfy the crowd (*ochlos*), the Matthean version asserts that it was at the request of "all the people" (*pas ho laos*). We will probably never be able to establish why this editorial change was made in the Gospel of Matthew.[27] What we do know, however, is that the dreadful *Wirkungsgeschichte* imposes a great deal of responsibility on those who interpret this verse. The recommendation in the Ten Points of Seelisberg, quoted above, is still perceptive and sagacious for those who seek an intrabiblical hermeneutics when addressing this issue.[28] And the fourth paragraph in the Roman Catholic document *Nostra Aetate* explicitly comments on this topic:

> True, the Jewish authorities and those who followed their lead pressed for the death of Christ; still, what happened in His passion cannot be charged against all the Jews, without distinction, then alive, nor against the Jews of today.

19
RENDERING THE RENDING OF THE VEIL
Matt 27:51, Mark 15:38, and Luke 23:45

The torn veil of the Jerusalem temple at the time of Jesus's death took on crucial meaning as Christians began to formulate their theological responses to that death.[1] According to Daniel M. Gurtner, the Greek word *katapetasma* was used exclusively to refer to this curtain in Christian texts for several centuries.[2]

Firstly, we should note that there is an impressive scholarly concord regarding one aspect of this event. The vast majority of New Testament scholars argue that the verb form *was torn* (*eschisthê*) should be read as a "divine passive" (Latin: *passivum divinum*), a form used to indicate that God is the agent: what is happening is an act of God.[3] The same verb (*schizein*) is used to describe what happens when Jesus is baptized by John in the Jordan River. At that moment the heavens "were torn apart" (*schizomenous*), and the Spirit descended like a dove on Jesus (Mark 1:10).

The *historical* event of the torn veil has demanded a *theological* interpretation.[4] The explanations range from Donald A. Hagner, who argues that Matthew did not need to explain the event because everyone understood what the rending of the veil meant, to Raymond E. Brown, who maintains that neither Matthew nor his readers understood it.[5] In other words, the theological implications are either totally obvious or absolutely obscure. The most common interpretation is that the torn veil is a sign that the death of Jesus has opened the way to God. However, this is not the only interpretation.[6]

The event is mentioned in three of the four New Testament Gospels—it does not occur in John—and there are important differences among the three synoptic accounts. In the Lukan account, the rending of the veil takes place *before* the death of Jesus. In the Markan narrative, it occurs immediately *after* his death, and in the Matthean version it is followed by miracles: an earthquake and the resurrection of the dead in Jerusalem. If the most common interpretation were correct—that the rending of the veil meant that it was not until Jesus's death that the way to God was opened—it would not have the support of the Lukan version, in which the veil is rent *before* the death of Jesus. Three interpretations of the rending of the veil will be presented and discussed in this chapter. They relate to three sentiments: *wrath, joyfulness*, and *sorrow*.

(a) *A sign of God's wrath?* The first interpretation sees the torn temple curtain resulting from and expressing divine wrath in response to the betrayal and execution of Jesus of Nazareth. The Gospels mention various religious and political groups cooperating to put Jesus out of the way, specifically representatives of the temple leadership and the occupying Roman power. Yet this has not been taken into consideration in interpretations of this text historically. Rather, the Jewish people *as a whole* has been named, not as the people that Jesus knew as his own, but as his executioners. This shift of emphasis—from various religious and political groups to the entire Jewish people—can be detected in the canonical Gospels, but it is even more evident in second-century texts. For three reasons, Melito's Easter homily *Peri Pascha* (On Easter) is often mentioned in this context. Firstly, it was written by an influential leader of the church. Melito (d. 180) was the bishop of Sardis, a city known in the Turkey of today as Sart Mustafa.[7] Secondly, it is a text that clearly accuses Jews as a people of the death of Jesus. Thirdly, the text is characterized by a *high Christology*, emphasizing that Jesus is more than human, that God was in Christ. Consequently, according to Melito, not just anyone was executed on the cross: God was murdered there.[8]

> But you cast your vote against your Lord.
> For him whom the gentiles worshipped.
> And uncircumcised men admired
> And foreigners glorified,
> Over whom even
> Pilate washed his hands,
> You killed him at the great feast.
> ...
> You killed your Lord in the middle of Jerusalem.
> ...
> Listen, all you families of the nations, and see!

Rendering the Rending of the Veil

An unprecedented [Greek *kainos*; i.e., "new," meaning
  "unparalleled"] murder has occurred in the middle of Jerusalem.
In the city of the law.
In the city of the Hebrews.
In the city of the prophets,
In the city accounted just.
And who has been murdered? Who is the murderer?
…
He who hung the earth is hanging;
He who fixed the heavens has been fixed;
He who fastened the universe has been fastened to a tree;
The Sovereign has been insulted;
The God has been murdered;
The King of Israel has been put to death
by an Israelite right hand.
O unprecedented [*kainou*] murder! Unprecedented [*kainês*] crime![9]

Only Jews are singled out for this unprecedented crime in Melito's text, as observed by Jeremy Cohen and others. Non-Jews—described as "gentiles," "uncircumcised," and "strangers"—worship and honor him, but the Jewish people killed him during the grandest of all Jewish feasts. Accused by this heinous crime is only one group: the Jews.

> Though the gospel stories of the Crucifixion allot important roles to Pilate and his Roman soldiers, Melito gives them no mention. He condemns Israel and Israel alone.[10]

Melito's Easter homily is an aggressive and damning interpretation of the death of Jesus. God's wrath comes upon the Jews for what they did. They did not see God in Christ and therefore lost the right to call themselves Israel: "But you did not turn out to be 'Israel'; you did not 'see God.'"[11] The background to this verdict is probably the popular—but etymologically impossible—view that the Hebrew word *Yisrael* should be interpreted as *ish raah El* (the one who saw God).

Unfortunately, Melito's Easter homily is not an exception. Rather, the legal proceedings against Jesus are often presented in a way that it is transmuted into a court case in which Jews stand accused: yesterday's Jews, today's Jews, all Jews of all times are accused of the death of Jesus.

Bishop Melito's Easter homily raises several questions: What were his sources? What were the relations between Jews and Christians in Sardis when he wrote his sermon? Was Melito addressing living Jews or presenting rhetorical characters? Did he have flesh-and-blood people in mind—or not?

Why does Melito direct his accusations only against the *Jewish people* when it is so obvious in the New Testament Gospels that *Roman soldiers* carried out the execution? Othmar Perler has argued that the source of Melito's homily is not primarily the canonical Gospels but the apocryphal Gospel of Peter, which was rediscovered in 1886–87 in a tomb in Akhmim, Egypt.[12] If Perler is correct, then this apocryphal gospel has played a tremendously important role in the Christian tradition, due to the fact that Melito's homily *Peri Pascha*, in turn, has inspired the *Improperia* (Latin for "Reproaches") in the Good Friday liturgy, blaming the Jewish people for the death of Jesus.[13]

What was found in the tomb in Akhmim in the 1880s was only a fragment of the original Gospel of Peter. The fragment commences in the middle of the trial against Jesus and concludes with the disciples going back home after the death of Jesus. What has been preserved, though, is enough for us to see the differences between this apocryphal gospel and the New Testament Gospels. One of these differences is found in the very first sentence: "But of the Jews, none washed their hands, neither Herod nor any one of his judges."[14] Then the author goes on to tell the story of how "the Jews" (*hoi Ioudaioi*) tortured Jesus, put a purple gown on him, and crucified him between two criminals. In other words, the Roman soldiers have totally vanished from the scene. In the Gospel of Peter, those who carry out the execution are *the Jews*![15]

In other words, we can regard the homily of Melito of Sardis, which probably is based on the Gospel of Peter, as an initial draft of the *Improperia* tradition, which was developed over time. This would mean that the tradition of reproaching Jews in the Good Friday service is not based on the canonical Gospels but on an apocryphal gospel that was never included in the canonical New Testament.

In the third century there was a heated discussion among Christians whether to celebrate Easter on the *date* in the Jewish calendar that Jesus died (the fourteenth in the month of *Nisan*), or on the *day* that he died (a Friday). The Quartodecimans (as in the number fourteen) argued that it was crucial for the commemoration to take place on the exact day of the month, not on the specific day of the week.[16] Since Melito was a Quartodeciman, his Good Friday commemoration did not necessarily take place on a Friday, but it always concurred with the Jewish Passover meal, and it is likely that this simultaneity affected his interpretation of texts and events. On the same day that Jews in Sardis were celebrating the departure from Egypt, one of the most important feasts in their calendar, Melito and his fellow Christians were commemorating and mourning the death of Jesus. This simultaneity may be discerned in the following passage from Melito's Easter homily.

> And you were making merry, while he was starving:
> You had wine to drink and bread to eat, he had vinegar and gall;
> Your face was bright, his was downcast;
> You were triumphant, he was afflicted;
> You were making music, he was being judged;
> You were giving up the beat, he was being nailed up;
> You were dancing; he was being buried;
> You were reclining on a soft couch, he in grave and coffin.[17]

This is not primarily referring to Jews being accused of crucifying Jesus but rather to the very specific circumstance that the Christian Good Friday fell on the very same day that the Jews in Melito's Sardis were celebrating Passover. A detail in the last stanza ("You were reclining on a soft couch, he in grave and coffin") is in all probability a reference to the practice of eating the Passover meal while sitting or leaning comfortably, as a remembrance and a celebration of no longer being slaves in Egypt. Jews today are reminded of this at Passover when singing the song *mah nishtanah ha-lailah ha-zeh mi-kol ha-leilot?* (Why is this night different from all other nights?). One of the questions posed by the youngest son is, "Why on this night are we all reclining?"

In short, this sociohistorical reading argues that the homily was influenced by the actual situation in Sardis during the time of Bishop Melito in the second century. The principal rationale for the aggression in Melito's Easter homily is the fact that Jews were celebrating Passover *at the very same time* in the very same city, perhaps in directly adjacent homes. This might have called into question his triumphalist interpretation of Christianity, which replaced the old order with the new. Cohen explains:

> For when the Jews of Sardis relived the Exodus at their Passover seder on the very night that the Quartodeciman Melito conducted the Easter vigil in his church, they implicitly declared that Christianity's New Testament had not replaced the Old.[18]

Cohen argues that the historical simultaneity of the Jewish *Pesach* and Melito's *Pascha* was a theological challenge. "For Melito, that amounted to nothing less than killing Christ on the cross, again and again and again."[19]

However, this raises another question: Are the Jews described in the Gospel of Peter, and the Israelites described in *Peri Pascha*, real people of flesh and blood, or are they primarily rhetorical figures? Too often, real Jews have been the victims when Christians have read sacred texts during Holy Week and responded with vengeful violence, but the question posed now is a different one: does Melito's account reflect the sociohistorical context in Sardis and other places? A number of scholars (including Lynn Cohick, Paula Fredriksen, Judith Lieu, Adele Reinhartz, and Miriam S. Taylor) question whether early anti-Jewish texts primarily reflect actual conflicts between Jews and Christians.[20] Cohick writes that Melito's *Peri Pascha*

> centers on defining Christianity over against a hypothetical "Israel" that the unknown author has created largely for rhetorical purposes.... This homily's anti-Jewish rhetoric is not the place to find evidence for Jews or Judaism of its time.[21]

This highlights a problem with sociohistorical interpretation that tends to seek a *historical* explanation for the *theological* outburst against Jews in Christian texts.[22] In parallel fashion, many New Testament scholars have argued that the reason for the Johannine "Jews" being described so negatively is that the Jews whom the evangelist met were behaving badly toward the Johannine Christians (see introduction, second challenge, and chapter 22). Cohick argues that the maxim of these scholars appears to be "where there's smoke, there's fire."[23] To paraphrase a well-known New Testament passage, in this situation biblical scholars tell us that the one who was *not* free from sin threw the first stone (cf. John 8:7). Some people *act* provocatively, while others simply *react* legitimately when in distress.

It has been suggested that the reason for the accusatory tone in Melito's Easter homily is Jews behaving badly toward Christ followers in Sardis. Irrespective of how many Jews and Christ followers there actually were in Sardis at that time, and the relations between these two groups, there is a tendency when interpreting these texts to describe the accusations in a way that seeks not only to *explain* but also implicitly to *justify* them. Some people tend to excuse the texts of their faith communities by blaming the behavior of another group. To repeat, other people *act*, while our people simply *react*.

For numerous readers of the Bible, *imitatio Dei* is a virtue. If the temple veil was rent as an expression of divine wrath over "the Jews" killing Jesus, why should Christians be more forbearing than God, according to this logic?[24] Thus, the main problem with this first interpretation is that it easily leads to antagonism and perhaps even aggression against the Jewish people. Of this interpretation we can say that "the tree is known by its fruit" (Matt 12:33). It is time to look at the second interpretation.

(b) A reason for joyfulness: Karl Barth was one of the most influential Christian theologians of the twentieth century. In his *Church Dogmatics*, he argues that there is a vast difference between, on the one hand, God's *revelation* and, on the other hand, *religion*—that is, between Christianity (which, according to his atypical nomenclature, is not, strictly speaking, a religion) and all other religious phenomena. A consequence of this strict dichotomy is that religiosity is something negative: a religious belief or behavior is not, as we might assume, an expression of a person's *belief*, but rather of his or her *unbelief*. The revelation of God is the abolition of religion.[25]

We need to revisit this dichotomy in our discussion of the torn veil because the second temple is often described in a Barthian way in theological literature. The torn veil is described as the end of the allegedly incorrect era of religiosity. It reveals something completely different, something that has nothing at all to do with the temple. According to this view, the second temple—the shrine that Jesus visited, according to the evangelists, and in which his disciples "always praised God"—became the symbol of humanity's vain efforts to reach out to God.[26] This line of thought seeks to suggest that the temple had become irredeemably defective. This approach shows a dogmatically motivated inability to appreciate the second temple as well as second-temple Judaism.

The death of Jesus is seen as the end of the era of erroneous religiosity, and the torn veil is a sign of this. Daniel M. Gurtner summarizes the history of this development with these words: "One of the few points of agreement among scholars who address the rending of the veil is that whatever else it means, it surely refers to the cessation of the veil's function."[27] The traditional view he describes is that "there is a new *accessibility* to God created through the removal of the separating function of the inner veil."[28] The theological message is that now there is access to God that was hindered before the veil was torn. Examples of this in the history of interpretation are legion. For example, in his *Lectures on the Gospel of Matthew*, published in 1868, William Kelly writes that before the veil was torn, it had been "the symbol that man could not draw near to God."[29] This second interpretation implies, accordingly, that the temple was a theological obstacle that hindered true worship.

There is sometimes an implicit ecclesiastical critique in this discourse of the torn veil. Numerous Christians believe that there is too much bureaucracy in their churches, that the liturgy is too complicated or old-fashioned, or that church leaders hinder people from encountering God. These Christians, therefore, are convinced that something new is needed, and this Christian self-criticism is not seldom expressed as a critique of second-temple Judaism.[30]

There are several objections to this widespread line of thought. First and foremost, Jewish temple service was one of the few phenomena in Judaism that the surrounding cultures did *not* see as strange. Non-Jewish contemporaries saw Judaism as peculiar in many ways—*but that had nothing to do with the Temple, nor with the offerings*.[31] It was more difficult to understand circumcision, food laws, and *shabbat*, as pointed out by Fredriksen:

> The thing most foreign to modern Western religiousness about ancient Judaism—the sacrifices and their attendant purity regulations—struck ancient observers as one of the few normal things Jews did.[32]

Anachronistic interpretations are widespread, not least on the internet, which hosts numerous simplistic interpretations of the torn veil. One example is the following text.

> The torn veil is the final verdict,
> Confirmed by the empty tomb three days later,
> The old ways are DEAD
> NO LONGER ARE WE SEPARATED FROM GOD
> Hallelujah!
> Rejoice!
> With the Torn Veil and the Empty Tomb GOD said it loud and clear:
> "No mortal, No Institution, No rules or laws, No human frailty Will come between ME and My Children"
> "You are free to seek Me EVERYWHERE!"
> Amen![33]

The temple of Jerusalem is presented here as an institution that was blocking the path between human beings and God. A similar theological reasoning is expressed in the following text:

> The curtain separated a holy God from sinful man.
> *Man created the veil by turning against God.*

> But he could not tear it down.
> It was too high
> and too thick.
> It was said that even the strongest horses tied to each side…
> could not pull the veil apart.
> Only *God* could tear the veil.
> …
> The barrier between *God* & humanity was removed.
> The veil was torn.[34]

The veil is presented not only as a hindrance but also as the very symbol of a people willfully turning away from God. However, the author clearly clashes with the Scriptures, according to which God *ordered* the people to build a tabernacle and *gave exact instructions* on how to build it. The specific instructions on how to build the tabernacle can be found in Exodus 26:31 and 33:

> You shall make a curtain of blue, purple, and crimson yarns, and of fine twisted linen; it shall be made with cherubim skillfully worked into it.…And the curtain shall separate for you the holy place from the most holy.

In other words, the supersessionist critique of the temple is so important in this line of thought that it induces its advocates to neglect what is explicit in Scripture: that building the tabernacle was *designed by God and commanded by God*. In the biblical narrative, the tabernacle and the temple are places for divine encounter, not symbols of alienation. They are not obstacles that *distance* people from God; they make it possible for humans to *draw near* to God, as in the famous opening words in Psalm 84:1f. and 4:

> How lovely is your dwelling place, O LORD of hosts! My soul longs, indeed it faints for the courts of the LORD; my heart and my flesh sing for joy to the living God.…Happy are those who live in your house, ever singing your praise.

Nevertheless, there is a widespread ambiguity in descriptions of the function of the temple and the implications of the death of Jesus. One example of this is Gurtner's commentary on the Matthean understanding of the temple. "This, however, is not a *rejection* of the temple.…Instead, it is an indication that the temple is *superfluous*: What it was intended to accomplish is *surpassed* by Jesus."[35] If something is superfluous and surpassed, is it, then, not thereby also rejected? Furthermore, Gurtner describes the torn veil (Latin: *velum scissum*) in the following manner:

> I can note here that the cessation of functions depicted by the *velum scissum* indicates, in some way, the cessation of the cultic necessity of distinctions between most holy and less holy, which therefore removes the need for such distinctions to be executed by a prohibition of physical and visual accessibility to God, and removes the cherubim that graphically depicts [*sic*] this distinction.[36]

In the same book, Gurtner describes Matthean Christology. "For Matthew, Jesus is the true Israel and the people of God are defined by their relationship to Jesus."[37] This would imply that a people no longer consisted of individuals, together forming what Benedict Anderson calls "an imagined community"; instead, they are embodied in an individual.[38]

Jesus is described in a similar way by N. T. Wright as "a new David, who will rescue his people from their exile, that is, 'waive his people from their sins.'"[39] This immediately raises the question of why the word "exile" no longer means "deportation" but is spiritualized instead. The obvious answer is that, otherwise, the theological scheme simply does not work. The sad irony is that Christianity concurred not with the end of an exile of the Jewish people but with its beginning. As we all know, it was after the two revolts against the Romans (66–73 CE and 132–135 CE) that a new era of exile began for the Jewish people.

Gurtner's analysis is a thorough and well-written study of the Matthean version of the rending of the veil; however, his conclusion that the death of Jesus implies the end of the era of the temple is problematic, even if not unusual. He writes that this is an understanding he shares with a consensus of New Testament scholars: "one of the few points of agreement among scholars who address the rending of the veil is that whatever else it means, it surely refers to the *cessation* of the veil's function."[40]

It must nevertheless be asked if this is the *only* possible conclusion. The temple fulfilled an important function for Jews in antiquity, and temple metaphors are still exceedingly important for Jews today. Can adherents to this interpretation genuinely seek to understand and appreciate the Jewish tradition? Or are the two alternatives mutually exclusive? Is it necessary to think of it as a crossroads whereby choosing one road eliminates the other?

The troubling question that remains is whether Christians are supposed to feel unmitigated *joyfulness* at the foot of the cross. If yes, what are the consequences for Christian views of torture and human suffering today? Are not the emotions we experience when encountering and pondering pain and agony in our world completely different from joy? This leads us to the third interpretation.

(c) An expression of divine sorrow? In Judaism there is an ancient tradition of tearing one's clothing at the loss of someone dear. The Hebrew term for this is *qeri'ah*. Nowadays this is done before or just after the funeral, or at the grave site, but in previous times it was at the time of death or upon hearing of the death that mourners tore their clothes.[41] This is described, for example, in 2 Samuel 13:30f.

> While they were on the way, the report came to David that Absalom had killed all the king's sons, and not one of them was left. The king rose, tore his garments (*wa-yiqra' et begadaw*), and lay on the ground; and all his servants who were standing by tore their garments (*qeru'ei vegadim*).

For several reasons, 2 Kings 2:12 is of special interest to us when pondering the New Testament passion narratives. Firstly, it is about Elijah (who is mentioned in the passion narratives in the New Testament). Secondly, the mourner tears his clothes. Thirdly, he tears them into two pieces. And, fourthly, a "father" is mentioned.

> Elisha kept watching [as Elijah ascended in a whirlwind into heaven] and crying out, "Father, father! The chariots of Israel and its horsemen!" But when he could no longer see him, he grasped his own clothes and tore them in two pieces.[42]

God, too, shows divine grief by tearing garments. In the words of Roger David Aus, "It was natural for the rabbis to think that God in mourning rent His royal purple garment in heaven when His dwelling on earth, the Temple, was destroyed by the Babylonians."[43] Hence, the Jewish tradition of tearing one's clothes must be considered when interpreting the torn veil in the New Testament.

The point has been made several times in this chapter that the temple was a manifestation of divine presence. It was a *meeting place* between God and humans, not a *hiding place* for God. The temple—including its curtain—was not something that separated humans from God. On the contrary, the temple and its curtain were symbols of the *presence* of God, not of divine *absence*.[44]

Seeing the temple as the manifestation of divine presence, it is not difficult to imagine that the tearing of the veil may have been understood as an expression of sorrow: God tore the divine robe when Jesus died.[45] Therefore, David Daube makes a convincing point:

> When we consider the stress laid in the New Testament on the complete splitting of the curtain into two—or, according to some readings, two parts—from top to bottom, it is safe to find here an allusion to the rite practiced as a sign of deepest sorrow.[46]

An interesting connection is noted by Abraham Joshua Heschel in *Heavenly Torah*. He cites a medieval text that highlights the similarities between the two words *qeri'ah* (tearing, rupturing) and *raqia'* (stronghold, firmament) and is used in creation narrative (Gen 1:6): "And God said, 'Let there be a dome in the midst of the waters, and let it separate the waters from the waters.'"[47] This connection can be seen in Matthew. In the hour of heavenly grief, as God rends the divine garment in mourning (*qeri'ah*), the "dome" (*raqia'*) trembles. The latter is reflected in the reference to an earthquake (27:51). In the presence of death, everything shakes: life falls apart and is torn to pieces.

According to this third interpretation, the rending of the veil may be understood as an expression of divine grief over what is happening. This has been suggested by several interpreters, including Claude G. Montefiore, David Daube, Roger David Aus, Rosann M. Catalano, and Paula Fredriksen.[48]

Yet another person who supports this thesis is, perhaps surprisingly, Melito of Sardis. In his *Peri Pascha* there is a passage that is relevant to this discussion. Melito's tone is reproachful of the Jewish people, yet it is nonetheless interesting to note the description of the one who grieves in the place of humans.

> For when the people did not tremble, the earth quaked;
> When the people were not terrified, the heavens were terrified;
> *When the people did not tear their clothes, the angel tore his.*[49]
> When the people did not lament, the Lord thundered out of heaven
>   and the Highest gave voice.[50]

In this antithetical presentation, one of God's angels fulfills what the people should have done. Melito implies that the veil is rent because God's angel rends his clothes in mourning when Jesus dies. Melito's text remains reproachful, yet we find these three small words in Greek, *perieschisato ho angelos* (the angel tore [his garment]), proving that this third interpretation can be traced all the way back to the second century.

Paul writes in 2 Corinthians 5:19 that God has entrusted him with *ton logon tês katallagês* (the message of reconciliation). This is often regarded as a reference to a Christian proclamation *about* reconciliation. But could we also see in this concise expression an exhortation to explain the biblical texts and message in a way that deepens understanding and allows them to *promote* reconciliation? If so, it would be apt when interpreting what happened at the time of the death of Jesus. It would prevent isolating the contents of the message from the reactions that are provoked among readers and listeners. Under the heading of being entrusted with the words of reconciliation, we will now study the consequences of the three key words: *wrath, joyfulness*, and *grief*.

In his book *Holy Week Preaching*, Krister Stendahl writes that the emphasis should be on the *consequences* of the events. "The mood is finality, not causality, as is the case so often in the Scriptures and in the teaching of Jesus."[51] Questions that emphasize *causality* focus on what led to the death of Jesus—what did they do then and there?—but those that emphasize *finality* investigate the consequences of his death—what does this mean for those who want to live as his disciples? In other words, he suggests that readers not ask "why?" but "what for?" Not "whence" but "whither?" In this chapter, three words have been in focus: *wrath, joyfulness*, and *grief*. Is it possible to describe the three interpretations in terms of "whither?" What are the consequences? Where do they take us? "When Christians come to the foot of the cross of Jesus," says Catalano, "they need a piety that honors God and all those whom God loves."[52]

The first interpretation, which centers on divine wrath, triggers a loaded question: Why is God so angry that the veil is torn, all the way from the top to the bottom? What feelings arise within the reader? We all know that Holy Week has been anything but holy for Jews. Indeed, for two thousand years it has been a *Via Dolorosa* (Latin for "Way of Suffering"). The main cause of this suffering is that Christians have been convinced that Jews as a people are collectively responsible for the death of Jesus. Writers who argue that the torn veil demonstrates the wrath of God at what happened during Holy Week are likely to evoke a similar anger in their readers. The history of the outcome of this first interpretation reveals how problematic and, indeed, dangerous it is.

The second interpretation, focusing on human joyfulness, presents the temple as an obstacle to people's relation with God. It portrays the temple that stood at the time of Jesus as the quintessential symbol of people's disbelief and lack of faith. This is a highly anachronistic interpretation. In antiquity, and especially in biblical times, temples were places for holy encounters. Temples were believed to be like the horizon: places where heaven and earth meet. This interpretation is also problematic in that it tends not to take suffering and grief seriously. Is there a risk that a theology that overemphasizes revelation might make us indifferent to suffering and death? Is there a risk that it leads to an insensitive elation, a merciless and triumphalist superiority?

The third interpretation suggests that the torn veil could be understood as an expression of divine grief over the death of Jesus. Readers would react very differently to this interpretation compared to the one of divine wrath. If divine grief is at the center, readers will ask themselves completely different questions: Why does God grieve so much? What occasions divine sorrow at this moment in the narrative? In *Mishnah Sanhedrin* 4.5 it is written that, "when a single human being dies, it is as though a whole world dies."[53] The reader who believes that *imitatio Dei* is a spiritual virtue thereby gains another way of thinking—that of mourning the death of one single human being as if an entire world has died, letting this grief be transformed into caring for other people, and remembering that every human being is a microcosm, a small world.[54]

In one of Abraham Joshua Heschel's poems we find a similar connection between God, expressing divine *sorrow* by a rending of clothes, and the exhortation to *care* for other people. These words may serve as a reminder that *theology* should never be isolated from *ethics*—and of the importance of feeling one's fellow human being's suffering as one's own:

> Like sparked logs lusting, thirsting for flames
> my eyes cry to You, God.
> Who rends His clothes in mourning for the world—
> Let us see how Your face is mirrored
> in the pupils of our eyes.
>
> And I have sworn:
> to let the pupils of my eyes to be mirror to each sunset,
> my heart never sealed
> my eyes never locked![55]

20
IS JOHN'S PRO-LOGUE ANTI-LOGOS?
John 1:1–18

In his classic introduction to the Fourth Gospel, *John, the Maverick Gospel*, Robert Kysar calls the Prologue "the first specimen of early Christian incarnational thought," and he continues: "Here the divine nature of the preexistent Logos is most clearly affirmed, and here the humanization or enfleshment of that Logos is flatly declared....Here is the heart of the Christian message articulated."[1] Now if Kysar is correct, and many a reader of the New Testament is certainly inclined to agree with him, then to study the Prologue's history of interpretation tells us a good deal about how this "heart of the Christian message" has been perceived and presented by New Testament scholars. The impact of the Prologue has been immense; this presentation will focus on questions of how its core message has been depicted in contrast to or continuity with the Jewish tradition.[2] Five interpretations will be presented in this chapter.

(a) Christian grace is the opposite of the Jewish Law: The influential maelstrom that posits Law *versus* Grace surfaces also in the interpretations of the Johannine Prologue. A notorious example is how *The Living Bible Paraphrased* renders the Prologue's message when rewording for today's readers the seventeenth verse: "For Moses gave us only the Law with its rigid demands and merciless justice, while Jesus Christ brought us loving forgiveness as well." We see in this paraphrase how the Jewish tradition—especially its long-established understanding of the Torah as the center of life and liturgy—is presented as a failure. Similar sweeping statements can be found in commentaries as well, for example, John Marsh's definition of *grace*: "Its characteristic use is to describe the love of God for men, stooping to initiate their redemption, in contrast to the legalism of the Jewish understanding of salvation."[3] He continues:

Though the light that was the Word had shone in the life of Israel, there is a great difference between that life and the life of the Church....The law was God's gift to Israel, and as such, to use Paul's words, holy, and just and good; but the gift that God had intended for life, had turned to man's undoing and death. That is the greatest mystery of iniquity, that it could turn a life-giving gift of God into an instrument of death! In contrast to the law, grace and truth have come *through* Jesus Christ.[4]

With an antithetical understanding of law and grace, John 1:16 becomes problematic. If the Jewish understanding of the Law as a vehicle for divine revelation is fundamentally flawed, why does the sixteenth verse state that there is "grace upon grace" (*charin anti charitos*), implying that grace is connected also to Moses and the Torah, which the strictly antithetical reading so vehemently disputes? Matthew Black has advocated a conjecture for this verse in the Prologue.[5] He proposes an Aramaic play on words behind the Greek text, which was misunderstood and, consequently, lost in translation: the first *chesed* goes back to the Aramaic word *chisda* (grace), describing what Jesus Christ has accomplished, and the second one to the word *chisuda* (condemnation, disgrace), referring to Moses and the Torah. Hence, according to Black, the original meaning of John 1:16 was distinctly antinomian:

> Because of his fullness we have all received, even grace instead of disgrace, mercy for condemnation. It is this thought which is continued in the following verse: "For the Law was given by Moses"—by which came condemnation—"but grace and truth came by Jesus Christ."[6]

Although widespread among Christians, particularly among Protestants, an antithetical reading this strict is not uncontested, as seen in, for example, Rudolf Schnackenburg's commentary:

> The greater fullness of grace under the new covenant, in contrast to the old, is not envisaged....John does not oppose the "law" as way of salvation....Thus John sees no absolute contradiction between Moses who gave the law (at God's command), and Jesus Christ who brought grace and truth....The verse [1:17] rather aims at showing the previous legal system has been surpassed by the reality of the grace of Jesus Christ....Behind both facts is the will of God.[7]

Is John's Pro-logue Anti-Logos?

The main difficulty for a strictly antithetical reading of the Prologue is that the Gospel of John on the whole does not support a denigration, let alone a defamation, of the Torah. In 10:34 the Johannine Jesus states that "the scripture cannot be annulled" (*ou dynatai lythênai hê graphê*).[8] It is difficult to imagine that the heart of the Christian message would be the very opposite of that verse. Scholarship does well to seek alternative interpretations.

(b) Reading the Prologue through Gnostic and Hermetic lenses: It is quite remarkable that, throughout history, the Gospel of John has always seemed to appeal to "orthodox" and dissenting readers alike. On the one hand, the first-known commentary to the Gospel was written c. 170 CE by a Gnostic by the name Heracleon.[9] Indeed, Gnostics and Gnosticizing readers have often appreciated the Fourth Gospel's emphasis on the spiritual world vis-à-vis this world, which is doomed; esoteric teaching has been nurtured by statements such as "Righteous Father, the world does not know you, but I know you" (17:25). On the other hand, the Prologue's Word-becoming-flesh theology has always attracted Christians who have emphasized incarnation—vis-à-vis both Docetism in antiquity (which denied that Christ had a real body) and hyper-"liberal" theologians today (stating that the historical Jesus of *Nazareth* has little, if anything, to do with the theological Jesus of *Nicaea*).[10] These observations help us understand why interpreters of the Gospel of John have walked in distinctly different directions. Quite obviously, there is in this Gospel enough theological food for thought to satisfy the appetite for various groups of famished readers.

In his commentary, C. H. Dodd argued that the closest parallel to the Gospel of John was the Hermetic literature. These works, stemming from second- and third-century Egypt, focus on Hermes Trismegistus, a sage who was deified after his death as the god Thoth.[11] To Dodd, the Gospel of John was intended for a non-Christian audience: "devout and thoughtful persons…in the varied and cosmopolitan society of a great Hellenistic city such as Ephesus under the Roman Empire."[12] However, his suggestion has been criticized. One objection is that many of the theological terms of importance in the Hermetic literature are absent from the Gospel of John: *athanasia* (immortality), *dêmiourgos* (Demiurge), *gnôsis*, and *mystêrion*.[13] In fact, the key vocabulary in the Gospel of John is far more often found in the Septuagint than in the Hermetic literature. This should give us pause when seeking to establish a connection between the Gospel of John and the Hermetic literature.

However, one conclusion of importance for the present work is that Dodd did not think of the Gospel of John as an arena for Jewish-Christian combat. Indeed, he argued that "Rabbinic Judaism, Philo and the *Hermetica* remain our most direct sources for the background of thought."[14] One could perhaps think of an operational priority here: before exploring parallels between the Prologue and Hermetic literature, one would like to pose a prior question: How would the Prologue be understood in a first-century *Jewish* context? This takes us to the next interpretation.

(c) John's Prologue as Jewish midrash: Most commentators acknowledge that the Prologue's Logos theology is illuminated more clearly in the light of contemporary Hellenistic writers, first and foremost Philo of Alexandria, who described the Logos not only as a manifestation of God but even as a "second God" (*deuteros theos*).[15] In his article on the Prologue in the *Jewish Annotated New Testament*, Daniel Boyarin states that "the *Logos* did not conflict with Philo's idea of monotheism" and that "Philo oscillates between presenting a separate existence of the *Logos* and depicting it as totally incorporated within the godhead."[16]

Similarly, Jewish sources in Hebrew and Aramaic develop concepts such as *Chokhmah* (Hebrew for "Wisdom"), *Davar* (Hebrew for "Word"), and *Memra* (Aramaic for "Word"), not merely as paraphrases for the name of God but even as "an actual divine entity functioning as a mediator."[17] This, he states, is of relevance to the development of Trinitarian theology in Christian doctrine:

> The use of the *Logos* in John's Gospel…is thus thoroughly Jewish. It is even possible that the idea of the Trinity began to develop precisely in pre-Christian Jewish conceptions on the second and visible divine being who played a mediating role between the heavenly and earthly sphere.[18]

Boyarin argues that the beginning of the Prologue is best understood as a midrash, a Jewish homily on Gen 1:1–5.[19] He asserts:

> In light of this evidence, the Fourth Gospel's Logos theology is not a new creation in the history of Judaism; its innovation is only, if even this, in its incarnational Christology, namely the taking on of flesh by the Logos in v. 14.…Until v. 14, John's Prologue is a piece of perfectly unexceptional Jewish thought that has been seamlessly woven into the christological narrative of the Gospel.[20]

Is John's Pro-logue Anti-Logos?

This astonishing statement obviously prompts a corollary question: what about the continuation of the Prologue? This takes us to the next interpretation.

(d) "Full of grace and truth" and incarnational theology: Boyarin's article on Logos theology in the *Jewish Annotated New Testament* prompts us to explore the expression "grace and truth" (Greek: *charis kai alêtheia*; Hebrew: *chesed we-emet*) in the Prologue's seventeenth verse. Whereas the key word "truth" occurs frequently in the Gospel of John, the word "grace" does not appear outside the Prologue, where it occurs four times. Lester Jacob Kuyper correctly indicates where to look in order to explore these two words together:

> When, therefore, John declares that the incarnate Word is full of grace and truth he is telling his readers to look for the meaning of this expression in the Old Testament, where it is descriptive of God. Let one reference suffice here for an Old Testament quotation which embodies other descriptive words about God: "The LORD passed before him [Moses] and proclaimed, 'The LORD, the LORD, a God merciful and gracious, slow to anger, and abounding in steadfast love and faithfulness'" (Exod. 34:6). "Abounding in steadfast love and faithfulness" becomes "full of grace and truth" in John's Gospel.[21]

It seems quite clear that the expression "full of grace and truth" is best understood as a reference to texts in the Scriptures that describe who God is and what God does. The Jewish tradition of referring to particular passages in Scripture by only vague allusions is attested elsewhere in the Gospels, for example, the passage about "the bush" in the Synoptic Gospels (Mark 12:26 and Luke 20:37). The fact that the allusion is even more oblique in the Prologue presupposes that it refers to a passage that was well-known to a first-century Jewish audience. The description of Jesus of Nazareth as "full of grace and truth" is undoubtedly a high-christological statement, and the depiction of him as "tabernacling" among his people is certainly a reference to the tabernacle in the desert, a visible sign of the invisible God: the Divine "Presence" (Hebrew: *shekhinah*) "tented" (Greek: *eskênôsen*) among them.[22] The glory of God has pitched its tent (Greek: *skênê*) in the midst of the people. This connection between the Scriptures, especially the theophanies in the book of Exodus and the Prologue in the Gospel of John, is often recognized. But how is it interpreted?

Göran Larsson has explored the expression "grace upon grace" in the sixteenth verse in the Prologue.[23] Building on an article by Gillis Gerleman, Larsson argues that it is quite likely the word *chesed* originally referred to "abundance" in a physical sense before it was interpreted and applied as the abstract theological term "grace."[24] In other words, divine grace could be likened to an abundant treasure in which one portion of the treasure does not replace or degrade another part of it. Furthermore, Larsson argues that a rabbinic principle of interpretation is of relevance here: there is no insignificant repetition or redundancy in the Torah (Hebrew: *ein bah ot yeter we-cheser* or *ein kephel ba-Miqra*). The notion that nothing is written in vain has been dubbed as the "the doctrine of omnisignificance" by James L. Kugel.[25] Hence, in a Jewish context, the two "graces" in John 1:16 could refer to two different aspects of divine grace. If this hermeneutical rule is applied here, how would the double *chesed* be interpreted? What Larsson suggests is that according to rabbinic hermeneutics the two *chasidim* (graces) in Exodus 34:6f. imply, firstly, one *realized* grace in connection with the renewal of the covenant in the Exodus narrative, and, secondly, one *promised* grace that has yet to be fulfilled in messianic times in the future. Hence, read in this way, the Prologue would remind a Jewish audience in late antiquity of the "tabernacling" of God's glory in the wilderness, and it would also perceive that this manifestation is repeated—now in the appearance of a human being. God is the agent in both cases. There was still more in God's rich treasure of grace than what had already been given through Moses and the Torah.

Larsson argues that the *nun rabbati* in Hebrew manuscripts to Exodus 34:7 strengthens his suggestion that Jewish Christians in the Johannine community could have interpreted the text as messianic. In Hebrew manuscripts the first letter of the word *notzer* (keeping) is majuscular—that is, somewhat larger than it ordinarily would have been (hence, *nun rabbati*, "[the letter] *nun* enlarged"). For a Jewish audience, *notzer chesed la-alaphim* (grace for thousands) in Exodus 34:7 could refer to something more than expected or ordinary—that is, to divine grace for future generations. Larsson also reflects on the possible connection between *notzer* and the name of the town Nazareth. Up until today, Christians are called *notzrim* in Hebrew, and he believes that Jewish Christians in antiquity may have interpreted the *nun rabbati* as an indication of the importance of the fact that their Master was called Jesus of *Nazareth*.[26]

Is the Prologue necessarily a revelation that *annuls* previous revelations? Does it *surpass* them? Or does it *intensify* them in such a way that, in fact, it reinforces and confirms them? There is much to suggest that the scriptural expression "full of grace and truth" is a veritable treasure chest for those who search for hidden resources for improved Jewish-Christian relations.

*(e) **The Roman Empire and Johannine Christology:*** The default setting in much of Christological thinking has been to articulate it in contradistinction to Jewish monotheism: both Jews and Christians have keenly insisted that high Christology is incompatible with Jewish belief—and both groups seem to have been quite content with drawing the line of demarcation between the two traditions precisely there.

However, various postcolonial readings of the New Testament provide us with fresh approaches also to Jewish-Christian relations. Indeed, if the opposite of Christian Christology is Jewish monotheism, then the two traditions are conceived as each other's opposites. If Jesus's teaching is the opposite of then-contemporary Jewish Torah piety, then these two ways of life are fundamentally incompatible. This book presents numerous such antithetical readings of various texts in the New Testament. But if the kingdom of God, as proclaimed in the New Testament, is the opposite of the Roman Empire (and not of Judaism), something happens with the conventional comparisons of Judaism and Christianity. As Tom Thatcher writes in his book *Greater than Caesar*: "Thus, the church becomes more than just another empire; the church is Rome in reverse."[27] According to Thatcher, there are Christological implications here as well: "John's Christology *is* his response to empire....John's thinking about Caesar was conflated with his portrait of Jesus, and vice versa, at the deepest level."[28]

Emperor Domitian, who ruled between 81 and 96 CE—to wit, when the Gospel of John most likely was written down—demanded that he be addressed *Dominus et Deus* (Lord and God). How can that not be relevant when reading the Gospel of John, in which Thomas exclaims "My Lord and my God" when meeting with the resurrected Christ (20:28)?[29]

While high Christology could have been explained as a phenomenological parallel to Jewish Torah piety, it has in practice most often been drafted solely in opposition to Jewish monotheism. The implication of this juxtaposition is not only that the historical context of Jesus is presented as his theological contrast, but also that the many ways in which high Christology must have constituted a serious challenge to the emperor cult in the Roman Empire have been toned down, ignored, and distorted.

In short, if the message of the Christ-believing movement is portrayed as the opposite of Jewish Torah piety, then Christianity will eventually come out as pro-Roman. But if this message is rendered within contemporary Judaism, as one of the "Judaisms" that sought to live a Jewish life under Roman occupation, then it will be obvious that Christian faith does not aspire to build an earthly empire, as the Johannine Jesus declares when standing before Pontius Pilate, the representative of the Roman Empire in Jerusalem: "My kingdom is not from this world" (18:36).

By way of conclusion, the Prologue's astounding idea to liken Jesus of Nazareth to the divine Logos is probably the most powerful, prominent, and persistent contribution of the Gospel of John to Christian theology. If language is the breath of God, then the Logos articulates God's mind and will—and, according to Christian theology, incarnates God's mind and will.

This divine Logos has often been presented as the opposite of or the substitute for the message of the Jewish Scriptures. Hopefully, this chapter has shown that there are other ways of understanding it, especially if we wish to take seriously how the texts may have resonated for a first-century Jewish audience. And it is quite plausible that a thoughtful Logos Christology may provide contemporary Christians with a language that helps them appreciate the Jewish reverence for the Torah when seeking to articulate the heart of the Christian message. In the words of Didier Pollefeyt:

> Jews have received from God the unique possibility to encounter the Logos through the Torah. This possibility is not given (in the same way) to the Christians. Christians have received the unique possibility to encounter the Logos through Christ, incarnating the Logos in a unique and irrevocable way. This experience is difficult to understand and experience (in the same way) from the Jewish perspective. It is God Himself who will bring together the final eschatological interpretations of Jews and Christians. From this hope, it is impossible that what has started as a deep and intimate bond *in* God will not be reconciled *by* God when all interpretations and all things come together. In the meantime, what remains for Christians is to recognise and express the lasting, indestructible dignity of Judaism.[30]

21

WHAT DID JESUS WRITE IN THE SAND?

John 7:53—8:11

Not surprisingly, this text raises many questions among readers. The Evangelist depicts a hostile situation: a defenseless woman is surrounded by men, who direct a serious accusation against her. There are also some details in the text that have puzzled many readers, especially two things.

Firstly, where is the man with whom she was together when caught in the act? Those who accuse her argue that the Law prescribes that "such women" (feminine in Greek: *tas toiautas*) should be punished, but this is not what is stated in the Scriptures. It says that both the woman *and the man* in such a situation be punished (cf. Lev 20:10 and Deut 22:22). Hence, where is the man? Secondly, what did Jesus write? It says that Jesus twice leaned forward and wrote something on the ground. What could he have been writing? We encounter various interpretations in art, homilies, and scholarship.

Biblical scholars have posed additional questions. One reason for this is that the story is actually missing in the oldest manuscripts and translations of the Gospel of John, and that is why it is often bracketed in translations. Raymond E. Brown writes that "it is only from c. 900 that it begins to appear in the standard Greek text."[1] The language as well as the literary style are more reminiscent of the Synoptic Gospels: it is, in fact, the only instance in the entire Gospel of John that the Mount of Olives is referred to, that "scribes" (*grammateis*) and "elders" (*presbyteroi*) are mentioned, that the expression *orthrou* (at daybreak) is used, that the verb *katakrinein* (to condemn) occurs, and that Jesus is called "master" (*didaskalos*).[2] Hence, much suggests that this is a text that originally was part of one of the other Gospels, probably the Lukan narrative, which often emphasizes the significance of mercy. And, indeed, we do have manuscripts in which the text is included in the Lukan narrative. At the end of the twenty-first chapter it says (v. 37f.):

> Every day he was teaching in the temple, and at night he would go out and spend the night on the Mount of Olives, as it was called. And all the people would get up early in the morning to listen to him in the temple.

The narrative in John begins with the following words (7:53—8:2):

> Then each of them went home, while Jesus went to the Mount of Olives. Early in the morning he came again to the temple. All the people came to him, and he sat down and began to teach them.

Now, if it is indeed a Lukan text, and if it originally was part of its twenty-first chapter, it belongs to the dramatic ending of the Lukan narrative, immediately before the story of the Passion begins. In Luke 22:1f. it says:

> Now the Festival of Unleavened Bread, which is called the Passover, was near. The chief priests and the scribes were looking for a way to put Jesus to death, for they were afraid of the people.

The twenty-first chapter in the Gospel of Luke begins with a story about a poor widow who gives everything she has to the temple: two copper coins. Hence, if this is the original context of the text now situated in John 8, then we have in this Lukan chapter two stories about two vulnerable women in the temple. How, then, has the story about the accused woman been interpreted? Three readings will be presented and discussed in this chapter:

(a) Jesus entrapped between Jews and Romans: The first interpretation is so common that many tend to think that it is the only possible one.[3] It is written in the sixth verse that the men who brought the woman to Jesus wanted "to test him [Jesus], so that they might have some charge to bring against him." Interpreters often describe how Jesus was put in what seemed to be an impossible situation, sandwiched between the law of the Roman Empire and what Judaism taught and demanded: they wanted to force Jesus to choose between obeying the Torah and thereby killing the woman, or not obeying the Torah and letting the woman go free. If Jesus obeyed the Torah

and commanded that she be stoned, then he would defy the Romans, because they had taken away from the Jewish people the mandate to impose the death penalty (cf. John 18:31). But if Jesus, by letting the woman go free, did not obey the Torah, then he would go against Judaism, and he would have disqualified himself as the Jewish Messiah and a rightful teacher of Israel. So, if Jesus chose the former alternative, he would act against the Romans—and if he chose the latter alternative, he would pit himself against "Judaism," which would be quite an anachronistic interpretation of this text. This line of thought concludes that Jesus did not choose either of these two alternatives but instead presented his own independent and innovative—alleged "non-Jewish"—reinterpretation.

It is often presented as an impossible equation: a cunning trap for Jesus, who finds himself caught between an alleged Jewish bloodthirstiness and Roman law.[4] This is an antithetical interpretation, in the sense that it takes for granted that there is a dialectical relationship both between the Roman Empire and Judaism, and, more fundamentally, between Jesus and Judaism. The interpreters claim that Jesus thinks, speaks, and acts in a way that would be completely unthinkable for a Jew of the time. Hence, this first interpretation is not only antithetical but also anachronistic because Jesus was a Jew, his mother was a Jew, his disciples were Jews—they all lived in a Jewish context. Judaism was not his theological contrast but his historical context. Therefore, this interpretation is so problematic that interpreters should readily refrain from it.

(b) "Do not judge, so that you may not be judged": The second interpretation could be called an existential one. Its starting point is the seventh and ninth verses where it says: "Let anyone among you who is without sin be the first to throw a stone at her....When they heard it, they went away, one by one, beginning with the elders; and Jesus was left alone with the woman standing before him." Many preachers have probably stuck to the last words: that it is the oldest—those who have come of age and those who, presumably, are more mature and wiser—who first leave the place. Is it not the case that, over the years, we become more aware of all our many shortcomings and limitations? There are other biblical statements that are reminiscent of this interpretation. In the Sermon on the Mount, the Matthean Jesus states (7:1–5):

> Do not judge, so that you may not be judged. For the judgment you give will be the judgment you get, and the measure you give will be the measure you get. Why do you see the speck in your neighbor's eye but do not notice the log in your own eye? Or how can you say to

your neighbor, "Let me take the speck out of your eye," while the log is in your own eye? You hypocrite, first take the log out of your own eye, and then you will see clearly to take the speck out of your neighbor's eye.

Similarly, the Johannine Jesus proclaims in the very same chapter where this text is now placed (8:15): "You judge by human standards; I judge no one."[5] It has been suggested that it was the many sins of the accusing men that Jesus wrote on the ground.[6] T. W. Manson points out that in Roman legal practice the judge first wrote the sentence and then read it aloud.[7] This accusing finger of Jesus is reminiscent of a story in the book of Daniel, in which a finger writes on the wall, *Mene, mene teqel u-pharsin*: interpreted as "You have been weighed on the scales and found wanting" (5:25).

The second interpretation thus emphasizes that since no one is completely innocent, we cannot judge or condemn others. This interpretation expresses empathy and sympathy with the woman in the narrative. Augustine famously wrote about the ending of this story: *relicti sunt duo, misera et misericordia* ([only] two remain: the distressed [woman] and mercy).[8]

But does the second interpretation end there? Would it not be natural to pose the question whether we can have a legal system in our society at all? If no one is flawless, if no one can ultimately judge anyone else—can we then have courts and judges? And if so, what happens to justice? Who then defends the weak, who advocates for the victims, and who assists the victims in our society? As Brown writes:

> Jesus is not saying that every magistrate must be sinless to judge others, a principle that would nullify the office of judge. He is dealing here with zealots who have taken upon themselves the indignant enforcement of the Law, and he has every right to demand that their case be thoroughly lawful and their motives be honest.[9]

This takes us to the third interpretation, which focuses on the theological and historical contexts of a first-century audience.

(c) An intra-Jewish reading: The starting point for this interpretation is that Jesus urges them to "be the first to throw a stone"—and Jesus's question to the woman, "Has no one condemned you?"

"To throw the first stone" has become a well-known expression—precisely because of this story in the Gospel of John, but it had appeared earlier in the Scriptures. Deuteronomy 17:7 states that witnesses throw the

What Did Jesus Write in the Sand?

first stones in order to emphasize their responsibility: they have literally taken a person's life into their own hands. A false testimony can mean that innocent people lose their lives, and if the witnesses are the ones who are to throw the first stones, they will be murderers who shed innocent blood.

It is quite plausible that this is what prompted Jesus's questions. A group of people come to Jesus to put him to the test. They claim to be faithful to the Scriptures, and Jesus challenges them in their own theological turf: the art of interpreting the Scriptures. He therefore urges the witnesses to appear; those who are "the first to throw a stone" is a synonym for "a witness," and at least two witnesses are needed. And since no witnesses wanted to appear, she must be acquitted—in accordance with the Torah. As in our own time—at least in some places—the rule is that any defendant is assumed innocent until proven guilty.

In the third interpretation, it is quite possible that the expression "the elders" (*presbyteroi*) does not refer to the oldest people; instead it is probably a reference to members of the Sanhedrin (the supreme Jewish legislative and judicial court; cf. Greek: *synedrion*, "council").[10] The first to leave were those who really knew the Torah, those who knew that without witnesses no one can be convicted.

J. Duncan M. Derrett has imaginatively suggested what Jesus wrote on the ground (Exod 23:1): "You shall not join hands with the wicked [to act as a malicious witness]." The reason, Derrett states, is that this verse

> was used by the rabbis to prove that in all situations, not merely in those of giving evidence in a trial, one should take care with whom one associates oneself, and to whose project one lends one's countenance and authority. It is a sin to join in, or help, or intervene in, an affair with an evil man.[11]

He even suggests that the last word not be vocalized *rasha'* (wicked), but *resha'* (crime), stating that "you shall not join hands with the crime." The reason, Derrett proposes, was that the husband had staged a conspiracy so that eyewitnesses would see and capture his wife. Then Jesus wrote, still according to Derrett, Exodus 23:7: "Keep far from a false charge [and do not kill the innocent and those in the right, for I will not acquit the guilty]."

This takes us to another question: was capital punishment practiced at the time of Jesus? It has already been mentioned that the Romans did not allow death penalties to be carried out by Jews. Around 30 CE the Romans deprived the Sanhedrin of the right to carry out the death penalty (cf. John 18:31: "We are not permitted to put anyone to death"). Furthermore, according to *Mishnah Makkot* 1.10, the Sanhedrin was considered *chovlanit* (Hebrew for "bloodthirsty," "tyrannical") if it imposed the death penalty once in *seven* years—or, according to Rabbi El'azar ben 'Azariah, once in *seventy* years. All this suggests that in practice the death penalty probably had been abolished at the time of Jesus. And even if the Romans had not yet prohibited it, the rabbis had made it so difficult to convict someone for crimes that led to capital punishment that it had been rendered inoperative. What is described in John 8, then, is a mob that wants to lynch the woman. A lynching is, by definition, an *extrajudicial* execution. But Jesus is on her side, and on the side of the Torah. Jesus says that those who claim to have the Law on their side must follow it.

The first century was a time of upheaval for the Jewish people. An uprising against the Romans was crushed, the temple was destroyed in 70 CE, and in connection with this the rabbis began to record the oral traditions. In that process, the death penalty was about to be abolished.

When we read a two-thousand-year-old text today, we must constantly be on our guard against anachronisms. Jesus's interpretation of the Torah was not non-Jewish; on the contrary, it was a very Jewish one. The Scriptures were relevant to him, so that he constantly interpreted and applied them in his teaching.

We cannot ascertain what the author of this narrative—be it Luke, John, or someone else—thought that Jesus wrote on the ground. He may have quoted biblical texts; maybe he did not. But hopefully this presentation of three interpretations of John 7:53—8:11 can be of assistance to us when reading biblical texts about life and death, about love and relationships, and about what was once impeccable but now is shattered. Augustine is presumably right—there are times in life when only two remain: *relicti duo, misera et misericordia* (the distressed [person] and [divine] mercy).

22

DEMONIZING ONE'S SPIRITUAL ADVERSARIES

John 8:31–59, esp. 8:44
(see chapter 1 and introduction, second challenge)

If one were to single out a verse that has negatively portrayed Jews of flesh and blood more than any other New Testament text, John 8:44 is quite likely the choice for many of those who are familiar with the painful story of Jewish-Christian relations through the centuries. New Testament scholar and child of Shoah survivors Adele Reinhartz writes in one of her books on the Gospel of John, "My heart still sinks every time I open the Gospel of John to 8:44 and read that the Jews have the devil as their father."[1]

The obvious problems with the antisemitic *Wirkungsgeschichte* of the Gospel of John cannot be narrowed down to this verse only, but studying this verse may provide readers of the New Testament with hermeneutical tools to be applied also when studying other passages in the Johannine literature and, indeed, the entire New Testament. It should also be added that the interpretations presented here are not mutually exclusive. Rather, although the motifs quite often overlap, they are emphasized to various degrees in commentaries, articles, and books. Hence, it is advantageous to present the motifs as follows.

(a) Jews as a race are inherently evil: For obvious reasons, John 8:44 was *gefundenes Fressen* for the racial antisemitism that preceded the Third Reich era and culminated during the Second World War.[2] Posters with the words *Der Vater der Juden ist der Teufel* (The father of the Jews is the devil) were frequently nailed to walls, and the verse was often quoted in newspapers, articles, and books—even in books intended for small children.[3] Doris L. Bergen, Robert P. Ericksen, Susannah Heschel, and others have shown how often biblical texts and motifs were referred to by the

Third Reich ideologues who were busy branding Jews as an existential threat to the Aryan race.[4] But, contrary to popular belief—or should one say wishful thinking?—the demonization of Jews did not end in 1945. The tendency to allude to or even quote biblical texts, and this verse in particular, is still prevalent today, for example, in white supremacy circles that propagate various conspiracies about alleged Jewish evil plots to obtain global power, adding fuel to the fire for antisemitic terrorists who attack synagogues and other Jewish institutions. Nor did the demonization of Jews begin with the rise of the Nazi movement in the twentieth century. In his classic study *The Devil and the Jews*, Joshua Trachtenberg surveys the medieval conception of the Jew as the devil. He demonstrates that the antisemitism of his own time—the book was originally published in 1943—was related to medieval motifs: "If the Jew is today despised and feared and hated, it is because we are heirs of the Middle Ages."[5] Trachtenberg makes it clear that the medieval preoccupation with demonizing the Jews cannot be detached from John 8:44. We may even say that the anti-Jewish texts, paintings, and sculptures of the Middle Ages were heirs of a number of influential interpretations of the New Testament, not least the Gospel of John. All this suggests that a genuinely self-critical reflection on the devastating impact of this verse belongs to the most important things a Christian can do.

(b) Cain is the son of the Evil One: Many commentators claim that John 8:44 most probably is a reference to the murder of Abel by Cain (Gen 4:8, cf. 1 John 3:12–15).[6] John's description "He was a murderer from the beginning" fits the story of the first fratricide in the Bible.

Ironically, the starting point for this claim is probably a midrash, namely, a *Jewish* interpretation of the obscure Hebrew text in Genesis 4:1. When Eve has given birth to Cain, she exclaims: *qaniti ish et-YHWH* (I have given birth [to a] man, [namely] the Lord). In a targum (a paraphrasing translation into Aramaic), we find the tradition that Eve became pregnant through the evil angel Sammael.[7] Those who embraced this interpretation of Genesis 4:1 reasonably interpreted the expression "children of the devil" literally: Cain was the devil's firstborn! Cain is often mentioned in both Jewish and Christian texts as the paradigm for an evil being with characteristic evil behavior. In the New Testament there are two explicit examples. In Jude 11, we read, "Woe to them! For they go the way of Cain," and in 1 John 3:12, "We must not be like Cain who was from the evil one [or 'son of evil'] and murdered his brother. And why did he murder him? Because his own deeds were evil and his brother's righteous."

Building on the Jewish midrash, Nils Alstrup Dahl—and subsequently Günter Reim—argued that the father is not the devil, but Cain (who, in turn, is the son of the devil).[8] Most commentators refer to this minority view, but few find it convincing.

However, the Greek in John 8:44 is difficult to interpret: *hymeis ek tou patrou tou diabolou este* translated quite literally would mean "you are from the father, [from] the devil." For this reason, it has been suggested that it ought to be understood as "You are from the father of the devil."[9] April deConick situates the text within pro-Gnostic circles with "a system where the Father of the Devil rules the world with his son, the Devil, just as the righteous Father rules the heavens with his Son, Jesus." She argues that the "architects of the foundational theology" of the Gospel of John are the ancestors of the second-century Gnostics.[10]

However, in an article jointly written by Stephen Robert Llewelyn, Alexandra Robinson, and Blake Edward Wassel, the traditional interpretation is defended, namely, that the two genitives ("from the father" and "[from] the devil") refer to one and the same being. Contending that there is nothing ungrammatical in the verse, they assert that this significantly weakens deConick's line of arguments.

(c) A response to the excommunication of Johannine Christians: One of the most influential books in Johannine scholarship is J. Louis Martyn's study, *History and Theology of the Fourth Gospel*, first published in 1968. He argues that there is a connection between the Johannine community's polemic against *hoi Ioudaioi* and the particular Christology of the Gospel of John. In the New Testament, the word *aposynagôgos* (excluded from the Synagogue) occurs three times, all in the Fourth Gospel: John 9:22, 12:42, and 16:2.

Martyn maintains that these three verses reflect the actual procedure when the *birkat ha-minim*, that is, the twelfth prayer of the Jewish *'amidah* prayer (also called *shmoneh 'esreh*, the "eighteen [prayers]" because it contains eighteen different moments of prayer), was revised.[11] The prayer, condemning heretics (Hebrew: *minim*), would make it virtually impossible for these Jewish Christ followers to be faithful to both their Judaism and their faith in Jesus as Christ. Anyone who could not recite the twelfth prayer therefore became an *aposynagôgos*. Martyn thus believes that the gospel's anti-Jewish polemic derives from Johannine Christians no longer being allowed to be part of the Jewish community of faith.

Bart Ehrman uses three prepositions to mark the radically changed conditions that the Johannine Christ followers underwent. In the first stage, the

Johannine Christ followers were *in* the Synagogue. This intra-Jewish belief is expressed in, for example, 20:30f.: "Jesus is the Messiah." During stage two they were excluded *from* the Synagogue. This stage is reflected as already shown in 9:22, 12:42, and 16:2. The third stage is characterized by the Johannine Christ followers turning *against* the Synagogue, perhaps most clearly in 8:44.[12] If Martyn is right, then the vehement anti-Judaism of the Fourth Gospel is the result of the Johannine Christ followers being mistreated by religious siblings who did not believe in Jesus as the Christ; it is John's way of *reacting* to the way they had been *acting*.[13] Quite simply, "they were the ones who started it!"

As D. Moody Smith summarizes Martyn's suggestion: the underlying assumption is that the statements about *aposynagôgos* mirror an actual historical situation and set of circumstances at the time of the evangelist, thus affording *primary* testimony for the circumstances under which it was written, but only *secondary* testimony for the times and events it claims to narrate.[14]

It has already been mentioned that Martyn's theory has been extremely influential. However, criticism of his hypothesis has been voiced by several (especially Jewish) scholars. Reuven Kimelman argues that *birkat ha-minim* should not be understood as a watershed between Jews and Christians in the first centuries.[15] Adele Reinhartz claims that the prayer "was not a ban but a filter."[16] Daniel Boyarin states that *birkat ha-minim* came into being almost two centuries after the destruction of the temple.[17] And Ruth Langer concludes: "Therefore, there is no way that the *birkat haminim* played a role in the exclusion of Christians from the synagogue described in the Gospel according to John."[18]

It is particularly important to remember that it is unlikely that the Christ-believing movement at that time was quite as substantial a theological challenge to Jewish *unity* as many today may assume. Whereas Jews and Judaism play a major role in early Christian texts, Christians and Christianity are an extremely marginal phenomenon in the earliest rabbinic literature. What conclusions should this imply? In Kimelman's words:

> We must be careful of anachronistically overestimating the impact of Christianity on Judaism in the first two centuries....Apparently, there never was a single edict which caused the so-called irreparable separation between Judaism and Christianity. The separation was rather the result of a long process dependent upon local situations and ultimately upon the political power of the church.[19]

In Ehrman's historical reconstruction, Johannine high Christology rather seems to be a response to an already realized antagonism. He believes that it is only when Jews and Johannine Christians go in different directions that the latter begin to develop their Christology in order to clarify for the other group and announce to their own why the division must take place. His view is thus that sociohistorical factors have greatly influenced theology—not the other way around. In a similar way, Reinhartz believes that the texts should be seen as an etiology:

> Hence the exclusion passages may have provided the Johannine community not with a direct reflection of their historical experience but rather with a divinely ordained etiology *in the time of Jesus* for a situation of separation which was part of their own experience....In this light, the exclusion passages, which may provide an etiology in the time of Jesus for the estranged relations between the Johannine and Jewish communities at the end of the first century C.E., also express the emotional tenor of that relationship and situate it in the christological framework of Johannine theology.[20]

To be sure, there is some form of connection between *theology* (e.g., Johannine high Christology) and *history* (the Johannine community's relationships with contemporary groups). It is, however, doubtful whether it should be expressed as cause and effect as in Martyn's book. Perhaps it is the other way around—that is, that high Christology pushed those Jews away who were not Christ followers? This question takes us to the next interpretation.

(d) Jewish worship, high Christology, and the exodus motif: In his book *Exodus and Revolution*, Michael Walzer has demonstrated the extraordinary importance that the exodus motif—the liberation from slavery in Egypt—has played in history.[21] This motif has been called Judaism's master story: the narrative that, more than any other, has shaped the group's beliefs, identity, expression, and actions.[22] At every Passover for millennia, Jews have read the most important texts from the Book of Exodus (cf. Greek: *exodos*, "a way out"), they have praised God in gratitude that they are no longer slaves, and they have exemplified the yoke of slavery in Egypt through the various dishes on the Passover meal table. A *crux interpretum* in Johannine scholarship is how to interpret the statement in 8:33: "We have descended from Abraham and have never been slaves to anyone." How could a group of Jews ever say, "We have never been slaves under anyone" (*oudeni dedouleukamen pōpote*)? How could they

ever forget the slavery in Egypt, ritualized in the Passover liturgy in the words '*avadim hayinu be-Mitzrayim* (We were slaves in Egypt)? And the Babylonian exile? And even if they had forgotten, how would they be able to ignore the ongoing Roman occupation?[23] There are only two possible interpretations here: either John is poorly informed about Jewish self-understanding or the text ought not be translated in the conventional way. Reinhartz suggests that the verb *douloun* (to serve, to be a slave) in this context does not refer to the *negative* servitude (slavery) but to the *positive* aspect (worship). Israel has been called out of Egypt and out of slavery to serve the God of Israel—and no one else.[24] See, for example, Deuteronomy 13:4: "The Lord your God you shall follow, him you shall fear, his commandments you shall keep, him you shall obey, him alone you shall fear."

Her interpretation would render the Johannine text meaningful in a Jewish context. What is intended, then, is not that the collective memory of the Jewish people does not contain any experiences of slavery, but that the Jews in this passage claim to have never served any other gods than the God of Israel. It is thus reasonably a discussion of Jewish strict monotheism versus Johannine high Christology:

> Read in this way, the Jews are neither lying nor boasting but simply explaining why they cannot believe in Jesus or continue in his word. To do so would be to violate the foundation of their faith and self-understanding as Jews....From the perspective of the Johannine Jews, belief in Jesus is the path *not* to the God of Israel but away from God to idolatry.[25]

This interpretation turns the table in John in regard to the question "Who is kicking out whom?" It is not *birkat ha-minim* but the high Christology of the Johannine Christ followers that makes it difficult for Jewish Christians to worship together with their Jewish kindred; it becomes impossible for other Jews to worship together with them. This interpretation and the previous one both seek to reconstruct a plausible historical context for the Gospel of John. Many have pointed out the weaknesses in Martyn's hypothesis; some may not be convinced by the inverted hypothesis that argues that high Christology pushed out non-Christ-believing Jews. Most will perhaps agree with D. Moody Smith when he states that "the sources available to us do not permit us to say exactly what transpired to produce the tension between Johannine Christianity and Judaism that is evident in the Fourth Gospel."[26]

*(e) **Befriending John:*** Reinhartz suggests four Jewish approaches to John: (1) a compliant reading that looks upon the beloved disciple as a mentor, (2) a resistant reading that thinks of him as an opponent, (3) a sympathetic reading that treats him as a colleague, and (4) an engaged reading that sees him as "Other." She points out that these four approaches are *her* readings, not *the* ultimate Jewish readings of John, and she also confesses that she has not succeeded fully in befriending the Beloved Disciple: "I still do not have a comfortable place for him in my own scheme of things. I continue to maintain my negative ethical judgment of him as (I believe) he would of me."[27]

What hermeneutical strategies can—or should one say *must?*—Christians apply when reading John, especially this passage, a text that has proven so lethal a weapon in anti-Jewish tirades over the centuries? Indeed, the question is whether there is any other New Testament verse that more acutely prompts a hermeneutical reflection than does John 8:44. A few reflections may be outlined here, informed by an insightful article by D. Moody Smith.[28]

(i) Quite clearly, this is one of the most heated discussions in the entire Gospel of John between the protagonist and some of "the Jews." There are no strictly grammatical reasons for adding the word "we" (Greek: *hêmeis*) in verse 41 (as it is implied in the word *gegennêmetha* [we were born]; this may be an indication that it should be emphasized in translation: "mind you, it is not *we* who are illegitimate children." Is the Johannine Jesus here accused of being conceived "out of wedlock?" If yes, is that a hint of the response of nonbelievers to the proclamation about "the man from heaven in Johannine sectarianism," to use the expression in Wayne A. Meeks's classic article?[29] Is it possible that we may even detect traces of the *Jesus ben Pantera* polemics (claiming that Jesus was the son of a Roman soldier by the name Panthera)?[30]

Be that as it may, on the narrative level, the protagonist's statement in verse 44 is uttered when he is distraught. But *we*—that is, readers of the Gospel of John today—are not always upset, at least not when reflecting theologically. And are we ourselves when we are angry? If not, how do we interpret biblical assertions that are conditioned by such a specific context?[31]

(ii) If we concur with the overwhelming majority of scholars who state that the message in verse 44 is the voice of the protagonist in the Johannine community, not of the historical Jesus, what conclusions do we draw? In a traditional red letter edition of the Bible (i.e., an edition that uses red ink for all statements attributed to Jesus), this passage is red, but not in the edition published by the Jesus Seminar (a group of scholars that assessed the statements attributed to Jesus in order to ascertain whether they go all the way back to the historical Jesus).[32] John's narrative and theology are different from the synoptic portraits of the protagonist, and they, in turn, are not identical with the teaching of the historical Jesus. We need to honor these differences between *story* and *history*—and not ignore them. It is highly unlikely that the Jew Jesus of Nazareth would express himself in this way. However, the statement is found in a book that is part of the Christian canon, and Christians have to develop hermeneutical tools in order to contend with these challenges. D. Moody Smith speaks of "the virtual certainty that Christians will continue to accord *John* a high, canonical authority in their own religion and theology," and continues: "But the seemingly anti-Jewish statements in the *Gospel of John* are disastrous theologically only on the basis of a rather narrow and literalistic conception of the authority of the New Testament Scriptures."[33] Given that there are several ways to read the Gospel of John, there is an acute need for self-critical hermeneutical reflection that takes into consideration the effects of these readings.

(iii) It is often stated that the Johannine community probably was a small group—indeed, it is often called a sect—at a time when, on the one hand, the Roman Empire insisted on the divinity of the emperor and, on the other hand, most Jews maintained that strict monotheism would be compromised if they embraced Johannine high Christology.[34] Meeks suggests that the Gospel of John be called "an etiology of the Johannine group":

> In telling the story of the Son of Man who came down from heaven and then re-ascended after choosing a few of his own out of the world, the book defines and vindicates the existence of the community that evidently sees itself as unique, alien from its world, under attack, misunderstood, but living in unity with Christ and through him with God.[35]

But that is not the most common scenario today. Most Christians—especially in countries and contexts in which a majority define themselves as Christians—do not face similar challenges. What happens when one takes such a *minority* text intended for a minority, and transfers it to a context in which the readers constitute a *majority*?

D. Moody Smith, when describing the Johannine Christ followers, writes that they had "the uncompromising zeal of new converts. They were not so much converts from Judaism to Christianity as converts to Jesus, filled with his spirit, born from above, filled with power and glory."[36] But the Johannine community matured. It is often pointed out that the commandment of love is called "new" in the Gospel (13:34), but "old" in the epistles (1 John 2:7), written down when Johannine Christianity, as D. Moody Smith writes, had "weathered the synagogue controversy and moved on to other concerns."[37] If Johannine Christ followers could do this already within a generation, so should Christianity today.

(iv) It seems likely that John 8:44 in one way or another is related to the midrash that suggests that Cain was the son of the serpent, the evil angel Sammael, or even the devil. If this is correct, then it was not a metaphorical expression but a statement that takes for granted that the author sees the antagonists quite literally as offspring of the devil. That assertion is difficult to translate into our contemporary world, in which we can count and classify chromosomes, ascertain our DNA, and even conduct genealogical studies to find out more about our ancestry. Moreover, the midrashic idea, if taken literally, provides no space whatsoever for the improvement of one's status. Put quite bluntly, people who are the children of the devil cannot change their DNA; neither assimilation nor emancipation can change this fact. They are what they have always been: the devil's offspring. Putting a finer point on it, that is why the Nazis rejected *assimilation* and repudiated *emancipation*; and that is why they advocated *annihilation*. What theological conclusions can we draw from this when reading the Gospel of John?

(v) This takes us to the crucial question whether the *Wirkungsgeschichte* of a text can be entirely irrelevant to the interpretation and actualization of the text. The dreadful reception history of John

8:44 and similar texts is painfully clear.³⁸ What conclusions are interpreters willing to draw? What reading strategies are suggested? In an article for the *Interpreters' Dictionary of the Bible*, Krister Stendahl famously distinguished between what the text once *meant* and what the text now may *mean*.³⁹ Few—if any—biblical texts demonstrate the necessity of this distinction more than does John 8:44.

(vi) Last but not least, is it not against the grain of Christianity's core proclamation of a love that goes beyond the boundaries of one's own group? This message is often spoken, but seems so difficult to apply to Jewish characters in Christian texts and—therefore—also to Jews of flesh and blood. Are Jews to be excluded from the commandment to love one's neighbor? Given the antisemitism in history, this is certainly not merely a rhetorical question. One example may suffice: Siegfried Leffler, one of the leaders of the *Deutsche Christen* movement, stated in 1936—to wit, a few months after the proclamation of the Nuremberg Laws but before the "Final Solution" was implemented—that

> in a Christian life, the heart always has to be disposed toward the Jew, and that is how it has to be. As a Christian, I can, I must, and I ought always to have or to find a bridge to the Jew in my heart. But as a Christian, I also have to follow the laws of my nation [*die Gesetze in meinem Volke*], which are often presented in a very cruel way so that again I am brought into the harshest of conflicts with the Jew [*in den härtesten Konflikt zum Juden*].... Even if I know "Thou shalt not kill" is a commandment of God or "Thou shalt love the Jew" because he too is a child of the eternal Father, I am able to know as well that I have to kill him, I have to shoot him, and I can only do that if I am permitted to say: Christ [*und ich kann das nur tun, wenn ich sagen darf: Christus*].⁴⁰

As Susannah Heschel writes,

> Leffler argues that Jews are not simply to be despised by Christians but are presented as a lethal danger that must be eradicated—*in the name of Jesus Christ*.⁴¹

A reader who overemphasizes Johannine theology—at the expense of the synoptic narratives and theologies—will not present a protagonist who teaches that one should love, care for, and pray for one's enemies. In the words of the Matthean Jesus in the Sermon on the Mount: "And if you greet only your brothers and sisters, what more are you doing than others? Do not even the Gentiles do the same?" (Matt 5:47). Reading John 8:44—or, for that matter, any biblical text—in a way that in the end demonizes Jews of flesh and blood runs counter to the Christian *euangelion* (good news). In short, *is the Christian "good news" necessarily bad news for Jews?*

23

PAULUS—MÄDCHEN FÜR ALLES?

1 Cor 9:19–23

One particular passage is often referred to in discussions of Paul, the apostle of Christ to the Gentiles, and especially his understanding of the validity of the commandments *for Paul personally*: "I have become all things to all people, that I might by all means save some" (1 Cor 9:22). Peter J. Tomson asserts that "it is the only one [passage] where Paul speaks about his actual behavior regarding what has come to be considered the central issue in his thought: the Law."[1] David J. Rudolph calls it "a hermeneutical lens for understanding Paul"[2] This discussion of 1 Corinthians 9:19–23 will limit itself to four interpretations.

(a) Paul changes his behavior depending on context: This is the mainstream interpretation, and it can be found as early as some of the writings of anti-Christian authors in late antiquity, for example, Porphyry's work *Kata Christianôn* (Against the Christians):

> The man who hypocritically pretends to be what he is not makes himself a liar in everything he does. He disguises himself in a mask. He cheats those who are entitled to hear the truth. He assaults the soul's comprehension by various tactics, and like any charlatan he wins the gullible over to his side.[3]

However, most biblical scholars do not criticize Paul's behavior as does Porphyry in this passage. Instead, it is almost always emphasized that he was able to adapt to different situations because Jewish *halakhah* had become completely meaningless to him, as C. K. Barrett writes: "He [Paul] could *become* a Jew only if, having been a Jew, he had ceased to be one and become something else. His Judaism was no longer of his very being, but a guise he could adopt or discard at will."[4]

Paulus—Mädchen für alles?

Although this interpretation is exceptionally widespread, it is not without problems. Firstly, is not Porphyry correct in questioning whether such an arbitrary behavior is laudable? Would the historical Paul, who describes himself as *amemptos* (blameless) in regards of the Torah (Phil 3:6), really conduct himself in such a way? And even if we assume, to use the traditional nomenclature, that he only regarded himself "blameless" when he was "still" Jewish, before "converting" to Christianity, is not Rudolph correct when stating that the mainstream interpretation quite simply portrays Jews as "simpletons," who allegedly did not notice that Paul was Torah observant only when he spent time with Jews? He points out that, according to Acts 18:7, Paul's congregation in Corinth met in a house next to the synagogue: *hê oikia ên synomorousa tê[i] synagôgê[i]* (the house was adjacent to the synagogue).[5] Secondly, is there a tendency to apply this mainstream interpretation only regarding Paul's attitude to Jewish *halakhah*, and not to the behavior of Gentiles? Mark D. Nanos rightly asks whether the passage could be interpreted to mean that Paul admits to behaving like those who worship the gods of other nations.[6] Thirdly, Nanos also points out that Paul *in the very same letter* decrees that Christ-believing Corinthians must not associate with those who have a manner unbecoming of their own ethics (1 Cor 5:11):

> But now I am writing to you not to associate [*synanamignysthai*] with anyone who bears the name of brother [or sister] who is sexually immoral or greedy, or is an idolater, reviler, drunkard, or robber. Do not even eat with [*synesthiein*] such a one.[7]

Nanos also refers to the gospel narratives about Jesus eating with prostitutes and tax collectors, a fact that does not suggest that he started behaving like them. Au contraire, when meeting with them, he urged them to stop doing what they did.[8]

These are quite serious objections to the mainstream interpretation, and one wonders if its popularity has to do with a pre-understanding of the alleged irrelevance of *halakhah* to the historical Paul. Ignoring the circularity of such reasoning, the text has supposedly proven that the Christ-believing Paul was not a Torah-observant Jew. Nanos writes, "Since the earliest commentators on Paul, 1 Cor 9:19–23 has been explained in terms of compromising his behavior according to the model of lifestyle adaptability."[9]

(b) *Text-critical rereading:* Tomson concludes his study *Paul and the Jewish Law* with a rereading of 1 Corinthians 9:19–23 based on text-critical observations. He suggests two omissions: firstly, the Greek word *hôs* (as) in the phrase "I became to the Jews as a Jew." The consequence of his rereading of this statement—without the word *hôs*—is that Paul, first and foremost, is stating that he was born a Jew, as he does elsewhere (Rom 9:3), rather than *pretending* to be a Jew without actually being one. Furthermore, Tomson argues that "to the weak I became weak" is a reference to his own weakness, which he describes as a "thorn in the flesh" in 2 Corinthians 12:5–10. Hence, it is not a matter of Paul pretending from time to time to live a Jewish life but a description of a Jew who lives a Jewish life, and a fragile person who reaches out to other people who, too, are fragile. Tomson argues that given the "progressive development of anti-Judaism, it is much easier to imagine its being added than its suppression."[10]

The second omission that Tomson proposes based on text-critical evidence is the entire phrase *mê ôn autos hypo nomon* (though I myself am not under the law). He argues that it is more reasonable that these words were added later rather than being omitted, and especially not omitted on purpose. The statement, Tomson argues, is tautological and "a sophism alien to Paul's passionate thought."[11] But if it is omitted, Paul's thought becomes clearer:

> Paul is not Law-less, not a non-Jew, "of God"—aptly translated "toward God" or more elaborately "under the aspect of God"; he is Law-respecting "under the aspect of Christ." This makes Pauline sense.[12]

Tomson's rereading is appealing, and perhaps primarily because it makes Paul's line of thought coherent rather than being based on strong textual evidence. However, when evaluating this suggestion, Rudolph states, "While Tomson's treatment of 1 Cor 8 and 10 has been well-received by many scholars, I am not aware of any who have adopted his text-critical argument for interpreting 1 Cor 9:1–23."[13] How does Rudolph interpret this text?

(c) Paul is imitating Jesus's open table fellowship: In the monograph *A Jew to the Jew*, primarily devoted to this Pauline passage, Rudolph criticizes the mainstream interpretation of 1 Corinthians 9:1–23 from various angles—intertextual, contextual, and textual—and offers his own reading of the text. He suggests that the key question is commensality: sharing food and eating together with others. He argues that Paul was and remained a Torah-observant Jew who, although imitating Jesus's stress on open table fellowship, nevertheless found ways to keep the Jewish *kashrut* regula-

tions. Hence, he neither ignored the rules altogether (*pace* the mainstream interpretation presented above) nor adhered to the strictest schools who were especially scrupulous in their interpretation and application of *halakhah* (who, according to Rudolph, are referred to as those "under the Law").[14] He writes, "In 1 Cor 9:21, Paul speaks of fulfilling Christ's *halakhah* by *visiting* the lawless one without *participating* in their lawlessness."[15] Rudolph portrays a Paul who seeks both to imitate Christ—by accepting invitations also from those who most probably did not offer him meals that were *kosher* according to the highest standard—and to accommodate in various situations so that he would not eat what obviously was non-*kosher*. In short, it is a matter of making it possible to have open table fellowship—but within the boundaries of *halakhah* as defined by Paul himself.

(d) *Not lifestyle adaptability, but rhetorical adaptability:* Mark D. Nanos points out that the mainstream interpretation does not suggest that Paul actually *becomes* both a Jew and a Gentile, both one who insists on keeping the commandments and one who does not.[16] Such an interpretation renders the keywords *Jew* and *Gentile* meaningless. Rather, the traditional interpretation describes that he *behaves* like a Jew or a Gentile, depending on the situation.

However, as we have already seen, Nanos and others have put forth a number of critical questions that severely weaken the mainstream interpretation that Paul in this paragraph gives vent to a lifestyle adaptability. Instead, Nanos proposes a different way to understand what Paul is describing, namely, that Paul changes his *rhetoric*, depending on his audience. Nano calls his own approach *rhetorical adaptability*. According to Nanos, Paul is describing his argumentative strategy: it is a question of arguments, not actions. Paul argues for his message "from the premises of each kind of person and group among which he finds himself."[17]

Nanos gives us an illuminating biblical example: In Acts 17, when arguing for his Christ-belief in a *non*-Jewish milieu (the Areopagus speech), the Lukan Paul relates to the inscription, "To an Unknown God" (v. 23), and a couple of passages from some of their own poets: "In him we live and move and have our being," and, "For we too are his offspring." Needless to say, this is a Lukan example, not the historical Paul himself preaching, but it is still relevant as a parallel to 1 Corinthians 9:19–23; when addressing non-Jews, the Lukan Paul is conveying his message *without* references to the Scripture, "without the Law" (*anomos*).

What Nanos suggests is that Paul does not confess to a chameleon-like conduct but articulates a willingness and ability to make his case verbally in various ways to various people.[18] Paul is willing to *argue* from the premises of any person or group, but not to *act* like those who do not share his convictions.

To conclude, four interpretations of this passage have been presented and discussed in this chapter. The first reading presented a Paul who is *inconsistent* in his behavior, simply because the commandments in the Torah are inconsequential to him as a Christ believer. The commandments simply serve the purpose of finding a forum when proclaiming his message among Jews. The second interpretation was a *text-critical rereading* of the passage, while the third focused on the question of *commensality* and portrayed a Paul who reminds some of us of a Jewish businessman today, who when traveling worldwide seeks ways to live a Jewish life. Finally, the fourth reading understood Paul's message to be one of *communication*. Paul expressed himself in different ways when meeting different audiences, but he remained a Jew. Although the first reading is well-known and widespread, it fails to convince those who have proposed alternative readings. The three suggestions forwarded by Tomson, Rudolph, and Nanos all have in common that they do not support the assertion that the historical Paul was indifferent to the commandments in the Torah. Indeed, all three argue that he remained a Torah-observant Jew also as a Christ follower. Hence, all three maintain that 1 Corinthians 9:19–23 should not be used as an argument for the suggestion that Paul—the Jew and the pagans' apostle—ceased to live a Jewish life in order to live a pagan's life.

24
REVIEWING VEILS AND REVELATIONS
2 Cor 3:4–18

The motif of blindfolded Jews has been extraordinarily influential in history—and unquestionably detrimental to Jews. It can be found not only in Christian teaching but in church architecture as well, known as the *Ecclesia et Synagoga* motif. One example of this is the pair of statues outside the cathedral of Strasbourg: whereas Judaism is portrayed as a grief-stricken, blindfolded woman with a broken spear and one of the tablets (or possibly both) of the Torah, Christianity is portrayed as a triumphant woman with a cross-topped staff in one hand and a chalice in the other. Other examples of this motif can be found in Bamberg, Freiburg Minster, and Minden in Germany; in Metz in France (as well as in Notre Dame, the cathedral in Paris that was destroyed in a fire during Holy Week in 2019); and in Lincoln, Rochester, Salisbury, and Winchester in England.[1]

The motif of exhibiting the synagogue (and thereby Jews and Judaism) as blindfolded is often traced back to Paul, who uses the veil metaphor in the third chapter in 2 Corinthians when presenting a series of binary pairs of words and expressions: old covenant *versus* new covenant, tablets of stone *versus* tablets of human hearts, written with ink *versus* written with the Spirit of the living God, letter that kills *versus* Spirit that gives life, ministry of death *versus* ministry of the Spirit, ministry of condemnation *versus* ministry of justification, and hardened minds *versus* acting with great boldness. Second Corinthians 3 has even been called "a shrunken version" of the epistle to the Hebrews because of this series of theological and rhetorical antitheses (see introduction, fourth challenge).[2]

How are we to understand this chapter, written toward the end of the 50s CE? Who are the blindfolded in the text, why are they blindfolded, and what does it take for them to be able to see (again)? Three suggestions will be explored in this chapter.

(a) Judaism per se is blindness: This first line of thought quite simply asserts that Christians see in Scripture what Jews fail to see: that is, that this is first and foremost a collection of texts about Jesus Christ. Consequently, all Jews who do not believe in Jesus as the Messiah are blindfolded by definition, and to read the texts non-Christologically is to misunderstand their purpose completely. There are, of course, numerous nuances here: some interpreters recognize the value of *pre*-Christian readings of the texts; it is only with the advent of the Christ that *non*-Christological Jewish hermeneutics ceased to be vibrant and vivacious. Other commentators would state that "the law was always meant by God as a transitory step toward the true covenant of those who are in Christ."[3] However, what unites all these interpretations is the claim that it is impossible to read the Scriptures in the decades after the death of Jesus of Nazareth in the same way as, say, one decade before his birth. And it is this construal that has given rise to the *Ecclesia et Synagoga* motif that depicts Jews as obdurate, obstinate, stiff-necked, unyielding, and blindfolded.

Now, the first critical question to pose to this first line of thought is whether it survives the acid test of anachronism. Is it plausible that Paul, perhaps as early as 57 CE, perceived "Judaism" as something completely separate from "Christianity," and that the former could be termed "the old covenant" (3:14; *palaia diathêkê*) and the latter "the new covenant" (3:6; *kainê diathêkê*)? If the answer is affirmative, Paul's legacy is indeed long-lasting, and he would probably not object to the *Ecclesia et Synagoga* motif in church art, since it represents in sculptures what he argued for in his writings: to be a Jew is to be blindfolded; to be a Christian is to be clear-sighted. However, if we believe that no one, as early as in the 50s CE, would be able to perceive and present the movement consisting of Gentile Christ followers, who believed in the God of Israel, as something entirely detached from Judaism, it cannot be a text that discusses how Christians should look upon members of another faith community.

The second critical question to pose is why Paul is so eager to find proof texts in the Scriptures—in the *Jewish* Scriptures—for his mission to the Gentiles. If the Scriptures "kill," if they contain a "ministry of death" and a "ministry of condemnation," why does he not simply abandon these texts? Why study texts that are deadly? When perusing his epistles, we see that everything suggests that Paul was convinced that it was precisely in these Scriptures he found his hermeneutical keys when seeking to interpret his mission in life. Peter J. Tomson, for one, argues that the text does not imply that Paul turned away from the Torah.[4] Furthermore, John M. G.

Barclay notes that the "ministry [of Moses] was not without its glory—in fact, [it was] so glorious that Moses' face was unbearably bright."[5] Hence, the point that Paul wishes to make is not that there is no radiance in the Scriptures. What this passage claims is that the people of Israel could not gaze at Moses because of the radiance from the glory of his face. In other words, it is not a lack of radiant glory but an *abundance* of it.

A third critical point is related to the issue of messianism, a complex topic that would require an extensive discussion. Suffice it in this context to underline that there was not, at the time of Jesus, one single, uniform, unchanging, and monolithic messianism, just waiting for Jesus, as if one picks up a glove from the street expecting it to fit perfectly, or walks into a store to buy a dress or a suit without trying it on.[6]

The answers to these three questions—the historical query about anachronism, the theological enquiry about Paul's recurrent usage of Scriptures, and the question of the manifold messianisms—should give us pause. We need to explore alternative interpretations.

(b) A reference to fellow Jews who did not "see" that God at the end of times is reaching out to the Gentiles: This line of thought argues that the key issue in this passage is that Paul's mission was questioned. All scholars agree that Paul belonged to those who believed that the end-times were near; many in antiquity agreed with him that it was a matter of a few years and not several generations. But far from everyone agreed with him that Jesus of Nazareth was the Messiah, and that his God had resurrected him, and that this, as Paula Fredriksen writes, was "the first swallow of the impending eschatological spring."[7] Nor did they agree with him that God at the end of times was ingathering the Gentiles from all over the world—and that this, too, proved that the end-times actually were near. However, today we know that Paul's times were not the end-times, and at that time many did not concur with Paul that it was God's time for reaching out to the Gentiles.

What is conveyed in this passage is Paul's frustration that his fellow Jews did not clearly see what God was achieving through the Pauline mission. The failure to perceive this is the *blindness* to which Paul is referring. To refuse to see that the Christ-believing Gentiles worshiped the God of Israel—a fact that, according to Paul, was preordained in the Scriptures—can be likened to wearing a veil when reading the Scriptures. In other words, this line of thought argues that what Paul specifically has in mind here is the relation between Jews and Gentiles. The one group could not be understood without the other. This is how Fredriksen interprets this passage:

We see how Paul linked his own gentile mission to Israel's divinely assured destiny. By working to turn pagans from their gods to his god, Paul worked as well, beneath a canopy of biblical promises, for the redemption of his own people.[8]

The benefit of this line of thought is that it avoids the anachronism that severely restricts the validity and applicability of the previous interpretation. Paul often refers to his opponents, and his second epistle to the Corinthians is no exception.[9] Indeed, oppositional rhetoric plays an important role in this passage, and, as a matter of fact, in the entire third chapter. It begins with the rhetorical question whether Paul needs "a letter of recommendation" (3:1; *systatikos epistolos*; cf. 5:12 and 10:12–17), and he answers the question in the negative—because the Christ-believing Corinthians constitute his letter of recommendation. This is the starting point for his exposé of the binary pairs of "letter" (*gramma*) and "Spirit" (*pneuma*).

In short, whereas the first interpretation does not hold water, the second does. But this presentation of interpretations would not be complete without a discussion of a third line of thought, to which we now turn our attention.

(c) Being unveiled is being "at home" in the texts: The starting point for the third line of thought is the endeavor to take into consideration to an even higher extent the historical and theological contexts of Paul, and this is what Yael Fisch does in her study *Written for Us: Paul's Interpretation of Scripture and the History of Midrash*. Examining Paul's hermeneutics of "unveiling" and comparing it to similar texts in the tannaitic literature, she argues that the Hebrew expression *giluy panim* (revelation of the face) is relevant here. *Giluy panim* denotes a *shameless* reading of the Scriptures. And, according to the rabbis of the tannaitic literature, the *tannaim*, a veiled reading is the traditional interpretation. This important observation is the starting point for the following musings.[10]

Historically, we must remember that Paul not only taught Gentiles *about* the stories in the Scriptures; he also had to teach them *how* to read the Scriptures. In other words, he taught them not only the contents of the central biblical texts but also the basics of formative biblical hermeneutics—and an important part of these reading strategies was the midrashic mode of interpreting the Scriptures.

Theologically, several elements in this passage are familiar to those who have acquainted themselves with Jewish hermeneutics, for example, the *qal wa-chomer* argument in 3:8 (*pôs ouchi mallon*... [how much more...])

is the first of the seven hermeneutical rules of Hillel.[11] As is well-known, the *qal wa-chomer* always compares something valid (although it may be deemed and described as "light") with something that is even more important ("heavy"). The purpose is not to contrast something that is null and void with something that is valid and worthy.

What New Testament parallels do we have to support this interpretation? One example may suffice: generally speaking, Christians have not interpreted Jesus's words "follow me, and let the dead bury their own dead" (Matt 8:22 and Luke 9:60) as a radical distancing from actually burying the dead. Indeed, both Jews and Christians in antiquity were known for showing respect for the dead by burying them. The point of Jesus's statement is that the commandment to live in imitation of Christ is *even more* important than the commandment to honor one's loved ones.

Furthermore, the theology of the "new" (or perhaps better "renewed") covenant of Jeremiah 31:31–33 and Ezekiel 36:26f. is also picked up in the rabbinic tradition; see, for example, *Talmud Bavli Berakhot* 17a where the people are admonished to "keep my Torah in your heart." In addition, the dialectics between what is put in writing and what is liberating is also attested in the rabbinic text, in, for example, *Mishnah Pirqei Avot* 6.2 where the similarity between the two words *charut* and *cherut* is noted and its meaning explained with the help of the *al tiqra...ellah* (do not read...but rather [read instead]) hermeneutics, which the rabbis employ when they want to reveal hidden meaning in the text:

> *The tablets were the work of God, and the writing was the writing of God, engraved [charut] upon the tablets* [Exod 32:16]. Do not read [the verse as], "engraved," [*charut*], but rather [read instead] "freedom" [*cherut*]—for no person is free except the one who labors in the study of Torah.

This revocalization does not imply that the commandments were not written down but that one must not contrast the act of writing them down with their inherent liberating force. Hence, there is no antithesis here between *writing* and *redeeming*, and this observation should assist us when interpreting the Pauline passage. It is quite unlikely that there is a fundamental ontological antithesis in Paul's thought between *scripta Dei* (the Scriptures of God) and *spiritus Dei* (the Spirit of God).[12]

Finally, it is also worthwhile to explore what the veil signifies. The word *kalymma* (veil) occurs only four times in the entire New Testament, and all four are found in this very text (vv. 13, 14, 15, and 16). Paul addresses a related issue in 1 Corinthians 11:1–16, whether one should or should not cover one's head when praying. Although the word *kalymma* does not occur in 1 Corinthians 11:1–16 (which discusses men's and women's head coverings), the passage must be considered in discussing 2 Corinthians 3:4–18.[13] The *kalymma* is what one wears when one is among strangers, but takes off at home when among family members. Thus, when interpreting the Scriptures in new ways, when one presents a *chiddush* (Hebrew for "new [interpretation]"), one is "at home" in the Scriptures, which is a sign that one is familiar with the texts. Is it possible that the new interpretations—homiletic *midrashim* intended for Christ followers—that Paul suggests reveal and "un-veil" the hidden meanings? In short, Paul is teaching the Christ-followers to read the Scriptures in a midrashic way—and there is always a striking boldness in the *midrashim*. Paul is aware that reading the Scriptures Christologically is a *new* way of interpreting them, and those who do not agree, those who prefer the traditional readings, are like those who read with a veil. John M. G. Barclay uses the expression "barefaced boldness" when describing Paul's hermeneutics, and this seems to capture what we are suggesting here.[14]

Is Psalm 104:29f. possibly a relevant parallel? "You [God] hide your face" (*tastir panekha*) is contrasted with God's Spirit that is sent forth, renewing "the face of the earth" (*penei adamah*)—and it is one and the same God who both conceals and reveals.[15]

What words do we use when talking about gaining knowledge and discernment? When reflecting on the meaning of the word under*standing*, we would perhaps say that we stand on someone else's shoulders, and that is why we see *farther* than previous generations of readers. *Higher* education is on a *higher* level than second-level education, which is on a higher level than primary education. The higher, the more advanced. In German, too, one speaks of under*standing*: *verstehen* comes from *stehen*, "to stand." Another way to express it is *begreifen* from *greifen* (to grasp), similar to the French verb *comprendre*, from *prendre* (cf. the English word "to comprehend"), to under*stand* or to *grasp* an idea.

But Paul is using another discourse: not *standing*, not *grasping*, but *seeing*. A new interpretation reveals what was previously concealed. Paul believed that the blueprint of his outreach to the Gentiles was already there in the Scriptures. It was a *déjà lu*—that is, he had a conviction that he had read about this before (*déjà lu* in French means "already read"). And his *déjà lu* led him to a kind of *déjà vu*: an in*sight*, as if he were saying: "now I *see*."

Reviewing Veils and Revelations

By way of conclusion, three readings have been presented in this chapter: first the *anti-Jewish interpretation* that has been so influential—and detrimental—in history, exhibiting Jews as blind because Judaism is a religion that fails to "see" that Jesus of Nazareth is the obvious and unquestionable focus of the Scriptures. If one does not see this, then one is blind, as if that were all there is to see in the Scriptures. If one does not say, "I see that Jesus is the Christ," then everything else is utterly meaningless, even if one is praying the same prayers that Jesus prayed, reading the same holy texts that Jesus read, and celebrating the same religious holidays that Jesus celebrated.

The second suggestion was a *pro-Pauline reading*. It interpreted the text as giving vent to Paul's strife for acceptance among his fellow Jews, when he compares some to those with a veil, because they do not concur with him on the importance of Gentile mission at the end of times. But it was not the end of times. In that sense, Paul is not clearsighted. On the contrary, he could not see what we see today. When reading Paul, this should give us pause.

The third reading takes this line of thought one step further and argues that Paul's exposition reveals so many Jewish hermeneutical and theological features that one ought to look upon it as an *intra-Jewish contribution* to an ongoing discussion within the Jewish community. In short, it is a text written by a *Jew* who applies *Jewish* hermeneutics in order to criticize some fellow *Jews* for the purpose of advancing his own *Jewish* understanding on how to look upon the fact that some non-*Jews* are observing some of the *Jewish* commandments and religious holidays. If that is not a description of an intra-Jewish discussion, what is?

It seems fitting to conclude by returning to the *Ecclesia et Synagoga* motif. In order to commemorate the fiftieth anniversary of the Roman Catholic declaration *Nostra Aetate*, promulgated on October 28, 1965, Saint Joseph's University in Philadelphia commissioned a sculpture by Joshua Koffman showing the *Ecclesia et Synagoga* motif—but now the two are in harmony. Both personifications wear crowns and hold their respective Holy Scriptures—the Jew holding a Torah scroll, the Christian a Christian codex—and, most significantly, they look at each other's Scriptures, hence sitting together and each learning from the other, as it is beautifully depicted in Psalm 133:1: *Hinneh mah tov u-mah na'im, shevet achim gam yachad* (How very good and pleasant it is when kindred sit together in unity).

25
DECIPHERING SARAH AND HAGAR IN GENESIS AND GALATIA
Gal 4:21—5:1

Of particular importance to the topic of this book is Paul's enigmatic midrash on Sarah and Hagar, and their children Isaac and Ishmael. Three readings will be presented in this chapter.[1]

(a) An allegory of covenantal contempt: The first interpretation is so well known that many readers may even take for granted that this is the only way to interpret Paul, to construe interreligious relations in the first century, and to present the relationship between the central motifs in the Hebrew Bible and in the New Testament. Those who subscribe to this interpretation start by noticing the verb *allêgorein* (to make an allegory) and the noun *diathêkê* (covenant) used in Galatians 4:24: "Now this is an *allegory*: these two women are two *covenants*" (emphases added). In the history of Christian interpretation, this text has indeed been allegorized: generations of Christians have taken for granted that Paul, a mere two decades after the death of Jesus, here defines and compares two distinct religious systems ("Judaism" *versus* "Christianity"), two key concepts ("Law" *versus* "faith"), and, indeed, two human attitudes toward life ("slavery" *versus* "freedom"). In addition, when the readers in Galatians 4:30 are asked to "drive out" what enslaves them, this has been understood as an exhortation to cleanse their Christian faith from everything Jewish: male circumcision (*peritomê*), a key term in this epistle, is often used as a shorthand description for a Jewish way of living defined by the 613 Jewish commandments. In other words, this first interpretation suggests that the Jewish covenant has been replaced by a Christian covenant, and that no Jewish way of thinking or living, which is by definition "enslaving," should be accepted in the new covenant. Hence, replacement

theology—the assertion that the advent of Christianity makes Judaism void—is the essence of the first interpretation.

What is quite remarkable, however, is that the rhetorical argument for this replacement theology reverses the roles of the characters in the Genesis narrative: it is as if Paul states that the heirs of Sarah ("the Jews") think that they are the children of the free woman, but they are actually in slavery. This is quite an indigestible proposition to Jews, who read not only Exodus but also Genesis as books about their own people's way to freedom. It is as the offspring of Isaac, the child of Abraham and Sarah, that they are freed from slavery under Pharaoh in order to serve God, and that they are free to follow not the whims of the capricious Pharaoh but the commandments of the Torah. *In short, Judaism for Jews is freedom, not slavery.* Torah for Jews is liberty, not captivity. Could it really be Paul's intention to *invert* the well-known narratives in the Book of Genesis? We have to ask ourselves what devout Jew, be it in antiquity or today, would be convinced by this logic and such a series of arguments? Is Paul so ill-informed of the fundamental pillars of Judaism? Is the "good news" (*euangelion*) of Jesus Christ and of Christianity that Jews must cease to be loyal to God and to the commandments of their covenant with God?

According to the first interpretation, the reason for Paul being so furious when writing this letter to the Galatians is that the recipients have reverted to Judaism "again" (4:9, 19; 5:1, 3; *palin*), after previously having been saved from Jewish deed-centered and worthless legalism to the freedom in Christ. Judaism, hence, is the exact opposite of the Christian gospel: obedience to the Law is the exact opposite of being a liberated Christian, and therefore Jews, whether they know it or not, are slaves, and, in that sense, children of the slave woman Hagar, although they boastfully proclaim themselves to be the children of the free woman Sarah. In short, according to the first reading of Galatians 4:21—5:1, the reason for Paul's inverting the traditional distribution of the four characters—Sarah and Isaac as the origin for Jews, and Hagar and Ishmael as the origin for non-Jews—is that Judaism is a theological failure, and whatever Jews do will be a self-aggrandizing project with only negative effects, such as the burdens of the Law, a bondage of the will, and an unavoidable oppression of other people. This line of thought continues throughout the ages: those who rely on the promises given to Abraham and Sarah seem inevitably to be entrapped in an enslaving enterprise, and the only way out of it is to realize that Judaism is not a liberating religion, either for Jews or for non-Jews.[2] Judaism constitutes a problem, and the only way to deal with this problem is to overcome it—or, to use the phrase in Galatians 4:30, to "drive out the slave." This way of thinking has been very influential in history, as James Carroll writes: "The imagination of the West has always defined itself positively against the negative other of Jewishness," and "Jews were the paradigmatic enemy within."[3]

There are a host of questions to be posed to this first interpretation, and some of them have already been hinted at: if this were an anti-Jewish appeal, why would a Jew who knows the narratives in Genesis ever be convinced by this audacious inversion of the characters, according to which Sarah becomes Hagar, and Isaac becomes Ishmael? An overwhelming majority of New Testament scholars agree that what is often called "the parting of the ways" (i.e., between Judaism and Christianity) took several centuries. At the time of Paul, then, the biblical characters Sarah and Hagar quite simply cannot correspond to two distinct religions. Obviously, Paul's Hagar can neither be a representative of *Islam* (several hundred years before the rise of Islam as a historical phenomenon) nor a symbol of *Judaism* (many decades, and perhaps even centuries, before the two religions, Judaism and Christianity, were defined as two separate religious systems). Furthermore, another fundamental error with the first interpretation is that it takes for granted that Paul was as ignorant about the fundamental pillars of Jewish thought—that is, the fact that the Torah has overwhelmingly positive connotations—as are some of today's Christian readers of the biblical texts. These observations on the shortcomings of the first line of thought take us to the second interpretation, which is a radical rereading of this particular passage in Paul's Epistle to the Galatians.

(b) *A parable about Jews persecuting Christ followers:* Thus, the first interpretation is not only *rhetorically flawed* (Jews would identify themselves as the children of Sarah, and not Hagar) but also *anachronistic* (because Judaism and Christianity were not seen as two distinct religious systems at the time of Paul). These realizations encourage us to look for an alternative reading, which, in order to avoid anachronisms, has to focus distinctly on the social circumstances in which Paul wrote this particular passage.

To begin, why would Hagar be connected to Mount Sinai? When studying the ancient biblical manuscripts, one sees that those who copied Galatians 4:25 were equally baffled by the arguments of the first interpretation of the text. The Greek text behind the translation "Mount Sinai is a mountain in Arabia" has been preserved in a number of variant readings, one reason being that the two Greek words *gar* (because) and *Hagar* are almost similar. The first variant is thus quite clear. Paul would here make use of a *geographical* criterion in his arguments: *because Mount Sinai is situated in Arabia*. According to another reading, he makes use of a *linguistic* argument: The word *Hagar* means "Mount Sinai" in Arabic.[4] Biblical scholars have spent much effort seeking to explain this.[5] It is true that the Arabic word *hadjar* means "stone," but one has to agree with Lloyd Gaston that it would be a "rather bizarre concept that Paul is using a pun on an Arabic word to convince the Galatians that Hagar ought to be connected with Sinai."[6] Another question, however, must also be posed: Would it be less bizarre to turn the descendants of Isaac into Ishmaelites because "Mount Sinai is a mountain in Arabia"? Has not Mount Sinai always been situated in "Arabia"? Paul does not seem to suggest that there was a continental shift, neither at the birth of Jesus nor at his death or resurrection. Hence, neither the *geographical* nor the *linguistic* argument provides a convincing rhetorical starting point for Paul's arguments. We must look elsewhere. In other words, there must be something particular in the context of the group of Christ followers in Galatia that corresponds with something similar in the biblical text.

In order not to lose the overview completely, it may be a good idea to remind ourselves of some basic facts: Paul introduces this passage in 4:21f. by referring to what the Torah says. Thus, it seems unlikely that he would fundamentally contest the obvious meaning of the biblical texts. If he did, his argument would not carry much weight. Indeed, it is difficult to conceive that he would actually mean that the Jewish people after Christ had lost all the promises that *he himself* mentions in Romans 9:4f.: "To them belong the adoption, the glory, the covenants, the giving of the law, the worship, and the promises; to them belong the patriarchs, and from them, according to the flesh, comes the Messiah." Could it really be his intention in Galatians 4 to claim that the Jewish people after Christ have lost all this, including *hai diathêkai* (the covenants)?

In his seminal article on Paul and the introspective conscience in the West, Krister Stendahl pointed out that Paul considered himself to be the apostle of the Gentiles (Rom 11:13; *ethnôn apostolos*) who had a particular mission, for he was sent by God with the good news "to the nations" (Gal 2:8; *eis ta ethnê*).[7] His primary purpose was to speak *on behalf of* Gentile Christ followers, and not to speak *against* any other group. His message was always one of Gentile inclusion, although, unfortunately in the course of history, it was understood as one of Jewish exclusion.

The starting point for this second reading—which is a radical rereading of the text, and a repudiation of the previous and very common interpretation—is the three words at the end of 4:29: *houtôs kai nun* (so it is now also). According to this line of thought, Paul points out that Isaac had to suffer because of what his elder brother did to him: Ishmael persecuted (*ediôken*) Isaac. Thus, he writes to the Galatians (4:28f.):

> Now you, my friends, are children of the promise, like Isaac. But just as at that time the child who was born according to the flesh persecuted the child who was born according to the Spirit, so it is now also.

The tone in the epistle indicates that there were major tensions between various groups in Galatia. Paul believes that he himself and those who follow him are being persecuted because of their convictions. Hence, the most probable answer according to the second reading is that Paul was searching for a biblical text that would speak to those who, for one reason or another, were being persecuted, one that would illustrate how siblings in faith sometimes attack one another, and how this persecution may serve as a confirmation that divine election is accompanied by suffering. Hence, anyone who wants to live a life following Christ must also expect persecution. The characters he chooses in the Bible are Sarah and Hagar, and Isaac and Ishmael. It is important to remember that not everything in Genesis about these four characters' lives is relevant in this context. He therefore chooses one aspect, namely, that which "corresponds" (4:25; *systoichei*) to the point that he intends to highlight: that even Isaac was persecuted.

The suffering of the righteous person is thus at the center of Paul's thought. However, in what sense can Isaac be said to be "persecuted" by Ishmael? The only verse on which Paul could build this reasoning is Genesis 21:9: "But Sarah saw the son of Hagar the Egyptian, whom she had borne to Abraham, playing with [*metzacheq*] her son Isaac." What does *metzacheq* [lit. "laughing"] mean? How has it been interpreted?

The study of the interpretation of this verse may help us understand the trajectory of a particular mode of biblical interpretation, which is the inclination to paint the portraits of the patriarchs and matriarchs with a broad brush, so that the main characters become virtuous and other characters are portrayed negatively.[8] The following paragraphs will analyze four versions of the Ishmael-Isaac encounter and will show that Ishmael gradually was portrayed increasingly unfavorably.

Firstly, as already mentioned, the Hebrew text of Genesis 21:9 states that when Sarah saw that Hagar's son was "laughing" at his brother, she sent Hagar and her son away into the desert. Numerous readers of the Bible must have felt that such a punishment for merely laughing at his brother was far too harsh, and therefore a tradition began to evolve that emphasized the mischievousness of Ishmael's behavior. The fact that the Hebrew verb form *piel* is used could indicate that it refers to scornful laughter, since *piel* often intensifies the act.[9]

Secondly, we see the result of this tendency already in the Septuagint, which says that Ishmael "was playing with Isaac" (*paizonta meta Isaak*). The verb *paizein* is actually mentioned only once in the New Testament. Occurring only in 1 Corinthians 10:7, it is a quotation from Exodus 32:6 referring to the incident with the golden calf:

> [The people of Israel] rose early the next day, and offered burnt offerings and brought sacrifices of well-being; and the people sat down to eat and drink, and rose up to revel [Greek: *paizein*; Hebrew: *le-tzacheq*].

Is the Septuagint claiming that what Ishmael did to Isaac was similar to when the people sinned and worshiped the golden calf at the foot of Mount Sinai, where Moses was about to receive the revelation?

The third version of the account is Paul's rewriting of the verse. He often quotes the Septuagint, but interestingly not this time. As already mentioned, he states that Ishmael "persecuted" his brother. Paul thus implies that it would not have been mere innocent play that caused this laughter.

Fourthly, the rabbinic text *Genesis Rabbah* 53.11 reproaches Ishmael for a number of crimes. It actually accuses Ishmael of rape, idolatry, and bloodshed—the three cardinal sins in the Jewish tradition.[10] Arguably the most relevant midrash is the statement by Rabbi 'Azariah, uttered in the name of Rabbi Levi: on one occasion, when Isaac and Ishmael were out in a field, Ishmael shot at his brother—and then he laughed and said that it was only a joke. "Like a maniac who shoots deadly firebrands and arrows, so is one who deceives a neighbor and says, 'I am only joking!'" (Prov 26:18f.). Locating this in a field alludes to Cain's murder of his younger brother, Abel, similarly while out in the field.[11] This midrashic tradition thus considers Ishmael's "laugh" as a euphemism for a real threat to Isaac's well-being.

When we place these four versions—the Hebrew Bible, the Septuagint, the New Testament, and one of the *midrashim*—next to one another, we see that Paul's epistle is part of this particular hermeneutical development that sought for and, in addition, found a satisfactory reason for Sarah's harsh decision.

Paul thus chose this text because the suffering of Isaac reminded him of his own suffering. His main concept is thus that he and his Christ-believing followers in Galatia correspond to Isaac. As a consequence, and only because of Paul's self-identification with Isaac, his opponents became identified with Hagar and Ishmael.

Given that this is an example of a Pauline midrash, a playful rereading of a biblical text, is there yet another aspect that may have contributed to Paul's peculiar reversal of the characters in Genesis and Galatians? A Jew is someone who has Jewish parents, whereas a Gentile Christ believer is someone who, "by faith in Christ" (or perhaps better translated as "by Christ's faithfulness"), has been grafted into the covenant (cf. Rom 11:17–24). Galatians 4:29 describes Ishmael as "born according to the natural order" (*ho kata sarka gennêtheis*), while Isaac is described as "according to the Spirit" (*ton kata pneuma*), and, in addition, in the previous verse as a child "of the promise" ([*teknon*] *epangelias*). This *could* imply that Paul here assumes that the Gentile Christ followers have been grafted into participation in the covenant, not "according to the order of nature" like Jews, but through their faith in Christ (or through Christ's faithfulness), a miraculous event, similar to the promise given to Abraham in Genesis 15:1–6.[12] To repeat, when interpreting the text in this way, one has to bear in mind that it is a Pauline midrash, to wit, one way of reading a scriptural passage that can be read in other ways.[13] As stated above, it is anachronistic to understand it as a dogmatic statement on the relation between the two world religions that we now know as Judaism and Christianity.

Furthermore, it does not further the discussion to keep calling this passage an "allegory," simply because it is not an allegory in the technical sense in which this term is used today by literary critics. It is true that Paul employs the verb *allêgorein* in 4:24, but today we would label this text a "parable." Read as a parable, this passage seeks to convey a message without requiring the reader to rely on the particulars in the story, as one does when analyzing an allegory.[14] As a parable, the sociopolitical *context* (the current circumstances in Galatia) and the *text* (Gen 21) simply "correspond" (4:25; *systoichei*) to each other.[15] In other words, Paul claims that righteous people must expect to be persecuted because of their convictions. His message is that divine election does not necessarily bring success—quite the contrary! The adversities that the Christ followers have to face in fact affirm that they, just like Isaac, are children of the promise. Furthermore,

Deciphering Sarah and Hagar in Genesis and Galatia

Paul's focus is on the individual person: if Gentile Christ followers seek to avoid suffering by adapting to the demands of the surrounding world (in this case for circumcision), they will not remain faithful to God's call. These Gentiles-in-Christ should rather persevere steadfastly in spite of the sufferings they may have to endure. When Paul in 4:24 refers to "these two women" as "two covenants," this could hardly be understood as a reference to an enslaving (Jewish) covenant and a liberating (Christian) covenant.

Paul's parable is also about *the opportunity to make a choice*, since in 5:1 he encourages his readers not to let anyone lay the yoke of slavery on them again. Once again, this cannot be an allegory about, to use anachronistic terms, "Judaism" and "Christianity," since the Gentile Christ followers who were the first readers of his letter had not previously been Jews: "Do *not* submit *again* to a yoke of slavery" (5:1; *mē palin*, emphases added). How could it refer to "Judaism" if these Gentiles had never before been Jews? Rather, this is Paul's encouraging them to remain Gentile Christ followers by not, in any sense whatsoever, returning to that state of alienation—slavery to lesser powers—in which they lived before they became Christians.

In other words, according to the second interpretation, Paul's text is not a comparison between Judaism and Christianity, simply because such a line of thought would be completely anachronistic. Instead, the second interpretation argues that Paul has internalized the biblical persons Sarah and Hagar, Isaac, and Ishmael. When he encourages the Gentile Christ followers to drive away the interior "slave woman and her son" from their lives, it is another way to express that they are to accept the freedom to which Christ has called them. The character Hagar is, of course, neither a representative of *Islam* nor a symbol of *Judaism* and an allegedly superseded covenant with the Jewish people. Both these readings are anachronistic. Instead, she is—and this is the focus of this second reading of Galatians 4—an embodiment and personification of the choice not to be made in a given situation.[16] In that sense, *and in that sense only*, she is to be driven out of the mind of the person who is about to make a choice in a given situation.

One of the strongest arguments in favor of the second reading is that it avoids the anachronistic supersessionism that is so manifest in the first interpretation. Replacement theology eventually became the main road taken by Christendom, but, in fact, it was not a dogmatic platform for Christian theology until several decades, if not centuries, after Paul's writings. It would be anachronistic to expect to find it in the very earliest layer of the New Testament, the epistles of Paul, which were written only some twenty years after the death of Jesus.

However, what the second reading does not take into account is that the epistle was written to people living in the *Roman* Empire. Rome's was a ruthless regime that did not stop at anything in order to uphold what, on the one hand, has been known in history books as Pax Romana but, on the other hand, concerned itself little with the subjugated *peoples'* own experience of peace. It was an era not of the presence of peace but rather of the absence of war. It was during this period that what would eventually become Christianity entered the scene and that Paul wrote his epistles to Christ-believing communities in the Roman Empire. Is it really likely that the only concern of the earliest Christian movement was whether and to what extent the commandments of the Torah apply to non-Jews, given that they all lived in a *Roman* province, in a *Roman* Empire, and under *Roman* occupation? This takes us to the third reading of Galatians 4, which firmly situates the Pauline parable in its *Roman* context.

(c) Reading Paul with vanquished peoples: The starting point for our third and final interpretation is the fact that the receivers of Paul's letter to the Galatians lived in a *Roman* Empire. Much of what has been written about this passage and indeed other parts of the Pauline Letters might give the reader the impression that the mightiest people at that time in the Mediterranean world were Jews, who, it might seem, had few other tasks to perform than to impose *halakhah* (i.e., Jewish Law) on Gentile Christ followers. This, quite obviously, was not the case. Hence, we constantly need to learn more about the social circumstances of the Epistle to the Galatians, and also about the Galatians within the structure of the Roman Empire.

This third reading of Galatians 4 is largely informed by Brigitte Kahl's impressive tome *Galatians Re-imagined*.[17] Drawing on ancient art and architecture, she illuminates imperial Roman constructs of power and identity. The results of her studies, which she calls reading this epistle "with the eyes of the vanquished," are highly relevant to this chapter.

She argues that the Celtic Gauls in the west and the Celtic Galatians in the east were more closely linked in the first-century Roman mind than we usually realize. This is because the Galatians were part of a continents-spanning culture that included the European Gauls and the Celts in general. Kahl convincingly argues that the Galatians were perceived as the prototype for the rebellious Other, who constantly had to be subjugated, humiliated, and conquered. Hence, Galatia was not a neutral geographical or ethnic description but, on the contrary, a region populated by the Celtic "counter nation," a peculiar species of "universal barbarians."[18] She writes:

> *Galatia* in antiquity is not a single carefully bounded geographical location, nor does it refer to a single ethnic identity standing neutrally among others, of any kind anywhere. It is a term soaked with memories, fears, and aggression that are completely absent from our New Testament dictionaries....For the Romans, the Galatians became a myth. That is, they played a constitutive role in a colonial/imperial discourse centered on war and victory, order and counterorder, Self and Other in the battle of civilization versus barbarism.[19]

In short, to be a Galatian was to be the archetypical barbarian, insubordinate at best, outright rebellious at worst. Galatians were recognized as the opposite of law and order.

There had been a constant "fear of the Galatians" (Latin: *metus Gallicus*) and therefore a need for "galatomachy," the seemingly never-ending battle against real or mythical Galatians. However, in the year of 52 BCE, the Galatians were conquered when their leader Vercingetorix was defeated; out of a total population of four million Galatians, one million were killed and one million were enslaved.[20] The sculptural motif of "the Dying Gaul" was installed all over the Roman Empire, lest people in the empire forget what happens to the rebellious. Despite the fact that they had been conquered by the time Paul wrote his epistle, "Galatians" were still mythological symbols of chaos and upheaval, the archetypes of lawlessness (*anomia*), rebellion, barbarian foreignness, and the opposite of order and law (*nomos*), proper religion and piety, the characteristics of the Pax Romana.[21]

During the reign of Claudius (41–54 CE), the Romans intensified their imperial presence in Galatia.[22] This is the social context of Paul's parable, giving him good reason to draw upon Scriptures describing how one person "persecuted" (Gal 4:29; *ediôken*) another. The Roman imperial cult of the period could be described as imperial monotheism, with the Roman emperor and the city of Rome at the center. Hence, Rome expected the Galatians to show loyalty to the Empire by taking part in various forms of the emperor cult. Disobedience could and probably would be interpreted as insubordination and a cause for stigmatization and even persecution.

The recognition that Paul wrote to the Galatians under the conditions of Roman domination reorients long-lived Christian readings of the basic conflict in Galatians. Paul composed the letter to the Gentile Galatians, not with hyper-halakhic Judaism as his adversary but with the imperial Roman religion as his overpowering opponent.

In other words, the paradigm of Jewish-burdensome-law versus Pauline-liberating-gospel, which has governed many Christians' reading of Galatians for centuries, is in urgent need of revision. There is certainly a clash in the epistle, but it is, so Kahl argues, between Paul's Jewish God-in-Christ and the imperial god-in-Caesar.[23] The consequences of this paradigm shift are far-reaching.

Paul's faith-versus-law dichotomy has to be correlated with the Roman imperial environment. He is primarily targeting not Jewish Torah but Greco-Roman imperial *nomos*. It was Roman law that decided, defined, and enforced what was licit or illicit. Hence, Kahl's interpretation of "justification by faith alone" suggests that Paul is here presenting a theology of resistance and transformation in the Roman Empire. Hence, if *nomos* at times refers to Roman law, then the expression "by works of the law" (2:16; 3:2, 5, 10; *ex ergôn nomou*), too, is an allusion to works of the imperial law, what is called *euergetism* (from *euergetein*, "to do good deeds"; *eu*, "good"; *ergon*, "work"); so in this context, good deeds not for the sake of goodness but in order to achieve a position in the Roman society.[24] In the light of this, "works of the law" are the outcome and expressions of imperial violence and competition. Furthermore, the Pauline expression "new creation" (6:15; *kainê ktisis*) should not be contrasted with the "old covenant" of Judaism but with Caesar's alleged "new creation" of the Roman imperial cult.[25] It has been suggested, similarly, that Paul's mention in 1:6 of *heteron euangelion* ("a different," "another," or "the other" gospel) could be a reference to the imperial cult.[26]

What, then, about the references to "special days, and months, and seasons, and years" (4:10; *hêmeras…kai mênas kai kairous kai eniautous*)? It is highly unlikely that they would be references to Passover, Pentecost, and the Feast of Booths (*Sukkot*), quite simply because the Galatians had never been Jews. More likely contexts are the Roman imperial feasts for the divine emperor. Once again, how could the allegation "how can you turn back again" (4:9; *pôs epistrephete palin*) be a reference to Jewish holidays if they had never been Jews? Kahl provides an alternative to the traditional understanding: September 23, the birthday of Augustus, was also celebrated as New Year's Day, and there were other days, months, and years that marked the rhythm of Rome's political, individual, and cosmic life.[27] It is this defiance of previous participation in the imperial religion that probably constitutes the actual storm center of the Galatian correspondence.[28]

All this provides us with good arguments for the assertion that the primary context for Paul's Christology in Galatians is not Judaism but Roman imperial monotheism: Judaism was belief in the One God, a God who was Other than Caesar, and Paul's theology concurred with this belief.[29]

However, a lingering question remains to be addressed: If Paul is so upset about the Galatians being too subservient to the Roman Empire, why does he explicitly and repeatedly discuss Jewish circumcision (2:7–9; 5:6, 11; 6:15; *peritomê*) in this epistle? Some of the Galatians had obviously done something that provoked him to call them "foolish Galatians" (3:1; *ô anoêtoi Galatai*).

In order to read Paul's epistle as firmly situated in the Roman Empire, one has to sense the profound vulnerability and victimhood of the Christ followers in Galatia. Mark D. Nanos calls them "outgrouped quasi-insiders."[30] They used to prove their loyalty to the emperor by taking part in the various expressions of this cult, but as Christ followers, Paul wanted them to abstain from these events. Now he is upset because the Galatians are choosing to accommodate to Roman imperial dominance by adopting an ethnic identity tolerated by the Romans: becoming circumcised Jews.

In short, Kahl argues that the lived context for Galatians is not a controversy over Torah observance between Jews and Christians—or Jewish Christians and Gentile Christians. Instead, the background is a Roman Galatian clash because of the demands of Roman imperial ideology: "law" in this context refers to *Roman* law; "good works" are deeds for the *Roman* emperor and for *Rome*, in order to gain favors, status, and security.

Furthermore, and this might have been the most challenging aspect of their faith, they were Christ-believing Galatians in a *Roman* Empire, who believed that the God of *Israel* had raised Jesus of Nazareth, a Jew who had been crucified by the *Romans*. This belief highlights the dynamic relationship between the Roman Empire and Paul's epistles and, indeed, the entire New Testament. The crucified Jew Jesus belonged to the transgressors of Roman law. By raising Jesus, the one God of Israel has openly challenged the singular power of the divine Caesar to define law and to impose death, and to restore life and righteousness to the vanquished at his discretion. This defied the codes of patronage and honor.[31]

For centuries, the Galatians had been the exemplary symbol of "lawlessness" in their rebellion against Rome. Was the Christ cult at this moment on its way to being understood as a new insurgency against Rome? In short, what Kahl is suggesting is that it was not fear of Jewish piety but of Roman reprisals that motivated some of the Galatians to impose the decisive cut into the flesh. Hence, the messianic identity of the Galatians is challenged, and they are pushed to clarify who they really are: either circumcised Jews or uncircumcised non-Jews, having to return to recognizable civic patterns of behavior shared by the rest of the non-Jews.[32] Enjoying limited autonomy, Jews were given permission to live, within bounds, according to their own law, the Torah. They were not necessarily respected, but they were tolerated, and it was this status that the Galatians wanted to attain. Kahl calls it "a flexible and relatively reliable mode of accommodation and inclusion."[33] Jews were, to a certain extent, safeguarded by Rome, but the Pauline interpretations and activities among Gentiles constituted illicit associations and unlicensed "atheism."[34]

Circumcision would not turn them into Jews "again" (*palin*), quite simply because they had never been Jews before, but it would, according to Paul, undo their being the nations (*ta ethnê*) who believed in Christ, which was a sign of the new creation, *kainê ktisis*. So as not to succumb to imperial ideology and idolatry, Paul wanted the Galatians to remain what he believed them to be: a new type of "transnational" obedience that included Jews and non-Jews alike. But the Romans saw it differently: they saw non-Jews behaving like Jews, which was disturbing, and according to Romans' way of remembering and describing history ("historiography"), they saw a typically Galatian behavior reemerging.[35] Circumcision, in this context, was prompted by political realism, not necessarily an expression of faithful, theologically motivated Jewish Torah obedience.[36]

The law that Paul confronts is not Jewish law per se but Jewish law in enforced servitude to Roman law. That is what makes Paul ferocious, and that is the raison d'être for his epistle. He is convinced that Christ belief cannot be combined with the Roman imperial cult because ultimately the Pauline gospel protests against Caesar worship. Hence, the antithesis—because there really is a fundamental clash in this epistle—is not between Jesus Christ and a Jewish God but between God-in-Christ and the "divine" Caesar.[37]

The center of attention in Kahl's rereading of Galatians is the exposure of two profoundly vulnerable persons: on the one hand, *the dying Gaul* in the legendary statue, and, on the other hand, *the dying Jesus of Nazareth*, a pious Jew—one of many—who was crucified by the Romans on a cross, and who is portrayed in churches and in Christian art all over the world. In less than two decades after the Epistle to the Galatians was written, Rome had, once again, defeated the Galatians, with Nero's victory over Gaius Julius Vindex in 68 CE, and later also the rebellious Jews in the year of 70

CE. This triumph over the Gauls and the Jews consolidated the Roman Empire.[38] Hence, less than two decades after Paul had written this letter, the Romans under General Titus would conquer Jerusalem, destroy its temple, and kill and sell into slavery hundreds of thousands of Jews. On top of its ruins, Emperor Hadrian would build a new city, into which Jews were forbidden to enter. Within three centuries, not only did Christianity become legal, but it also became the state religion and eventually even the only legal religion. The only exception to this rule was Judaism, which remained technically "a licit religion" (Latin: *religio licita*), but in practice it was despised and shunned. Indeed, it seems that "the Jew" in Christian imagination and collective memory replaced "the Gaul" as the prototype for the rebellious other, who had to be subjugated, humiliated, and conquered, or, as we saw in the first interpretation of 4:30, "drive[n] out [as] the slave." The *galatomachy* (the battle against the Galatians) was eventually transmuted into *Judeophobia* (a fear of what is considered too "Jewish"), generating a constant urge to combat "Judaizers" who in every age threatened to taint the essence of pure Christianity.

Three readings have been presented in this chapter. The first line of thought was a traditional and triumphalist reading. For two millennia, it has been conventional wisdom to view Paul's epistle to the Galatians as a text that encourages the Christian reader to cast out all that is Jewish, which, by definition, is invalid, burdensome, and enslaving. This first reading is noticeably *anti-Jewish* and is an expression of a time-honored legacy in Christian biblical interpretation: Judaism is a problem, and Christianity is the solution to that problem.

The second reading focuses on the persecuted. It was pointed out that, although Paul uses the Greek verb for "being an allegory" in 4:24, strictly speaking, the text is not in the genre of an allegory but a parable. The words "and so it is now also" in 4:29 give a starting point for understanding its message: the readers of the parable were at risk of being persecuted, and this is the issue that Paul wants to address. The second interpretation perceives the parable of Sarah and Hagar as an expression of an *intra-Jewish* debate, which addresses this question: Are Christ followers a part of the Jewish people and, therefore, expected to live a genuinely halakhic life, or are they, as Paul argues, an eschatological manifestation of the ingathering of the Gentiles, which means that they should continue living their lives as Gentiles?

The third reading highlights the issues of the vanquished peoples in the Roman Empire. This interpretation underscores the fact that Christ followers in a Roman world were at risk of being persecuted by the Romans. Hence, the third interpretation detects the inevitable *anti-Roman* implications of a Christ-believing life in Galatia in the 50s CE. We have seen that Gaul and Galatia for centuries had been for Romans the primordial Other to be humiliated and defeated. Seen in this light, the Pauline teaching in Galatia inevitably created a stir. What were Christ followers expected to do and not to do? Kahl argues that Paul did not criticize his antagonists from a "Christian" point of view because of their "Judaizing" apostasy. Rather, he criticized them from a Jewish messianic viewpoint of an idolatrous apostasy in bowing to Rome.[39] This third interpretation, which could be seen as an extension of the second reading, emphasizes that Jewish monotheism constituted a problem for Rome. Jews had been tolerated, but the status of the new Christ-believing group of Gentiles in Galatia was yet to be determined. Furthermore, Jesus was executed by the Roman Empire. Any proclamation that he had been raised by God could be interpreted as an insult to the emperor and a challenge to his authority. The proclamation in the Roman Empire of the crucified and raised Jesus of Nazareth may have amounted to sedition. Paul's theology presented Jesus as the Son of God, and this was a threat to the imperial religion of Rome, in which the emperor was divine.

The third reading of Galatians underlines the cruel nature of the Roman oppression, indeed, of any occupation—there is no such thing as a benevolent or benign occupation. It seeks to foster *sympathy* with oppressed people and peoples, but without resorting to traditional Christian *supersessionism* as in the first interpretation of Galatians 4:21—5:1. This interpretation opens the path to a profound sympathy with oppressed people and peoples in the past as well as today.

26
"THE ISRAEL OF GOD" IN GALATIANS
Gal 6:16

The cornerstone in supersessionist theology is the claim that the church has replaced the Jewish nation as God's people, and that the church is now "the new Israel." Although scriptural support is scarce for such a position, it is often promoted as being biblical and classic. This prompts us to explore the only instance in which the expression "the Israel of God" (Greek: *ho Israêl tou Theou*) occurs in the New Testament: Galatians 6:16. Susan Grove Eastman described it as having a "puzzling syntax":

> *kai hosoi tô[i] kanoni toutô[i] stoichêsousin, eirênê ep' autous kai eleos kai epi ton Israêl tou Theou.*
> (And for as many as will walk according to this rule: peace upon them, and mercy, and upon God's Israel.)[1]

The word *kai* occurs three times in this verse, and the key question is how the last *kai* is to be interpreted: is it "and" (continuative), or "also" (additive), or "even" (emphatic), or "namely" (explicative)? The answer to that question decides whether Paul in this verse is referring to *one* (if it is explicative) or *two* groups (if it is continuative, additive or emphatic). If it is only one group, then those who walk according to the Pauline instructions do seem to constitute "the Israel of God." But what if Paul is referring to two different groups here? Three interpretations will be presented and discussed.

(a) The church is the new Israel: Although this undoubtedly is the majority interpretation, both in history and in biblical scholarship, we must point out that no other texts equate the church and Israel before Justin

Martyr's *Dialogue with Trypho*, and that text was written more than a century after Paul's epistle.[2] Hence, nowhere else in the New Testament—neither in the Gospels, nor in Acts, nor in the epistles, nor in Revelation—is the church described as "Israel," which should give us pause. E. P. Sanders, undoubtedly a trailblazer in this field of studies, points out how idiosyncratic this verse is if interpreted as a majority of scholars have assumed:

> Thus, although Paul thought of the members of the church as heirs of the promises to Israel, he did not (*with one exception* [i.e., Gal 6:16]) give them the name. The title "Israel of God" would be truly appropriate only when all the physical descendants of Jacob had been accounted for, at the end, when the polar distinction "my people" and "not my people" would cover everyone. Meanwhile, however, we must recognize the extent to which the church constituted, in Paul's view, a third entity, which stood over against both the obdurate part of Israel and unconverted Gentiles.[3]

The majority view maintains that in Galatians 6:16 Paul is referring to only one group that is described in two ways: Paul is only addressing the loyal Paulinists in Galatia—that is, those who live according to the set of rules that he has presented—and *they* are now "the Israel of God."

However, as we have seen, there are several obstacles to such an assertion. Firstly, the *contextual* argument: there are no parallels to this theology anywhere else in the New Testament. In other words, apart from this single verse, the term "Israel" always refers to the Jewish people: Israel is Israel "according to the flesh" (*kata sarka*; cf. Rom 9:3 and 1 Cor 10:18).[4] As S. Lewis Johnson writes, "Is not that very relevant to the interpretation of Galatians 6:16?"[5] Secondly, the *historical* argument: it takes more than one hundred years for Christian writers to equate the church and Israel. This suggests that there *are* non-supersessionist readings of the Pauline epistle. To explore such readings is the main purpose of the present book. And, thirdly, the *grammatical* argument: the mainstream interpretation requires that the last *kai* in Galatians 6:16 is understood in the explicative sense—that is, "namely," which is extremely unusual. S. Lewis Johnson concludes that it is "highly unlikely" that this interpretation is to be preferred grammatically.[6]

To recap, according to the first interpretation—which in history has been the majority position—"the Israel of God" here refers to the church. However, is it not awkward to build an ecclesiology on this single verse, given that its syntax is puzzling and that we have no parallels in earliest

Christianity before the writings of Justin Martyr, written down more than a century after Paul's epistle? S. Lewis Johnson's verdict over the first interpretation is quite stern:

> If there is an interpretation that totters on a tenuous foundation, it is the view that Paul equates the term "the Israel of God" with the believing church of Jews and Gentiles. To support it, the general usage of the term *Israel* in Paul, in the NT, and in the Scriptures as a whole is ignored. The grammatical and syntactical usage of the conjunction *kai* is strained and distorted—and the rare and uncommon sense accepted when the usual sense is unsatisfactory—only because it does not harmonize with the presuppositions of the exegete.[7]

With these harsh words ringing in our ears, we proceed to the second interpretation.

(b) Jewish Christians are "the Israel of God": In two articles, the first published in 1949 and the second in 1950, Gottlob Schrenk argued that the term "the Israel of God" refers to Jewish Christianity.[8] Hence, the third *kai* in Galatians 6:16 does indeed distinguish between two groups (as *kai* usually would do): Paul is first addressing *Gentile* Christ followers and then *Jewish* Christ followers (who are called "the Israel of God"). If this is correct, it means that the distinction between Israel and Gentiles is still valid and meaningful to Paul, despite—or should we say because of?—his belief in Jesus as the Christ.

In Romans 11:5, Paul is referring to "a remnant that was chosen by grace" (*leimma kat' eklogên charitos gegonen*). Is this a parallel to this interpretation of Galatians 6:16—that is, that Jewish Christians are "the [remaining] Israel of God"? Against this assertion, however, it could be argued that Paul's rationale when writing this is that God has *not* rejected his people (v. 2; cf. 1 Sam 12:22 and Ps 94:14). Why would the Jews cease to be "the Israel of God" if God has *not* rejected the people of Israel? However, what we do find in the Pauline epistles are statements that claim that within Israel there are those who believe and behave in a way that is more in accordance with what is expected of Israel (to wit, according to Paul), perhaps most clearly in Romans 9:6: "For not all Israelites truly belong to Israel [*ou gar pantes hoi ex Israêl houtoi Israêl*]." But this hardly amounts to an advanced supersessionist theology that claims that Israel has been replaced by the church. As Charles E. B. Cranfield writes:

But this does not mean what it has so often been taken to mean—that only part of the Jewish people is the elect people of God. Paul is not contriving to disinherit the majority of his fellow-Jews, to write a charter of Christian anti-semitism....All Jews, *pantes hoi ex Israêl*, are members of God's elect people. This is an honour—and it is no small honour—of which no member of this race can be deprived.[9]

Hans Dieter Betz, who questions Schrenk's hypothesis, points out that, at the time of Paul, the demarcations between various groups were most probably not as distinct as we often tend to take for granted,

that at the time of Galatians the borderline between Christianity and Judaism was not yet clearly drawn, that a diversity of Christian and Jewish movements and groups tried to come to grips with the issue of Christ, and that the claim expressed in "Israel of God" could be made by different groups at the same time. Thus, Paul extends the blessing beyond the Galatian Paulinists to those Jewish-Christians who approve of his *kanôn* ("rule") in v 15.[10]

(c) Paul refers to both Christ-believing Gentiles (not Israel) and Jews (Israel): Since Paul nowhere else refers to Christ followers as "the Israel of God," is it, then, not likely that this term here quite simply refers to the people of Israel, be they Christ followers or not? In other words, is Paul here referring to—indeed, *blessing*—two distinctly different groups: first Gentile Christ followers and then also the Jewish people? S. Lewis Johnson, one of those who argues that the term refers to the "all Israel" of Romans 11:26, locates the blessing in the future.[11]

Eastman, too, maintains that two groups are addressed in this verse, but her interpretation is slightly different: she argues that he is pronouncing a blessing of "peace" specifically to the former group—the Gentile Christ followers—and a prayer that divine mercy is bestowed on the latter—"the Israel of God."[12]

And so, as he draws his polemical letter to a close, Paul pronounces peace on all those who remain faithful to his vision of the gospel, which makes a new creation in which the distinction between circumcision and uncircumcision no longer matters. But then, precisely because the undoing of that distinction thoroughly shuts the door on Jewish privilege and identity markers, thereby calling Israel's destiny into question, he also prays for God's saving mercy on unbelieving

Israel: "And peace be upon as many as walk in line with this rule, and mercy even upon the Israel of God."[13]

That Paul, who has not forgotten his people, cannot imagine that God would have rejected the chosen people is what Eastman calls the "Jewish horizon to Paul's thought."[14] There are other texts in the New Testament that not only uphold the distinction between Jews and Gentiles but, in addition, address these two groups in different ways. Many are reminded of this dichotomy in the Nunc Dimittis prayer (Luke 2:32):

- a *light for revelation* to the Gentiles and
- for *glory* to your people Israel.

Another example—this time from the Pauline texts—is the paragraph in Romans 15:7–13 in which Paul articulates in what ways a belief in Jesus as the Christ may resonate differently within the two groups:

- For I tell you that Christ became a servant to the circumcised to show God's truthfulness, in order to confirm the promises given to the patriarchs,
- and in order that the gentiles might *glorify God for his mercy*.

Eastman notes that this text connects the Gentiles to the motif of divine mercy: they are the outsiders who have been included by the grace of God.[15] Her suggestion is ingenious, and, although it may not convince everyone, her interpretation is a clear example of the third line of thought presented here—that is, that Paul's expression, "the Israel of God," refers to the Jewish people.[16]

To sum up, several arguments indicate that Galatians 6:16, rather than supporting supersessionism, sustains the fundamental distinction in Pauline theology between Jews and Gentiles. Since Paul sees himself as the apostle to the Gentiles specifically, this is what he emphasizes in his teaching and preaching: his message is about *Gentile inclusion*, not *Jewish exclusion*.

As Shaye J. D. Cohen notes, Paul here may well be adapting a traditional benediction, extending it to become a *double* blessing on *two* groups.[17] In the Psalms, we already find the expression "peace [be] upon Israel" (Hebrew: *shalom 'al Yisrael*; see, e.g., Ps 125:5 and 128:6); Cohen notes its expansion in later liturgy. Hence, for Paul, Israel remains Israel, while the inclusion of the Gentiles is a foretaste of the world to come. Paul has asserted precisely this in the preceding verse, before addressing

Gentiles as well as Jews: "…it is a new creation! As for those [Gentiles] who will follow this rule—peace be upon them, and mercy, and also upon the Israel of God." Paul here *extends* the wishes of peace when *including* non-Jews. He does not *restrict* it by redefining it and thereby *excluding* Israel. In short, it is not about uncircumcision being correct and circumcision being wrong but that both are right for different groups of people. The good news is not that Jews have been *excluded* (one cannot but wonder why that so often has been proclaimed as "the good news") but that those who do not belong to the people of Israel have been *included*, nonetheless still not being Israel.[18]

We thus see that the first interpretation *repudiates* that the Jewish people are Israel, the second interpretation *redefines* the concept of Israel so as to constrict it only to Christ followers, and the third interpretation *reinforces* that Israel remains "the Israel of God," despite various differences, however painful these disagreements may be for Paul, his followers, and his antagonists.

27
"MR. G., TEAR DOWN THIS WALL!"
Eph 2:11–22

When seeking a deeper understanding of the historical and theological development of the earliest Christian movement, it is of utmost importance to recognize that it consisted of two distinct groups: *Jewish* Christ followers and *Gentile* Christ followers.[1] In other words, one group was made up of Jews who were familiar with the Scriptures, most probably had participated in synagogue services all their lives, and may have sacrificed in the temple of Jerusalem at the major holidays of Passover, Pentecost, and the Feast of Booths (*Sukkot*). The other group of Christ followers were Gentiles: non-Jews who had become interested in the Jewish Scriptures, Jewish theological reasoning, and Jewish liturgy. Belief in Jesus as the Christ was their path to the God of Israel. We can cite a well-known verse in the New Testament to describe what these Gentiles surely felt: none of them would have come to the Father except through the Son (cf. John 14:6). Thus *the path to God for Gentile Christ followers was radically different from the path for Jewish Christ followers*. If we ignore this irrefutable fact, we will have difficulties comprehending some of the most fundamental motifs in the New Testament and early Christian writings. No other passage in the New Testament is likely to make this clearer than Ephesians 2:11–22, which uses spatial metaphors when describing how belief in Christ brings people closer to God, as in the thirteenth verse: "But now in Christ Jesus you who once were far off have been brought near by the blood of Christ." This quotation reminds us that the fundamental perspective in the New Testament epistles, and not only in the epistles that are Pauline, is that the ministry, life, death, and resurrection of Jesus is the way God chose to come to Gentiles—that is, non-Jews—and make them people of God.[2]

Today, when the Christian calendar is used in many parts of the world, it is easy to forget that the New Testament was written in a radically different situation. At that time a group of Christ-following Gentiles gathered in communities where *Jewish* texts were read, *Jewish* terminology was used, and *Jewish* holidays probably were celebrated (though perhaps with renewed meaning). The expressions "far off" and "near" were used in Ephesians because *parts of the non-Jewish population were approaching the Jewish faith and the Jewish people.* By reading from the Scriptures and using Jewish terminology, they asserted that God had appeared to the people of Israel in a historically unique way (Deut 7:7f.):

> It was not because you were more numerous than any other people that the Lord set his heart on you and chose you—for you were the fewest of all peoples. It was because the Lord loved you and kept the oath that he swore to your ancestors, that the Lord has brought you out with a mighty hand, and redeemed you from the house of slavery, from the hand of Pharaoh king of Egypt.

It was most likely obvious to the earliest Gentile Christ followers that their faith was intrinsically related to the Jewish people, who had long been in covenant with the God of Israel. To approach the Jewish people was to approach the God of Israel, and to approach the God of Israel was to join with the Jewish people in their worship, albeit without becoming Israel, and certainly not by replacing Israel.

The second chapter of Ephesians is the key text in considering that this experience breached a formerly impenetrable wall. There are many reasons to believe that the epistle is primarily directed toward Gentiles, "who once were far off…[and now had] been brought near by the blood of Christ." In antiquity, as Moshe Halbertal argues, sacrificial offerings brought people closer to God (cf. the verb *li-qrov*, "to come near," "to approach").[3] By using this language, the passage asserts that, likewise, Christ brings Gentiles closer to God.

Now, what is meant by "the dividing wall" (*to mesotoichon tou phragmou*) in Ephesians 2:15? Five interpretations will be presented and discussed.

(a) A fence in the temple: Commentators often advance the interpretation that it represents the fence (Hebrew: *soreg*) in the temple of Jerusalem between the courtyard of the Gentiles and the courtyard of Israel.[4] It was a fence that was ten cubits high (approx. eighty centimeters).[5] If we assert that *to mesotoichon tou phragmou* in Ephesians refers to this *soreg*, we may need to find a better phrase than "dividing wall," because the word *wall* does not bring to mind a fence that is barely a meter tall.[6] An argument

against this interpretation is that the term in Ephesians is not used by the Jewish historian Josephus when he describes the temple of Jerusalem.[7]

According to this first interpretation, "the dividing wall" is not strictly a metaphor but a reference to an actual, physical fence. If Ephesians is a deutero-Pauline epistle (not written by Paul but perhaps by one of his disciples), it may have been written after the fall of the temple in 70 CE, making it highly relevant in this context. Does the author mean that the boundary between Jews and non-Jews was abolished after the destruction of the temple? In Acts 21:28f., Luke writes that there were *reports* that Paul *supposedly* had brought Greeks (i.e., non-Jews) to the temple in Jerusalem. But Luke also states that this was an *incorrect* rumor, as he writes previously in the chapter: "Thus all will know that there is *nothing* in what they have been told about you [i.e., Paul], *but that you yourself observe and guard the law*."[8] Hence, the Lukan understanding of this incident is that Paul did not behave in a manner contrary to the halakhic restrictions in the temple. But perhaps the author of Ephesians, who wrote the epistle several decades after Paul's epistles, interpreted Gentile mission in light of the fall of the temple. Did this author argue that faith in the God of Israel flourished among Jews and Gentiles alike, in spite of the catastrophe in 70 CE? We cannot know. The first line of thought leaves several questions unanswered.

(b) A fence around the Torah: The second interpretation suggests that the "dividing wall" refers to a notion we find in rabbinic literature: "a fence around the Torah" (Hebrew: *seyag la-Torah*).[9] Is the author of Ephesians objecting to the growing attempts of the rabbinical movement to extend the application of the commandments? The rabbinical expression *seyag la-Torah* is unfortunately often misunderstood by Christians, which is rather peculiar, as much of the teaching in the Sermon on the Mount actually could be described as *seyag la-Torah*, that is, an attempt to interpret the commandments maximalistically, such as applying the commandment not to kill *also* to those who are angry at and therefore insult a brother or sister (see chapter 2).[10] Is it really plausible that Ephesians is on a collision course with the Sermon on the Mount? The argument that the author of Ephesians would object specifically to *seyag la-Torah* is unconvincing.

(c) The dividing wall between heaven and earth: A third interpretation is that it refers to an ontological dividing wall between heaven and earth, between the eternal and temporal worlds, between God and humanity.[11] However, this interpretation, too, raises a number of questions. Does the author claim that nothing separates heaven and earth from each other following the life, death, and resurrection of Jesus?[12] Is it plausible that the

author is stating that previously it had not been possible to approach God, that a covenantal relationship with God did not exist when the Scriptures were written down? Is the author really asserting that the psalmists wrote and sang without any theological knowledge of who God is, and that the prophets did not speak on behalf of God? All these questions indicate that this simply is not a convincing interpretation.

(d) The Jewish Law: The fourth interpretation combines the reference to the "dividing wall" with the reference to the Law per se in the following paragraph. In other words, it is asserted that Christ's mission was to abolish the Torah completely, to tear it down as a diving wall could be torn down.[13] This has been a particularly influential interpretation, not least in the Lutheran tradition. The ulterior—and problematic—reasoning is that the greatest mistake a person can make is to believe that the Law can save a person, and that a person can be saved by obeying the Law. One wonders, however, in what way this interpretation can be reconciled with the statement that the message is "peace for those who are near." If the Torah is the fundamental problem of humanity, and if Jesus came to abolish the Torah (and, implicitly, Jewish faith and tradition), how could this possibly be conceived as a message of peace by Jews? Nor would many Jews identify with the description of being "saved" by "observing the commandments." Jews who keep the commandments in the Torah do so because God has sanctified them with the commandments (cf. Hebrew: *qiddeshanu bemitzwotaw*).[14] Hence, this interpretation is also questionable.

Tet-Lim N. Yee argues that *aspects* of the Law that differentiated Jew from Gentile no longer apply. He describes this as a biblically motivated ethnic antagonism:

> What is at stake, however, is not the law *per se* but the law as the Jews had used it to consolidate their Jewish identity....This, the enmity between Jew and Gentile, lies not with the Torah *per se* but with the human attitude that perverted the gifts of God into signs of separation and exclusiveness. However, the law...is now abolished through the death of Christ.[15]

Yee wrote his dissertation for Durham University, where James D. G. Dunn was active for many years. Dunn is the scholar who introduced the "New Perspective on Paul" (see introduction, third challenge). Yee's book extensively expresses Dunn's perspective on the writings and theology of Paul, namely, that Paul objected to the way the Jewish Law put up boundaries that separated Jews from Gentiles.[16] Yee concludes that the death of

Jesus abolishes the Jewish commandments. As we have seen elsewhere, for him Jewish observance of the commandments in the Torah seems to be a problem to solve, not a life to live. Furthermore, this raises the question about every group identity—including that of the Paulinists in the earliest Christian movement—creating some form of boundary to its surroundings. We come to the need for a fifth interpretation.

(e) The wall as a metaphor: The four interpretations above are not convincing. How, then, should we understand the discourse of "the dividing wall?" The fifth and most persuasive interpretation is that the expression truly is a *metaphor*. Now, what is a metaphor? In the words of Nelson Goodman, a metaphor is "teaching an old word new tricks."[17] The phrase "they cried rivers of tears" contains a metaphor (that is, "rivers of tears"). The statement, "The Nile is the world's longest river" does not; nor does the statement, "they shed many tears." "Complaints flood in" is a metaphor, but neither the word *complaint* nor *flood* is. If the Greek expression *to mesotoichon tou phragmou* were simply a reference to the temple of Jerusalem, it would not be a metaphor. If it is an image depicting something else, then it is a metaphor. If it refers to the things that truly divide people, namely, mistrust, enmity, and hatred, then it is a metaphor. This is what the sixteenth verse states explicitly. Enmity (Greek: *hê echthra*) is the true dividing wall between individuals and peoples—and it is much higher than ten hands! The true dividing wall between people is not diversity but intolerance. The greatest obstacles to genuine understanding are not differences but schisms.

A question briefly touched upon above demands a more comprehensive response. What is the meaning of the statement in 2:15: "He has abolished the law with its commandments and ordinances [*ton nomon tôn entolôn en dogmasin katargêsas*]"?[18] The word *nomos* (Law) is used in several ways in the epistles, and its meaning, therefore, has to be established in each and every case. A complicating factor in this case is that it occurs only here in Ephesians. If the epistle is indeed a deutero-Pauline text, we have even less contextual framework because it cannot be read in the light of Pauline epistles such as Romans and Galatians.

But the answer to the question cannot possibly be that all the Scriptures are negated. The earliest Christian movement was not a lawless religion. Quite obviously, even the very first generation of Christ followers held ethical principles.[19] Could it be that the expression "the law with its commandments and ordinances" refers to the commandments that apply *only to Jews*, in other words, the ordinances that theologically excluded Gentiles?

The Gentiles, having been brought near, were no longer excluded by the Scriptures. Through Jesus, the commandments that excluded Gentiles could do so no longer because God had opened a way, as Paul writes in Rom 3:21, "apart from law [*chôris nomou*; or literally 'without law'], as attested by the law and the prophets." Lionel J. Windsor argues that it is "not a claim that the law of Moses has been rendered invalid in all respects. Rather, it is a claim that Christ's death renders unnecessary some of the key functions of the law's commandments as interpreted by Jewish authorities in the first century."[20]

The Greek expression, translated as "dividing wall," is a metaphor. Importantly, the author of Ephesians emphasizes the *enmity* between people as the problem, not the destruction of the temple as a prerequisite for improved relations between Jews and non-Jews.

Yee seems to take for granted that Jewish exclusivism is the main problem, and that it must be broken down and abolished for there to be peace between those who are far off and those who are near. But can we assume that Jewish exclusivism is the main problem? And today, is an alleged Jewish self-confidence the greatest challenge to Christian faith? A renewed understanding of Ephesians 2 is needed. An interesting—and yet rarely cited—parallel is to be found in 2 Baruch. The author of that text is unknown. Writing under the pseudonym of Baruch, who served as a secretary to the prophet Jeremiah, the author places the writing of the text at the time of the destruction of the first temple of Jerusalem, Solomon's temple, in 586 BCE.[21] The passage 2 Baruch 54.3–5 is particularly relevant here, as it reveals yet another possible interpretation of the text on the dividing wall in Ephesians:

> He who reveals to those who fear him what awaits them, so that from here on he will console them, he makes known the mighty deeds to those who do not know—he breaks the barrier [Syriac: *suga*] for those who are not persuaded, and enlightens the darknesses and reveals what is hidden to those who are without blemish, those who have subjected themselves in faith to you and to your Torah.[22]

The text of 2 Baruch was probably written after the fall of the second temple in 70 CE. Albertus Frederik Johannes Klijn suggests that 2 Baruch was written down between 100 and 120 CE, Liv Ingeborg Lied argues that it came about one or two decades after 70 CE, and Matthias Henze asserts that it was written down during the period between the two Jewish revolts against Rome: between the years 70 and 132 CE.[23] In other words, if

Ephesians is deutero-Pauline, the two texts would have been written approximately during the same period. The source of the preserved Syriac manuscript was probably a Hebrew original that was also the source of a paraphrased fragment in Greek found in Oxyrhynchus, Egypt.[24] As a theological response to the destruction of the (second) temple in 70 CE, the book addresses the challenges that faced Jewish societies following that cataclysmic historical event.[25]

It is interesting to note that the author of 2 Baruch writes of a dividing wall that has been torn down, but in this case it is not an alleged Jewish exclusivism that is the problem (as Yee claims is the case in Ephesians); rather, it is people's lack of knowledge, which God will cure by revealing mighty deeds. "You pull down the enclosure *for those who have no experience and enlighten the darknesses*."[26] This motif appears in several texts, for example, in Isaiah 25, as a veil shrouding all the *non-Jewish* peoples, but that shall one day be destroyed.

> On this mountain the LORD of hosts will make for all peoples [*le-khol-ha-'ammim*] a feast of rich food, a feast of well-aged wines, of rich food filled with marrow, of well-aged wines strained clear. And he will destroy on this mountain the shroud that is cast over all peoples [*kol-ha-'ammim*], the sheet that is spread over all nations [*kol ha-goyim*].[27]

Yet again, it is a matter of the nations of the world gaining spiritual enlightenment, not of the covenantal markers of the Jewish people being destroyed.[28] This appears as well in Isaiah 19:24:

> On that day Israel will be the third [*shlishiyah*, "a triad"] with Egypt and Assyria, a blessing in the midst of the earth, whom the Lord of hosts has blessed, saying, Blessed be Egypt my people, and Assyria the work of my hands, and Israel my heritage.

This perspective can be found yet again in sections of Isaiah that were written later, in, for example, 60:1–4:

> Arise, shine; for your light has come, and the glory of the Lord has risen upon you. For darkness shall cover the earth, and thick darkness the peoples [*le-ummim*]; but the Lord will arise upon you, and his glory will appear over you. Nations [*goyim*] shall come to your light, and kings to the brightness of your dawn. Lift up your eyes and look

around; they all gather together, they come to you [*kulam niqbetsu vau lakh*]; your sons shall come from far away [*banayikh merachoq yavou*], and your daughters shall be carried on their nurses' arms."²⁹

The text in Isaiah that is most similar to the one in Ephesians can be found in 57:19: *shalom shalom la-rachoq we-la-qarov, amar Adonay* ("Peace, peace, to the far and the near," says the LORD).³⁰ The message of peace thus applies to *both* those who were once far away *and* those who were already near.

In sum, it is not the theological insights of the Jewish tradition that constitute the theological problem, but the Gentiles' lack of knowledge. The point, then, is not that the Gentile Christ followers are superior to Jews but that the Gentiles through Christ have been granted a covenantal relationship similar to the one the people of Israel already has.³¹

There is a specific difficulty with Ephesians: If this epistle was written by Paul, then it can and should be read in light of his other epistles. If it was not, then we cannot draw parallels in the same way between the genuine Pauline epistles. In New Testament research there is no consensus on the author of Ephesians. As a result, the new models of interpretation generally accepted in the study of the undisputed Pauline epistles have been less applied to Ephesians.³²

The dramatic change is that those who were far off have been brought close—not that those who were close only believed they were although they were not, or that those who were close have now been driven far off. It is interesting to relate the spatial metaphors to the discourse of sacrifice as an act that brings humans *closer to God*—remembering that the author of the Epistle to the Ephesians writes that the Gentiles have been brought near to God "by the blood of Christ." The ministry, life, death, and resurrection of Jesus are compared to the sacrifices in the temple, to that which, during the existence of the temple, brought people close to God. The existential exile of the Gentiles has been replaced by a covenantal relationship: in Christ the Gentiles gain a theological citizenship. The author uses legal language in 2:19: the Gentiles are no longer "strangers and aliens" (*xenoi kai paroikoi*) but "citizens" (*sympolitai*).

The recipients of the epistle are encouraged to no longer live as Gentiles (4:17): "Now this I affirm and insist on in the Lord: you must no longer live as the Gentiles live." In spite of this quite explicit appeal of the author, the epistle has oddly enough often been understood as a call for Jews to no longer live as Jews! But it is not an alleged Jewish exclusivism that separates Jew from non-Jew in Ephesians. No, the epistle's good news is not that Jews have been disinherited but that the Gentiles have become fellow heirs: they are members of the same body, and sharers in the promise in Christ Jesus, through the gospel (cf. 3:6).

By way of summary, a closer analysis of the second chapter of Ephesians has been fruitful for a number of reasons. Firstly, the second chapter in Ephesians is the New Testament text that most explicitly uses *spatial metaphors* when describing how belief in Christ brings Gentiles, who once were far off, near. The epistle is clearly directed primarily to Gentile Christ followers (see, e.g., 4:17: "you must no longer live as the Gentiles live"). It is directed to those who were "aliens from the commonwealth of Israel, and strangers to the covenants of promise." "Now in Christ Jesus," they "who once were far off have been brought near"; that does not mean that everything God previously did for Israel and with Israel is abolished. The author of Ephesians writes of breaking down a dividing wall, obviously a metaphor for the enmity that actually separates people.

Secondly, the author of the epistle uses *sacrificial terminology* to express how the ministry of Christ accomplishes inclusion for those who are far away. Sacrifice is used as a concept because of the importance of the temple of Jerusalem, not because it was a theological obstacle or a manifestation of the enmity between God and humanity. By using the temple metaphor, the author describes the Gentile mission. The Gentiles, who had been far off, are brought near by God through Christ. That is why "the blood of Christ" is mentioned in 2:13. The temple metaphor expresses the ingathering of the Gentiles into the covenant.

Thirdly, the basis of the epistle is *not an antinomian theology*. The similarity to the quoted passage in 2 Baruch is striking. In that text, obedience to the Torah and grief at the fall of the temple are the obvious theological bases. The dividing wall is ignorance; the barrier is a lack of insight.

In this chapter we have seen that two early groups—Jewish Christ followers and Gentile Christ followers—must be kept in mind when interpreting Ephesians. We have argued that the text about the torn-down dividing wall cannot be understood as a rejection and even less as a condemnation of "those who were near"; instead, it is an invitation to those who previously had been "far off." It was their sight—and indeed, insight—that previously had been obstructed by something that could be likened to a dividing wall. When that separating wall or veil of ignorance is taken away, they not only may worship the God of Israel but also learn to respect the covenantal life of the Israel of God.

28

PAUL AND PROFANITY
Phil 3:7–14

In this passage there is a Greek word, the meaning of which is much discussed. Paul writes in the eighth verse that there are things that he regards as *skybala* (singular: *skybalon*) compared to "the surpassing value of knowing Christ Jesus [his]...Lord" (*to hyperechon tês gnôseôs Christou Iêsou tou Kyriou mou*). The word *skybala* is a *hapax legomenon* in the New Testament (i.e., occurring only once), and translators discuss whether it should be translated as "waste" or even "excrement." As a matter of fact, it is a *hapax legomenon* also in the Septuagint: in Sirach 27:4 it says that "When a sieve is shaken, the refuse appears; so do a person's faults [*skybala anthrôpou*] when speaking." Four interpretations will be presented and discussed in this chapter.

(a) Judaism is a revolting religion: For those who want to draw an abysmal gap between Judaism and Christianity, this text has come to play an important role. Using this verse as proof, they assert that Paul finds everything Jewish offensive and even disgusting.[1] Furthermore, they claim that this text demonstrates that, on the road to Damascus, Paul left the Jewish world, converted from Judaism to Christianity, and became a Christian instead of—as before—a Jew. Friedrich Lang, in his article on *skybalon* in the *Theological Dictionary of the New Testament*, states that

> the striving for self-righteousness by one's own achievement is unmasked as *pepoithenai en sarki* [to have confidence in the flesh] (v. 3), as a carnal and worldly enterprise the complete antithesis of faith....To the degree that the Law is used in self-justification, it serves the flesh and is not just worthless but noxious and even abhorrent.[2]

But the problem with these assertions is not only that they are anachronistic (in Paul's time it was not possible to speak of two essentially different religions), but also that Paul immediately before this passage, in exceptionally positive terms, describes his Jewish identity: he is circumcised on the eighth day (i.e., not in his maturity), he belongs to the people of Israel (i.e., he is not a proselyte who has been grafted into the people), and he is of the tribe of Benjamin (i.e., he belongs to the tribe of King Saul); in the matter of Torah interpretation (*kata nomon*) he is a Pharisee (i.e., he is an expert in the Law), and in righteousness according to the Law, he is "blameless" (3:6; Greek: *amemptos*; cf. Hebrew: *tam*; cf. Rom 9:4f.).[3]

In addition to these two arguments—firstly, that it would be anachronistic to assume that Paul is comparing two religious systems, and, secondly, that it does not take into consideration the literary context in Philippians—we can add a third reflection. The word *skybalon* occurs some two hundred times in Greek texts, out of which almost half are found in medical literature. Most importantly, it is not found in comedy, mime, or other genres where one may encounter vulgarity.[4] Hence, is it likely that a word often occurring in texts written by doctors, historians, and philosophers is a swear word or was understood as a rude word?

In short, this suggests that Paul is neither referring to Judaism in toto nor using a word that invokes revolting feelings. Hence, we need to look for alternative interpretations that do better justice to Paul's self-understanding.

(b) Paul—the persecutor became a persecuted person: Peter J. Tomson sees this passage in the third chapter of Philippians as a description between "two phases of his life" that contrast sharply with each other. In Galatians 1:13f. Paul describes the first phase:

> You have heard, no doubt, of my earlier life [*tên emên anastrophên pote*] in Judaism, I was violently persecuting the assembly of God [*tên ekklêsian tou Theou*] and was trying to destroy it. I advanced in Judaism beyond many among my people of the same age, for I was far more zealous for the traditions of my ancestors.[5]

Paul then continues by describing how God, who had set him apart before he was born, called him through his grace, and revealed his Son in him (i.e., in Paul), so that he "might proclaim him among the Gentiles" (v. 16).[6] Thus began the second phase in Paul's Jewish life. Hence, Tomson argues that what Paul is comparing—and indeed contrasting—is, on the one hand, the phase when he was a zealous persecutor, and, on the other hand, his mission to be an apostle to the Gentiles (cf. Rom 11:13 and Gal

2:8). Thus, the extraordinarily strong language in this passage is an expression of Paul's "frank remorse" for his previous behavior. He was turning away from a wrong and wrongheaded manner of life toward his calling in the service of Jesus Christ. He was *rejecting* neither his Jewishness nor his Torah piety, and certainly not the God of Israel. But he *loathed* having been someone who—and according to his own understanding, he went further than any of his contemporaries—persecuted the Christ followers.[7] The strong language he uses reflects what he felt about having been a person who persecuted and destroyed those whom the God of Israel had called. That is why he calls his previous life *skybala*. But he does not despise his Jewish belief—on the contrary, it is his firm conviction that the God of Israel has called him to reach out to the Gentiles.

(c) Paul is comparing what is incomparable: Paul's terminology is taken from two different arenas: partly from the business world, when in verse 7 he describes how an accountant records something as "profit" (*kerdos*) or "loss" (*zêmia*); partly from the sports world, when in verse 14 he writes that he is pressing on toward "the goal for the prize of the heavenly call of God in Christ Jesus." The fact that he compares himself to a runner helps us understand that he wants to focus on one thing and one thing only—that is, what now has become the most important thing in his life: he wants "to know Christ and the power of his resurrection" (v. 10). In comparison, everything else necessarily fades away, not because it is bad but because it is not the most important thing in his life. Indeed, is not his rhetorical strategy, as elsewhere in the New Testament, that he compares the most important thing with something that is *also* significant?[8]

What parallels support this interpretation? At least three can be mentioned: firstly, in general, Christians have not interpreted Jesus's words "Let the dead bury the dead" (Matt 8:22 and Luke 9:60) as a radical distancing from traditional burial customs. Indeed, both Jews and Christians in antiquity were known for showing respect for the dead by giving them a funeral. Even today, it is a great honor for Jews to belong to the *chevrah qadisha* (Aramaic for "holy fellowship"), the group that cares for the dead and prepares them for burial. The point of Jesus's statement is probably that the commandment to live in imitation of Christ is *even more important* than the commandment to honor one's loved ones.

A second example is the statement in Luke 14:26: "Whoever comes to me and does not hate father and mother, wife and children, brothers and sisters, yes, even life itself, cannot be my disciple." Now, if this does not mean that discipleship abrogates even the Decalogue, then it is yet another example of how following Christ is *even more important* than the commandment to honor one's parents.

The third parallel is the Matthean parable about the person who one day finds a precious pearl on the market and thereupon sells everything he owns in order to buy this magnificent pearl (Matt 13:45f.; cf. Gospel of Thomas 76). This parallel from the marketplace may be the most illuminating text of all the three examples. It has already been mentioned that Paul uses the business terms *kerdos* and *zêmia* for "profit" and "loss," so it is not too far-fetched to suggest that Paul considers all his inherited merits not worthless (if so, how could he possibly trade them for what he wanted to acquire?), but rather so precious that he is bold enough to list them in the very sentence in which he expresses his deep desire to live with Christ.

Finally, in the previous chapter in his epistle, Paul encourages his readers to imitate Christ's humility. Possibly quoting a hymn, Paul describes how Christ, "though he was in the form of God, did not regard equality with God as something to be exploited, but emptied himself, taking the form of a slave, being born in human likeness" (2:6f.). The Greek verb behind "emptied himself" (*ekenôsen*; infinitive: *kenoun*) has given name to a theological pattern that is tremendously important in Christological thinking: the *kenosis* (self-emptying) of Christ. Is Paul suggesting, in terms of *kenosis*, that there is a parallel between him and Christ, both self-emptying: Christ of his divine status, and Paul of his Jewish tradition? In the words of Charles A. Wanamaker, "In short, just as Christ divested himself of his claim to equality with God, Paul divested himself of his claim to special status with God through his Jewish identity."[9] If that is correct, he is certainly not likening his Jewish upbringing and the Jewish tradition to something that is meaningless.

(d) Torah and Gospel are not antithetical but chronological: Christopher Zoccali, too, argues that what Paul is indicating in this passage is that "*in comparison to knowing Christ even the most highly regarded things infinitely pale in significance.*"[10] Hence, Paul's comparison rests on an extraordinarily high value placed upon his Jewish identity—not that it would be worthless. That is why Paul poses the question in Romans 3:1: "Then what advantage has the Jew? Or what is the value of circumcision?"—and immediately answers his own question: "Much in every way [*poly kata panta tropon*]." Hence, in one word, what Paul is describing here is not the *abandoning* but the *subordination* and alteration of his Pharisaic-Jewish identity.[11]

However, Zoccali, goes one step further when seeking to understand this Pauline passage. He argues that the Torah plays several roles in Paul's theology. In terms of salvation-history or the divine economy—Zoccali uses both expressions—the Christ event has accomplished the total defeat of sin and death, but that does not imply that the Torah "ceases altogether to play an important role for Jews in particular, and the Christ community collectively."[12] The *telos* of the Torah—the Greek word *telos* in Romans 10:4 is often translated as "end," but it should be translated as "goal"—is "freedom from sin and death, but *clearly not from the Torah itself.*"[13]

What Zoccali is arguing is that the two keywords *Torah* and *euangelion* (gospel) are not *antithetical*—as so often assumed in scholarship and Christian preaching; they are *chronological*, "with the former depending on the advent of the latter for its ultimate fulfillment (cf. Matt 5:17–18)."[14]

Four interpretations have been presented in this chapter. Whereas the first line of thought quite clearly claims that Paul in this passage unambiguously repudiates any inherent value in his Jewish faith, the three other suggestions all have in common that Paul here is not claiming that he has departed from Judaism.[15]

By way of conclusion, it is perhaps a bit ironic that some readers seem to be more concerned about the fact that Paul may be using foul language in this passage than presumably likening the entire Jewish tradition to manure. However, as we have seen, we lack strong arguments for understanding *skybalon* as sheer vulgarity. One cannot help but wonder whether the popular suggestion that Paul here uses an extraordinarily strong word for something that he finds revolting has been triggered by the unlikely presumption that, when comparing Judaism and Christianity, he likens Judaism to manure. The general advice in the New Testament epistles is to abstain from unwholesome speech, as in Ephesians 4:29:

> Let no evil talk [*logos sapros*] come out of your mouths, but only what is useful for building up, as there is need, so that your words may give grace [*charin*] to those who hear.

Indeed, given the importance of food laws (*kashrut*) in an intra-Jewish context, the teaching of Jesus stresses this to an even higher extent: even more important than being careful about what goes into the mouth is to be cautious about what comes out of the mouth (see chapter 9).

29
DID PAUL THE PERSECUTOR ACCUSE THE JEWS OF PERSECUTING?
1 Thess 2:13–16

An overwhelming majority of New Testament scholars consider Paul's first letter to the Christ followers in Thessalonica to be the oldest of all his letters, probably written in 49 or 50 CE, and, hence, the oldest New Testament text. It is also, therefore, the oldest text, preserved to posterity, that gives witness to the history and theology of the very earliest Christ-believing communities.

In the present book it has often been argued that we can detect a trajectory of accumulating anti-Jewish hostility in the Christian movement. Accordingly, in the very earliest text, one ought *not* to find instances of the kind of stereotyping occurring in later texts. However, 1 Thessalonians 2:13–16 seems to counter such an understanding of early Jewish-Christian relations. Hence, interpreting this passage is particularly important when seeking to establish a trajectory of Pauline thought on the topic of Jews and Jewish tradition, from his earliest to his latest writings.

In a research overview, Matthew Jensen argues that this section has received a more thorough examination than any other part of 1 Thessalonians.[1] Much could therefore be said about this passage; the following discussion will have to limit itself to presenting merely four interpretations of 1 Thessalonians 2:13–16.

(a) "The Jews killed the Lord Jesus": It is virtually impossible to disregard the similarities between 1 Thessalonians 2:13–16 and the antisemitic discourse that has been nurtured by elements from the Christian tradition. David Fox Sandmel calls this passage "a succinct summary of classical Christian anti-Judaism."[2] Given the disheartening history of antisemitism in the parts of the world where Christianity has been particularly influential,

this is by no means an overstatement. Indeed, not recognizing the connection seems to amount to taking history—and also what can be learned from history—lightly. Is Paul, then, the father of "classical Christian anti-Judaism?"

Jeffrey S. Lamp points out that the text gives rise to three key questions: (1) Who are "the Jews?" (2) What are the persecutions that are referred to in this passage? (3) What is the wrath that has *eis telos* ("finally," or perhaps "in full measure") come upon "the Jews"?[3] We will discuss these three questions in turn.

Firstly, this passage does seem to be at odds with Paul's understanding of the Jewish tradition and his relation to his own Jewishness; elsewhere he is quite positive toward his Jewish heritage (Gal 1:14 and Phil 3:5f.), and he proudly calls himself a Jew (Gal 2:15 and Rom 11:1). When describing Paul's positive statement in Romans 9 as "passionately solicitous words," Peter J. Tomson labels 1 Thessalonians 2 as a "hostile passage." Between these "two extremes"—those are Tomson's own words—he posits 2 Corinthians 11, "where Paul continues to cling to the importance of his Jewish descent, though with pain."[4] Hence, Paul the Christ follower was and remained a Jew. So why would Paul *the Jew* accuse "the Jews" for killing Jesus? Although a frequent accusation in history, it is not one we find elsewhere in the Pauline epistles. "Nowhere else does Paul write quite like this," as Ernest Best states.[5] Elsewhere, Paul's focus is on the *finality* of the cross event, which is the resurrection, and not on the *causality* of the death of Jesus.[6] Indeed, Judas is not mentioned anywhere in his epistles, and when Paul does discuss the death of Jesus in 1 Corinthians 2:8, he actually states that it was "the rulers of this age" (*tôn archontôn tou aiônos toutou*)—that is, the Romans—who factually killed Jesus. As Richard S. Ascough writes about the passage in 1 Thessalonians: "It remains troublesome, not simply for its seeming promotion of anti-Judaism but its contradiction with other Pauline texts."[7]

Secondly, what about the persecutions? Even if *hoi Ioudaioi* here is to be understood in a geographical and not an ethnic sense—that is, "Judaeans" rather than "Jews"—it is still unclear how this expression could be used to justify persecution of *Judaean* Christ followers—simply because the persecuted were no less Judaean than the persecutors. And why does he not mention anything about his own prehistory as one of the fiercest persecutors of Christ followers, attested both in his own epistles and in Acts, where it is stated that "Saul approved of their killing him" (Acts 8:1)? Certainly, this is a Lukan comment, but it is supported by Paul's own self-critical

Did Paul the Persecutor Accuse the Jews of Persecuting?

reflections in his epistles (e.g., 1 Cor 15:9f., Gal 1:13–23, and Phil 3:5f.). How can one of the fiercest persecutors of Christ followers accuse "the Jews" (or possibly "the Judaeans") for what he, too, previously had done?

Thirdly, what does the text refer to when stating that the divine wrath finally has come upon *hoi Ioudaioi*? The Greek expression *eis telos* (lit. "to [the] end") can be understood in either a temporal or a modal way—that is, either "at the end" or "to the utmost." The text seems to refer to a specific event, but scholars do not agree what that event might be. It may refer to Emperor Claudius's eviction of the Jews from Rome in 49 CE, but that remains a guess. Hence, all these question marks have prompted scholars to look for alternative readings.

(b) The interpolation hypothesis: The single most influential work on this topic was published in 1971. In a seminal article, slightly revised and republished in 1997 in a collection of essays, Birger A. Pearson argued that 1 Thessalonians 2:13–16 was not written by Paul but is, rather, an interpolation.[8] Pearson presents a large number of arguments in order to show that the passage is an addition to the Pauline epistle, of which the following six may be mentioned.[9] (1) The choice of words in the concluding sentence in this passage suggests that the author refers to the destruction of Jerusalem in 70 CE: "but God's wrath has overtaken them at last" (v. 16: *ephthasen de ep' autous hê orgê eis telos*). The verb *ephthasen* is an aorist form of *phthanein* (to happen, to take place); it is likely that it refers to a specific event, something that has already happened and that can be considered to be an expression of *orgê* (wrath) that afflicts the Jewish people *eis telos*. If this expression were not found in a text that is dated to approximately 50 CE, it is quite probable that many historians spontaneously would assume that it is a reference to the catastrophic events in 70 CE. Pearson argues that this proposal is far more likely than it being a theological interpretation of the emperor's decision to expel the Jews from Rome in 49 CE. (2) It has already been mentioned that Paul never accuses "the Jews" of being Christ killers. If a group is to be blamed, it is the Romans: "the rulers of this age" (see 1 Cor 2:8). Indeed, one can go one step further: in 1 Corinthians 11:23 he writes, "On the night when Jesus was betrayed, he took a bread and…" But does this really refer to Judas ("the Jew") as responsible for the death? Because it is not improbable that the Greek word behind "was betrayed" (*paredideto*) here rather ought to be translated as "was handed over [i.e., by God]." As a matter of fact, the verb occurs twice in this sentence, and in the other instance it means "to hand over"—that is, the tradition that Paul has received and also faithfully handed over (*paredôka*) to other

Christ followers. This makes the text even less relevant as a parallel to 1 Thessalonians 2:15. (3) It has also been pointed out that Paul calls himself a "Jew" and an "Israelite." In his letters he never calls himself a "Christian." Although Paul disagrees with many of his fellow Jews, he remains a Jew: he looks upon himself as a *Jewish* apostle to the Gentiles. Why, then, would he accuse "the Jews" for the death of Jesus and for persecutions of Christ followers? (4) Pearson states that there is no evidence that Jews persecuted Christians between 44 and 66 CE. Hence, if this section were Pauline, it would be the only evidence of such an extensive persecution perpetrated by "the Jews," and that they would be "against every person" (*pasin anthrôpois enantiôn*). (5) Pearson points out that the transition from verse 12 to verse 17 is unproblematic. In an article on the linguistic evidence for the interpolation hypothesis, Daryl Schmidt states that verses 13–16 neither fit well into 1 Thessalonians nor into Pauline thought in general. He argues that the section intrudes into the overall structure of the whole letter. Hence, the linguistic evidence suggests that it is not written by the same author as the rest of the letter; rather, it is built around a conflation of Pauline expressions.[10] (6) Pearson also argues that the introduction to the letter (1:2) and this passage (2:13) are strikingly similar. This supports the hypothesis that verses 13–16 are an interpolation by someone who wanted to copy Paul's way of writing. (On the other hand, the fact that a passage in a Pauline epistle bears Pauline features could, of course, be an indication that it is Pauline. But what Pearson suggests is that it is likely that someone imitated the Pauline style.)

(7) To Pearson's solid arguments an additional can be added, which certainly weighs no less heavily than those already stated. The question has already been posed above: has Paul completely forgotten that he himself once was one of the most fierce opponents of the Christ-believing movement? In Galatians 1:13f. he writes that he "was violently persecuting [*ediôkon*] the assembly of God and was trying to destroy it [*eporthoun*]."[11] He describes himself as more zealous (*zêlôtês*) than anyone else.

Pearson has put forth a series of strong arguments in favor of the interpolation hypothesis, and other scholars have continued the discussion and refined the arguments. Jensen summarizes the discussion by stating that there are four arguments in favor of the interpolation hypothesis—that is, form-critical/literary, grammatical/syntactical, historical, and theological. He states that "none are without weaknesses."[12] Although a growing number of scholars seem to be convinced by the arguments when they are considered as a whole, there are other scholars who interpret this passage as an integral part of Pauline thought.[13] This takes us to our next interpretation.

(c) A relevant Jewish parallel? Lamp has analyzed parallels between the concluding words in 1 Thessalonians 2:16 ("and the wrath of God has come over them to the end") and *Testament of Levi*, a Jewish text that has been transmitted and reworked by the church. Its sixth chapter retells the story in Genesis 34 of the rape of Dinah and the vengeance taken on Shechem and his people on the third day when the men were recovering from their circumcision:

> But I knew that God's sentence was for evil upon Shechem, because they wanted to do to Sarah just as they did to Dinah, our sister, but the Lord prevented them. And likewise, they persecuted Abraham, our ancestor, when he was a stranger, and they trampled the flocks against him while they were pregnant, and they exceedingly mistreated Jeblae,[14] who was born in Abraham's house. And, indeed, likewise they do to all strangers, seizing their women with force and banishing them. *But the Lord's wrath has come upon them.*[15]

Lamp argues that a parallel is also the fact that the entire city was punished for Shechem's rape of Dinah: "The reckoning of culpability was made on the basis of corporate identification."[16] Lamp suggests that Paul is making a similar, generalized statement of culpability. Hence, Lamp argues that Paul,

> rather than engaging in an indiscriminate and emotional anti-Jewish polemic, is making a reasonable—though passionately convinced— assessment of the generally negative Jewish response to God's work in Jesus Christ and continuing activity through the ministry of the apostles. This opposition has reached the point where God's wrath in judgment has come upon the Jews finally and decisively…the use of generalizing language neither consigns all individuals within the group "the Jews" to perdition nor implies that all individuals within this group are guilty of any or all points of Paul's indictment against any group.[17]

However, Lamp's article does not give an exhaustive answer to the question why Paul, who identified as a Jew, and who, in addition, had been one of the fiercest persecutors of the Christ-believing community, can accuse "the Jews" for this very persecution. Nor is it clear why we do not have any parallels in the Pauline epistles to the accusation that "the Jews killed the Lord Jesus." But the parallels between 1 Thessalonians 2:16 and *Testament of Levi* 6.11 do indeed point in the direction of interpreting the expression "but God's wrath has overtaken them at last" as something of a proverbial saying, which is not necessarily to be taken literally, and this takes us to the fourth and final reading of this text.

(d) Is it a rhetorical hyperbole? If this passage is indeed authored by Paul, how are we to understand its generalizations about "the Jews"? It has been stated several times in this discussion that the author (allegedly Paul) does not include himself in this category in this text, although he does so in other letters. Elsewhere, he defines himself as a "Jew" (Gal 2:15), "of the people of Israel" (Phil 3:5), and as an "Israelite" (Rom 11:1). In other words, *Ioudaioi* cannot simplistically be translated as "Jews" here. One is reminded of how the word is used in the Gospel of John where Jews can be afraid of "the Jews" (7:13, 9:22, 19:38, and 20:19; see introduction, second challenge). Peter J. Tomson, who claims that it is advisable to read the passage as an authentic Pauline statement ("except perhaps for the final part"), suggests that Paul is here using "existent polemic expressions in an attempt to encourage the church of Thessalonica; they are being persecuted just as the prophets who spoke in Jesus' name had been."[18]

Now, if the historical Paul is the author of this passage, (1) he uses the word *Ioudaios* in an astounding way; (2) he refers to a transformative tragedy that had recently afflicted the Jewish people; and (3) he is silent over his own rage against Christ followers only a few years earlier.[19] Abraham J. Malherbe writes that "Paul is highly polemical....It is the nature of polemic to verge on vituperation and hyperbole."[20] He refers to Carol J. Schlueter, who argues that Paul's exaggeration should be termed "polemic hyperbole."[21]

A hypothetical example may illuminate the remarkable hyperbole in the passage in 1 Thessalonians: How are we to interpret a statement by an American claiming that it was "the Americans who killed Abraham Lincoln"? To what extent is this an intelligible statement, given that Abraham Lincoln was an American—and that all but one American did *not* kill the president? And how does the person who states this relate to being an American?

In conclusion, this passage is indeed a *crux interpretum*. Is it an interpolation as many scholars argue? Or is it a genuine Pauline statement? If we prefer the latter alternative, we need to pose the question whether Paul has completely forgotten that he himself was once one of the most violently

Did Paul the Persecutor Accuse the Jews of Persecuting?

passionate persecutors of the Christ followers in Judaea. Is it a rhetorical hyperbole about "the Jews," authored by Paul, the Jewish apostle to the Gentiles? We have no conclusive answers to these questions, and, as Jensen states, "this debate will continue until a definitive work comes to hand."[22]

Until then interpreters need to take into consideration that this is either a non-Pauline interpolation (not reflecting Pauline theology) or a Pauline polemical hyperbole. As such, it does not refer to all Jews (since Jesus was a Jew, he himself was a Jew, and many Christ followers were Jews), and it does not reflect his overall understanding of the cause for the death of Jesus, who was executed by "the rulers of this age" (i.e., the Romans) and perhaps even handed over to them by God (1 Cor 11:23; see chapter 17). John C. Hurd, not convinced by the interpolation hypothesis, argues that in this early epistle, Paul was "ahead of his time," in the sense that some decades later similar anti-Jewish statements would be more prevalent: "But…it is my conviction that there is evidence that Paul grew in his appreciation of the wideness of God's love and came to hope for the inclusion of all men in God's salvation."[23] Hence, Hurd suggests, on the one hand, that Paul here gives vent to a theology that eventually would become widespread in the Christian tradition, and, on the other hand, that, later in life, Paul himself articulated a far less hostile theology. In other words, whereas it is the young Paul who has been more influential in this respect, the more mature Paul would have distanced himself both from the anti-Judaism of later times and from the line of thought in his very own epistle.

It has already been mentioned that David Fox Sandmel sees in this passage "a succinct summary of classical Christian anti-Judaism: the Jews killed Jesus, persecuted his followers, and threw them out of the synagogues; God has therefore rejected and punished them." It is impossible not to see the connection between what is stated in 1 Thessalonians 2:13–16 and accusations against the Jewish people in history up until today. Interpreters of the New Testament need to take this into consideration. Several suggestions have been presented in this chapter: the interpolation hypothesis, the intra-Jewish apocalyptic framework, and the importance of recognizing the characteristics of rhetorical hyperbole. If it is indeed a Pauline passage, it ought to be read in the light of other Pauline texts. Leaving vindication to God, and God alone, Paul writes in Romans 12:19–21, "Beloved, never avenge yourselves.…Do not be overcome by evil, but overcome evil with good."[24] Rabid antisemites need to search elsewhere for a rationale for their hateful speech and vicious acts.

30
WHAT ARE THE MEMBERSHIP REQUIREMENTS FOR "THE SYNAGOGUE OF SATAN"?

Rev 2:9 and 3:9

A well-known request in the last book in the New Testament is that readers be either "hot" (*zestos*) or "cold" (*psychros*), not "lukewarm" (*chliaros*) (Rev 3:15f.). Indeed the very book in which this statement is found has seldom been read in a lukewarm manner by Christians. Because of its apocalyptic discourse, similar to Daniel and parts of Ezekiel in the Hebrew Bible, it is either "hot" (i.e., often read and quoted, and at the very center of one's often apocalyptic theology) or "cold" (i.e., almost completely ignored, due to its pronounced apocalypticism).

In this chapter, the very last in the present work, the expression "the Synagogue of Satan," occurring twice in Revelation, will be discussed. This phrase, as well as the expression "those who say that they are Jews and are not," appears twice in the book in describing two different situations. Claudia Setzer therefore draws the conclusions that they were "slogans" in their historical context.[1]

The expression "Synagogue of Satan" has been used in a figurative sense as an epithet for forms of Christianity that numerous other Christians find despicable; antisemites have written these words on the doors and walls of synagogues; these words have been shouted at Jews, be they secular or religious; and, since the expression occurs in the New Testament, it is also regularly and solemnly read in some churches.[2] All this constitutes the rationale for and the importance of studying the expression.

Firstly, an initial observation: it is intriguing that the Greek word *synagōgē* is translated in different ways depending on the context in the New Testament. In James 2:2, there is a discussion about persons of different social status walking into a *synagôgê*. This is often translated as "if a person…comes into your assembly," "meeting" or "congregation," thereby helping the readers to approach the text with an *intra muros* perspective—that is, it is a text that has to do with the Jesus movement (which is correct, since it is part of a letter written by and for Christ followers). However, in Revelation 2:9 and 3:9, the very same word—*synagôgê*—is typically not translated but merely transcribed, which gives the reader the impression that it is a reference to something that has to do solely with Judaism, situated outside the Jesus movement. Three interpretations will be presented and discussed below.

(a) The supersessionist interpretation: The first reading argues that what is referred to is what we today know as two different religions: Judaism and Christianity—and that Christianity has replaced Judaism. The implication is that Jews are no longer Jews. In the classic *Letters to the Seven Churches in Their Local Setting*, Colin J. Hemer writes:

> The simplest explanation of "those who say they are Jews and are not" (Rev. 2.9) is that which identifies them with the Jewish community in Smyrna *per se*, which preserved its identity and claimed to constitute exclusively the people of God.…[The author] insists that the true people of God is a spiritual nation, not an ethnic group. The Christians were now the true Jews; those who maintained a racial separation had rejected the Christ, according to John, and were of Satan.[3]

In short to be a Jew in the traditional sense, taking for granted that Jews are those who belong to the Jewish people, is to be "of Satan," and they no longer have the right to call themselves Jews.

(b) Christians were persecuted by Jews—and Revelation responds to this: The second interpretation—which is not so much an alternative interpretation as a rationale for what the previous interpretation suggests that John claims—emphasizes that Revelation was written when Christians were being brutally persecuted, possibly during the reign of Emperor Nero (54–68 CE) or more probably Emperor Domitian (81–96 CE).[4] What if some Jews took part in these persecutions? Hence, Robert Henry Charles writes, "The persecution with which the Church is here threatened shows that the *Jews* are *acting in concert with the heathen authorities*."[5] Similarly, George Bradford Caird writes that "the Christians have been subjected to active hostility…instigated by the Jews.…The Jews of Philadelphia have rejected the Messiah, thereby forfeiting their right to be called Jews."[6]

David Frankfurter correctly points out that such apologetic justification for Revelation's discourse has had "the unfortunate effect of blaming Jews as well as Romans for persecutions of Christians. The text's criticism of 'so-called Jews' and their 'synagogues of Satan'…has typically been taken as referring to real Jews who, it follows, were persecuting John's 'Christians.'"[7] In other words, scholarship has turned the text's "vindictive fantasy into righteous political critique."[8]

Time and again, it has been pointed out in the present volume that the consequence of this bias is that the violent discourse in the New Testament texts is not nuanced but legitimized by an alleged persecution *by Jews*. In this sense, the reading strategies of Revelation are related to the Gospel of John, which also contains the word *Jews*—but with one important difference: "the Jews" in the Fourth Gospel are probably Jews who do not believe in Jesus of Nazareth as the divine Logos. In contrast, according to the conventional interpretation at least, those who are disparaged in Revelation 2:9 and 3:9 are those who merely claim to be Jews but, in the author's judgment, are no longer Jews because they do not believe in Jesus. Hence, John the Evangelist and John of Patmos seemingly use the word *Jew* in two different ways, as D. Moody Smith points out:

> *Revelation*, interestingly enough, reflects less hostility toward Jews than does John's Gospel. The term *Ioudaioi* appears only twice in *Revelation* (2:9; 3:9), in both cases in an indirectly positive sense. That is, members of the "synagogue of Satan" are said to claim to be Jews although in reality they are not. The presumption is that it is good to be a Jew. "Jew" is still used in a positive sense, even as it is in Paul's *Letter to the Romans* (2:17, 28, 29; cf., 3:1).[9]

Hence, the second line of thought seems to be too apologetic, which should always give us pause. And there are critical questions to pose to the first interpretation, which forms the basis for the second. Is it really consistent with what we know about the early Christ-believing movement? It seems anachronistic that John of Patmos would consider "non-Christian Jews" to be so wrong that they would cease to be ethnic Jews. As Setzer points out: "Normally 'Jew' is not a particular title of honor in early Christian literature. It would be more characteristic of early Christians to say others are not true Israelites, true Hebrews, or true descendants of Abraham (Phil 3:5; Rom 9:6)."[10] Furthermore, Frankfurter asks whether it is plausible that John of Patmos is pitting himself against the Jewish community as radically as against the Roman Empire.[11] If not, we need to proceed to the third interpretation.

(c) Critique of those who claim to be Jews: David Frankfurter argued that, when studying this biblical text, scholarship has not taken into consideration the extent to which the Jesus movement was an entirely *intra-*Jewish sectarian movement: "if we qualify 'Jewish' to indicate a range of *practices*, then the outlines of conflict around John of Patmos begin to emerge with more precision."[12] Frankfurter argues that John identifies "the so-called Jews" not with the Smyrnaean and Philadelphian Jews *outside* the Jesus movement but rather with a constituency *within* the Jesus movement who were claiming the label "Jew" in a manner that John found illegitimate.[13] Frankfurter asserts that the real Jews are those who, like John of Patmos himself, followed a strict, priestly interpretation of *halakhah*, especially with respect to dietary laws (2:14 and 20) and sexual purity laws (2:2–22, 14:4 and 22:14f.).

According to this line of thought, the persons in the texts who are not Jews—although they themselves assert that they are Jewish—are those Gentile Christ followers who claim an affiliation with Judaism *without being Jewish*, and *without living a Jewish life*.[14] One example may suffice: in Revelation 2:14 and 20, John accuses his opponents of eating meat sacrificed to idols. The same question is discussed by Paul, but he reaches a different conclusion (see, e.g., 1 Cor 8). John is criticizing Gentiles for laying false claim to some type of "Judaism." Purity is, Frankfurter suggests, "the arbiter of the sainthood he is encouraging among the Jesus-believers in his orbit."[15]

In other words, it is quite possible that this text is castigating pagan Christ followers who claimed to be Jewish without being ethnic Jews. This is a line of thought that also has implications for Jewish-Christian relations today. Do these two passages in this biblical book actually criticize those who blur the distinction between Jews and non-Jews, more exactly those who claim to be "the true Israel" or "the new Israel"—without being Jewish? The reason for claiming to be a Jew may be that these Christ followers sought to avoid persecution, since Judaism was a *religio licita* (permitted religion), and Christianity—if that terminology be used at this early stage—was not. To put it bluntly, those who persecuted Christ followers were not Jews (as suggested in the previous interpretation, *[b]* above), but representatives of the Roman Empire.

If Frankfurter is correct, then there is a considerable tension in this regard between the theologies of John of Patmos and Paul of Tarsus. Now, the fact that one can find a wide variety of theological positions in the New Testament is not a new observation: attitudes of either *submission* to the ruler who "beareth not the sword in vain" (Paul in Rom 13:4, the famous expression in the King James Version) or *insubordination* against a persecuting, satanic power (John of Patmos) are often referred to in these discussions.[16] Another well-known example is the tension between Paul and James when they describe the intrinsic relation between faith and deeds: Paul argues that deeds without faith are insufficient (Rom 4:1–6), and James, that faith without deeds is dead (2:17).[17] If Frankfurter's thesis is accurate, he points to yet another example of the tensions within the New Testament.

However, there is a lingering question that needs to be addressed. It is argued in the present work that Paul did not think of Gentile Christ followers as Jews. To the contrary, the distinction between Jews and Christ-believing Gentiles seems to be one of considerable importance to him (see chapter 26). Consequently, is Revelation a response to a *misunderstood* Pauline theology on Jews and Gentiles? Indeed, are these two passages actually a rebuke of those who say that they are Paulinists, but in fact they are not?[18]

CONCLUDING REMARKS

The sheer number of interpretations offered the readers of the present volume lays bare the fact that there was never only one way to interpret the New Testament texts: this is due partly to the fact that they were written in *koinê* Greek almost two thousand years ago, partly because none of the original documents is extant today and that the existing copies differ from one another, and, even more importantly, because texts—including the books in the New Testament—by definition are multifaceted.[1] In the thirty exegetical chapters that constitute the main bulk of this book, a series of interpretations of each passage has been presented, often ranging from *contrast and conflict* with people who identified with then-contemporary Judaism to *context and continuity* with the Jewish tradition.

In the introduction it was spelled out that the perspective in these thirty studies is that the earliest Christian movement was *a Christ-centered worship of the God of Israel, with predominantly Gentile followers* rather than a very early form of the caustic anti-Jewish Christendom that eventually evolved in the coming centuries. No one can deny that far more often than not throughout history Christians have read the New Testament in ways that have presented Jews as nothing but adversaries to the Christian religion: a blindfolded people unable to perceive fundamental spiritual truths because they are reading the Scriptures erroneously. This portrayal of Jews and Judaism has been exceptionally influential far beyond the border of the ecclesiastical milieux in which it was fostered, as Amy-Jill Levine writes:

> While I do not believe the road to Auschwitz begins with the gospel, interpretations of the gospels contribute to that infrastructure. Therefore, the Shoah should not be taught as if Christianity, and Christian biblical interpretation, had no part to play.[2]

The veracity of her words cannot be questioned; to do so would ridicule historical and theological scholarship on the development of antisemitism throughout history. But the question we ought to pose is whether there are ways to read the New Testament that do not contribute to such an anti-Jewish infrastructure in the world. For this reason, five topics will be discussed in these concluding remarks: *anachronism*, *allegorization*, *antinomianism*, *anti-Judaism*, and *apologetics*.

(a) Anachronism is mentioned first because anachronism is, in a manner of speaking, the original sin of historians, in the sense that it enters the equation early and that its consequences are transmitted from generation to generation. The outcome is rarely correct if the proposition is wrong—and not taking into account the historical context of the New Testament texts often leads to anachronistic results.

The most problematic anachronism in this area of research is the idea that, at the time of Paul and the other authors of the New Testament, one could distinguish between two distinct religions—Judaism and Christianity—and that those who heard or read the New Testament texts would be able to identify these two systems. We have in several of the thirty chapters identified this problematic approach to the New Testament. It is not anachronistic to argue that these texts from late antiquity may be relevant as we face serious challenges today; quite the opposite, the willingness to listen to and learn from insights of previous generations is often valuable and of great assistance. But it is problematic to assume more or less simplistically that antiquity addresses our current questions. We cannot ignore the broad shoulders upon which we stand: those who have informed us and, indeed, formed us during the last two thousand years give us perspectives that people in antiquity did not have.

The driving force for anachronism among readers of the New Testament is often *a yearning for relevance*. It is understandable that Christians today want the text to make sense and to be meaningful; therefore, it is all the more important to approach the texts with an awareness of the risk of anachronistic interpretations. Furthermore, this yearning for relevance often assumes that Jesus of Nazareth was *unique* in his teaching. In discussing doctrine, such a statement makes sense for Christians. Several scholars have argued, though, that a *theological* affirmation of an absolute uniqueness of Jesus—being the sole Son, the *monogenês*, "the only begotten"—has been transferred to a *historical* statement—for example, that no one had ever called God "Father" as Jesus did.[3] But, as E. P. Sanders states:

It is very bad theology to hang a confession of faith on a verbal detail. Doing it creates bad Christology. This little detail and that are unique.

They prove that Jesus was the Son of God. The basis is inadequate for the Christological confession....The claim of Christianity historically has not been that Jesus said six things which no one else said. When scholars put themselves into the awkward position of proving his greatness by finding unique sayings, they unwittingly reduce him to the level of a phrase-maker. Classical Christianity claimed that in Jesus' life, death and resurrection God acted for the good of the world. Sayings, no matter how original, will not prove that, and trying to prop up faith by specious arguments for uniqueness not only denigrates Judaism, it demeans Christianity.[4]

Moreover, Lloyd Gaston correctly argues that after the Enlightenment Jesus's alleged uniqueness was no longer a given but had to be argued for, which was done by contrasting him with his historical context. Thus, the only thing left of the uniqueness of Jesus was that he stood in sharp contrast to the Judaism of his days. These are "highly charged theological postulates disguised as historical method."[5] Similarly W. D. Davies and Dale C. Allison state that

the claim to find in the synoptic logion profound originality seems ill-conceived and probably stems more from Christian apologetics than from an objective examination of the texts...the truth of his [i.e., Matthew's] Lord's teaching did not necessarily hinge upon its novelty.[6]

Some Christians think of the *ontological* uniqueness of Jesus Christ, but they articulate this belief—which arguably is central to Christian faith—in terms of an alleged *historical* uniqueness, resulting in him as appearing to be non-Jewish. As we have noted repeatedly in this volume, the starting point for bad Christian theology is often the de-Judaization of Jesus.

In short, firstly, when the New Testament was written, Judaism and Christianity were not two separate religious systems. Therefore, we should not approach the texts with such an anachronistic presupposition. Secondly, the quest for the *historically unique* Jesus is often an expression of *theologically weak* Christology.[7] It does not mean that a Christian should seek to find the minutiae of the Apostolic and Nicene Creeds in every text in the New Testament—quite the opposite, actually. But it does mean that the relevance of Jesus of Nazareth for Christians today is not dependent on an alleged uniqueness in his *teaching*.[8] In short, if your interpretation requires of the historical Jesus that he was the only person in antiquity who conveyed the values of the twenty-first century (which happen to concur with your own), then you have every reason to suspect that it is anachronistic.

(b) Allegorization was shunned by Adolf Jülicher, but it reappears over and over again when the New Testament parables are reread as salvation-historical descriptions of the history of the Jewish people: the immoral characters in the parables signify Jews, the Jewish people collectively, the Old Testament, and the old covenant.[9] The virtuous characters represent Christians, the church, the New Testament, and the new covenant.

When discussing the parable of the good Samaritan, we saw that in Augustine's reading the two men who ignored the wounded man represented the old covenant: they were unwilling, and the old covenant was unable to assist the person who needed their help. We also noted that although contemporary scholarship takes pains to distance itself from such allegorizing interpretations, it still often claims that it was Jewish purity regulations that made it impossible for them to reach out to their compatriot. Hence, ironically, the Augustinian allegorization prevails in this aspect: the message of the text is that Judaism cannot "save" a person. Similarly, it has been suggested that the anonymous rich man did not reach out to the impoverished Lazarus outside of his house simply because Judaism hindered him from doing so. Once again, we see that "the Jewish background" is essentialized as the opposite of the vision and mission of the kingdom of God that the New Testament writers wish to offer their readers. To put it bluntly, it is Judaism that prevents Jews from behaving as they ought to behave: as good Samaritans, or as good Christians, which is really the same thing. In order to avoid such allegorization, readers of the New Testament parables need to treat the parables as parables.

(c) Antinomianism in this context refers to the understanding that the message of Jesus and Paul was that the Torah is a burden that has to be removed in order to free people for service in the Kingdom of God. Now, to state that the Torah is such an unbearable yoke may be characteristic of much of Christian teaching, especially in the Protestant tradition, but it is certainly not representative of Judaism, and without understanding the fundamental pillars of Judaism, we will undoubtedly misunderstand the first Christ followers, since earliest Christianity began as an intra-Jewish movement.

The Torah with its commandments is similar to what a sacrament is in much of Christian theology: a visible sign of the invisible grace of God. Therefore, to state that the Torah is a burden—and that Jesus's mission was to abolish it—is to misunderstand the earliest Christian perspective. In several of the thirty chapters we saw how Jesus by various interpreters has been presented as a person who was brave enough to challenge the "pettifogging" Jews and their insistence on reading the Torah literally and following its many commandments. Two recommendations may be of assistance:

> Firstly, remember that *Paul of Tarsus* was reaching out to Gentiles, who, by definition, were *not* Jews—and he argued that they *not* become Jews, to wit, *not* be Torah-observant Jews, but to remain what they were when they were called (cf. 1 Cor 7:17–20). Hence, keeping the Jewish commandments was not their way of worshiping the God of Israel. If the main focus of an article, lecture, or sermon presents "the Law" as a problem, and if Paul manages to solve that problem, then the text is most probably antinomian.
> Secondly, reflect on the Word-of-God theology that developed already in the New Testament, according to which *Jesus of Nazareth* was the Word of God, the breath of God, the articulation of the will of God: he was Torah incarnated. The Creed and the church fathers do not speak of him as *heteroousios* (i.e., the Son being fundamentally different from the Father) but of *homoousios* (i.e., that he was of the same essence as the Father). This discourse was, of course, developed much later, but it may still be useful as we read the New Testament. To repeat, if the main point of an article, lecture, or sermon is that Jesus more than anything else had to abrogate the commandments of the Torah, then the proclamation is antinomian. Certainly there is an ongoing and vivid discussion in the Gospels about the application of the commandments in the Torah, but this is because of their enduring *significance, not* their *insignificance*. For example, the purpose of discussions about *shabbat* in intra-Jewish contexts is not whether to abolish it but how best to apply it. As theologians tend to state, *abusus non tollit usum* (abuse does not cancel the use).

(d) Anti-Judaism: This is a topic that is difficult to approach. Who wants to be anti-Jewish; who wants to admit being anti-Jewish? Nevertheless, the problems will not go away by themselves; we have to address them, however uncomfortable the process may make us. In a radio speech subsequently published in German and translated into English, Ernst Käsemann stated that he believed that "the apostle's real adversary is the devout Jew [*Der eigentliche Gegner des Apostels ist der fromme Jude*], not only as the mirror-image of his own past—though that, too—but as the reality of the religious man."[10] It is correct that Käsemann here presents the Jew as a representative of a larger problem—"the religious man"—but that is quite typical in anti-Jewish discourse: the Jew is the typical Bolshevik or capitalist or anything or everything else that is condemned. It is to be noted that Käsemann is not stating that Paul's true adversary is a *hypocrite* (but those who are sincere and humble), or only a fraction, for example, *the Pharisees*; no, he is stating that Paul's antagonist is *the devout Jew*. Later in the same radio speech he argues that

> in and with Israel he [i.e., Paul] strikes at the hidden Jew in all of us [*In und mit Israel wird der verborgene Jude in uns allen getroffen*], at the man who validates rights and demands over against God on the basis of God's past dealings with him and to this extant is serving not God but an illusion.[11]

And this is a speech that has been published in a book, the second edition of which was translated into English! There are many stations on the way for the author to modify his statements on *der fromme Jude* and *der verborgene Jude*, but he simply chose not to do so. Now, one cannot but wonder that if this is not a textbook generic example of theological anti-Judaism, what is? And as previously stated: the problem is there—and it has to be addressed.

An observation repeatedly made in the present volume is that we can detect in the New Testament texts, when studied chronologically, an evolving anti-Jewish trajectory that begins within the New Testament and subsequently escalates in later texts from the earliest Christian movement. If we are able to identify an *increased* anti-Judaism in the texts the later they are, should we not also seek to detect *decreased* anti-Judaism in the very earliest texts, assuming that these are closer to the original events that are depicted? Four examples may suffice: Firstly, we saw that the people going out into the desert in order to listen to John the Baptist's teaching are not criticized in the Gospel of Mark, as they are in the Gospel of Matthew, and even more in the Gospel of Luke. Secondly, the person who discusses the greatest commandment with Jesus is in the Gospel of Mark presented as genuinely interested in the topic, whereas in the other Synoptic Gospels he is posing the question merely because he wants to put Jesus to a test. Thirdly, the character Judas is depicted in increasingly gloomy colors the later the texts are written: hence, John is more negative than the Synoptics, and Papias goes even further in his depiction of the fate of Judas. Fourthly, the later the sources are, the less emphasis is put on the responsibility of the Romans for the death of Jesus, and more on the Jewish authorities, and, subsequently, on the Jewish people as a whole. Given that there is such a trajectory from the earliest to later sources, what role do these observations play as we seek to reconstruct the original historical events and interpret the texts responsibly today?

Furthermore, anti-Jewish theology diverges from the purpose of theology proper—"theology" literally means "word[s] about God"—in order to focus on something else: it is blaming Jews instead of praising God, and it is criticizing Jews instead of scrutinizing oneself. It transmutes the theological *mea culpa* into an anti-Jewish *tua culpa*. Journalists often state that their task is "to comfort the afflicted and afflict the comfortable"—anti-Jewish theology, when passing judgment on Jews instead of its Christian readers, inverts this programme: it transmutes parenetic theology into a polemical *Schadenfreude*.[12] In that sense, anti-Jewish theology could be described as a *secularization* of the Christian message?

In the survey of interpretations of the parable about the widow who frequently visits a judge, we saw that a certain uneasiness about the judge representing the Heavenly Judge may have caused some readers to think of him not as a depiction of the God of Israel but of a typical Jewish judge at the time of Jesus. At times it seems that an anti-Jewish prism is imported into texts where it is not called for, perhaps because, for one reason or another, traditional God-centered readings are problematic. In the introductory chapter we referred to David Nirenberg, who argues that "anti-Judaism is not simply an attitude toward the action of real Jews and their religion, but *a way of critically engaging the world.*"[13] Our observations about various anti-Jewish readings of the New Testament support his proposition.

(e) Apologetics: The fifth and final topic also addresses the issue of the driving force for anti-Jewish readings of the New Testament. One may wonder why the supersessionist paradigm has been so exceptionally influential in history. There are probably two main reasons for its success story. Firstly, one should not underestimate the fact that *supersessionism is so easy to convey in teaching and preaching*: old vs. new, failure vs. success, promises vs. fulfilment, Old Testament vs. New Testament, Jews vs. Christians. As Paula Fredriksen writes about scholarship on Paul (but her words can undoubtedly be applied to Jesus research as well), "This Paul—anti-Jewish, antiritual, anti-Torah—continues to flourish in academic publications, not

least of all because he is so usable theologically."[14] These dichotomies are rhetorically appealing in presentations of Christianity in various contexts. They are also aesthetically attractive in church art: divisions of altar paintings or stained-glass windows into two halves, one depicting Adam and Eve being driven away from the Garden of Eden (and, therefore, how the rest of the Old Testament is nothing but a theological failure), and one showing how Jesus Christ through his life and death opens the way to Paradise (and, hence, that the New Testament restores what the Jewish master story is unable to achieve). It is far more challenging for Christian theology to seek to do justice to the Jewish self-understanding.

Secondly, as has already been pointed out, *supersessionism is self-aggrandizing*: it claims that a fundamental part of Christian theology is that Christianity is better than Judaism, and for this reason it is eager to import Jews and Judaism into almost any conversation about virtually every biblical text. It is noteworthy that, whereas it only took some *two generations* for Christ followers to realize that their imminent eschatology had to be revised, it took almost *two thousand years* to start repudiating supersessionism. The reason for this discrepancy is that supersessionism is both triggered by and triggers a self-aggrandizing self-understanding, and that is as complicated to address as was the suspension of the eschaton in antiquity.

> After two thousand years of supersessionism, it takes a lot of work to articulate a Christian theology which is fulfilment without supersessionism—but not as much work as the first generations of Christ believers had to devote to de-eschatologizing their message in order to be able to hand it over to future generations of Christians.[15]

Hence, we need to discern and question the triumphalistic theology that promotes this yearning for an unhistorical *uniqueness* of the teaching of Jesus (e.g., "no one has ever said what he said") and *paradigmatic* significance of his teaching (e.g., "Jesus came in order to teach us that we no longer should..."). Krister Stendahl said in an interview that

> apologetics, defending the Bible—defending God, for that matter—is a rather arrogant activity. Who is defending whom? I love to use the old Swedish expression, "It is pathetic to hear mosquitoes cough." I don't know why that is funny, but in Swedish it is funny. And apologetics is mosquitoes coughing. It kills so much of the joy in reading and practicing the love of the scriptures.[16]

Concluding Remarks

These five topics—*anachronism, allegorization, antinomianism, anti-Judaism,* and *apologetics*—are certainly not the only recurring problems for interpreters of the New Testament, but they are arguably significant when seeking to understand Judaism not *as the theological contrast* but as *the historical context* of Jesus and Paul.

It has already been stated that the perspective in the present book is that the earliest Christian movement was *a Christ-centered worship of the God of Israel, with predominantly Gentile followers*—rather than *a very early form of the caustic anti-Jewish Christendom that eventually evolved in the coming centuries.* Interpreted in this way, the message is that the nations rejoice *together with* God's people Israel, not *instead of* Israel.[17]

Hopefully this perspective appeals to readers, and perchance this book provides them with a set of hermeneutical keys that celebrate such a perspective. A key can be used in two ways: One can *close* a door with a key; the words *kleis* in Greek and *clavis* in Latin are related to words that remind us of this aspect of what a key does—*kleiein* in Greek and *claudere* in Latin both mean "to lock," and they have given rise to new words, for example, *claustrophobia*. But a key can also be used in order to *open* doors into new rooms or to let guests into your house. The Hebrew word for *key* draws attention to this dimension, since the root of *maphteach* is *p-t-ch*, which means "to open" (cf. *Ephphata*—"Be opened!" in Mark 7:34). Once again, the purpose of this book is to provide the reader with hermeneutical keys that *open up* the texts.

To read the New Testament texts apologetically tends to close them. But to read them unapologetically may well open them up and sustain us with new—textual as well as existential—meanings, as in the beautiful words of Psalm 145:16. Recited at meals through the centuries, the root of its first word is the same as in *key*:

Poteach et yadekha u-masbia' le-khol chai ratzon.
(You open your hand, satisfying the desire of every living thing.)

NOTES

INTRODUCTION

1. There are a few well-known exceptions, e.g., the Syrophoenician (Canaanite) woman (Matt 15:21–28 and Mark 7:24–30), some Roman soldiers, and Pontius Pilate, but practically everyone else is Jewish.

2. For a similar list (albeit with seven points—"a good biblical number"), see Amy-Jill Levine, *The Misunderstood Jew: The Church and the Scandal of the Jewish Jesus* (San Francisco: HarperSanFrancisco, 2006), 124–66, esp. 124f.

3. Cf. Matt 11:30.

4. Cf. Matt 5:39 and 41.

5. Cf. John 18:36.

6. Cf. Matt 6:28.

7. Amy-Jill Levine, *Short Stories by Jesus: The Enigmatic Parables of a Controversial Rabbi* (New York: HarperCollins, 2014), 168, and "Supersessionism: Admit and Address Rather than Debate or Deny," *Religions* 13 (2022), https://doi.org/10.3390/rel13020155 (accessed March 23, 2023).

8. *King James Version*. Cf. the *New Revised Standard Version*: "are you envious because I am generous?"

9. In his paradigmatic study on supersessionism, R. Kendall Soulen describes three supersessionist models: *punitive, economic,* and *structural supersessionism*. The *punitive* model asserts that God punishes Israel by abrogating the covenant because of Israel's rejection of Christ (and, in the most extreme version, the responsibility for killing him); the *economic* model claims that Israel's role in God's plan for the world (Greek: *oikonomia*; hence, "economic") was merely to prepare for salvation in its spiritual and universal form; and, finally, the *structural* model interprets the Christian canon in such a way that it marginalizes or even trivializes the Jewish Scriptures and Jewish self-understandings; see *The God of Israel and Christian Theology* (Minneapolis: Fortress, 1996), 28–33. Another influential distinction has been forwarded by David Novak; he distinguishes between *hard* and *soft* supersessionism. The former asserts that "God has elected Christians to displace the Jews in the covenant between God and His people. Christianity is taken to be Judaism's necessarily total successor or 'fulfilment.'" The latter claims that "Christianity brings something new (a *novum testamentum* [i.e., a new covenant]) to the

covenant between God and Israel"; see, e.g., "Supersessionism Hard and Soft," *First Things* (February 2019) https://www.firstthings.com/article/2019/02/supersessionism-hard-and-soft (accessed April 19, 2023).

10. David Nirenberg, "Anti-Judaism as a Critical Theory," *The Chronicle of Higher Education* (January 28, 2013), B10–B13 (emphasis added). See also his tome *Anti-Judaism: The Western Tradition* (New York: Norton, 2013), 3.

11. Cf. Clark M. Williamson and Ronald J. Allen, *Interpreting Difficult Texts: Anti-Judaism and Christian Preaching* (Philadelphia: SCM / Trinity, 1989), 2: "What we Christians have done for a long time...is to criticize as 'Jewish' everything that goes wrong in Christianity."

12. *Shoah* is the Hebrew word for "catastrophe." *Holocaust*, although widespread, is not without complications, since it is the term in the Septuagint for burnt offerings: *holokauston* (*holos*, "thoroughly and completely"; *kaustos* from *kaiein*, "to burn"). Hence, *holokauston* in the Bible is not an abomination but the term for a rite that God has ordained (Lev 1:9): "an offering by fire of pleasing odor to the L ORD."

13. Gavin I. Langmuir, *Toward a Definition of Antisemitism* (Berkeley: University of California Press, 1990), 311.

14. Helen Fein, "Dimensions of Antisemitism: Attitudes, Collective Accusations, and Actions," in *The Persisting Question: Sociological Perspectives and Social Contexts of Modern Antisemitism*, ed. Helen Fein (New York: Walter de Gruyter, 1987), 67. For the applicability of various definitions when studying texts from antiquity, see Peter Schäfer, *Judeophobia: Attitudes toward the Jews in the Ancient World* (Cambridge, MA: Harvard University Press, 1997), 197–211.

15. Marc Saperstein, *Moments of Crisis in Jewish-Christian Relations* (Philadelphia: SCM / Trinity, 1989), esp. 26–37 (the chapter on the age of the Reformation). See also Guy G. Stroumsa, "From Anti-Judaism to Antisemitism in Early Christianity?," in *Contra Iudaeos: Ancient and Medieval Polemics Between Christians and Jews*, ed. Ora Limor and Guy G. Stroumsa (Tübingen: Mohr, 1996), 26: "It is this perception of the continued existence of Judaism as a perpetual threat to the very survival and truth of the Christian religion that was to prove so ominous in the future."

16. James Bernauer, *Jesuit Kaddish: Jesuits, Jews, and Holocaust Remembrance* (Notre Dame: University of Notre Dame Press, 2020), 28. For a survey of Lazare's life and writings—and the importance of the Dreyfus affair for the development of his thinking—see Nelly Jussem-Wilson, "Bernard Lazare's Jewish Journey: From Being an Israelite to Being a Jew," *Jewish Social Studies* 26 (1964): 146–68.

17. The word *Jüden* is spelled with an umlaut in the original.

18. Saperstein, *Moments of Crisis in Jewish-Christian Relations*, 41.

19. James Carroll, *Constantine's Sword: The Church and the Jews; A History* (Boston: Houton Miflin, 2001), 22. Similarly Stroumsa, "From Anti-Judaism to Antisemitism in Early Christianity?," 19: "Judaism had been

Notes

deprived of religious value and respect long before the Jews were disenfranchized legally."

20. John Connelly, *From Enemy to Brother: The Revolution in Catholic Teaching on the Jews, 1933–1965* (Cambridge, MA: Harvard University Press, 2012), 173 (emphasis added).

21. Zygmunt Bauman, "Jews and Other Europeans, Old and New," *European Judaism: A Journal for the New Europe* 42 (2009): 125.

22. Ruth Gruber, "Allosemitism (noun)—Jews as the Perpetual 'Other,'" *Jewish Journal* (August 7, 2008) (accessed April 13, 2023).

23. Bernauer, *Jesuit Kaddish*, 28–31. On p. 30 he writes that asemitism found its name in twentieth-century Poland.

24. Bernauer, *Jesuit Kaddish*, 30.

25. Quoted in, e.g., Bernauer, *Jesuit Kaddish*, 122f. The historical context for Heschel's statement was discussions about various drafts of *Nostra Aetate*, and especially the issue of Catholic mission to the Jewish people. *Ad maiorem Dei gloriam* is the Latin motto of the Jesuits (the Society of Jesus).

26. Soulen, *The God of Israel and Christian Theology*, 33 (emphasis in the original). See also p. 31: "The standard model [of the Christian Bible as a whole]...*unifies the Christian canon in a manner that renders the Hebrew Scriptures largely indecisive for shaping conclusions about how God's purposes engage creation in universal and enduring ways*" (emphases in the original).

27. Jonathan Culler, "Defining Narrative Units," in *Style and Structure in Literature: Essays in the New Stylistics*, ed. Roger Fowler (Ithaca, NY: Cornell University Press, 1975), 123.

28. In this context *Torah* seldom refers only to the Pentateuch but includes all texts in the Scriptures (*ha-Miqra*).

29. Scholarship on the Pharisees is vast; see, e.g., James C. VanderKam, "Foreword," in Anthony J. Saldarini, *Pharisees, Scribes and Sadducees in Palestinian Society: A Sociological Approach*, 2nd ed. (Grand Rapids: Eerdmans, 2001), xi–xxv, and Jacob Neusner and Bruce D. Chilton, eds., *In Quest of the Historical Pharisees* (Waco: Baylor University Press, 2007). The most recent and comprehensive study (including an extensive section on the reception history of the Pharisees) is Joseph Sievers and Amy-Jill Levine, eds., *The Pharisees* (Grand Rapids, MI: Eerdmans, 2021). David Rosen can claim some birthing privileges of the book, as he suggested the topic for the conference that gave rise to this collection of essays.

30. Gary Tyra, *Defeating Pharisaism: Recovering Jesus' Disciple-Making Method* (Colorado Springs, CO: Authentic, 2009), 6.

31. An example from my native Sweden is Hugo Odeberg's immensely influential book *Pharisaism and Christianity*, trans. J. M. Moe (St. Louis: Concordia, 1964 [Swedish: 1943, and three subsequent editions]), 7: "the antithesis is...fundamental in the sense that a Pharisaism which assumes Christian lines of thought ceases to be Pharisaism, and a Christianity which incorporates Pharisaic lines of thought likewise ceases to be Christianity....

Particularly Christianity has repeatedly been in danger of incorporating Pharisaical lines of thought, and the great fathers of the church have always stressed the fact the [*sic*] Pharisaism is not something that can be combined with Christianity, but something that, if it is permitted to extend its influence, will work as a deadly poison which is bound to destroy the Christian life. Thus Luther, like no one else, took up Paul's battle against Pharisaism and vigorously pursued it." On Odeberg's scholarship, see Jesper Svartvik, *Bibeltolkningens bakgator: Synen på judar, slavar och homosexuella i historia och nutid*, 2nd ed. (Stockholm: Verbum, 2022), 118–45, and Susannah Heschel, *The Aryan Jesus: Christian Theologians and the Bible in Nazi Germany* (Princeton, NJ: Princeton University Press, 2008), 13, 64, 103, 145–48, and 235.

32. *Mishnah Pirqei Avot* 1.2. This is attributed to Shimon *ha-Tzaddiq* (the righteous) who was a high priest, but that piece of information is suppressed here, probably because the text wishes to marginalize the importance of the priesthood after the destruction of the temple.

33. For the group known as "the men of the great assembly," see, e.g., Ephraim E. Urbach, *The Sages: Their Concepts and Beliefs*, trans. Israel Abrahams, 2 vols. (Jerusalem: Magnes Press, 1987), 564–76.

34. Emily Brontë, *Wuthering Heights* (Hertfordshire: Wordsworth, 1992 [orig. 1847]), ch. 5.

35. See, however, Shaye J. D. Cohen, "The Forgotten Pharisees," in *The Pharisees*, ed. Joseph Sievers and Amy-Jill Levine (Grand Rapids, MI: Eerdmans, 2021), 291: "Ultimately, the Pharisees will be seen as the molders and shapers of Judaism, as if they had been links in the chain of tradition all along."

36. Annette Yoshiko Reed, "When Did Rabbis Become Pharisees? Reflections on Christian Evidence for Post-70 Judaism," in *Envisioning Judaism: Studies in Honor of Peter Schäfer on the Occasion of His Seventieth Birthday*, ed. Ra'anan S. Boustan et al., 2 vols. (Tübingen: Mohr Siebeck, 2013), 2:862. Shaye J. D. Cohen argues that Jerome was the first to identify the then-contemporary rabbis as Pharisees; see *The Significance of Yavneh and Other Essays in Jewish Hellenism* (Tübingen: Mohr Siebeck, 2010), 70. Annette Yoshiko Reed maintains that we have proof for this as early as the Syrian-Christian (i.e., Matthean) context; see "When Did Rabbis Become Pharisees?," 2:884f.

37. Craig E. Morrison, "Interpreting the Name 'Pharisee,'" in *The Pharisees*, ed. Joseph Sievers and Amy-Jill Levine (Grand Rapids: Eerdmans, 2021), 19.

38. In a passage in *Talmud Bavli Sotah* 22b, seven categories of *perushin* (=Pharisees?) are discussed, the first five of which are criticized for being selfish or hypocritical. However, it is not crystal clear whether this is actually a discussion about those belonging to the religious school—i.e., the "Pharisees"—or about people in general who abstain (*p-r-sh*) from something in particular.

39. Harold W. Attridge, "Pharisees in the Fourth Gospel and One Special Pharisee," in *The Pharisees*, ed. Joseph Sievers and Amy-Jill Levine (Grand Rapids, MI: Eerdmans, 2021), 198 (emphasis added).

40. John Chrysostom, *Commentary on Saint John the Evangelist and Apostle: Homilies 48–88*, trans. Sr. Thomas Aquinas Goggin (New York: Fathers of the Church, 1960), 437 (Homily 85). For additional reflections, see Attridge, "Pharisees in the Fourth Gospel and One Special Pharisee," 195.

41. Attridge, "Pharisees in the Fourth Gospel and One Special Pharisee," 196.

42. Paula Fredriksen, "Paul, the Perfectly Righteous Pharisee," in *The Pharisees*, ed. Joseph Sievers and Amy-Jill Levine (Grand Rapids, MI: Eerdmans, 2021), 135.

43. For additional examples of "good" Pharisees, see, e.g., Luke 13:31 and Acts 5:33–39.

44. This alludes to *In Quest of the Historical Pharisees*, a collection of essays edited by Jacob Neusner and Bruce D. Chilton. That title, in turn, is a tongue-in-cheek reference to the English translation of Albert Schweitzer's famous book on Jesus research: *The Quest of the Historical Jesus*, indicating that it is analogously difficult to reconstruct the teachings of the Pharisees.

45. Josephus, *Jewish Antiquities* 18.1.2–6 (§11–25) and 17.2.4 (§41).

46. Fredriksen, "Paul, the Perfectly Righteous Pharisee," 119.

47. See, e.g., Yair Furstenberg, "The Shared Image of Pharisaic Law in the Gospels and Rabbinic Tradition," in *The Pharisees*, ed. Joseph Sievers and Amy-Jill Levine (Grand Rapids, MI: Eerdmans, 2021), 203, 209, and 213.

48. Basing it on the writings of Ernest Crawley, Sigmund Freud coined this expression in 1917.

49. T. W. Manson, *The Sayings of Jesus as Recorded in the Gospel according to St Matthew and St Luke Arranged with Introduction and Commentary* (London: SCM, 1949 [1937]), 295.

50. See Manson, *The Sayings of Jesus*, 295: "To the Sadducees, and probably to them alone in Judaism, the words 'treasure in heaven' meant nothing at all."

51. Manson, *The Sayings of Jesus*, 295.

52. Clement of Alexandra, quoted in Eusebius, *Church History* 6.14.7.

53. On ambiguity in C. G. Jung's thinking, see, e.g., Bent Falk, *Att vara där du är: Samtal med människor i kris*, trans. Margareta Brandby-Cöster (Stockholm: Verbum, 2005 [Danish: 1996]).

54. Kaufmann Kohler, "New Testament," in *Jewish Encyclopedia*, ed. Isidore Singer, 12 vols. (New York: Funk & Wagnalls, 1901–06), 9:251.

55. Adele Reinhartz, *Befriending the Beloved Disciple: A Jewish Reading of the Gospel of John* (New York: Continuum, 2001), 13.

56. D. Moody Smith, "Judaism and the Gospel of John," in *Jews and the Christians: Exploring the Past, Present and Future*, ed. James H. Charlesworth (New York: Crossroad, 1990), 78.

57. See, e.g., David Nirenberg, "Mass Conversion and Genealogical Mentalities: Jews and Christians in Fifteenth-Century Spain," *Past & Present* 174 (2002): 3–41.

58. D. Moody Smith, "Judaism and the Gospel of John," 81.

59. Malcolm Lowe, "Who Were the ΙΟΥΔΑΙΟΙ? *Novum Testamentum* 18 (1967): 101–30. See, however, D. Moody Smith, "Judaism and the Gospel of John," 81: "That 'the Jews' are residents of Judea is probably the case in most instances, but simply to translate *Ioudaioi* as 'Judeans' will not do. They are both more and less than 'Judeans.'"

60. Franz Mussner, *Tractate on the Jews: The Significance of Judaism for Christian Faith*, trans. Leonard Swidler (Philadelphia: Fortress / SPCK, 1984), 184. See also Urban C. von Wahlde, "The Johannine 'Jews': A Critical Survey," *New Testament Studies* 28 (1982): 33–60.

61. D. Moody Smith, "Judaism and the Gospel of John," 82. (Probably by mistake emphasized "*Jewish leaders*" in the original.)

62. Robert Kysar, *John, the Maverick Gospel*, 3rd ed. (Louisville, KY: Westminster John Knox, 2007), 83. Adele Reinhartz has discussed this in several books and articles, e.g., *Cast Out of the Covenant: Jews and Anti-Judaism in the Gospel of John* (Lanham, MD: Fortress Academic, 2018), 67–108. Similarly Michael J. Cook, *Modern Jews Engage the New Testament: Enhancing Jewish Well-Being in a Christian Environment* (Woodstock, VT: Jewish Lights, 2008), 225: "'Jews' for John represent *those who stubbornly disbelieve when it is they who ought to believe*" (emphases in the original). Samuel Sandmel argues that the Gospel of John reflects "one side of a *reciprocal bitterness*, [in] a two-sided animosity"; see *Anti-Semitism in the New Testament* (Philadelphia: Fortress, 1978), 119 (emphases in the original).

63. Is it possible to detect a Semitic popular etymology behind 1:31, in which it says that Jesus will be seen by Israel? It triggers the mind that the name "Israel" here perhaps is interpreted as *ish raah El*, "the one who saw God." For another text in Greek that may give vent to this unscientific etymology, see Melito of Sardis, *On Pascha*, 82. For Greek text and English translation, see Melito of Sardis, *On Pascha and Fragments*, ed. Stuart George Hall (Oxford: Clarendon Press, 1979).

64. Dorothy Savage, "Jews and Judaism in Protestant / Christian Curriculum," in *Removing the Anti-Judaism from the New Testament*, ed. Howard Clark Kee and Irvin J. Borowsky (Philadelphia: American Interfaith Institute / World Alliance, 2000), 157.

65. See, e.g., *Talmud Bavli Bava Metzia* 31b. For additional comments on this hermeneutical concept, see, e.g., Abraham Joshua Heschel, *Heavenly Torah: As Refracted through the Generations*, ed. and trans. Gordon Tucker with Leonard Levin (New York: Continuum, 2005 [Hebrew: 1962–65]), 47–49.

66. D. Moody Smith, "Judaism and the Gospel of John," 78.

67. Joshua D. Garroway, *The Beginning of the Gospel: Paul, Philippi, and the Origins of Christianity* (Cham: Palgrave Macmillan, 2018), 1.

68. These three approaches to Pauline theology on the Law have previously been presented in Jesper Svartvik, "'East Is East, and West Is West': The Concept of Torah in Paul and Mark," in *Mark and Paul: Comparative Essays*, part 1: *Two Authors at the Beginnings of Christianity*, ed. Oda Wischmeyer, David C. Sim, and Ian J. Elmer (Berlin: Walter de Gruyter, 2014), 157–85.

69. Two examples of the importance of this interpretation of the Law: Philipp Melanchthon called the Epistle to the Galatians (in which, it was believed, this understanding of the Law was particularly well articulated) *Christianae religionis compendium* (a summary of the Christian faith) and that Martin Luther wrote that he treasured it as highly as Katharina von Bora—that is, to him it was as adorable and indispensable as his own wife. Luther's scriptural hermeneutics centered much on the principle of *was Christum treibet* (what promotes Christ), which was not Christology in general, but which always referred to a particular type of forensic Christology, namely, that the death of Jesus absolves humanity from guilt and the demands of the Law. Humans are justified by faith in Christ and not by their deeds.

70. Needless to say, Christians have not been opposed to observance of the Decalogue; only the so-called *ritual* commandments have been questioned.

71. Paula Fredriksen, *Paul: The Pagans' Apostle* (New Haven, CT: Yale University Press, 2017), 86.

72. At times, one gets the impression that a "Jew" is anyone who is self-sufficient, a person who needs neither God nor God's grace, and "to Judaize" is what Christians do when they keep the covenantal commandments and have too positive an understanding of Judaism.

73. Pamela Eisenbaum, *Paul Was Not a Christian: The Original Message of a Misunderstood Apostle* (San Francisco: HarperOne, 2009), 244.

74. Krister Stendahl, "The Apostle Paul and the Introspective Conscience of the West," *Harvard Theological Review* 56 (1963): 199–215, and previously "Paulus och samvetet," *Svensk Exegetisk Årsbok* 25 (1960): 62–77.

75. K. Stendahl, "The Apostle Paul and the Introspective Conscience of the West," 200.

76. James D. G. Dunn, "The New Perspective on Paul," *Bulletin of the John Rylands Library* 65 (1983): 94–122.

77. For this argument, see, e.g., Francis Watson, *Paul, Judaism and the Gentiles: A Sociological Approach* (Cambridge: Cambridge University Press, 1986), 21f.: "If in one sense it is true that Paul sought to break down the barrier between Jew and Gentile, he nevertheless did so only to reestablish exclusiveness in a new form." For important reflections on universalism, see Krister Stendahl, *Final Account: Paul's Letter to the Romans* (Minneapolis: Fortress, 1995), 43f.: "But universalism is always the root of imperialism....The Jewish scholar David Hartman has written a new model of theology in which he says: salvation is the recognition of limits."

78. See, however, Matthew Thiessen, *Paul and the Gentile Problem* (Oxford: Oxford University Press, 2016), 169: "This radical new perspective fails to live up to its name. It is neither *new*, since Luke had already portrayed

Paul in ways that anticipated the work of these scholars, nor is it *radical*, inasmuch as Christian tradition situated Luke's portrayal of a law-observant Paul within its authoritative canon" (emphases added).

79. Fredriksen, *Paul*, xii.

80. K. Stendahl, *Final Account*, ix.

81. Although *pistis Christou* habitually is translated as "faith in Christ," it is quite likely that the meaning rather is "the faithfulness of Christ." However, the former interpretation also emphasizes that "faith" in both biblical Hebrew (*emunah*) and Greek (*pistis*) equals "trust" and "confidence" (not affirmation of a series of dogmas); see, e.g., Peter J. Tomson, *Presumed Guilty: How the Jews Were Blamed for the Death of Jesus*, trans. Janet Dyk (Minneapolis: Fortress, 2005), 125. See also Fredriksen, *Paul*, 125: "[A Gentile] *can* overcome his difficulties, but only *in* Christ, through his *pistis*, his confidence in or fidelity toward Christ" (emphases in the original).

82. For a survey of the figure of Moses primarily (but not exclusively) in Jewish thought, see Avivah Gottlieb Zornberg, *Moses: A Human Life* (New Haven, CT: Yale University Press, 2016).

83. Fredriksen, *Paul*, 110 and 130.

84. Another example in the very same chapter is v. 29 where it is emphasized that God is the God "also of the Gentiles," not "instead of the Jews," as it so often is being presented.

85. Hence, in the present work it is argued that Paul taught neither that God had relinquished Israel nor that he required that Israel relinquish the Torah, *pace* N. T. Wright, *Climax of the Covenant: Christ and the Law in Pauline Theology* (New York: T&T Clark, 1991), 248: "there is no reason why she [Israel] should not herself be subsequently saved, and indeed every reason why she should. All she has to do is relinquish her frantic grip on the Torah."

86. This section about the fourth challenge is a revised edition of the article "The New Testament's Most Dangerous Book for Jews," *Christian Century* (September 22, 2021), https://www.christiancentury.org/print/pdf/node/38881 (accessed May 26, 2023).

87. See, e.g., Andrew Lincoln, *Hebrews: A Guide* (New York: T&T Clark, 2006), 58: "Hebrews is pervaded by the comparison and contrast between two dispensations of revelation, the old covenant and the new covenant, stressing the superiority of the latter." For a comprehensive survey of its history of interpretation and influence, see Craig R. Koester, *Hebrews: A New Translation with Introduction and Commentary* (New York: Doubleday, 2001), 19–63.

88. See, e.g., Earl S. Johnson, *Hebrews* (Louisville, KY: Westminster John Knox, 2008): "The old covenant that demanded absolute obedience to the Hebrew law and required animal sacrifice is no longer operative. It is *obsolete*, it is *negans, nada*, antiquated, out of date, old. God will make all things new (Isa. 43:19; Rev. 21:5). Do you not see it?" (emphases in the original).

89. Robert P. Gordon, *Hebrews*, 2nd ed. (Sheffield, UK: Sheffield Phoenix Press, 2008), 24: "Hebrews is the only New Testament document to use the

word 'better'—which it does on several occasions—in making comparisons between Christianity and Judaism, and to the disadvantage of the latter."

90. In 13:22 the author describes the text as *tou logou tês paraklêseôs* (a word of exhortation). Thomas G. Long describes it as "a sermon that was preached *in absentia*, and when it was sent to the congregation, certain 'epistle-like' additions were posted to the end"; see *Hebrews* (Louisville, KY: John Knox, 1997), 148. On its genre, see, e.g., Lincoln, *Hebrews*, 9–22 and 69.

91. Eusebius, *Church History* 6.25.11–14.

92. The latter date has to do with when 1 Clement was written, since Hebrews is most probably alluded to in 1 Clement 36:1–5.

93. Marie E. Isaacs, "Why Bother with Hebrews?," *The Heythrop Journal* 43 (2002): 71.

94. Peter J. Tomson, *"If This Be from Heaven": Jesus and the New Testament Authors in Their Relationship to Judaism* (Sheffield, UK: Sheffield Academic Press, 2001), 362.

95. This is Psalm 101 in the Septuagint.

96. Jesper Svartvik, "Reading the Epistle to the Hebrews without Presupposing Supersessionism," in *Christ Jesus and the Jewish People Today: New Explorations of Theological Interrelationships*, ed. Philip A. Cunningham, Joseph Sievers, Mary C. Boys, Hans Hermann Henrix, and Jesper Svartvik (Grand Rapids, MI: Eerdmans, 2011; Italian trans. 2012), 77–91.

97. "'The Gifts and the Calling of God Are Irrevocable' [Rom 11:29]: A Reflection on Theological Questions Pertaining to Catholic-Jewish Relations on the Occasion of the 50th Anniversary of '*Nostra Aetate*' [No. 4]": (https://www.vatican.va/roman_curia/pontifical_councils/chrstuni/relations-jews-docs/rc_pc_chrstuni_doc_20151210_ebraismo-nostra-aetate_en.html) (accessed March 14, 2023).

98. Ernst Käsemann, *The Wandering People of God: An Investigation of the Letter to the Hebrews*, trans. Roy A. Harrisville and Irving L. Sandberg (Minneapolis: Augsburg, 1984 [German 2nd ed. 1957]), 240 (emphases in the original).

99. William G. Johnsson, "The Pilgrimage Motif in the Book of Hebrews," *Journal of Biblical Literature* 97 (1978): 239–51.

100. Richard B. Hays, "'Here We Have No Lasting City': New Covenantalism in Hebrews," in *The Epistle to the Hebrews and Christian Theology*, ed. Richard Bauckham et al. (Grand Rapids: Eerdmans, 2009), 166f. On pp. 168–73, using Stanley Fish's terminology, Hays argues that Hebrews is a "self-consuming artifact," that is (p. 170) "meant to lead the reader beyond its own rhetoric to an encounter with the living God." Similarly, A. J. M. Wedderburn argues that the writer's presuppositions are self-subverting, see "Sawing Off the Branches: Theologizing Dangerously *Ad Hebraeos*," *Journal of Theological Studies* 56 (2005): 413: "It is that New Testament author who has most conspicuously put on a Platonic garb whose apparel is then seen to be coming apart at the seams."

101. Cf. Lincoln, *Hebrews*, 79: "there appears to be more of an emphasis on continuity in the sections of paraenesis and more of an emphasis on discontinuity in the sections of theological exposition." See also Graham Hughes, *Hebrews and Hermeneutics: The Epistle to the Hebrews as a New Testament Example of Biblical Interpretation* (Cambridge, UK: Cambridge University Press, 1979), 54–73.

102. Williamson and Allen, *Interpreting Difficult Texts*, 53.

CHAPTER 1

1. The first two chapters in Matthew and Luke contain the birth narratives (and Luke also recounts the story of the twelve-year old Jesus in the Temple).

2. Matt 3:7, which differs only slightly from Luke 3:7.

3. W. D. Davies and Dale C. Allison, *The Gospel according to Saint Matthew*, 3 vols. (Edinburgh: T&T Clark, 1988–97), 1:301.

4. See, e.g., Aaron M. Gale, "The Gospel according to Matthew," in *The Jewish Annotated New Testament*, 2nd ed., ed. Amy-Jill Levine and Marc Zvi Brettler (Oxford: Oxford University Press, 2017), 15, and Amy-Jill Levine, "The Gospel according to Luke," in *The Jewish Annotated New Testament*, 2nd ed., ed. Amy-Jill Levine and Marc Zvi Brettler (Oxford: Oxford University Press, 2017), 116. Samuel Tobias Lachs points out that the serpent is not a symbol of hypocrisy; he suggests that the Greek *echidna* is a mistranslation of an Aramaic original *aph'a* ("spotted cat," "leopard," or possibly "hyena"), not *effe* (viper); see *A Rabbinic Commentary on the New Testament: The Gospels of Matthew, Mark, and Luke* (Hoboken, NJ: Ktav, 1987), 42.

5. "Why Did John the Baptist Refer to the Pharisees as a Brood of Vipers?," https://www.gotquestions.org/brood-of-vipers.html (accessed June 18, 2022).

6. Eduard Schweizer, *The Good News according to Matthew*, trans. David E. Green (London: SPCK, 1976 [German: 1973]), 50.

7. Needless to say, not all of them went out into the desert: it is stated that many of the Pharisees and Sadducees went there (*pollous tôn Pharisaiôn kai Saddoukaiôn*).

8. See, e.g., Henry Pattarumadathil, "Pharisees and Sadducees Together in Matthew," in *The Pharisees*, ed. Joseph Sievers and Amy-Jill Levine (Grand Rapids, MI: Eerdmans, 2021), 139. Cf. Lachs, *A Rabbinic Commentary on the New Testament*, 42: "The Pharisees and the Sadducees did not come to be baptized, but in order simply to *witness* the proceedings."

9. Davies and Allison, *The Gospel according to Saint Matthew*, 1:304.

10. For arguments that the historical John the Baptist had little if any relation to Jesus, see Tamás Visi, "John the Baptist: A Jewish Preacher Recast as the Herald of Jesus," https://www.thetorah.com/article/john-the-baptist-a-jewish-preacher-recast-as-the-herald-of-jesus (accessed March 24, 2023).

Notes

11. E. P. Sanders, *Paul and Palestinian Judaism: A Comparison of Patterns of Religion* (Philadelphia: Fortress, 1977), 422. Davies and Allison refer to this concept when summarizing their understanding of the text, see *The Gospel according to Saint Matthew*, 1:309: "Thus the Baptist is not overturning the fundamental idea of covenant but rather repudiating the popular understanding of what the Abrahamic covenant entailed. John does away not with covenant but with popular covenantal nomism." Their and Sanders's usages of "covenantal nomism" do not seem to concur.

12. Gale, "The Gospel according to Matthew," 15. For additional information about the concept *zekhut avot*, see Arthur Marmorstein, *The Doctrine of Merits in Old Rabbinical Literature* (Oxford: Oxford University Press, 1920), and Solomon Schechter, *Aspects of Rabbinic Theology*...(Woodstock, VT: Jewish Lights, 1993 [1909]), 170–98. As a matter fact, Schechter also discusses the Merit of the Mothers; see pp. 172f. According to rabbinic hermeneutics, "there is no before and after in the Torah" (*ein muqdam u-meuchar ba-Torah*, see, e.g., *Mekhilta Shirata* 7); hence Abraham can be delivered through the merits of Jacob (!) because of *zekhut banim* (merits of the children); see *Leviticus Rabbah* 36.4f. For additional examples of *zekhut*, see C. G. Montefiore and H. Loewe, *A Rabbinic Anthology: Selected and Arranged with Comments and Introductions* (Philadelphia: Meridien / Jewish Publication Society of America, 1963 [1938]) 38, 337, 676, and 689.

13. W. D. Davies, *Paul and Rabbinic Judaism: Some Rabbinic Elements in Pauline Theology* (London: SPCK, 1962), 272. Cf. Rom 9:6–8.

14. See, e.g., Schweizer, *The Good News according to Matthew*, 49f.

15. Cf., e.g., Hab 2:4, which in the *New Revised Standard Version* is translated "the righteous live by their faith," but it could also mean that one should live in accordance with one's belief.

16. Schechter, *Aspects of Rabbinic Theology*, 173. (*Petra* is the Greek word for "rock"; cf. the wordplay about Simon Peter's name and mission in, e.g., Matt 16:18.)

17. Cf. wordplays on *banim* (children) and *bonim* (builders) (ch. 10).

18. *Genesis Rabbah* 12.9 and 15.4.

CHAPTER 2

1. "Lady Mobster (1998)," https://www.youtube.com/watch?v=g1u8 qLM_OHc (accessed June 21, 2022).

2. Benno Jacob, *The Second Book of the Bible Exodus Interpreted by Benno Jacob* (Hoboken, NJ: Ktav, 1992), 650.

3. For a bibliography (until the early 1990s), see Willard M. Swartley, ed., *The Love of Enemy and Nonretaliation in the New Testament* (Louisville, KY: Westminster John Knox Press, 1992).

4. Bernard S. Jackson, "The Problem of Exod. XXI 22–5 (Ius talionis)," *Vetus Testamentum* 23 (1973): 273.

5. Raymond Westbrook and Bruce Wells, *Everyday Law in Biblical Israel: An Introduction* (Louisville, KY: Westminster John Knox Press, 2009), 78.

6. Davies and Allison, *The Gospel according to Saint Matthew*, 1:551 and 552. They list a number of Jewish parallels.

7. Davies and Allison argue that the accusation specifically to annul the *prophets* does not make so much sense: "one wonders whether such an accusation was ever brought against Christians or their Lord." The most plausible conclusion is that those words are a redactional addition, "which has made for an awkward construction." This, subsequently, is evidence for the remaining part not being redactional: "Do not think that I have come to abolish the *Torah*"; see *The Gospel according to Saint Matthew*, 1:484.

8. Lachs points out that this only applies to square script, since in old Hebrew script the *yud* was no smaller than any of the other letter; see *A Rabbinic Commentary on the New Testament*, 88. Does Matthew 5:18 indicate that square script was in use in the first century?

9. It is difficult to ascertain to what extent the *ketarim* were in use at the first century. Matthew 5:18 certainly points in the direction that they actually were written in manuscripts at that time.

10. Cf. Davies and Allison, *The Gospel according to Saint Matthew*, 1:550: Jesus *surpasses* the OT [i.e., Old Testament] teaching" (emphasis added). See also p. 1:566: "Yet it is precisely because it [i.e., the Sermon on the Mount] is always before us and never within reach that our gospel's window on the ideal, like a guiding star, even beckons the faithful to move forward." Similarly, Levine, *The Misunderstood Jew*, 47: "Jesus does not 'oppose' the Law; he extends it." Reinhard Neudecker, too, argues that Jesus does not oppose the Torah itself; however, he argues that Jesus's teachings "seem to stand in opposition to Scribal and Pharisaic interpretations, legislations, or practices concerning these biblical injunctions"; see *Moses Interpreted by the Pharisees and Jesus: Matthew's Antitheses in the Light of Early Rabbinic Literature*, 2nd ed. (Rome: Gregorian & Biblical Press, 2015), 39. Davies and Allison list as many as nine interpretations of *plêroun* (to fulfill), see *The Gospel according to Saint Matthew*, 1:485f.

11. Exod 21:23–25, Lev 24:19f., and Deut 19:21. It is the version in Leviticus that most explicitly speaks about retribution. The rabbis chose the parallel in Exodus as the starting point for their interpretations.

12. Annika Wenemark, "'Öga för öga, tand för tand': En biblisk vedergällningslag?" (Bachelor's thesis, Lund University, 2013). Her four interpretations are presented here in a somewhat modified form, to suit the purpose in this chapter, which primarily focuses on the Matthean text.

13. One rare exception is the case of the *nokmim* (Revengers) who after the end of the Second World War sought revenge against the Germans for the Holocaust, but this group, consisting of circa fifty fanatics, is certainly not representative; see Dina Porat, *Nakam: The Holocaust Survivors Who Sought Full-Scale Revenge* (Redwood City, CA: Stanford University Press, 2022).

Notes

14. John Piper, *"Love Your Enemies": Jesus' Love Command in the Synoptic Gospels and in the Early Christian Paraenesis; A History of the Tradition and Interpretation of Its Uses* (Grand Rapids, MI: Baker Book House, 1991), 89 (emphases in the original). On the same page, he writes: "Jesus' command not to resist evil...demands the opposite of the Old Testament legal principle, 'an eye for an eye and a tooth for a tooth'....If and when Jesus' word is binding, then the other is not."

15. Schweizer, *The Good News according to Matthew*, 110, 133, and 136 (emphasis added).

16. Jonathan Klawans, "The Law," in *The Jewish Annotated New Testament*, 1st ed., ed. Amy-Jill Levine and Marc Zvi Brettler (Oxford: Oxford University Press, 2011), 517. His wordings are slightly revised in the second edition (2017); see p. 656: "the Torah's literal sense does not define Jewish law, whether for the rabbis, the Dead Sea sectarians, or for Jesus and his followers."

17. Martha T. Roth (author) and Piotr Michalowski (ed.), *Law Collections from Mesopotamia and Asia Minor* (Atlanta: Scholars Press, 1995), 217. Isaac Kalimi, too, argues that the passages in the Torah limit "primitive vengeance which was often quite out of proportion to the alleged offense"; see "Targumic and Midrashic Exegesis in Contradiction to the Peshat of Biblical Text," in *Biblical Interpretation in Judaism and Christianity*, ed. Isaac Kalimi and Peter J. Haas (New York: T&T Clark, 2006), 14.

18. Hans Jochen Boecker, *Law and the Administration of Justice in the Old Testament and Ancient East* (Minneapolis: Augsburg, 1980), 174.

19. The fact that the scriptural authority for the fifth criterion for pecuniary compensation was the verse "you shall cut off her hand" (Deut 25:12) proves that its original sense had long been a dead letter; see David Daube, *The New Testament and Rabbinic Judaism* (Peabody, MA: Hendrickson, reprint of 1956), 263–65. However, if this biblical verse deals with *preventing* harm, not with *retributing* harm, this argument is somewhat weakened.

20. *Talmud Bavli Bava Qamma* 83b.

21. Lachs, *A Rabbinic Commentary on the New Testament*, 103f. Cf. Jackson, "The Problem of Exod. XXI 22–5 (Ius talionis)," 280f.

22. Daube, *The New Testament and Rabbinic Judaism*, 255 (emphases added).

23. Daube, *The New Testament and Rabbinic Judaism*, 257: "He was not combating talion in the case of mutilation."

24. Daube, *The New Testament and Rabbinic Judaism*, 265. He even calls this hermeneutical trajectory "a plain instance" of the evolution from Scripture via the New Testament to the early rabbinic texts.

25. Benno Jacob, *Auge um Auge: Eine Untersuchung zum Alten und Neuen Testament* (Berlin: Philo, 1929), 25–48.

26. See, e.g., Nahum M. Sarna, *The JPS Torah Commentary: Exodus...* (New York: Jewish Publication Society, 1991), 126: "Rabbinic tradition understood the biblical formulation to mean monetary payment and not physical retaliation." As a matter of fact, there is only one deviant opinion: as so often,

it is Eli'ezer ben Hyrcanus who is in favor of a literal interpretation—that is, physical retaliation. All other rabbis argue in support of monetary compensation. Interestingly, in Numbers 35:31 it is stated that one cannot accept compensation for a murderer's life; hence, one *can* accept monetary compensation in other cases. Daube argues that Jesus omitted the first clause "Life for life" because it belonged to criminal law, but the other clauses to private law; see *The New Testament and Rabbinic Judaism*, 258.

27. See, e.g., Davies and Allison, *The Gospel according to Saint Matthew*, 1:545.

28. Cf. Davies and Allison, *The Gospel according to Saint Matthew*, 1:542.

29. Davies and Allison, *The Gospel according to Saint Matthew*, 1:540 and 1:542.

30. The Greek original in v. 19 only says, "the Wrath." The two quotations are from Deut 32:35 and Prov 25:21f.

31. Lenn E. Goodman, *Love Thy Neighbor as Thyself* (Oxford: Oxford University Press, 2008), 15.

32. Raphael Jospe, "'Love Your Fellow as Yourself': Universalism and Particularism in Jewish Exegesis of Leviticus 19:18." *Jewish-Christian Relations* (https://www.jcrelations.net/articles/article/love-your-fellow-as-yourself.html) (accessed April 3, 2023).

33. For Jewish commentaries on Lev 19:18, see, e.g., James L. Kugel, *In Potiphar's House: The Interpretive Life of Biblical Texts* (New York: HarperSanFrancisco, 1990), 214–46.

34. Lachs, *A Rabbinic Commentary on the New Testament*, 107.

35. Davies and Allison pose the question how the commandment to love one's enemies is to be harmonized with "the vituperations so frequently hurled at the Jewish leaders"; see *The Gospel according to Saint Matthew*, 1:563.

36. In a book published in Swedish in 1944, Daniel Brick argues that it is unthinkable that Jesus, who was a scribe and who knew the Scriptures ("som var skriftlärd") and therefore must have known what was written, would have said anything like that. He concludes that this statement in the Sermon on the Mount must be the result of some kind of misinterpretation. See *Varför anklagar man judarna?* (Stockholm: Albert Bonnier, 1944), 27. It is intriguing that the Qumran scrolls were discovered only a couple of years later, in which, as a matter of fact, there is a most relevant parallel. Probably the first to notice this similarity was Morton Smith, "Mt. 5.43: 'Hate Thine Enemy,'" *Journal of Biblical Literature* 45 (1952): 71–73, esp. 71. However, Smith does not argue that Matthew ("to say nothing of Jesus") was actually criticizing the teaching of the Qumran community. He merely points out the similarity. His own suggestion is that a Galilean *targum* may have glossed "you shall love your neighbor" with the words "and hate your enemy," similar to the gloss "that which is hateful to you, do not do to him." But is not a nonexistent Galilean *targum* less convincing than an existent Judean parallel?

37. The fact that it is quoted in *Mishnah Pirqei Avot* 4.19 (*Siddur* 4.24) is evidence for the centrality of this admonition.

38. *The Community Rule* [1QS] 1.9–11, cf. 1.4 and 9.21–23. Translated as in *Outside the Bible* 3:2929. Levine, too, writes that the Matthean text "perhaps" is reflecting the saying from the Qumran community; see *Short Stories by Jesus*, 93.

39. Cf. Amy-Jill Levine and Marc Zvi Brettler, *The Bible with and without Jesus: How Jews and Christians Read the Same Stories Differently* (New York: HarperOne, 2020), 217: "The irony is that, despite the frequent Christian claim that Jews take texts literally whereas Christians understand their spiritual value, here it is Christians who are reading the Torah literally and imposing that literal reading on Judaism."

40. Davies and Allison, *The Gospel according to Saint Matthew*, 1:565.

CHAPTER 3

1. Immanuel Kant, *Groundwork of the Metaphysics of Morals: With On a Supposed Right to Lie on Philanthropic Concerns*, 3rd ed., trans. James W. Ellington (Indianapolis: Hackett, 1993 [German: 1785]), 30. The term "Golden Rule" can be traced back to the end of the Middle Ages; see Hans Dieter Betz, *The Sermon on the Mount* (Minneapolis: Fortress, 1995), 509.

2. Davies and Allison, *The Gospel according to Saint Matthew*, 1:687.

3. Davies and Allison, *The Gospel according to Saint Matthew*, 1:686f. and George Foot Moore, *Judaism in the First Centuries: The Age of Tannaim*, 3 vols. (Peabody, MA: Hendrickson, 1960 [1927–30]), 2:87f. For more extensive surveys, see Albrecht Dihle, *Die goldene Regel: Eine Einführung in die Geschichte der antiken und frühchristlichen Vulgärethik* (Göttingen: Vandenhoeck & Ruprecht, 1962), and Philip S. Alexander, "Jesus and the Golden Rule," in *Hillel and Jesus: Comparative Studies of Two Major Religious Leaders*, ed. James H. Charlesworth and Loren L. Johns (Minneapolis: Fortress, 1997), 363–88.

4. For a similar prohibition, see, e.g., *Mishnah Pirqei Avot* 2.4: "and judge not your fellow until you have come into his position" (*we-al tadin et-chaverkha 'ad she-tagia' li-mqomo*).

5. The terminology is not consistent, probably partly because of the similarity between the Hebrew words *kol* (everything), *kelal* (rule), and *kelalah* (its [i.e., the *Torah*] rule): hence "the whole Torah" (*kol ha-Torah*), "a rule in the Torah" (*kelal ba-Torah*), "a rule of the Torah" (*kelalah shel Torah*), and "a rule in which the whole Torah is included" (*kelal she-kol ha-Torah kelalah bo*) are variants of the same tradition, see, e.g., Menahem Kister, "The Golden Rule and Ancient Jewish Biblical Exegesis: The Pluriformity of a Tradition," *Journal of Biblical Literature* 141 (2022): 722 and 730.

6. Davies and Allison, *The Gospel according to Saint Matthew*, 1:685f.

7. *Talmud Bavli Shabbat* 31a. Cf. Tob 4:15 and *Testament of Issachar* 5.2 and 7.6, *Testament of Zebulun* 5.1f., and *Testament of Benjamin* 3.3.

8. W. A. Spooner, "Golden Rule," in *Encyclopaedia of Religion and Ethics*, ed. James Hastings, 10 vols. (New York: Charles Scribner, 1928), 6:311f.

9. G. B. Caird, *The Gospel of Saint Luke* (Harmondsworth: Penguin, 1963), 104f.

10. Schweizer, *The Good News according to Matthew*, 174 and 175 (emphases added).

11. Moore, *Judaism in the First Centuries*, 2:87f.

12. Davies and Allison, *The Gospel according to Saint Matthew*, 1:687: "It also bears remarking that the negative and positive versions appear in early Christian literature with little discussion of their differences." It is noteworthy that the Western text (e.g., Codex Bezae [D]) adds a *negative* form of the Golden Rule to the Apostolic Decree in Acts 15:20 and 29. As Bruce M. Metzger writes, the Western text has "a fondness for paraphrase"; see *A Textual Commentary on the Greek New Testament...*, 3rd ed. (Stuttgart: United Bible Societies, 1975), xviii. The purpose of the decree was to settle the question whether Gentile Christ followers are obligated to keep the commandments in the Law. The Apostolic Council decided that they only need to keep a few commandments. Hence, the *negative* form if the Golden Rule in this manuscript is a summary of what gentile Christ followers are mandated to do. For additional comments on the Apostolic Decree, see, e.g., Jesper Svartvik, *Mark and Mission: Mk 7:1–23 in Its Narrative and Historical Contexts* (Stockholm: Almqvist & Wiksell International, 2000), 119–28.

13. Davies and Allison, *The Gospel according to Saint Matthew*, 1:687.

14. Similarly, in Galatians 5:14, Paul also quotes Leviticus 19:18, and adds, in the following verse, "If, however, you bite and devour one another, take care that you are not consumed by one another."

15. Davies and Allison, *The Gospel according to Saint Matthew*, 1:689.

16. Kister, "The Golden Rule," 723.

17. Kister, "The Golden Rule," 724.

18. Davies and Allison, *The Gospel according to Saint Matthew*, 1:688.

19. *Avot de-Rabbi Natan* (version B), ch. 26. For Kister's translation (with a few minor changes), see "The Golden Rule," 720.

20. *Sifra Qedushim* 2.2 (ed. Weiss 89b).

21. Kister, "The Golden Rule," 735.

22. See, e.g., Richard Kugelman, *James and Jude* (Dublin: Veritas, 1980), 27.

23. Martin Dibelius and Heinrich Greeven, *James: A Commentary on the Epistle of James*, ed. Helmut Koester, trans. Michael A. Williams (Philadelphia: Fortress, 1975 [German: 1964]), 143 and 142 (in that order).

24. Dibelius and Greeven, *James*, 142.

25. Dibelius and Greeven, *James*, 144.

26. It is not clear, however, exactly how this conclusion is related to their statement that "it is a Christian law, and consequently it is not obeyed by being ever so careful in tiny matters, but rather by fulfilling the great com-

mandment of love," which does not seem to be consistent with their general understanding of the expression "royal law"; see Dibelius and Greeven, *James*, 144.

27. Krister Stendahl and Emilie T. Sander, "Biblical Literature: New Testament Literature," in *The New Encyclopaedia Britannica (Macropaedia)*, 15th ed., 30 vols. (Chicago: Encyclopaedia Britannica, 1975), 2:969.

28. The two rules are criticized differently: it is often stated that the "Jewish" form of Golden Rule is *only* negative (whereas Jesus's—better—version is positive), and the "Jewish" way of interpreting Leviticus 19:18 *only* applies to fellow Jews (whereas the—better—Christian interpretation widens it to everyone).

CHAPTER 4

1. The order in the Gospel of Thomas 47 is inverted.

2. See David Flusser's analysis "Do You Prefer New Wine?" *Immanuel* 9 (1979): 26.

3. Alistair Kee, "The Old Coat and the New Wine: A Parable of Repentance," *Novum Testamentum* 12 (1970): 18.

4. Kee, "The Old Coat and the New Wine," 14.

5. S. MacLean Gilmour, "The Gospel according to St. Luke," in *Interpreter's Bible*, ed. George Arthur Buttrick, 12 vols. (New York: Abingdon-Cokesbury Press, 1952), 8:110, and D. E. Nineham, *The Gospel of St. Mark* (Harmondsworth: Penguin, 1969), 102.

6. Schweizer, *The Good News according to Matthew*, 227.

7. Schweizer, *The Good News according to Matthew*, 227.

8. Huub van de Sandt and David Flusser, *The Didache* (Minneapolis: Fortress, 2002), 293: "The instruction in Did 8:1 does not seem to presuppose a situation in which Jews and Christians fasted two days every week but rather implies a discussion as to which two days are preferable once an individual or a community had indeed decided to fast." The reason for choosing Wednesdays and Fridays may be that these two days had a certain prominence in the solar calendar that was used by the Essenes of the Qumran community. For additional aspects on the two calendars in first-century Judaism, see Annie Jaubert, *La date de la Cène* (Paris: Gabalda, 1957).

9. Davies and Allison, *The Gospel according to Saint Matthew*, 2:115.

10. Davies and Allison, *The Gospel according to Saint Matthew*, 2:112.

11. Kee is even harsher in his assessment (p. 16): "To attribute the idea of incompatibility to Jesus, as a way of describing his relationship to Judaism, is *bad theology* and *bad history*. It is also *bad exegesis* of the Reply to the Question about Fasting" (emphases added).

12. Joachim Jeremias, *The Parables of Jesus*, trans. S. H. Hooke (London: SCM, 3rd ed. 1972 [German: 1970]), 118.

13. Kee, "The Old Coat and the New Wine," 19. New wineskins that burst are mentioned in, e.g., Joshua 9:13 and Job 32:19.

14. Davies and Allison, *The Gospel according to Saint Matthew*, 2:115.
15. Kee, "The Old Coat and the New Wine," 17.
16. Kee, "The Old Coat and the New Wine," 20.
17. For further comments, see, e.g., Uwe-Karsten Plisch, *The Gospel of Thomas: Original Text with Commentary*, trans. Gesine Schenke Robinson (Stuttgart: Deutsche Bibelgesellschaft, 2008), 123–26.
18. Kee, "The Old Coat and the New Wine," 13.
19. *Sifrei Devarim* 48 (ed. Finkelstein, p. 111, emphasis added).
20. Cf. Meir Zlotowitz and Nosson Scherman, *Pirkei Avos: Ethics of the Fathers...* (New York: Mesorah, 1984), 41.
21. Flusser, "Do You Prefer New Wine?," 30.
22. Flusser, "Do You Prefer New Wine?," 31.

CHAPTER 5

1. In *Mishnah Pirqei Avot* 3.5 the term *'ol malkhut* refers not to the kingdom of Heaven but to the rules and conditions of an earthly power. In *Talmud Bavli Avodah Zarah* 5a the word refers to the yoke of repentance.
2. Cf. Davies and Allison list three interpretations: (1) those burdened by the Pharisaic establishment, (2) those suffering from the costly demands of discipleship, and (3) those suffering under the weight of sin, see *The Gospel according to Saint Matthew*, 2:288.
3. For a theology that contrasts "the yoke of self-righteousness" and Christian faith, see, e.g., "What Does It Mean When Jesus Says 'My Yoke Is Easy and My Burden Is Light' (Matthew 11:30)?" https://m.youtube.com/watch?v=pOMgDwMZ1v8 (accessed April 6, 2023).
4. Rudolf Bultmann, *Primitive Christianity in Its Contemporary Setting*, trans. R. H. Fuller (London: Collins, 1960 [German: 1949]), 78 (emphasis in the original).
5. Otto Bauernfeind, *anapausis*, 1:350f., in *Theological Dictionary of the New Testament*, ed. Gerhard Kittel and Gerhard Friedrich; trans. and ed. Geoffrey W. Bromiley (Grand Rapids, MI: Eerdmans, 1964–76 [German: 1933–49]), 1:351.
6. Schweizer, *The Good News according to Matthew*, 274.
7. Schweizer, *The Good News according to Matthew*, 272.
8. An (in)famous example of the discussion between the two houses: Should one tell a bride that she is unattractive? Whereas Shammai, referring to Exodus 23:7, declared that one should not lie, Hillel said that every woman is "beautiful and attractive" (*naah wa-chasudah*) on her wedding day (*Talmud Bavli Ketubbot* 16b–17a). In matrimonial issues, however, Hillel was more lenient, *seen from the male perspective*, e.g., a man was allowed to divorce a woman even if she had only burned a meal (*Talmud Bavli Gittin* 90a).
9. *Talmud Bavli 'Eruvin* 13b.
10. Floyd V. Filson, *A Commentary on the Gospel according to St. Matthew*, 2nd ed. (London: Adam & Charles Black, 1971), 144.

Notes

11. Davies and Allison argue from *solution* to *plight* when stating "that the yoke of Christ alone brings true rest, and that therefore all...who have not come to Jesus must be deprived of rest, that is, must be weary and burdened"; see *The Gospel according to Saint Matthew*, 2:288. For reflections on the from-solution-to-plight hermeneutics, see Sanders, *Paul and Palestinian Judaism*, 543–56, esp. 554. Jacques E. Ménard argued that the topic in the Gospel of Thomas was celibacy; see *L'Évangile selon Thomas* (Leiden: Brill, 1975), 192.

12. It is noteworthy that Martin Hengel's chapter "Crucifixion among the Jews" is only two (!) pages long; see *Crucifixion in the Ancient World and the Folly of the Message of the Cross*, trans. John Bowden (Philadelphia: Fortress, 1977 [German: 1976]), 84f.

13. Matt 11:29, 12:43, Luke 11:24, Rev 4:8, and 14:11.

14. *Anapausis* occurs in, e.g., the Gospel of Thomas 50, 60, and 90. (In logion 90 *anaupasis* [*sic*] is obviously a spelling error for *anapausis*. For additional references to text stemming from "Gnostic circles," see Davies and Allison, *The Gospel according to Saint Matthew*, 2:288.

15. The Hebrew term behind the Greek, probably *beit midrash* or possibly *beit musar*, indicates, as Benjamin G. Wright III writes, "a formal setting of pedagogy," adding that scholars "debate about what a 'school' would have looked like in this period"; see "Wisdom of Ben Sira," in *Outside the Bible: Ancient Jewish Writings Related to Scripture*, ed. Louis H. Feldman, James L. Kugel, and Lawrence H. Schiffman, 3 vols. (Philadelphia: Jewish Publication Society, 2013), 3:2350.

16. *Mishnah Pirqei Avot* 3.5 states that the one who accepts "the yoke of the Torah" (*'ol Torah*) is excused from societal duties (*'ol malkhut*; lit. "the yoke of the kingdom") and mundane care (*'ol derekh eretz*), For the expression "the yoke of the kingdom," see also *Mishnah Berakhot* 2.2.

17. It is often pointed out that the language in the preceding passage is more Johannine than one usually finds in the Synoptic Gospels. It has even been called a "bolt from a Johannine blue"; see, e.g., Davies and Allison, *The Gospel according to Saint Matthew*, 2:282. They state that Karl von Hase coined the expression in 1876.

CHAPTER 6

1. See, e.g., *Apostolic and Post-apostolic Times*, trans. Robert A. Guelich (Grand Rapids, MI: Baker Books House, 1970 [German: 1962]).

2. The introduction to the fourth volume is called "The Historical Jesus Is the Halakic Jesus"; see John P. Meier, *A Marginal Jew: Rethinking the Historical Jesus* (New Haven, CT: Yale University Press, 2009), 4.1–25. (Whereas Meier chose the transliteration "halakic," the present book prefers "halakhic.")

3. Leonhard Goppelt, *Jesus, Paul and Judaism: An Introduction to New Testament Theology*, trans. Edward Schroeder (New York: Nelson, 1964 [German: 1954]), 43, 61, and 63.

4. Goppelt, *Apostolic and Post-apostolic Times*, 74.

5. E. P. Sanders, *Jesus and Judaism* (Philadelphia: Fortress, 1985), 404.

6. Leonhard Goppelt, *Theology of the New Testament*, ed. Jürgen Roloff; trans. John E. Alsup, 2 vols. (Grand Rapids, MI: Eerdmans, 1981–82 [German: 1975–76]), 1:94.

7. Davies and Allison, presenting eight suggestions, prefer a Christological interpretation; see *The Gospel according to Saint Matthew*, 2:310f.

8. Francis White Beare, "The Sabbath Was Made for Man?," *Journal of Biblical Literature* 79 (1960): 133.

9. E. P. Sanders, "Jesus and the Constraints of the Law," *Journal for the Study of the New Testament* 17 (1983): 20.

10. In Acts 1:12 we find the expression *sabbatou hodos*, "a sabbath's way," which refers to the distance one was allowed to walk on *shabbat*. The biblical foundation for not traveling on *shabbat* is Exodus 16:29, where it says that one is not allowed to go "from one's place" (*mi-meqomo*). Indeed, we cannot know that this rabbinic decree was in force at the time of Jesus. It is quite possible that the regulations were even stricter at that time—that is, less than one thousand meters. Several *techum* signs from antiquity have been discovered; the purpose of these signs was to inform visitors and citizens how far they were allowed to walk on *shabbat*.

11. Beare, "The Sabbath Was Made for Man?," 133.

12. Davies and Allison, *The Gospel according to Saint Matthew*, 2:304. For the rabbinic expression, see *Mishnah Chagigah* 1.8: "The rules about *shabbat*…are as mountains hanging by a hair, for the [teaching of] Scripture [thereon] is scanty and the rules many."

13. See *Talmud Bavli Shabbat* 128a.

14. David Flusser (with R. Steven Notley), *The Sage from Galilee: Rediscovering Jesus' Genius* (Grand Rapids, MI: Eerdmans, 2007), 35.

15. Krister Stendahl, "Kvinnan i Bibeln och Kyrkan," in *Handlingar rörande prästmötet i Stockholm den 2, 3 och 4 juni 1975* (Stockholm: Stockholms stift, 1975), 70.

16. See, e.g., *Talmud Bavli Yoma* 85b.

17. Solomon Zeitlin, *Who Crucified Jesus?* (New York: Harper, 1942), 129.

18. In Mark 2:26 it says that Avyatar was the chief priest, but according to 1 Samuel 21:1 it was his son Achimelekh. The Matthean and Lukan versions do not state his name.

19. Y. D. Gilad, "On Fasting on the Sabbath." *Tarbiz* 52 (1983): 1–15 (Hebrew).

20. See, e.g., *John R. Donahue*, "Recent Studies on the Origin of 'Son of Man' in the Gospels," *Catholic Biblical Quarterly* 48 (1986): 484–98, and Davies and Allison, *The Gospel according to Saint Matthew*, 2:43–53, who present four categories: (1) an established messianic title in first-century Judaism, (2) a background in the Scriptures, (3) an Aramaic idiom, perhaps a substitute for the personal pronoun "I," and (4) reference to the First/Primal Man.

On p. 50 they write that "we are inclined to think that Jesus used the son of man idiom on more than one occasion in a novel or quasititular manner with the intent of directing his hearers to Dan 7, and that he saw in Daniel's eschatological figure a prophecy of his own person and fate," and on p. 52: "in Matthew 'the Son of man' is a title whose first function is to tell the reader that Jesus is the figure seen in the vision of Dan 7."

21. Beare, "The Sabbath Was Made for Man?," 131.

22. *Talmud Bavli Yoma* 85b and *Mekhilta de-Rabbi Yishmaʻel* (commenting on Exod 31:14; ed. Lauterbach 3.198).

23. *Mekhilta de-Rabbi Yishmaʻel* 3.198.

24. Davies and Allison, *The Gospel according to Saint Matthew*, 2:311.

25. Beare, "The Sabbath Was Made for Man?," 134.

26. Davies and Allison, *The Gospel according to Saint Matthew*, 2:305: "But where exactly does that leave the ordinary Christian? Is the situation depicted normative or exceptional? And is the sabbath abrogated or modified?"

27. The Greek word *meizon* (larger) is in the neuter (referring to the event per se), not masculine (which could and would refer to the person Jesus). For the perspective that gentiles who keep the *shabbat* are included, see, e.g., Isa 56:6f.

28. The same expression also occurs in Acts when describing Paul's behavior on *shabbat*; see Acts 17:2: "And Paul went in[to the synagogue], *as was his custom*" (emphases added).

CHAPTER 7

1. *Mishnah Kilayim* 2.8f. and 3.2. It remains, of course, for these scholars to provide evidence that the prohibition was in force at the time of Jesus. The fact that the Matthean version has the expression "in his field" may point in that direction, but it is not a very strong argument. However, Lachs argues that it is "most likely" that Matthew was aware of the rabbinic regulations (and that Luke was not cognizant of them); see *A Rabbinic Commentary on the New Testament*, 225.

2. Bernard Brandon Scott, *Hear Then the Parable: A Commentary on the Parables of Jesus* (Minneapolis: Fortress, 1989), 376.

3. Scott, *Hear Then the Parable*, 383 and 387.

4. Scott, *Hear Then the Parable*, 387.

5. Lachs, *A Rabbinic Commentary on the New Testament*, 224f.

6. Ryan S. Schellenberg, "Kingdom as Contaminant? The Role of Repertoire in the Parables of the Mustard Seed and the Leaven," *Catholic Biblical Quarterly* 71 (2009): 532f.

7. A topic outside the scope of this chapter is to explore possible reasons for the differences between the two gospels: why a mountain (*oros*) in Matthew and a mulberry tree (*sykaminos*, cf. "sycamine") in Luke? Did Luke misread *sinapi* (mustard) as *sykaminos*?

8. Klyne R. Snodgrass, *Stories with Intent: A Comprehensive Guide to the Parables of Jesus* (Grand Rapids, MI: Eerdmans, 2008), 221.

9. Levine, *Short Stories by Jesus*, 168.

10. Davies and Allison, *The Gospel according to Saint Matthew*, 2:415.

11. Snodgrass, *Stories with Intent*, 220.

12. Possibly in Greek: *poiei kladon megan*. The word *tar* (branch) is a *hapax legomenon* (occurring only once) in the Gospel of Thomas.

13. Davies and Allison, *The Gospel according to Saint Matthew*, 2:418.

14. T. W. Manson, *The Teaching of Jesus: Studies of Its Form and Content* (Cambridge, UK: Cambridge University Press, 1948), 133.

15. Scott, *Hear Then the Parable*, 67.

16. For additional comments, see, e.g., Davies and Allison, *The Gospel according to Saint Matthew*, 2:420.

17. Robert W. Funk, *Honest to Jesus: Jesus for a New Millennium* (San Francisco: HarperSanFrancisco, 1996), 157.

18. Funk, *Honest to Jesus*, 157.

19. Funk, *Honest to Jesus*, 157.

20. Funk, *Honest to Jesus*, 157.

21. Schellenberg, "Kingdom as Contaminant?," 538.

22. For his long list of beneficial effects, see *Natural History* 20.87 (§236–40). Pliny writes in 19.54 (§170f.) that mustard grows wild (*nulla cultura*) and has the healthiest effects on the body (*effectus ac saluberrimum corpori*).

23. Levine, *Short Stories by Jesus*, 181.

24. Levine, *Short Stories by Jesus*, 174. She does not, however, develop this observation.

25. Levine, *Short Stories by Jesus*, 168.

CHAPTER 8

1. On leaven in Jewish thought and life at that time, see, e.g., Shemuel Safrai, "Religion in Everyday Life." In *The Jewish People in the First Century: Historical Geography, Political History, Social, Cultural and Religious Life and Institutions*, ed. Shemuel Safrai and Menachem Stern, with David Flusser and W. C. van Unnik, 2 vols. (Philadelphia: Fortress, 1974–76), 2:808–10.

2. Funk, *Honest to Jesus*, 157 (emphasis added).

3. Levine, *Short Stories by Jesus*, 129.

4. C. H. Dodd, *The Parables of the Kingdom* (Glasgow: Collins, 1978 [1935]), 144.

5. Schweizer, *The Good News according to Matthew*, 306 and 307.

6. Filson, *A Commentary on the Gospel according to St. Matthew*, 162.

7. See, e.g., Levine, *The Misunderstood Jew*, 36. For an example of a Christian text that actually refers to what is leavened positively, see, e.g.,

Macarius, *Homily* 25.3: "We have not yet been leavened with *the leaven of sincerity,* but are still in the leaven of wickedness" (emphasis added).

8. See, e.g., Hugo Odeberg, "Senapskornet och surdegen," *Erevna* 11 (1954): 56f.

9. Davies and Allison, *The Gospel according to Saint Matthew*, 2:424.

10. The Greek word is *saton* (plural: *sata*), which is a loan word from the Aramaic *sata* and the Hebrew *seah*. Lachs points out that *seah* was used for a variety of measures (e.g., five Jerusalem *seah* were equal to six desert *seah*); see *A Rabbinic Commentary on the New Testament*, 226.

11. Jeremias, *The Parables of Jesus*, 147.

12. It is less important that Sarah is baking "cakes" (Hebrew: *'ugot*), not bread. In biblical Hebrew an *'ugah* is not a "cookie" as in modern Hebrew; see Exod 12.39.

13. Levine, *Short Stories by Jesus*, 136. Referring to 2 Esdras 4:39f. and Romans 8:22, she is suggesting that the yeast in the bread parable may be a reference to pregnancy; we see here, she argues, a "common metaphor that associates pregnancy and childbirth with the messianic age."

14. Levine, *Short Stories by Jesus*, 136.

15. Davies and Allison, *The Gospel according to Saint Matthew*, 2:423.

16. Levine, *Short Stories by Jesus*, 137.

CHAPTER 9

1. See, e.g., Menahem Kister, "Law, Morality and Rhetoric," in *Studies in Ancient Midrash*, ed. James L. Kugel (Cambridge, MA: Harvard University Press, 2001), 154: "Transmitted in a different, nonhalakhic and sometimes antinomistic context, this saying [Matt 15:11 and Mark 7:15] came to be the most radical antinomistic saying in the Synoptic Gospels." For a survey of the role of Matt 15:1–20 and Mark 7:1–23 in the quest for the historical Jesus, see Svartvik, *Mark and Mission*, 13–108.

2. See, e.g., Annette Aronowicz, "Translator's Introduction," in Emmanuel Levinas, *Nine Talmudic Readings*, trans. and with an intro. by Annette Aronowicz (Bloomington: Indiana University Press, 1994), xxii.

3. Boyarin, *The Jewish Gospels*, 117f.

4. Boyarin, *The Jewish Gospels*, 106.

5. The fact that liberal Judaism at times has referred to this statement by Jesus as a positive example does not change the fact that *in antiquity* Jewishness was defined by, for example, food laws observance. For liberal Judaism's appreciation of this statement, see, e.g., Claude G. Montefiore, *The Synoptic Gospels: Edited with an Introduction and a Commentary*, 2nd ed., 2 vols. (London: Macmillan, 1927), 1:170: "According to the principle laid down by Jesus, no *thing* can make you unclean. You can only make yourself unclean by sin. The principle seems profoundly true. It destroys with a prophet's blow the terrible incubus from which all ancient religions suffered, that

certain objects or physical states are in themselves taboo or religiously unclean" (emphasis in the original).

6. Eduard Schweizer, *The Good News according to Mark*, trans. Donald H. Madvig (London: SPCK, 1971 [German: 1967]), 146f. (emphasis added).

7. Ezra Palmer Gould, *A Critical and Exegetical Commentary on the Gospel according to St. Mark* (Edinburgh: T&T Clark, 1907 [1896]), 126 (emphasis added). The word "this" refers to the expression "the traditions of the elders."

8. Ernst Käsemann, *Essays on New Testament Themes*, trans. W. J. Montague (Philadelphia: Fortress, 1982 [German: 1960]), 101.

9. Robert W. Funk, *The Gospel of Mark: Red Letter Edition* (Sonoma, CA: Polebridge, 1991), 126 (emphasis added).

10. Richard S. McConnell, *Law and Prophecy in Matthew's Gospel: The Authority and Use of the Old Testament in the Gospel of St. Matthew* (Basel: Reinhardt, 1969), 79f. (emphasis added).

11. C. E. B. Cranfield, *The Gospel according to Saint Mark* (Cambridge, UK: Cambridge University Press, 1959), 244 (Greek letters in the original). However, it is far more likely that *telos* in Romans 10:4 means "climax," not "end."

12. Herbert Braun, *Jesus: Der Mann aus Nazareth und seine Zeit* (Stuttgart: Kreuz, 1969), 73 (emphases added).

13. See, e.g., Sigurd Grindheim, "Jesus and the Food Laws Revisited," *Journal for the Study of the Historical Jesus* 31 (2020), for a recently published article that claims that the historical Jesus (p. 76) "did not consider himself to be completely bound by the Mosaic law, at least not the food laws and purity laws."

14. Kister, "Law, Morality and Rhetoric," 152.

15. Heikki Räisänen, "Jesus and the Food Laws: Reflections on Mark 7:15," *Journal for the Study of the New Testament* 16 (1982): 79–100, republished in *The Torah and Christ: Essays in German and English on the Problem of the Law in Early Christianity* (Helsinki: Finnish Exegetical Society, 1986). See also E. P. Sanders, *Jesus and Judaism*, 264–67, esp. 267: "as the saying now stands it can hardly be authentic."

16. Montefiore, *The Synoptic Gospels*, 1:133.

17. Norman Perrin, *Rediscovering the Teaching of Jesus* (London: SCM, 1967), 150.

18. This is how Roger P. Booth paraphrases the meaning of the statement, *Jesus and the Laws of Purity: Tradition History and Legal History in Mark 7* (Sheffield, UK: Sheffield Academic Press, 1986), 214: "There is nothing outside a man which cultically defiles him as much as the things coming from a man ethically defile him."

19. Barbara Trainin Blank, "Portrait of Joseph Telushkin," *Hadassah Magazine* 81 (April 2000): 28. The transliteration of *lashon ha-ra'* as in the article. For the concept *lashon ha-ra'*, see the fifth interpretation below.

20. Gedalyahu Alon, *Jews, Judaism and the Classical World: Studies in Jewish History in the Times of the Second Temple and Talmud* (Jerusalem: Magness, 1977), 232. See also Yair Furstenberg, "Defilement Penetrating the Body." *New Testament Studies* 54 (2008): 199. The living-like-priests theory was first advanced by Adolf Büchler, *Der galiläische 'Am-ha 'Areṣ des zweiten Jahrhunderts: Beiträge zur innern Geschichte des palästinischen Judentums in den ersten zwei Jahrhunderten* (Wien: Hölder, 1906).

21. Furstenberg, "Defilement Penetrating the Body," 178. He argues that the logion was "a reaction against then-current innovations in the field of purity."

22. Furstenberg, "Defilement Penetrating the Body," 199. He notes that the member of the Qumran community did not wash their hands; instead, they fully immersed before every meal.

23. Furstenberg, "Defilement Penetrating the Body," 186.

24. Furstenberg, "Defilement Penetrating the Body," 193f. Hence, far from being an originally priestly custom, handwashing was, according to Furstenberg, a product of everyday behavior.

25. Furstenberg, "Defilement Penetrating the Body," 196f. Whereas the position of the synoptic Pharisees is situated within the *rabbinic* system, Jesus's arguments gave vent to the *levitical* system (by Furstenberg also called "the biblical law"). Hence, the Matthean and Markan Jesus takes the conservative position in this discussion.

26. Furstenberg, "Defilement Penetrating the Body," 184.

27. This is Daniel Boyarin's conclusion of Furstenberg's explanation, see *The Jewish Gospels*, 121.

28. Boyarin, *The Jewish Gospels*, 115. Hence, the accusation against the Pharisees that they "cross sea and land to make a single convert" (cf. Matt 23:15) does not refer to the proselytizing of gentiles, but to concerted efforts to persuade Jews to adhere to the Pharisaic interpretations of *halakhah*.

29. Boyarin, *The Jewish Gospels*, 116.

30. Boyarin, *The Jewish Gospels*, 118: "This is a debate between Jews about the correct way to keep the Torah, not an attack on the Torah."

31. Boyarin, *The Jewish Gospels*, 126.

32. E. P. Sanders, *Jewish Law from Jesus to the Mishnah: Five Studies* (Philadelphia: SCM / Trinity Press International, 1990), 28. See also *Jesus and Judaism*, 267, and E. P. Sanders and Margaret Davies, *Studying the Synoptic Gospels* (Philadelphia: SCM / Trinity Press International, 1989), 314.

33. Boyarin, *The Jewish Gospels*, 108f.

34. *Tosefta Peah* 1.2. Cf. James 3:1–12.

35. Matt 5:22 and, e.g., *Talmud Bavli Sanhedrin* 107a.

36. For an interesting parallel in the Apostolic Fathers, see *The Shepherd of Hermas* 2.2.3: *kai gar hautê ouk apechetai tês glôssês, en hê[i] ponêreutetai* (For she also does not refrain her tongue, with which she sins).

37. http://www.shamash.org/listarchives/oldflame/sheminii1.oldflame.95 (accessed January 31, 2000; emphases added).

CHAPTER 10

1. Aaron A. Milavec, "A Fresh Analysis of the Parable of the Wicked Husbandmen in the Light of Jewish-Christian Dialogue," in *Parable and Story in Judaism and Christianity*, ed. Clemens Thoma and Michael Wyschogrod (Mahwah, NJ: Paulist Press, 1989), 81.

2. With Soulen's definition this amounts to *punitive supersessionism*: "Because the Jews obstinately reject God's action in Christ, God in turn angrily rejects and punishes the Jews"; see *The God of Israel and Christian Theology*, 30.

3. Schweizer, *The Good News according to Matthew*, 412 and 414.

4. Schweizer, *The Good News according to Mark*, 241. Davies and Allison dismiss as *eisegesis* (i.e., reading into the text one's own ideas) the interpretation that the (Matthean) parable speaks about "the final dismissal of the Jews"; see *The Gospel according to Saint Matthew*, 3:190.

5. Schweizer, *The Good News according to Mark*, 241.

6. John Dominic Crossan, *In Parables: The Challenge of the Historical Jesus* (Sonoma, CA: Polebridge Press, 1992 [1973]), 94. See also "The Parable of the Wicked Husbandmen," *Journal of Biblical Literature* 90 (1971): 464.

7. Dodd, *The Parables of the Kingdom*, 16.

8. E.g., Crossan, "The Parable of the Wicked Husbandmen," *In Parables*, 84–94, *The Historical Jesus*, 351f., and *The Power of Parable: How Fiction by Jesus Became Fiction about Jesus* (New York: HarperOne, 2012), 134.

9. It is stated in the parable that the season of fruit drew near, hence it can hardly be less than *three* years. Given that it was a new vineyard, the *four*-year regulation in Leviticus 19:23–25 is relevant; see Lachs, *A Rabbinic Commentary on the New Testament*, 355. J. Duncan M. Derrett, argues that it probably took *five* years between the planting of the vineyard and the first payment; see, *Law in the New Testament* (London: Darton, Longman & Todd, 1970), 290.

10. Crossan, *The Historical Jesus*, 351.

11. See, e.g., Wilson, "'Thomas' and the Growth of the Gospels," 239, and Scott, *Hear Then This Parable*, 238.

12. The context from which his words are taken: "The parable of the Wicked Husbandmen helps to illuminate those sayings of Jesus in which He foretells His own death and the disaster to fall upon the Jews…by implication it may be said to 'predict' the death of Jesus, and the judgment to fall upon His slayers"; see Dodd, *The Parables of the Kingdom*, 98.

13. Matthew Black, "The Parables as Allegory," *Bulletin of the John Rylands Library* 42 (1960): 283.

14. Richard Valantasis, *The Gospel of Thomas* (New York: Routledge, 1997), 144. However, also in other logia (47 and 64), in which the same word cannot refer to divine messengers, a fact that complicates his conclusion.

15. Scriptural references do not occur in the Gospel of Thomas because the text does not situate the protagonist in a distinctly *Jewish* context.

Notes

16. Jane E. Newell and Raymond R. Newell, "The Parable of the Wicked Tenants," *Novum Testamentum* 14 (1972): 236.

17. Newell and Newell, "The Parable of the Wicked Tenants," 236.

18. Levine, *Short Stories by Jesus*, 224 (when discussing the parable in Matt 20:1–16).

19. Malcolm Lowe, "From the Parable of the Vineyard to a Pre-Synoptic Source," *New Testament Studies* 28 (1982): 257–63, and David Stern, *Parables as Midrash: Narrative and Exegesis in Rabbinic Literature* (Cambridge, MA: Harvard University Press, 1991), 189–97.

20. Milavec, "A Fresh Analysis of the Parable of the Wicked Husbandmen in the Light of Jewish-Christian Dialogue," 104.

21. Milavec, "A Fresh Analysis of the Parable of the Wicked Husbandmen in the Light of Jewish-Christian Dialogue," 87.

22. See his article "The Heresy That Necessitated Mark's Gospel," in *The Interpretation of Mark*, 2nd ed., ed. William R. Telford (Edinburgh: T&T Clark, 1995), 91.

23. Theodore J. Weeden, *Mark—Traditions in Conflict* (Philadelphia: Fortress, 1979 [1971]), 50f. He is aware of the fact that Mark, according to his interpretation, "deviate[s]…radically from the trend in the rest of Christian literature."

24. Weeden, *Mark—Traditions in Conflict*, 52.

25. Cf. the title of Elizabeth Struthers Malbon, "Fallible Followers: Women and Men in the Gospel of Mark," *Semeia* 28 (1983): 29–48.

26. It should be noted that "the kingdom of God" is not a typically Matthean expression; avoiding the name of God, Matthew prefers "the kingdom of heaven."

27. Matt 28:19; Davies and Allison, *The Gospel according to Saint Matthew*, 3:189.

28. Avrohom Chaim Feuer (with Nosson Scherman), *Tehillim: A New Translation with a Commentary Anthologized from Talmudic, Midrashic and Rabbinic Sources*, 2 vols. (New York: Mesorah, 1985), 2:1411.

29. See, e.g., *The Koren Siddur: With Introduction, Translation and Commentary by Rabbi Sir Jonathan Sacks* (Jerusalem: Koren, 2009), 301.

30. Cf. Joel Marcus, *Jesus and the Holocaust: Reflections on Suffering and Hope* (New York: Doubleday, 1997), 19–33, esp. 27.

31. Krister Stendahl, "'And Why Is This Granted to Me?,'" *Harvard Divinity Bulletin* 24 (1995): 24.

32. For the wordplay between *ben* (son) and *even* (stone), see, e.g., Klyne R. Snodgrass, *The Parable of the Wicked Tenants: An Inquiry into Parable Interpretation* (Eugene, OR: Wipf & Stock, 2011 [1983]), 113–18, and *Stories with Intent*, 296.

33. Davies and Allison, *The Gospel according to Saint Matthew*, 3:189.

34. Milavec, "A Fresh Analysis of the Parable of the Wicked Husbandmen in the Light of Jewish-Christian Dialogue," 110. He is discussing the Markan version of the parable.

35. Milavec, "A Fresh Analysis of the Parable of the Wicked Husbandmen in the Light of Jewish-Christian Dialogue," 117 (emphases added).

CHAPTER 11

1. Schweizer, *The Good News according to Matthew*, 425: "they are (together) the 'great' commandment because they are the *only* ones that need to be obeyed" (emphasis in the original).

2. Schweizer, *The Good News according to Matthew*, 426. (There is a typographical error in the quoted text: "unerlines.")

3. Schweizer, *The Good News according to Mark*, 253.

4. Lachs, *A Rabbinic Commentary on the New Testament*, 281.

5. Philo, *On the Decalogue* 22 (§108–110), cf. *Special Laws* 2.15 (§63).

6. Mark 12:28 (*eperôtan*), Matt 22:35 (*peirazein*), and Luke 10:25 (*ekpeirazein*) (emphases added).

7. Laurence M. Wills notes that "the [Markan] *scribe* answers Jesus positively and Jesus responds in kind." He describes Jesus's concluding word "You are not far from the kingdom of God" as "a warm response from Jesus"; see "The Gospel according to Mark," in *The Jewish Annotated New Testament*, 2nd ed., ed. Amy-Jill Levine and Marc Zvi Brettler (Oxford: Oxford University Press, 2017), 96 (emphasis in the original).

8. Schweizer, *The Good News according to Mark*, 252.

9. Jay B. Stern, "Jesus' Citation of Dt 6:5 and Lv 19:18 in the Light of Jewish Tradition," 312–16, in *Catholic Biblical Quarterly* 28 (1966): 315.

10. However, it is absent in the Matthean version. The Greek preposition *epi* means "in connection to": *epi tou batou* (Mark); *epi tês batou* (Luke).

11. Stern, "Jesus' Citation of Dt 6:5 and Lv 19:18 in the Light of Jewish Tradition," 316.

12. Since the second exhortation in Micah 6:8 does not contain a verb, this was perhaps originally not a *thrice*-divided exhortation but one consisting of only *two* exhortations: (1) both to do justice and to exercise *ahavat chesed* (approx. "loving kindness"), and (2) to walk humbly with God. See Jesper Svartvik, *Konsten att bli vän med nåden* (Stockholm: Verbum, 2018), 52f.

13. *Talmud Yerushalmi Nedarim* 9.4 and *Sifra Qedushim* 2.4 (ed. Weiss 89b). Cf. *Genesis Rabbah* 24.7.

14. Moore, *Judaism in the First Centuries*, 2:85 (emphases added).

15. Michael Fagenblat, "The Concept of Neighbor in Jewish and Christian Ethics," in *The Jewish Annotated New Testament*, 2nd ed., ed. Amy-Jill Levine and Marc Zvi Brettler (Oxford: Oxford University Press, 2017), 649f.

16. Goodman, *Love Thy Neighbor as Thyself*, 31.

17. The *Shemaʿ* consists of Deut 6:4–9, 11:13–21, and Num 15:37–41.

18. Daube, *The New Testament and Rabbinic Judaism*, 250.

19. Kister, "The Golden Rule," 727.

20. On the risk of collapsing love of God into love of neighbor in "a good deal of American theology toward the end of the last century," see Meier, *A Marginal Jew: Law and Love*, 4:494.

21. Quoted in Nahum N. Glazer, *Franz Rosenzweig: His Life and Thought*, 2nd ed. (New York: Schocken, 1961), 31.

CHAPTER 12

1. Dodd, *The Parables of the Kingdom*, 13.

2. Dodd, *The Parables of the Kingdom*, 13f. Augustine, *Questions on the Gospels* 2.19. (Incidentally, in most dictionaries of biblical Hebrew the words *Jerusalem* and *Jericho* are listed next to each other.)

3. Caird, *The Gospel of Saint Luke*, 148f. Cf. Eduard Schweizer, *The Good News according to Luke*, trans. David E. Green (Atlanta: John Knox, 1984 [German: 1982]), 186: "The priest, God's professional servant, and the Levite, his subordinate, have fulfilled the law that defines their position; they have done what they have to do. They are impassioned fighters on behalf of God's honor....And so they 'see' the injured victim but not God, who waits within him, demanding and thus also giving."

4. In *Talmud Bavli Megillah* 3b it is stated that "As between the study of Torah and attending to a *met mitzwah* [a neglected corpse], attending to a *met mitzwah* takes precedence....As between *'avodah* [liturgy, i.e., the Temple service] and attending to a *met mitzwah*, attending to a *met mitzwah* takes precedence."

5. This is pointed out by Levine, *Short Stories by Jesus*, 101.

6. Levine, *Short Stories by Jesus*, 101.

7. Snodgrass, *Stories with Intent*, 355: "First, Jews were required on religious grounds to bury a neglected corpse....Second, at least for most Jews, nothing—not even purity laws—legitimately stood in the way of saving a life. Laws were suspended when life was endangered." Similarly, Levine, *Short Stories by Jesus*, 100: "To follow Torah, the priest should have checked to see if the man was alive and, finding him alive, should have helped him. Should he have discovered a corpse, he should have covered it and then immediately gone for help."

8. Levine, *Short Stories by Jesus*, 100.

9. This covenantal triad (priest, Levite, and Israelite) is a common way to classify three categories within the people of Israel: A *Levite* is a descendant of Levi, the son of Jacob and Leah (Num 3:6–10), a *priest* is a descendant of Aaron (who was a Levite), and *Israelite* is a designation for the rest of the people. In today's synagogue services on *shabbat*, a priest is first invited to read a portion from the Torah, then a Levite, and finally an Israelite; see, e.g., *The Koren Siddur*, 504f.

10. See, e.g., Jacob Mann, "Jesus and the Sadducean Priest: Luke 10. 25–37," *Jewish Quarterly Review* 6 (1916): 415–22; Israel Abrahams, *Studies in Pharisaism and the Gospels*, 2 vols. (Cambridge, UK: Cambridge University

Press, 1917–24), 2:33–40; and Lachs, *A Rabbinic Commentary on the New Testament*, 282.

11. Manson, *The Sayings of Jesus*, 262. He defines the third person as "a Jew who did not attend with proper strictness to the details of the legal system, a Jew who was not a 'practising' Jew."

12. Cf. Levine, *Short Stories by Jesus*, 80: "In many Christian contexts, the Samaritan comes to represent the Christian who has learned to care for others or to break free from prejudice, whereas the priest and the Levite represent Judaism, understood to be xenophobic, promoting ritual purity over compassion, proclaiming self-interest over love of neighbor, and otherwise being something that needs to be rejected."

13. Fagenblat, "The Concept of Neighbor in Jewish and Christian Ethics," 649: "It is only later Amoriac rabbis who regard them as Gentiles."

14. See, e.g., Levine, *Short Stories by Jesus*, 112.

15. Some scholars argue that first-century Jews believed that accepting aid from a Samaritan would delay the redemption of Israel, but we lack evidence for maintaining that this was a widespread notion among first-century Jews. Snodgrass states that such an assertion is based on "inadequate evidence" in an anthology compiled by Hermann L. Strack and Paul Billerbeck; see Snodgrass, *Stories with Intent*, 342 and 696. Levine (*Short Stories by Jesus*, 109f. and 317) adds that it probably entered scholarship through a book by Walter Grundmann, see *Die Geschichte Christi* (Berlin: Evangelische Verlagsanstalt, 1957), 90. It should be added that, during the Second World War, Grundmann was the director of an institute that sought to eradicate Jewish "influence" from Christianity (*Institut zur Erforschung und Beseitigung des jüdischen Einflusses auf das deutsche kirchliche Leben*). For more information about the institute, see, e.g., S. Heschel, *The Aryan Jesus*, esp. 67–105.

16. For a reception-historical study of Lev 19:18 (except for rabbinic literature), see Kengo Akiyama, *The Love of Neighbour in Ancient Judaism: The Reception of Leviticus 19:18 in the Hebrew Bible, the Septuagint, the Book of Jubilees, the Dead Sea Scrolls, and the New Testament* (Leiden: Brill, 2018). Akiyama argues in favor of interpreting *kamokha* ([you shall love your neighbor] like you) *adjectively* (i.e., [who is] like you), not *adverbially* (i.e., like [you love] yourself); see 57–60.

17. Levine, *Short Stories by Jesus*, 94: "He may be the only person in antiquity to have given this instruction."

18. Manson, *The Sayings of Jesus*, 261 (emphases added). Cf. Fagenblat, "The Concept of Neighbor in Jewish and Christian Ethics," 649: "Jesus' point was not to redefine the category of 'neighbor' to include Gentiles but to emphasize that neighbors are those who *show* love" (emphasis in the original). Fagenblat states that it is only later (i.e., amoraic) rabbis who regard Samaritans as Gentiles; in earlier texts they were not defined as Gentiles.

19. Levine, *Short Stories by Jesus*, 114f.

Notes

CHAPTER 13

1. Jonathan Knight, *Luke's Gospel* (London: Routledge, 1998), 120, and Paul Trudinger, "Exposing the Depth of Oppression (Luke 16:1b–8a)," in *Jesus and His Parables: Interpreting the Parables of Jesus Today. With a Foreword by Seán Freyne*, ed. V. George Shillington (Edinburgh: T&T Clark, 1997), 121. Lachs, stating that there are no rabbinic parallels, nevertheless identifies several phrases that can be traced to Semitic origins; see *A Rabbinic Commentary on the New Testament*, 310. David Flusser argues that the Semiticisms "dishonest wealth" and "the children of light" indicate that the parable originally was directed against the Essenes (hence, the children of this age being wiser than the Essenes); see "The Parable of the Unjust Steward: Jesus' Criticism of the Essenes," in *Jesus and the Dead Sea Scrolls*, ed. James H. Charlesworth (New York: Doubleday, 1992), 183f. and 191.

2. In Latin: *vilicus* (or, less correctly, *villicus*); in rabbinic texts: *iqonomos* or *inqolomos*.

3. Joseph A. Fitzmyer, *The Gospel according to Luke: Introduction, Translation, and Notes*, 2 vols. (New York: Doubleday, 1981–85) 2:1097 and 2:1099. Cf. Joseph's assignment in Gen 39:5f.

4. Dodd, *The Parables of the Kingdom*, 26. Therefore, Trudinger writes, "interpretations that point to the parable's original meaning in the light of the moralistic pronouncements in verses 8b–13 are dubious"; see "Exposing the Depth of Oppression (Luke 16:1b–8a)," 125.

5. Snodgrass, *Stories with Intent*, 406–9.

6. It is not uncommon that Luke refers to Jesus as *ho Kyrios*; see, e.g., Luke 18:6. Furthermore, not only do we not know to whom the word *kyrios* in verse 8 refers, but the meaning of the praise is also open to discussion: is it perhaps an *ironical* statement (Stanley E. Porter, "The Parable of the Unjust Steward [Luke 16:1–13]: Irony *is* the Key," in *The Bible in Three Dimensions Essays in Celebration of Forty Years of Biblical Studies in the University of Sheffield*, ed. David J. A. Clines et al. [Sheffield, UK: Journal for the Study of the Old Testament, 1990], 127–153, and Flusser, "The Parable of the Unjust Steward," 176–97) or uttered *in anger* (Trudinger, see below).

7. Manson, *The Sayings of Jesus*, 295.

8. Caird argues that it probably was Luke himself who inserted the criticism of the Pharisees, and continues, "There is no evidence that they were addicted to avarice to the same extent as either the Sadducees or the tax gatherers, but they did tend, with ample justification from the Old Testament, to regard prosperity, or at least their own prosperity, as the reward of godliness" (*The Gospel of Saint Luke*, 188). However, Caird does not refer to any sources that support this pejorative statement.

9. N. T. Wright, *Jesus and the Victory of God* (London: SPCK, 1996), 332 and 638 ("there is a strong probability that Jesus intended a reference to the present Jewish nation and its current leaders"), and *Luke for Everyone*

(London: SPCK, 2001), 194: "The master is God; the steward is Israel....But Israel...has failed in the task, and is under threat of imminent dismissal."

10. George A. Buttrick, *The Parables of Jesus* (New York: Harper & Brothers, 1928), 117.

11. Tertullian, *On the Flight under Persecution*, 13.

12. Wright, *Luke for Everyone*, 194.

13. Wright, *Luke for Everyone*, 194. Hence, a (less allegorical) variant of the first interpretation argues that the steward is the Pharisaic party that has mismanaged the (divine) "economy" (cf. the Greek term *oikonomia*), and, indeed, in the Lukan setting, it is the Pharisees who ridicule Jesus upon hearing his teaching (16:14). Similarly, Caird (*The Gospel of Saint Luke*, 187) argues that "the parable is an attack on the niggling methods of scriptural interpretation by which the Pharisees managed to keep their religious principles from interfering with business, and an appeal for a whole-hearted service of God."

14. Wright, *Luke for Everyone*, 195.

15. Snodgrass, *Stories with Intent*, 410: "That some parables involving masters and servants point to God and Israel does not mean that every such parable does."

16. Snodgrass, *Stories with Intent*, 410, and Trudinger, "Exposing the Depth of Oppression (Luke 16:1b–8a)," 124 (emphasis in the original).

17. Manson, *The Sayings of Jesus*, 292.

18. Caird, *The Gospel of Saint Luke*, 185.

19. Scholars have discussed the meaning of the Greek preposition *ek* in v. 9: Does it mean "with the help of" (cf. Prov 3:9: "Honor the LORD with your substance") or "apart from," "without" unrighteous wealth? See, e.g., Flusser, "The Parable of the Unjust Servant," 193, and Snodgrass, *Stories with Intent*, 409.

20. Hans Kosmala, "The Parable of the Unjust Steward in the Light of Qumran," *Annual of the Swedish Theological Institute* 3 (1964): 115 and 120.

21. Trudinger, "Exposing the Depth of Oppression (Luke 16:1b–8a)," 136 (emphases in the original). Since Trudinger does not present his own reading until the penultimate page of his article, it is not developed at length. Cf. Crossan, *In Parables*, 106–8, and William R. Herzog II, *Parables as Subversive Speech: Jesus as Pedagogue of the Oppressed* (Louisville, KY: Westminster John Knox, 1994), 7: "What if the parables of Jesus were neither theological nor moral stories but political and economic ones?...What if the parables are exposing exploitation rather than revealing justification?"

22. Fitzmyer, *The Gospel according to Luke*, 2:1097.

23. Margaret Dunlop Gibson, "On the Parable of the Unjust Steward," *Expository Times* 14 (1902–3): 334.

24. Fitzmyer, *The Gospel according to Luke*, 2:1101: "It means that the debtor actually owed his master only fifty jugs of oil, and that the other fifty were the manager's commission." However, the *atokos* system is different from the *syn hêmiolia* (with a half) type, in which the interest of 50 percent is explicitly recorded.

Notes

25. Josephus, *Jewish Antiquities* 18.6.3 (§157).
26. J. Duncan M. Derrett, "Fresh Light on St Luke xvi." *New Testament Studies* 7 (1960–61): 216f. Cf. Levine, "The Gospel according to Luke," 148f.: "the steward has created for him [i.e., the rich man] the reputation of generosity, which he would not want to counter."

CHAPTER 14

1. Fitzmyer, *The Gospel according to Luke*, 2:1131.
2. Fitzmyer, *The Gospel according to Luke*, 2:1130.
3. Scholarship has focused on parallels, especially between this parable and Egyptian sources (Hugo Gressmann), but also on the writings of Lucian of Samosata (R. F. Hock) and the *Book of Jannes and Jambres* (Richard Bauckham). It seems wise to agree with Outi Lehtipuu, *The Afterlife Imagery in Luke's Story of the Rich Man and Lazarus* (Boston: Brill, 2007), 38: "All in all, it is obvious that the significance of the Egyptian and Jewish stories has been grossly overestimated," and also with her conclusion that "the reversal of fate of rich and poor after death was a well-known folkloric motif that circulated all over the Hellenistic world."
4. Levine quotes several scholars (e.g., David B. Gowler, William R. Herzog, and Klyne R. Snodgrass) who all argue that Lazarus was ritually impure, see *Short Stories by Jesus*, 280 (on purity regulations, see ch. 9).
5. Levine, *Short Stories by Jesus*, 282.
6. C. H. Cave, "Lazarus and the Lukan Deuteronomy," *New Testament Studies* 15 (1969): 323. See also Crossan, *In Parables*, 65f.
7. Scott, *Hear Then the Parable*, 142.
8. If it is a Christ-centered rereading of the Scriptures, the Lukan concluding chapter is an obvious parallel: the discussion on the way to Emmaus, in which the expression "Moses and all the Prophets" occurs in v. 27 (cf. v. 44).
9. Snodgrass, *Stories with Intent*, 425. Levine correctly points out that the question in John 9:2 is not economic status but blindness; see *Short Stories by Jesus*, 335.
10. Arland Hultgren, *The Parables of Jesus: A Commentary* (Grand Rapids: Eerdmans, 2000), 116.
11. Jeremias, *The Parables of Jesus*, 184, and also *Jerusalem in the Time of Jesus: An Investigation into Economic and Social Conditions during the New Testament Period*, trans. F. H. Cave and C. H. Cave. (London: SCM, 1969 [German: 1967]), 116–19. However, it is not stated in the parable that he was a *beggar* (*pace* Jeremias), nor that he was *pious*—only that he was *poor*. And whereas the rich man is anonymous, Lazarus has a name, which is a terse theological statement: although *poor*, he is still a *person*.
12. Julie Adler Pelc has suggested that it is better to translate *lo dibbartem elay nekhonah* as "you have not spoken *to* me what is right"; see Jesper Svartvik, *Reconciliation and Transformation: Reconsidering Christian Theologies of the*

Cross, trans. Karen Hagersten (Eugene, OR: Cascade, 2021 [Swedish: 2014]), 104f.

13. John Dominic Crossan, *How to Read the Bible and Still Be a Christian: Struggling with Divine Violence from Genesis through Revelation* (San Francisco: HarperOne, 2015), 98.

14. C. G. Montefiore, J. Edwin Odgers, and S. Schechter, "The Doctrine of Divine Retribution in the Old Testament, the New Testament, and the Rabbinical Literature," *The Jewish Quarterly Review* 3 (1890): 1–51.

15. Levine, *Short Stories by Jesus*, 273. She also points out that the Hebrew word for "almsgiving" (*tzedaqah*) comes from the same root as the term for "righteousness" (*tzedeq*)—and we could add "righteous" (*tzaddiq*) as well—which underlines that charity is not a matter of sentimentality but of justice (cf. also the Arabic word for "charity": *sadaqah*).

16. Levine, *Short Stories by Jesus*, 276.

17. Lehtipuu, *The Afterlife Imagery in Luke's Story of the Rich Man and Lazarus*, 38.

18. Levine, *Short Stories by Jesus*, 274.

19. Levine, *Short Stories by Jesus*, 270.

20. The expression can be traced back to a letter from Fr. Pedro Arrupe in a letter written in 1968 and sent to the Jesuits of Latin America. It was developed by Gustavo Gutiérrez in *A Theology of Liberation: History, Politics, and Salvation*, 2nd ed. (London: SCM, 1988 [Spanish 1st ed.: 1971]).

21. See, e.g., Bo Johnson, "Något om bibelanvändningen i latinamerikansk befrielseteologi," *Svensk Teologisk Kvartalskrift* 60 (1984): 64–70, esp. 69f.

22. Levine, *Short Stories by Jesus*, 277. See also p. 272: "He [i.e., the rich man] is not serving God or neighbor; he is the epitome of one who is self-serving." On p. 274 she refers to Gary Anderson, who discusses the rabbinic concept of "drawing down one's treasury in this world"; see *Sin: A History* (New Haven, CT: Yale University Press, 2009), 230.

23. See, e.g., Levine, *Short Stories by Jesus*, 278 and Scott, *Hear Then the Parable*, 149.

24. Fitzmyer, *The Gospel according to Luke*, 2:1134.

25. Levine, *Short Stories by Jesus*, 296.

CHAPTER 15

1. Plutarch, *Moralia: Sayings of Kings and Commanders: Philip the Father of Alexander* 31 (179D).

2. *Talmud Yerushalmi Berakhot* 9.1.

3. William Barclay, *The Parables of Jesus* (Louisville, KY: Westminster John Knox, 1999), 116: "The point is not the *likeness*, but the *contrast* between God and men." (His book was previously published in 1952 under the title *And Jesus Said*. That book was reissued with minor alterations in 1970, and republished in 1999.)

Notes

4. See, e.g., Fitzmyer, *The Gospel according to Luke*, 2:1177.

5. W. Barclay states that it must have been a *Roman* judge since under Jewish law one single person could not constitute a court; see *The Parables of Jesus*, 114.

6. Levine, *Short Stories by Jesus*, 247f. and 332. She is quoting, respectively, Luke Timothy Johnson, Brad H. Young, Mary W. Matthews, Richard Q. Ford, and Luise Schottroff. (However, the last quotation is from p. 247 in Schottroff's book, not p. 277, as stated in Levine's book.)

7. Amy-Jill Levine with Maria Mayo, *Short Stories by Jesus: The Enigmatic Parables of a Controversial Rabbi; Participant Guide* (Nashville: Abingdon, 2018), 86. See, e.g., Exod 22:22; Deut 10:18, 14:29, 27:19; and Isa 10:2.

8. Levine, *Short Stories by Jesus*, 239. Cf. p. 240: "Jesus's parables give women agency."

9. Cf. the widow who put a gift into the treasury in the temple (Luke 21:1–4). It is explicitly stated that she was poor (*tina chêran penichran*). The word used to describe her economic status (*penichros*) refers to persons that are working for their daily living, as opposed to a beggar (*ptôchos*).

10. Levine, *Short Stories by Jesus*, 247.

11. If indeed a victim, she is not necessarily a victim because the society is too *Jewish*. Levine refers to Carolyn Osiek who shows that churches in antiquity sought to make widows dependent on bishops and deacons; see "The Widow as Altar: The Rise and Fall of a Symbol," *Second Century* 3 (1983): 159–69.

12. Barbara E. Reid, "Beyond Petty Pursuits and Wearisome Widows: Three Lukan Parables," *Interpretation* (2002): 293. See also her article "A Godly Widow Persistently Pursuing Justice: Luke 18:1–8," *Biblical Research* 45 (2000): 25–33. That the widow represents God has previously been suggested by Megan McKenna, *Parables: The Arrows of God* (Maryknoll, NY: Orbis, 1994), 105, and by Mary W. Matthews, Carter Shelley, and Barbara Scheele, "Proclaiming the Parable of the Persistent Widow (Luke 18:2–5)," in *The Lost Coin: Parables of Women, Work and Wisdom*, ed. Mary Ann Beavis (New York: Sheffield Academic Press, 2002), 68–70.

13. Reid, "Beyond Petty Pursuits and Wearisome Widows," 293.

14. Reid, "Beyond Petty Pursuits and Wearisome Widows," 293.

15. Scott (*Hear Then the Parable*, 185) repudiates this interpretation because "a chief characteristic of a widow is her defenselessness. Why should a judge fear physical attack from her? They are an uneven match." But this is exactly the point that Levine et al. are trying to make—that is, they *are* an even match. Adolf Jülicher, too, argued in favor of the physical abuse interpretation; see *Die Gleichnisreden Jesu*, 2nd ed., 2 vols. (Tübingen: Mohr Siebeck, 1910 (1st ed. 1888), 2:282.

16. Snodgrass, *Stories with Intent*, 449.

17. Levine, *Short Stories by Jesus*, 265.

18. Emphases added.

19. Generally in this book, the first interpretation emphasizes *contrasting* and the last *contextual*, but in this chapter, it is the second line of thought that is the most contrastive.

CHAPTER 16

1. Scott, *Hear Then the Parable*, 96.
2. This is often pointed out; see, e.g., Michael Farris, "A Tale of Two Taxations (Luke 18:10–14b)," in *Jesus and His Parables: Interpreting the Parables of Jesus Today; With a Foreword by Seán Freyne*, ed. V. George Shillington (Edinburgh: T&T Clark, 1997), 29, and Levine, *Short Stories by Jesus*, 194. John Dominic Crossan suggests that the parable's original impact could be likened to the following statement from a Roman Catholic pulpit on a Sunday morning: "A Pope and a pimp went into St. Peter's to pray"; see *Raid on the Articulate: Comic Eschatology in Jesus and Borges* (New York: Harper & Row, 1976), 108.
3. Biblical texts that are important for this theological tradition are, e.g., Gen 15:6, Hab 2:4, and Rom 1:17.
4. Levine, *Short Stories by Jesus*, 210.
5. Levine, *Short Stories by Jesus*, 199. Timothy A. Friedrichsen, "The Temple, a Pharisee, a Tax Collector, and the Kingdom of God: Rereading a Jesus Parable (Luke 18.19–14a)," *Journal of Biblical Literature* 124 (2005): 95–97.
6. Levine, *Short Stories by Jesus*, 184.
7. See, e.g., 2 Kings 5:18, 24:4, Ps 25:11, 78:38, 2 Chron 6:30, Lam 3:42, Dan 9:19.
8. Bultmann, *Primitive Christianity in Its Contemporary Setting*, 83f.
9. Snodgrass does not believe that the characterizations of the Pharisee and the tax collector are caricatures; see *Stories with Intent*, 472.
10. Farris, "A Tale of Two Taxations (Luke 18:10–14b)," 27.
11. Friedrichsen, "The Temple, a Pharisee, a Tax Collector, and the Kingdom of God," 94.
12. See, e.g., Scott, *Hear Then the Parable*, 96, Levine, *Short Stories by Jesus*, 203, and Friedrichsen, "The Temple, a Pharisee, a Tax Collector, and the Kingdom of God," 110. Friedrichsen rightly criticizes Kenneth E. Bailey for suggesting that the prophet Amos had "some sharp words for this type of religion" (cf. 4:4); see *Through Peasant Eyes* (Grand Rapids, MI: Eerdmans, 1980), 152. For Christ followers fasting twice a week, see *Didache* 8.1 (i.e., not on Mondays and Thursdays, but on Wednesdays and Fridays).
13. Friedrichsen, "The Temple, a Pharisee, a Tax Collector, and the Kingdom of God," 111.
14. Fitzmyer argues in favor of the comparative interpretation and refers to 13:2 and 4; see *The Gospel according to Luke*, 2:1188. Bo Johnson maintains that *dikaios* (righteous) is never a matter of comparison in the New Testament; see *Rättfärdigheten i Bibeln* (Gothenburg: Gothia, 1985), 19 and 87f.

15. Levine, *Short Stories by Jesus*, 208f., and Friedrichsen, "The Temple, a Pharisee, a Tax Collector, and the Kingdom of God," 116.
16. Friedrichsen, "The Temple, a Pharisee, a Tax Collector, and the Kingdom of God," 117.
17. For additional information about the concept *zekhut avot*, see Marmorstein, *The Doctrine of Merits in Old Rabbinical Literature*, and Schechter, *Aspects of Rabbinic Theology*, 170–98. For additional examples of *zekhut*, see Montefiore and Loewe, *A Rabbinic Anthology*, 38, 337, 676, and 689.
18. Friedrichsen, "The Temple, a Pharisee, a Tax Collector, and the Kingdom of God," 117.
19. Levine, *Short Stories by Jesus*, 206.
20. Levine, *Short Stories by Jesus*, 209.
21. Abrahams, *Studies in Pharisaism and the Gospels*, 2:103.

CHAPTER 17

1. Andrew Lloyd Webber, *Jesus Christ Superstar*.
2. Ragnar Blix, *De 5 Aar* (Copenhagen: Berlingske Forlag, 1945), [no page number]. Torgny Söderbergh, the editor in chief of the newspaper, was an ardent anti-Nazi. Winston Churchill used "Quisling" metaphorically in a speech for the U.S. Congress in 1941.
3. Anthony Cane, *The Place of Judas Iscariot in Christology* (Burlington, VT: Ashgate, 2005), 62.
4. See, e.g., William Klassen, *Judas: Betrayer or Friend of Jesus?* (Minneapolis: Fortress, 1996), 32–34.
5. A fact that weakens the probability of this interpretation is that Simon, the father of Judas, is also called "Iscariot" in John 6:71, 13:26, and 13:2 (although there are several variations in the manuscripts).
6. Gustaf Dalman, *The Words of Jesus: Considered in the Light of Post-biblical Jewish Writings and the Aramaic Language*, trans. D. M. Kay (Eugene, OR: Wipf & Stock, 1997 [1902] [German: 1st ed. 1898]), 52 (the word *Iskariôt* is written in Greek letters in the English edition).
7. Various interpretative types have been suggested; see, e.g., Klassen, *Judas*, 4–8 (four interpretations; similar to the four in the present survey, but in another order), and Richard G. Walsh, *Three Versions of Judas* (New York: Routledge, 2014 [2010]), who, inspired by Jorge Luis Borges's 1962 book with the same name, presents—obviously—three interpretations: Judas as necessary for the *divine plan*, a *determined outsider*, and *demonic*.
8. Oscar Quensel, *Judas Iskariots bild psykologiskt belyst* (Stockholm: Svenska kyrkans diakonistyrelses bokförlag, 1914), 12, emphasis in original.
9. Karl Barth, *Church Dogmatics* 2.2, §34f. Barth's preface is dated *Pfingsten* (Whitsuntide) 1942. Paul S. Chung states that the section on election and Israel was written in approximately 1940; see *Karl Barth: God's Word in Action* (Eugene, OR: Cascade, 2008), 377.

10. Barth, *Church Dogmatics* 2.2, 92 (§34); *Kirchliche Dogmatik* 2.2, 316.

11. Barth, *Church Dogmatics* 2.2, 274 (§35); *Kirchliche Dogmatik* 2.2, 518f.

12. Barth, *Church Dogmatics* 2.2, 277 (§35); *Kirchliche Dogmatik* 2.2, 521.

13. Barth, *Church Dogmatics* 2.2, 313 (§35) (the word *paradidous* written in Greek letters); *Kirchliche Dogmatik* 2.2, 562.

14. Derek Alan Woodard-Lehman, "Saying 'Yes' to Israel's 'No': Barth's Dialectical Supersessionism and the Witness of Carnal Israel," in *Karl Barth: Post-Holocaust Theologian?*, ed. George Hunsinger (London: Bloomsbury / T&T Clark, 2018), 75. His purpose is (p. 69) to "think beyond Barth, yet still think with and through Barth. Moreover, we *must* say that, on his own grounds, Barth not only *need not* say what he says in paragraphs 34 and 35, but *should not* say what he says there. We can rethink his ecclesiological formulation of election in terms that are more consistent with his best insights" (emphases in the original).

15. See, e.g., Lars Fischer, "Karl Barth's Letter to Friedrich-Wilhelm Marquardt (5 September 1967): 'I Am Decidedly Not a Philosemite,'" https://jnjr.div.ed.ac.uk/primary-sources/contemporary/karl-barths-letter-to-friedrich-wilhelm-marquardt-5-september-1967-i-am-decidedly-not-a-philosemite/ (accessed March 25, 2023).

16. See, e.g., Steven M. Sheeley, "Judas Iscariot," in *Eerdmans Dictionary of the Bible*, ed. David Noel Freedman, Allen C. Myers, and Astrid B. Beck (Grand Rapids: Eerdmans, 2000), 749.

17. *Triclinium* (Greek: *triklinos*; *tri*, "three"; *klinê*, "couch") is the name both for the couches that were placed next to each other forming a "U" around a low table, and, more properly, for the room in which they were placed.

18. Klassen, *Judas*, 35.

19. Klassen, *Judas*, 90.

20. However, in Matt 27:9 it is stated that this is a quotation from *Jeremiah*. The explanation may be that it is recounted in Jer 32 that Jeremiah buys a field.

21. Pinchas Lapide, *Wer War Schuld an Jesu Tod?*, 2nd ed. (Gütersloh: Mohn, 1989), 23f. (quoted in Klassen, *Judas*, 98).

22. There are several variations in the manuscripts, see Metzger, *A Textual Commentary on the Greek New Testament*, 239f.

23. Klassen, *Judas*, 174.

24. Raymond E. Brown, *The Death of the Messiah: From Gethsemane to the Grave*, 2 vols. (New York: Doubleday, 1994), 2:1410.

25. There are actually two versions in Papias: the longer version quoted here, and a shorter version ("Judas lived his career in this world as an enormous example of impiety. He was so swollen in the flesh that he could not pass where a wagon could easily pass. Having been crushed by a wagon, his entrails poured out"); see R. E. Brown, *The Death of the Messiah*, 2:1408–1410. The

longer version is clearly legendary, but, as Brown states (2:1410): "historical probability cannot be assigned to any of the different deaths."

26. Klassen, *Judas*, 3.

27. Candida Moss, "A Note on the Death of Judas in Papias," *New Testament Studies* 65 (2019): 397.

28. Klassen, *Judas*, 47. Henry George Liddell and Robert Scott, *A Greek-English Lexicon...*, 9th ed. with a revised supplement (Oxford: Clarendon, 1996), s.v. "*paradidômi*."

29. Klassen, *Judas*, 48. Klassen states on p. 57 that Judas is called "traitor" (*prodotês*) only once in the entire New Testament: Luke 6:16.

30. Matt 26:26–29, Mark 14:22–25, Luke 22:15–20, and 1 Cor 11:23–25; cf. John 6:22–59 (emphases added).

31. Klassen, *Judas*, 61.

32. R. E. Brown, *Death of the Messiah*, 1:211. See also 1:211–13 and 2:1394–418.

33. Klassen, *Judas*, 203.

34. David Weiss Halivni argues that there is no transgression that merits a punishment like the *Shoah*. Therefore, he avoids the concept *hester panim* (the hiding of [God's] face) because this arises as a consequence of sin, but he finds the kabbalistic notion of *tzimtzum* helpful when analyzing the immense suffering during the *Shoah*: "*They suffered and died, but for nothing they had done. The cause of their suffering was cosmic*"; see *Breaking the Tablets: Jewish Theology after the Shoah*, ed. and introduced by Peter Ochs (Lanham, MD: Rowman & Littlefield, 2007), 34 (emphases in the original).

35. It is also possible that the expression "before the foundation of time" refers to the names written in the Book of Life.

36. Quoted in, e.g., R. E. Brown, *The Death of the Messiah*, 1:xii.

37. Cf. the title of Malbon, "Fallible Followers: Women and Men in the Gospel of Mark."

38. K. Stendahl disapproves of the tradition of meditation and preaching that sees a denying Peter, a betraying Judas, and a wavering Pilate in everyone. Instead he wants to come closer to "an earlier and deeper perspective, where the mysterious death of Jesus Christ[,] the Son of God[,] absorbs our minds so fully that we almost forget the bystanders and the moral lessons"; see *Holy Week Preaching*, 2nd ed. (Philadelphia: Fortress, 1985), 12.

39. For a narrative-critical study of Peter, see Richard J. Cassidy, *Four Times Peter: Portrayals of Peter in the Four Gospels and at Philippi* (Collegeville, MN: Liturgical Press, 2007).

40. Klassen, *Judas*, 6. Cf. p. 38: "Judas Iscariot was one of the twelve disciples of Jesus, possibly from Jerusalem, who probably served as treasurer of the itinerant group....Committed to a faith in God's rule, he had responded to the call to follow Jesus and was a devoted and trustworthy disciple of Jesus of Nazareth. He was in the inner circle, one of the Twelve."

41. Weeden, *Mark—Traditions in Conflict*, 50.

42. Woodard-Lehman, "Saying 'Yes' to Israel's 'No,'" 74.

43. Cf. Cane, *The Place of Judas Iscariot in Christology*, 61: "For Barth, Judas is never simply an individual who acts in a particular way, but always a representative figure, a type, whether of the rejected as a totality, Israel, *or the apostolic group*" (emphasis added).

44. Edgar Lee Masters, "Simon Surnamed Peter," *Songs and Satires* (London: T. Werner Laurie, 1916), 43 (emphases added).

CHAPTER 18

1. Montefiore, *The Synoptic Gospels*, 2:365. (Since he is commenting on the Markan text, he does not refer explicitly to Matt 27:25.)

2. Although the combination of the two verbs obviously is a Septuagintism (i.e., Greek imitating Hebrew), the first verb "responding" nevertheless emphasizes that the statement is a response to what Pilate has just said.

3. See, e.g., Rainer Kampling, *Das Blut Christi und die Juden: Mt 27,25 bei den lateinischsprachigen christlichen Autoren bis zu Leo dem Grossen* (Münster: Aschendorff, 1984).

4. Richard C. H. Lenski, *Commentary on St. Matthew's Gospel 15–28* (Minneapolis: Augsburg Fortress, 1943), 1096f. (In his text the words *pas ho laos* are written with Greek letters.) See also, e.g., Schweizer, *The Good News according to Matthew*, 509: "All the people, not just their leaders…unequivocally reject Jesus, after the manner of a legal formula (Josh. 2:19), calling down Jesus' blood on themselves and their descendants in case of a miscarriage of justice." On the word for "people," see his comment on p. 414 that "[*laos* is] the word, hallowed by Biblical tradition, that designates Israel as the people of God."

5. Daniel Marguerat, *Le jugement dans l'Évangile de Matthieu*, 2nd ed. (Geneva: Labor et Fides, 1995), 376 (the words "le judaïsme tout entier" are emphasized in the original). He refers to S. Légasse, who states that the Matthean position is that "Par là, Israël s'efface lui-même de l'histoire du salut," see "L''antijudaïsme' dans l'Évangile selon Matthieu." In *L'Évangile selon Matthieu: Rédaction et théologie*, ed. M. Didier (Gembloux: Duculot, 1972), 424. However, Légasse states that the misfortunes of the Jewish people throughout history cannot be justified by this cry: "Il ne saurait être question, par contre, d'y voir un appel au châtiment divin, une auto-malédiction que viendraient justifier tous les malheurs endurés par les Juifs au cours de leur histoire."

6. However, in Luke 23:13 it is said that "Pilate then called together the chief priests, the leaders, and the people [*kai ton laon*]," indicating that *laos* here refers to those who are neither priests nor leaders, i.e., the crowd (cf. "laicity" and "laity").

7. Cf. Fredriksen, *Paul*, 23.

8. Davies and Allison, *The Gospel according to Saint Matthew*, 3:592.

Notes

9. Davies and Allison, *The Gospel according to Saint Matthew*, 3:591: "If Pilate has tried to dissociate himself from innocent blood, 'all the people' now accept responsibility."

10. Hans Kosmala, "'His Blood on Us and on Our Children' (The Background of Mat. 27,24–25)." *Annual of the Swedish Theological Institute* 7 (1968–69): 118.

11. Gale, "The Gospel according to Matthew," 62 and 64.

12. On shedding of innocent blood, see, e.g., 2 Baruch 64.1–5.

13. Davies and Allison, *The Gospel according to Saint Matthew*, 3:592.

14. Timothy B. Cargal, "His Blood Be upon Us and upon Our Children: A Matthean *Double Entendre*?" *New Testament Studies* 37 (1991): 101–12. Catherine Sider Hamilton notes that Amy-Jill Levine in *The Social and Ethnic Dimensions of Matthean Salvation History* (p. 269) was the first to observe this, see *The Death of Jesus in Matthew: Innocent Blood and the End of Exile* (Cambridge, UK: Cambridge University Press, 2017), 4.

15. Davies and Allison, *The Gospel according to Saint Matthew*, 3:592.

16. Hamilton wishes to steer away from a dichotomy that has governed much of scholarship: either the *extra muros* perspective (i.e., Matthew writing about Judaism from an *outside* position) or an *intra muros* perspective (Matthew defining himself *within* Judaism), see *The Death of Jesus in Matthew*, 5.

17. Hamilton, *Death of Jesus*, 233 and 235.

18. International Council of Christians and Jews, *Reports and Recommendations of the International Conference of Christians & Jews: Seelisberg 1947* (Geneva: International Council of Christians and Jews, 1947), 15f. (emphases in the original).

19. Desmond Sullivan, "New Insights in Matthew 27:24–25," *New Blackfriars* 73 (1992): 454.

20. Sullivan, "New Insights in Matthew 27:24–25," 457.

21. Sullivan, "New Insights in Matthew 27:24–25," 457.

22. Davies and Allison argue that the Matthean text emphasizes that they made their decision "under the influence of evil leaders"; see *The Gospel according to Saint Matthew*, 3:592.

23. Warren Carter offers five different verdicts in history on Pilate: (1) a villain: a cruel anti-Jewish tyrant, (2) a weak leader without conviction, (3) a typical and insensitive Roman official, (4) a Christian convert, and (5) a saint; see *Pontius Pilate: Portraits of a Roman Governor* (Collegeville, MN: Liturgical Press, 2003), 3–11, and on pp. 154–59 he suggests what Pilate's defense strategies may have been.

24. Filson, *A Commentary on the Gospel according to St. Matthew*, 291.

25. Philo, *The Embassy to Gaius* 38 (§302).

26. Joseph B. Tyson, "The Death of Jesus," in *Seeing Judaism Anew: Christianity's Sacred Obligation*, ed. Mary C. Boys (Lanham, MD: Rowman & Littlefield, 2005), 45 (emphases added).

27. In Luke 23:13 it is stated that Pilate called together the chief priests, the leaders, "and the people" (*kai ton laon*), which implies that "the people" are those who are neither priests nor leaders, i.e., laity.

28. For a recent decalogue for improved Jewish-Christian dialogue, see Philip A. Cunningham, *Maxims for Mutuality: Principles for Catholic Theology, Education, and Preaching about Jews and Judaism* (Mahwah, NJ: Paulist Press, 2022).

CHAPTER 19

1. Previous versions of this chapter have been published in a *Festschrift* and a monograph; see Jesper Svartvik, "Rendering the Rending of the Veil: What Difference Does It Make?," in *Making a Difference: Essays on the Bible and Judaism in Honor of Tamara Cohn Eskenazi*, ed. David J. A. Clines, Kent Harold Richards, and Jacob L. Wright (Sheffield, UK: Sheffield Phoenix Press, 2012), 257–76, and *Reconciliation and Transformation*, 72–95.

2. Daniel M. Gurtner, *The Torn Veil: Matthew's Exposition of the Death of Jesus* (Cambridge, UK: Cambridge University Press, 2007), 76.

3. See R. E. Brown, *The Death of the Messiah*, 2:1100.

4. The focus here is not the question of whether it actually *happened*. Rather, the main question is the way in which the descriptions in the Synoptic Gospels have been *interpreted*.

5. Donald A. Hagner, *Matthew*, 2 vols. (Dallas: Word Books, 1993–95), 2:849, and R. E. Brown, *The Death of the Messiah*, 2:1102.

6. For a list of interpretations, see Roger David Aus, *Samuel, Saul and Jesus: Three Early Palestinian Jewish Christian Gospel Haggadoth* (Atlanta: Scholars Press, 1994), 156f.

7. Sardis was the capital of the ancient kingdom of Lydia. The synagogue that was rediscovered in 1962 is 120 meters long and 18 meters wide. It had space for about a thousand worshipers. According to a manuscript written by Josephus, the Jewish congregation had been in Sardis "since the beginning" (Greek: *ap' archês*); see *Jewish Antiquities* 14.10.24 (§259–61).

8. See Erik Werner, "Melito of Sardis: The First Poet of Deicide," *Hebrew Union College Annual* 37 (1966): 191–210.

9. Melito, *On Pascha* 92–97. The Greek words *hypo dexias Israêlitidos* literally mean "by an Israelite right [hand]." It is possible that Melito wants to emphasize the force and power of Israel by explicitly writing *dexias*. Cf. Ps. 73:23: "Nevertheless I am continually with you; you hold my right [*yemini*] hand."

10. Jeremy Cohen, *Christ Killers: The Jews and the Passion from the Bible to the Big Screen* (Oxford: Oxford University Press, 2007), 59. As a matter of fact, Melito does mention Pilate, but only that he washed his hands.

11. Melito, *On Pascha* 82. Cf. Exod 32:30 and Philo, *On the Change of Names* 12 (§81): *ho de Israêl horôn ton Theon kaleitai*.

Notes

12. Othmar Perler, "L'Evangile de Pierre et Méliton de Sardis," *Revue Biblique* 71 (1964): 584–90 (reprinted in *Sapientia et caritas: Gesammelte Aufsätze zum 90. Geburtstag [von] Othmar Perler*, ed. Dirk Van Damme, Otto Wermelinger, and Flavio Nuvolone [Freiburg (Switzerland), 1990], 331–37).

13. Cf. Micah 6:2f., "for the Lord has a controversy with his people, and he will contend with Israel. O my people, what have I done to you?" See, e.g., Patrick J. Morrisroe, "Improperia," in *Catholic Encyclopedia*, ed. Charles G. Herbermann et al., 15 vols. and index (New York: Encyclopedia Press, 1907–14), s.v.: "The Improperia are the reproaches which in the liturgy of the Office of Good Friday the Saviour is made to utter against the Jews, who, in requital for all the Divine favors and particularly for the delivery from the bondage of Egypt and safe conduct into the Promised Land, inflicted on Him the ignominies of the Passion and a cruel death."

14. Gospel of Peter 1. Compare this statement with Melito's homily *On Pascha* 77 and 92.

15. Cf. John 19:16 where it is stated that Pilate in handing over Jesus "to them [i.e., the chief priests] to be crucified."

16. Cf. Lev 23:5: "On the fourteenth day of the month" (Latin: *quarta decima die mensis*).

17. Melito, *On Pascha* 79f.

18. J. Cohen, *Christ Killers*, 62.

19. J. Cohen, *Christ Killers*, 65. See also Daniel Boyarin, *Dying for God: Martyrdom and the Making of Christianity and Judaism* (Stanford, CA: Stanford University Press, 1999), 13: "For these [Quartodeciman] Christians, Easter or Pascha was simply the correct way to observe the Pesah."

20. See Paula Fredriksen, "*Excaecati occulta justitia Dei*: Augustine on Jews and Judaism," *Journal of Early Christian Studies* 3 (1995): 322; Miriam S. Taylor, *Anti-Judaism and Early Christian Identity: A Critique of the Scholarly Consensus* (Leiden: Brill, 1995), 8; Judith Lieu, *Image & Reality: The Jews in the World of the Christians in the Second Century* (Edinburgh: T&T Clark, 1996), 199–240; Lynn Cohick, "Melito of Sardis's PERI PASCHA and Its 'Israel,'" *Harvard Theological Review* 91 (1998): 351–72; and Adele Reinhartz, "'Jews' and Jews in the Fourth Gospel." *Anti-Judaism and the Fourth Gospel*, ed. Reimund Bieringer, Didier Pollefeyt, and Frederique Vandecasteele-Vanneuville (Louisville, KY: Westminster John Knox, 2001), 213–27.

21. Cohick, "Melito of Sardis's PERI PASCHA and Its 'Israel,'" 372.

22. This has been suggested by Fredriksen, "*Excaecati occulta justitia Dei*," 322: "To place Christian anti-Jewish invective in such a context is to rationalize it, to give it some sort of reasoned and reasonable explanation."

23. Cohick, "Melito of Sardis's PERI PASCHA and Its 'Israel,'" 365.

24. Gurtner, *The Torn Veil*, 7: "Other scholars have suggested that the rending of the veil is simply an act of vengeance on the part of God for the unjust execution of his son."

25. Karl Barth, *Church Dogmatics* 1.2, 280–361. An introduction to his "The Revelation of God as the Abolition of Religion" can be found in

Christianity and Pluralism: Classic and Contemporary Readings, ed. Richard J. Plantinga (Malden, MA: Blackwell, 1999), 223f. Barth is quoted on pp. 223–42.

26. Luke 24:53. It is worth noting that Abraham Joshua Heschel argued the exact opposite, that it is God who constantly seeks out humans. See *God in Search of Man: A Philosophy of Judaism* (New York: Farrar, Straus & Giroux, 1955), 136–44.

27. Gurtner, *The Torn Veil*, 47.

28. Gurtner, *The Torn Veil*, 188 (emphasis added).

29. William Kelly, *Lectures on the Gospel of Matthew* (London: Morrish, 1868), 398, quoted in Gurtner, *The Torn Veil*, 15.

30. See Nirenberg, *Anti-Judaism*, e.g., 254: "After all, Jews and their synagogue had long been the whipping boys of preachers and exegetes"; and 259: "The strategy of Judaizing Christian 'error' is as old as Christianity itself."

31. For pagan discussions about Jewish aniconism, abstinence from pork, *shabbat*, and circumcision, see Schäfer, *Judeophobia*, 34–105.

32. Paula Fredriksen, *Jesus of Nazareth, King of the Jews: A Jewish Life and the Emergence of Christianity* (New York: Knopf, 1999), 52.

33. www.youtube.com/watch?v=SU1mSKuwNN0 (uppercased in original; accessed September 23, 2010).

34. Dan Stevers, "The Veil." www.youtube.com/watch?v=UcpTiV_DzVE&feature=related (emphases in original; accessed May 30, 2023).

35. Gurtner, *The Torn Veil*, 190 (emphases added).

36. Gurtner, *The Torn Veil*, 71.

37. Gurtner, *The Torn Veil*, 198.

38. Benedict Anderson, *Imagined Communities: Reflections on the Origin and Spread of Nationalism*, 2nd ed. (New York: Verso, 1991).

39. N. T. Wright, *The New Testament and the People of God* (London: SPCK, 1992), 386.

40. Gurtner, *The Torn Veil*, 47 (emphasis added).

41. For a brief introduction, see Isaac Klein, *A Guide to Jewish Religious Practice: A Supplement by Rabbi Joel Roth* (New York: Jewish Theological Seminary of America, 1992), 278f., and Joseph Ozarowski, "*Keri'ah*: The Tearing of the Garment," in *Jewish Insights on Death and Mourning*, ed. Jack Riemer, foreword by Sherwin B. Nuland (New York: Schocken, 1995), 121–26 (originally published as *Wrestling with the Angel*).

42. 2 Kings 2:12 (Hebrew: *wa-yiqra'em li-shnayim qera'im*; Greek [Septuagint]: *kai dierrêxen auta eis dyo rhêgmata*). For additional viewpoints, see David Daube, *The New Testament and Rabbinic Judaism*, 23.

43. Aus, *Samuel, Saul and Jesus*, 151. Gurtner, however, considers this assertion to be "highly speculative"; see *The Torn Veil*, 186.

44. Jacob Milgrom, *The JPS Torah Commentary: Numbers…*(Philadelphia: Jewish Publication Society, 1990), 20: "Since the inner Tabernacle curtains were anointed (Lev. 8:10), they theoretically had the same sacred status as the sancta (Exod. 30:29)."

Notes

45. Daube, *The New Testament and Rabbinic Judaism*, 25. Daube points out that "the word *pargodh*, which in the Targum stands for the curtain separating the holy of holies from the outer chamber, may also denote a tunic."

46. Daube, *The New Testament and Rabbinic Judaism*, 24. For a list of occasions of particularly great sorrow: *Mishnah Sanhedrin* 7.5, *Talmud Bavli Bava Qamma* 25b, and *Mo'ed Qatan* 26a.

47. Cf. Heschel, *Heavenly Torah*, 124. See also the translator's note 46 on the same page.

48. Daube, *The New Testament and Rabbinic Judaism*, 23–26; Paula Fredriksen, *From Jesus to Christ: The Origins of the New Testament Images of Jesus* (New Haven, CT: Yale University Press, 1988), 183; Aus, *Samuel, Saul and Jesus*, 147–57; and Rosann M. Catalano, "A Matter of Perspective: An Alternative Reading of Mark 15:38," in *Seeing Judaism Anew: Christianity's Sacred Obligation*, ed. Mary C. Boys (Lanham, MD: Rowman & Littlefield, 2005), 195. Most often, however, the rent veil is seen as an expression of divine grief that the temple will soon be destroyed. The first modern commentator to suggest that the tearing of the veil was an expression of grief was most likely Montefiore, see *The Synoptic Gospels*, 2:388. For a bibliography of early Christian writing that interprets the rending of the veil as an expression of grief, see Gurtner, *The Torn Veil*, 18.

49. Emphases added (Greek: *tou laou mê perieschismenou perieschisato ho angelos*).

50. Melito, *On Pascha* 98.

51. K. Stendahl, *Holy Week Preaching*, 23.

52. Catalano, "A Matter of Perspective," 198.

53. The text continues, "and whoever saves a single human being, Scripture credits this person as though a whole world has been saved." This section from the Mishnah is often cited in Jewish contexts, such as on the memorial for Swedish diplomat Raoul Wallenberg at Yad Vashem in Jerusalem.

54. Cf. Catalano, "A Matter of Perspective," 196: "The question the text occasions is not 'Why is God angry?' but 'What is God mourning?' What occasions divine sorrow at this moment in the narrative?" For the view of the human being as a microcosm and the church as *makro-anthropos* (Greek for "macro-being"), see Vladimir Lossky, *The Mystical Theology of the Eastern Church* (New York: St. Vladimir's Seminary, 1976 [French: 1944]), 114 and 178.

55. Abraham Joshua Heschel, "Untitled" (Yiddish: *On a nomen*), *The Ineffable Name of God: Man. Poems.* Trans. from the Yiddish by Morton M. Leifman. Intro. by Edward K. Kaplan (New York: Continuum, 2004), 193. The shift from second (Yiddish: *tzu dir*; English: *to You*) to third person (Yiddish: *zikh*; English: *His*) may reflect the way Jewish prayers transition from second to third person. For example, "Blessed be *you*…who consecrate us by *his* laws."

CHAPTER 20

1. Kysar, *John, the Maverick Gospel*, 45.
2. See, e.g., Michael Theobald, *Die Fleischwerdung des Logos: Studien zum Verhältnis des Johannesprologs zum Corpus des Evangeliums und zu 1 Joh* (Münster: Aschendorff, 1988), 6–161.
3. John Marsh, *The Gospel of Saint John* (Harmondsworth: Penguin, 1968), 109.
4. Marsh, *The Gospel of Saint John*, 111. On the same page he writes about "that saving act of kindness (grace) which was *intended*, but, through man's perversity, only *foreshadowed*, in the law given through Moses" (emphases added).
5. Matthew Black, "Does an Aramaic Tradition Underlie John 1, 16?," *Journal of Theological Studies* 42 (1941): 69f.
6. Black, "Does an Aramaic Tradition Underlie John 1, 16?," 70.
7. Rudolf Schnackenburg, *The Gospel according to St John*, trans. Kevin Smyth, Cecily Hastings, Francis McDonagh, David Smith, Richard Foley, and G. A. Kon, 3 vols. (New York: Crossroad, 1990 [German: 1965–75]), 1:276.
8. The Gospel of John uses *nomos*, habitually translated into English as "Law," also for the Book of Psalms, as in this case, as well as in 15:25.
9. See, e.g., Elaine H. Pagels, *The Johannine Gospels in Gnostic Exegesis: Heracleon's Commentary on John* (Nashville: Abingdon Press, 1973).
10. For a liberal portrayal of the "Jesus the iconoclast" who became "Christ the icon," see, e.g., Funk, *Honest to Jesus*, 31–45.
11. C. H. Dodd, *The Interpretation of the Fourth Gospel* (Cambridge, UK: Cambridge University Press, 1954), 11. See also Raymond E. Brown, *The Gospel according to John: Introduction, Translation, and Notes*, 2 vols. (New York: Doubleday, 1966–70), lviii.
12. Dodd, *The Interpretation of the Fourth Gospel*, 9.
13. See R. E. Brown, *The Gospel according to John*, lix, who refers to G. D. Kilpatrick, "The Religious Background of the Fourth Gospel," in *Studies in the Fourth Gospel*, ed. F. L. Cross (London: Mowbray, 1957), 36–44.
14. Dodd, *The Interpretation of the Fourth Gospel*, 133 (emphasis in the original).
15. Philo, *Questions and Answers to Genesis* 2.62.
16. Daniel Boyarin, "Logos, A Jewish Word," in *The Jewish Annotated New Testament*, 2nd ed., ed. Amy-Jill Levine and Marc Zvi Brettler (Oxford: Oxford University Press, 2017), 689. See also his article "The Gospel of Memra: Jewish Binitarianism and the Prologue of John," *Harvard Theological Review* 94 (2001): 243–84.
17. Boyarin, "Logos, A Jewish Word," 689.
18. Boyarin, "Logos, A Jewish Word," 688.
19. Boyarin, "Logos, A Jewish Word," 691.

20. Boyarin, "Logos, A Jewish Word," 691. He also states that "the idea is so abundant in late antique Jewish writing that it is best read as the product of a common tradition shared by (some) messianic Jews and (some) non-messianic Jews."

21. Lester Jacob Kuyper, "Grace and Truth," *Interpretation* 18 (1964): 3. See also p. 14: "One wonders why the word grace was dropped. Let me suggest an answer. The Evangelist abandons the word because he intends to let the word truth carry the full import of the concept within the expression, grace and truth."

22. It is interesting to note that the Hebrew and Greek words are so similar: *shekhinah* in Hebrew (where the root consonants are *sh*, *k*, and *n*) and *skênê* (consonants: *s*, *k*, and *n*) in Greek. Is it not worth pondering that the words in the two parts of the Christian Bible for divine presence in this world are so similar in the two biblical languages Hebrew and Greek?

23. Göran Larsson, *Bound for Freedom: The Book of Exodus in Jewish and Christian Traditions* (Peabody, MA: Hendrickson, 1999), 258–62, and *Fönster mot Gud: Ikonernas budskap i Svenska teologiska institutets kapell i Jerusalem* (Lund: Arcus, 2011), 94–104.

24. Gillis Gerleman, "Das Übervolle Mass: Ein Versuch Mit Ḥaesaed," *Vetus Testamentum* 28 (1978): 151–64.

25. James L. Kugel, *The Bible as It Was* (Cambridge, MA: Belknap, 1998), 21.

26. The most common suggestion is Isaiah 11:1, where the word appears in a messianic context. Of course, it is difficult to ascertain how old the tradition is to write *notzer* with an enlarged nun.

27. Tom Thatcher, *Greater than Caesar: Christology and Empire in the Fourth Gospel* (Minneapolis: Fortress, 2009), 139.

28. Thatcher, *Greater than Caesar*, 125. On the same page: "I...find it impossible to believe that John's views of Roman power were neutral. Political neutrality, if such a thing exists, is a luxury that only the privileged can afford."

29. This is pointed out by, e.g., Tomson, "*If This Be from Heaven*," 373.

30. Didier Pollefeyt, "Unrevoked Covenant—Revoked Consensus—Indestructible Love? The Reception of *Nostra Aetate* 4 in Jewish-Catholic Relations," in *Res Opportunae Nostrae Aetatis: Studies on the Second Vatican Council Offered to Mathijs Lamberigts*, ed. Dries Bosschaert and Johan Leemans (Bristol, CT.: Peeters, 2020), 498.

CHAPTER 21

1. R. E. Brown, *The Gospel according to John*, 1:335.

2. In this text the vocative form *didaskale* (O master) is used. In John the Greek word *Ioudaioi* is frequently used, habitually translated as "Jews" (see introduction, second challenge).

3. R. E. Brown compares this dilemma to the story about the Roman coin in Mark 12:13–17; see *The Gospel according to John*, 2:337. See also J.

Duncan M. Derrett, "Law in the New Testament: The Story of the Woman Taken in Adultery," *New Testament Studies* 10 (1963–64): 25.

4. R. E. Brown, *The Gospel according to John*, 2:337.

5. See also John 7:24.

6. This idea can be traced back as far as Jerome, and in a tenth-century Armenian manuscript it is explicitly written that "he wrote the sins of the accusers"; see, e.g., R. E. Brown, *The Gospel according to John*, 1:333.

7. T. W. Manson, "The Pericope de Adultera (Joh 7,53–8,11)," *Zeitschrift für die neutestamentliche Wissenschaft* 44 (1952): 255f.

8. Augustine, *Tractate on John's Gospel* 33.5.

9. R. E. Brown, *The Gospel according to John*, 1:338.

10. The word *presbyteroi* is a *hapax legomenon* (occurring only once) in John, but it is quite common in the Synoptics.

11. Derrett, "Law in the New Testament: The Story of the Woman Taken in Adultery," 20.

CHAPTER 22

1. Reinhartz, *Befriending the Beloved Disciple*, 167.

2. See, e.g., Eliezer Berkovits, *Faith after the Holocaust* (Jerusalem: Maggid, 2019 [1973]), 18: "The most scurrilous of all Nazi antisemitic publications, Streicher's *Der Stürmer*, drew heavily on the Gospel passages about the Jews for support. As a young student in Berlin, I was introduced to the New Testament by the showcases in which *Der Stürmer* was so widely displayed in the streets of the German capital."

3. Kathleen Gallagher Elkins, "The Jews as 'Children of the Devil' (John 8:44) in Nazi Children's Literature," *Biblical Interpretation* 30 (2022): 1–17. Did these books, published for children in the Third Reich, influence adults? Strictly speaking, these publications illustrate to what degree even children were influenced by antisemitism, but they do not prove that these young children behaved in antisemitic ways, because as children they were not very influential in the society. Rather, they are *Augenblicksbilder* (snapshots) of that era, illustrating the extent to which people, even children, were indoctrinated toward antisemitism.

4. See, e.g., Doris L. Bergen, *Twisted Cross: The German Christian Movement in the Third Reich* (Chapel Hill / London: University of North Carolina Press 1996), Robert P. Ericksen, *Theologians under Hitler: Gerhard Kittel, Paul Althaus and Emanuel Hirsch* (New Haven, CT: Yale University Press, 1985), and S. Heschel, *The Aryan Jesus*. Hugo Odeberg, in a book first published in 1943, argued that John 8:44 clarifies *the* difference between [alleged Pharisaic] Judaism and Christianity, see *Pharisaism and Christianity*, 48.

5. Joshua Trachtenberg, *The Devil and the Jews* (New Haven, CT: Yale University Press, 1943), xiv.

6. E.g., R. E. Brown, *The Gospel according to John*, 1:358.

Notes

7. *Targum Pseudo-Jonathan* to Gen 4:1f. On the nonexistence of a particular "Cainite" sect of Gnostics, see Birger A. Pearson, *Gnosticism, Judaism, and Egyptian Christianity* (Minneapolis: Fortress, 1990), 95–107. For a more positive role of Cain in Gnostic texts, see his book, *Ancient Gnosticism: Traditions and Literature* (Minneapolis: Fortress, 2007), 122–24.

8. Nils Alstrup Dahl, "Der Erstgeborene Satans und der Vater des Teufels (Polyk. 7.1 und Joh 8.44)," in *Apophoreta: Festschrift für Ernst Haenchen zu seinem siebzigsten Geburtstag am 10. Dezember 1964,* ed. Walther Eltester (Berlin: Alfred Töpelmann, 1964), 70–84, and Günter Reim, "Joh 8.44—Gotteskinder / Teufelskinder: Wie antijudaistisch ist 'Die wohl antijudaistischste Äusserung des NT?,'" *New Testament Studies* 30 (1984): 619–24.

9. See, e.g., R. E. Brown, *The Gospel according to John*, 1:357.

10. April deConick, "Why are the Heavens Closed? The Johannine Revelation of the Father in the Catholic-Gnostic Debate," in *John's Gospel and Intimations of Apocalyptic*, ed. Catrin H. Williams and Christopher Rowland (London: T&T Clark, 2013), 178. See also R. E. Brown, *The Gospel according to John*, 1:357f.: "The Gnostics took it thus in their opposition to the God of the OT [i.e., Old Testament], whom they regarded as the source of evil because He was responsible for the existence of matter."

11. For this prayer, see especially Ruth Langer, *Cursing the Christians? A History of the Birkat Haminim* (Oxford: Oxford University Press, 2012).

12. Barth Ehrman, *The New Testament: A Historical Introduction to the Early Christian Writings*, 4th ed. (New York: Oxford University Press, 2008), 179–82.

13. However, as D. Moody Smith emphasizes, "If, in fact, Johannine Christians were persecuted by some Jews or Jewish authorities, as Saul at first persecuted the Christian sectarians, this is obviously no justification for Christians' persecuting Jews subsequently"; see "Judaism and the Gospel of John," 88.

14. D. Moody Smith, "Judaism and the Gospel of John," 84.

15. Reuven Kimelman, "*Birkat Ha-Minim* and the Lack of Evidence for an Anti-Christian Jewish Prayer in Late Antiquity," in *Jewish and Christian Self-Definition*, ed. E. P. Sanders et al. (Philadelphia: Fortress, 1981), 2:244.

16. Reinhartz, *Befriending the Beloved Disciple*, 39.

17. Daniel Boyarin, *Border Lines: The Partition of Judaeo-Christianity* (Philadelphia: University of Pennsylvania Press, 2004), 71f.

18. Langer, *Cursing the Christians?*, 34.

19. Kimelman, "*Birkat Ha-Minim* and the Lack of Evidence for an Anti-Christian Jewish Prayer in Late Antiquity," 2:233 and 2:244.

20. Reinhartz, *Befriending the Beloved Disciple*, 50 and 51 (emphases in the original).

21. Michael Walzer, *Exodus and Revolution* ([New York]: Basic, 1985). On p. 149 he condenses this important motif into three points: (1) "wherever you live, it is probably Egypt," (2) "there is a better place, a world more attractive, a promised land," and (3) [quoting W. D. Davies:] "'the way to the land is

through the wilderness.' There is no way to get from here to there except by joining together and marching."

22. For the importance of master stories, see, e.g., Michael Goldberg, *Jews and Christians, Getting Our Stories Straight: The Exodus and the Passion-Resurrection*, 2nd ed. (Philadelphia: Trinity Press International, 1991), 13.

23. R. E. Brown, *The Gospel according to John*, 1:355.

24. Both the Hebrew and Greek words are used both for slavery in a *negative* sense and worship and discipleship in a *positive* sense (Hebrew: *la-'avod*; Greek: *douloun*). On the dialectics of servitude (negative for the Egyptian Pharaoh, and positive for the God of Israel), see, e.g., Jon D. Levenson, *The Hebrew Bible, the Old Testament, and Historical Criticism: Jews and Christians in Biblical Studies* (Louisville, KY: Westminster John Knox Press, 1993), 127–59.

25. Reinhartz, *Befriending the Beloved Disciple*, 92 and 93 (emphasis in the original). Similarly, Levine, *The Misunderstood Jew*, 109: "Perhaps it is John, not the synagogue, who is seeking to separate the communities and force those who confess Jesus to disassociate with 'the Jews.'"

26. D. Moody Smith, "Judaism and the Gospel of John," 87.

27. Reinhartz, *Befriending the Beloved Disciple*, 167.

28. D. Moody Smith, "Judaism and the Gospel of John," 76–99.

29. Wayne A. Meeks, "The Man from Heaven in Johannine Sectarianism," *Journal of Biblical Literature* 91 (1972): 44–72.

30. See, e.g., Raymond E. Brown, *The Birth of the Messiah: A Commentary on the Infancy Narratives in the Gospels of Matthew and Luke*, updated ed. (New York: Doubleday, 1993), 534–42, and Christopher B. Zeichmann, "Jesus 'ben Pantera': An Epigraphic and Military-Historical Note," *Journal for the Study of the Historical Jesus* 18 (2020): 141–55. It is plausible that the name Panthera was seen as a mocking allusion to the Greek word *parthenos* (virgin; cf. Isa 7:14), see, e.g., John Dominic Crossan, *Jesus: A Revolutionary Biography* (New York: HarperCollins, 1994), 18.

31. For a survey of four of the imprecatory psalms (Ps 58, 109, 137, and 139), see Elisabet Nord, *Vindicating Vengeance and Violence? Commentary Approaches to Cursing Psalms and Their Relevance for Liturgy* (Lanham, MD: Lexington Books / Fortress Academic, 2023).

32. For a critique of the criteria for authenticity applied by the Jesus Seminar, see Birger A. Pearson, *The Gospel according to the Jesus Seminar: Occasional Papers of the Institute for Antiquity and Christianity; Number 35* (Claremont: Claremont Graduate School, 1996).

33. D. Moody Smith, "Judaism and the Gospel of John," 88 (emphases in the original).

34. See, e.g., Thatcher, *Greater than Caesar*, 9–11.

35. Meeks, "The Man from Heaven in Johannine Sectarianism," 69f.

36. D. Moody Smith, "Judaism and the Gospel of John," 94.

37. D. Moody Smith, "Judaism and the Gospel of John," 90. To be exact, he is here commenting on the Farewell Discourse, which, he says, is "closer to these epistles than to the rest of this gospel."

38. See, e.g., Elkins, "The Jews as 'Children of the Devil' (John 8:44) in Nazi Children's Literature."

39. Krister Stendahl, "Biblical Theology, Contemporary," in *The Interpreter's Dictionary of the Bible*, ed. G. A. Buttrick, 4 vols. (Nashville: Abingdon Press, 1962–78), 1:418–32.

40. Quoted in Susannah Heschel, "Race as Incarnational Theology: Affinities between German Protestantism and Racial Theory," in *Prejudice and Christian Beginnings: Investigating Race, Gender, and Ethnicity in Early Christian Studies*, ed. Laura Nasrallah and Elisabeth Schüssler Fiorenza (Minneapolis: Fortress, 2009), 214f. (quoted almost verbatim). German original in Tord Fornberg and Göran Larsson, ed. *Förskjutningar: Avgörande skiften i relationen mellan judar och kristna* (Skellefteå: Norma, 2022), 14.

41. S. Heschel, "Race as Incarnational Theology," 214.

CHAPTER 23

1. Peter J. Tomson, *Paul and the Jewish Law: Halakha in the Letters of the Apostle to the Gentiles* (Assen: Van Gorcum / Fortress, 1990), 275.

2. David J. Rudolph, *A Jew to the Jews: Jewish Contours of Pauline Flexibility in 1 Corinthians 9:19–2...*, 2nd ed. (Eugene, OR: Pickwick, 2016), 209.

3. Due to Christian censorship, Porphyry's writings can only be reconstructed with the help of quotations in Christian writings. No manuscripts of his text have survived antiquity. Macarius Magnes, *Apocritus* 3.31, quoted in Mark D. Nanos, *Reading Corinthians and Philippians within Judaism* (Eugene, OR: Cascade, 2017), 96.

4. C. K. Barrett, *A Commentary on the First Epistle to the Corinthians*, 2nd ed. (London: Adam & Charles Black, 1973), 211 (emphasis in original). However, Barrett eventually changed his mind about Paul changing his behavior (!); see *A Critical and Exegetical Commentary on the Acts of the Apostles*, 2 vols. (Edinburgh: T&T Clark, 1998), 2:1013.

5. Rudolph, *A Jew to the Jews*, 12. The verb *synomorein* (to be next to, to border on) is a *hapax legomenon* (occurring only once in the New Testament).

6. Nanos, *Reading Corinthians and Philippians within Judaism*, 107.

7. In the preceding passage (5:6–8) Paul writes about the yeast in the bread that leavens the whole batch of dough, and that Jesus Christ is "our paschal lamb." Hence, the very rhetoric depends on an intra-Jewish understanding of the prohibition against *chametz* during Passover.

8. Nanos, *Reading Corinthians and Philippians within Judaism*, 100.

9. Nanos, *Reading Corinthians and Philippians within Judaism*, 86.

10. Tomson, *Paul and the Jewish Law*, 277.

11. Tomson, *Paul and the Jewish Law*, 278. He also states that, to him, they sound "rather pedestrian."

12. Tomson, *Paul and the Jewish Law*, 280.

13. Rudolph, *A Jew to the Jews*, 14.

14. Rudolph, *A Jew to the Jews*, 196f. He compares these distinctions to *charedim* (ultra-Orthodox) and *masortiim* (traditional) in contemporary Israeli parlance.

15. Rudolph, *A Jew to the Jews*, 207 (emphases added).

16. Nanos, *Reading Corinthians and Philippians within Judaism*, 94.

17. Nanos, *Reading Corinthians and Philippians within Judaism*, 99.

18. Nanos, *Reading Corinthians and Philippians within Judaism*, 106. Tomson suggested something similar, see *Paul and the Jewish Law*, 278: "Paul, being a Jew, can *communicate* with Jews and also with gentiles as one of them, although he is not actually a gentile" (emphasis added).

CHAPTER 24

1. Heinz Schreckenberg, *The Jews in Christian Art: An Illustrated History* (New York: Continuum, 1996), 31–66. The Strasbourg sculptures are depicted on p. 47.

2. The quotation is ascribed to John MacArthur, see Bruce Hurt, "2 Corinthians 3:12–14 Commentary," https://www.preceptaustin.org/2corinthians_312-14_commentary (accessed February 20, 2023).

3. Alan J. Avery-Peck, "The Second Letter of Paul to the Corinthians," in *The Jewish Annotated New Testament*, 2nd ed., ed. Amy-Jill Levine and Marc Zvi Brettler (Oxford: Oxford University Press, 2017), 358. (This is not necessarily how Avery-Peck understands this passage; he simply describes an influential interpretation.)

4. Tomson, "*If This Be from Heaven*," 178.

5. John M. G. Barclay, "2 Corinthians," in *Eerdmans Commentary on the Bible*, ed. James D. G. Dunn and John W. Rogerson (Grand Rapids, MI: Eerdmans, 2003), 1360.

6. For the wide variety of Jewish Messianisms in antiquity, see, e.g., the classic Jacob Neusner, William Scott Green, and Ernest S. Frerichs, eds., *Judaisms and Their Messiahs at the Turn of the Christian Era* (Cambridge, UK: Cambridge University Press, 1987), and, more recently, Matthew V. Novenson, *Christ among the Messiahs: Christ Language in Paul and Messiah Language in Ancient Judaism* (Oxford: Oxford University Press, 2012) and *The Grammar of Messianism: An Ancient Jewish Political Idiom and Its Users* (Oxford: Oxford University Press, 2017).

7. Fredriksen, *Paul*, 6.

8. Fredriksen, *Paul*, 166.

9. See, e.g., Dieter Georgi, *The Opponents of Paul in Second Corinthians: A Study of Religious Propaganda in Late Antiquity*, trans. supervised by Dieter Georgi (Philadelphia: Fortress, 1986 [German: 1964]).

10. See Yael Fisch, *Written for Us: Paul's Interpretation of Scripture and the History of Midrash* (Leiden: Brill, 2023), esp. 131–60. See also her article, "The Origins of Oral Torah: A New Pauline Perspective," *Journal for the Study of Judaism* 51 (2020): 43–66.

11. See *Tosefta Sanhedrin* 7.11, *Sifra* 1.7 (ed. Weiss 3a), and *Avot de-Rabbi Natan* (Version A) ch. 37; Günter Stemberger, *Introduction to the Talmud and Midrash*, 2nd ed., trans. and ed. Markus Bockmuehl (Edinburgh: T&T Clark, 1996), 18.

12. Tomson points out that the members of the Qumran community applied the expression "a new covenant" (Jer 31:31) to themselves—needless to say, without abolishing the Torah, see "*If This Be from Heaven*", 178. He, too, asserts that there is no antithesis between law and spirit in Pauline thought (cf. Rom 8:2). However, Daniel Boyarin argues that there is a fundamental dialectics between *en grammati* (in [the] letter) and *en pneumati* (in [the] Spirit), see *A Radical Jew: Paul and the Politics of Identity* (Berkeley: University of California Press, 1994), 86.

13. Alan F. Segal, in *Paul the Convert: The Apostolate and Apostasy of Saul the Pharisee* (New Haven, CT: Yale University Press, 1990), 152–55, suggests that the veil in Paul's text is not merely a metaphor; he is possibly also speaking of "a communal practice." Paul is referring, Segal argues, to the ritual of veiling one's head in Judaism. Segal suggests that Paul is writing before the custom of reverent head covering for worship had evolved. Hence, is it an admonition not to pray as (some) Jews prayed? Is it primarily a question of liturgical behavior? Did Paul advocate that gentile Christ followers not veil their heads with a *tallit*?

14. Barclay, "2 Corinthians," 1360.

15. Cf. Alfred Lord Tennyson, "In Memoriam," in *Poems of Tennyson*...(London: Oxford University Press, 1917), #5 (p. 320): "For words, like Nature, half reveal And half conceal the Soul within."

CHAPTER 25

1. This chapter is based on a previously published essay; see Jesper Svartvik, "The Children of Sarah and Hagar, and the 'Mother City' of Jerusalem," in *Enabling Dialogue about the Land: A Resource Book for Jews and Christians*, ed. Philip A. Cunningham, Ruth Langer, and Jesper Svartvik (Mahwah, NJ: Paulist Press, 2020), 160–90.

2. Donald K. Guthrie suggests that Paul here is thinking of slavery in two senses: Jerusalem under Roman occupation, and also Paul's "primary thought must be of slavery to law. Pharisaism had so superimposed upon the law a mass of minute regulations that observance of it had become a burden." See his commentary *Galatians*, 2nd ed. (London: Marshall, Morgan & Scott, 1974), 125.

3. James Carroll, "What Donald Trump Doesn't Understand about Anti-Semitism," *The New Yorker* (February 23, 2017).

4. This is not a reference to the person named Hagar, since the word is preceded by the definite article in the neuter (Greek: *to*).

5. It has been pointed out that a certain Christoph Harant Freiherr von Polschitz already in 1598 during a journey to Mount Sinai noted that *Den Berg Synai nennen die Arabische und Mauritanische Heyden* [sic] *Agar oder Thur: Weissenberg* (the Arabian and Mauritanian heathens call Mount Sinai Agar or Thur: [the] White Mountain). See Friedrich Sieffert, *Der Brief an die Galater. Von der 6. Auflage an neu bearbeitet* (Göttingen: Vandenhoeck & Ruprecht, 1899), 285.

6. Lloyd Gaston, *Paul and the Torah* (Vancouver: University of British Columbia, 1987), 91.

7. For the arguments in favor of Paul as an apostle to the gentiles, see K. Stendahl, "The Apostle Paul and the Introspective Conscience of the West," 199–215.

8. See, e.g., Tikva Frymer-Kensky, *Reading the Women of the Bible: A New Interpretation of Their Stories* (New York: Schocken, 2002), 226: "Several midrashim try to solve the ethical issue by finding fault with Hagar." And as we see in this case, with Ishmael as well.

9. Wilhelm Gesenius translated the verb form *piel of tzachaq* (laughed) as *scherzen* (to kid) and refers to Gen 19:14; see *Hebräisches und Aramäisches Handwörterbuch über das Alte Testament*, 16th ed. (Leipzig: Vogel, 1915).

10. For a discussion of the three cardinal sins, see, e.g., *Talmud Bavli Sanhedrin* 74a.

11. This is actually stated explicitly in the Septuagint, in which Cain says to Abel, "Let us go into the field" (*dielthômen eis to pedion*).

12. Cf. Fredriksen, *Paul*, 106: "The gentiles, then, are like Isaac, children of the promise." However, she argues that the sons of Hagar are "those who receive his competitor's gospel."

13. For a discussion of the midrashic genre, see, e.g., Barry W. Holtz, "Midrash," in *Back to the Sources: Reading the Classic Texts*, ed. Barry W. Holtz (New York: Summit, 1984), 177–211.

14. Arguably, the most well-known example of an allegory is George Orwell's novel *Animal Farm: A Fairy Tale* (London: Secker & Warburg, 1945).

15. Nor should the verb *systoichein* (correspond) mislead the interpreter. The noun *stoichos* means "a pillar." Gaston, *Paul and the Torah*, 83, correctly points out, "No one really knows what the verb means, and the only place where it occurs in ancient literature throws little light on Galatians 4:25." Thus we cannot know exactly what is being compared to what.

16. Frymer-Kensky writes that Hagar is an archetype of Israel and that the story of Sarai and Hagar "is not a story of conflict between 'us' and 'other,' but between 'us' and 'another us.' Hagar is the type of Israel, she is the redeemed slave, she is 'us'"; see *Reading the Women of the Bible*, 233 and 236.

17. Brigitte Kahl, *Galatians Re-imagined: Reading with the Eyes of the Vanquished* (Minneapolis: Fortress, 2010). Kahl's book is not a traditional verse-by-verse commentary; she gives a plethora of examples of the sheer bru-

tality in the Roman Empire and a great quantity of information about Galatia, but, at times, less about the Epistle to the Galatians. See also her article "No Longer Male: Masculinity Struggles behind Galatians 3.28?," *Journal for the Study of the New Testament* 79 (2000): 37–49. Although not concurring with this particular reading, John M. G. Barclay, nevertheless, counts Kahl as one of the four most important interpreters of Galatians (along with the three readings of Martin Luther, James D. G. Dunn, and Louis Martyn), see *Paul and the Gift* (Grand Rapids: Eerdmans, 2015), 339–50.

18. Kahl, *Galatians Re-imagined*, 33 and 49. Mark D. Nanos mentions that the Galatians are Celts, but without drawing as far-reaching conclusions as does Kahl about the Galatian as the typical barbarian; see *The Irony of Galatians: Paul's Letter in First-Century Context* (Minneapolis: Fortress, 2002), 232 and 263. The main purpose of his book is to identify those who encourage circumcision; see, e.g., 6, 183, 207, and 317.

19. Kahl, *Galatians Re-imagined*, 51.

20. Kahl, *Galatians Re-imagined*, 56, 59, and 70.

21. Kahl, *Galatians Re-imagined*, 126 and 212.

22. Kahl, *Galatians Re-imagined*, 186.

23. Kahl, *Galatians Re-imagined*, 166.

24. Kahl, *Galatians Re-imagined*, 263, defines it as "the myriads of ways of upholding and reproducing the 'combat order' of the imperial world construct with the victorious self at the top." When *nomos* refers to Scripture (e.g., 4:21), it is not a reference to Roman law. Cf. p. 227: "The term *nomos* in Galatians thus necessarily oscillates between a Jewish and a Roman connotation, the latter being the predominant one." For *erga nomou* in Romans, see 2:15; 3:20, and 27f.

25. Kahl, *Galatians Re-imagined*, 161.

26. See, e.g., Nanos, *The Irony of Galatians*, 289.

27. Kahl, *Galatians Re-imagined*, 225. This has previously been suggested by Troy Martin, "Pagan and Judeo-Christian Time-Keeping Schemes in Galatians 4:10 and Colossians 2:16," *New Testament Studies* 42 (1996): 120–32.

28. Kahl, *Galatians Re-imagined*, 220. She here refers to other scholars who have also suggested this, e.g., Bruce Winter, Mark Nanos, Thomas Witulski, and Justin Hardin.

29. Kahl, *Galatians Re-imagined*, 144.

30. Nanos, *The Irony of Galatians*, 98.

31. Kahl, *Galatians Re-imagined*, 205.

32. Kahl, *Galatians Re-imagined*, 209.

33. Kahl, *Galatians Re-imagined*, 216. Kahl points out that the limited autonomy of the Jews was especially prevalent in the cities of the Roman East, i.e., where the recipients of Paul's epistle actually lived.

34. Kahl, *Galatians Re-imagined*, 221.

35. Kahl, *Galatians Re-imagined*, 222. Kahl quotes Fredriksen, who writes in *Jesus of Nazareth*, 135: "Paul walked these Gentiles-in-Christ into a

social and religious no man's land. In the time before the Parousia [the end of times], they had literally no place to go." Hence, it was Paul's eschatology, in Fredriksen's words, "his foreshortened perspective on time," that did not leave much room for a Gentile Christ-believing community to maneuver.

36. Kahl, *Galatians Re-imagined*, 226.
37. Kahl, *Galatians Re-imagined*, 227 and 257.
38. Kahl, *Galatians Re-imagined*, 293.
39. Kahl, *Galatians Re-imagined*, 301f.

CHAPTER 26

1. Susan Grove Eastman, "Israel and the Mercy of God: A Re-reading of Galatians 6.16 and Romans 9–11," *New Testament Studies* 56 (2010): 371. Her translation: "And for as many as will walk in line with this rule, peace be upon them and (even) mercy and (even) upon the Israel of God."
2. S. Lewis Johnson, "Paul and the 'Israel of God: An Exegetical and Eschatological Case-Study,'" *Master's Seminary Journal* 20 (2009): 43: "It is well-known that Justin Martyr in his *Dialogue with Trypho* is the first author to claim an identification of the term *Israel* with the church. Of the commentators, Chrysostom is one of the earliest apparently to identify the church with Israel, affirming that those who keep the rule are 'true Israelites'" (emphases in the original). Johnson's article was originally published in 1986.
3. Sanders, *Paul, the Law and the Jewish People*, 176 (emphases added).
4. Eastman, "Israel and the Mercy of God," 380. For "Israel according to the flesh" in Jewish thought, see Daniel Boyarin, *Carnal Israel: Reading Sex in Talmudic Culture* (Berkeley: University of California Press, 1993); for early Christianity and noncarnality, see Peter Brown, *The Body and Society: Men, Women and Sexual Renunciation in Early Christianity* (New York: Columbia University Press, 1988).
5. S. L. Johnson, "Paul and the 'Israel of God,'" 50.
6. S. L. Johnson, "Paul and the 'Israel of God,'" 49.
7. S. L. Johnson, "Paul and the 'Israel of God,'" 54 (emphases in the original).
8. Gottlob Schrenk, "Was bedeutet 'Israel Gottes?,'" *Judaica* 5 (1949): 81–95, and "Der Segenwunsch nach der Kampfepistel" *Judaica* 6 (1950): 170–90.
9. C. E. B. Cranfield, *A Critical and Exegetical Commentary on the Epistle to the Romans*, 2 vols. (Edinburgh: T&T Clark, 1975–79), 2:473 and 474 (*pantes hoi ex Israêl* is written in Greek letters in the original).
10. Hans Dieter Betz, *Galatians: A Commentary on Paul's Letter to the Churches in Galatia* (Philadelphia: Fortress, 1979), 323 (Greek letters in the original).
11. S. L. Johnson, "Paul and the 'Israel of God,'" 52.
12. Eastman, "Israel and the Mercy of God," 372.

13. Eastman, "Israel and the Mercy of God," 390. Hence, she argues that (p. 382): "Here Paul neither redefines 'Israel' nor creates a temporary distinction *within* Israel, an 'Israel within Israel.'" Cf. p. 367: "Paul invokes peace on those who live according to the new creation, and mercy on Israel" (who are not Christ believers, but nevertheless remain the Israel of God). Peter Richardson (*Israel in the Apostolic Church* [Cambridge, UK: Cambridge University Press, 1969], 79) suggests a repunctuation that results in a similar reading: "May God give peace to all who will walk according to this criterion, and mercy also to his faithful people Israel." He argues that Paul is giving "an ironical twist" to the Jewish prayer *shemoneh 'esreh* (The Eighteen [Prayers]). However, Betz is critical, questioning why Paul would use "mercy" ironically; see *Galatians*, 322.

14. Eastman, "Israel and the Mercy of God," 389.

15. Eastman, "Israel and the Mercy of God," 380.

16. Cf. Rom 11:25–36, where Paul clearly distinguishes between "Israel" and "you" (the recipients of the epistle, who are not Israel).

17. Shaye J. D. Cohen, "The Letter of Paul to the Galatians," in *The Jewish Annotated New Testament*, 2nd ed., ed. Amy-Jill Levine and Marc Zvi Brettler (Oxford: Oxford University Press, 2017), 386f. Cf. Betz, *Galatians*, 321: "This benediction is not only different from other benedictions Paul uses, but it is also remarkably similar to Jewish benedictions…: *sim shalom tovah u-vrakhah chen we-chesed 'aleinu we-'al kol Yisrael 'amkha* ('bestow peace, happiness and blessing, grace and loving-kindness and mercy upon us and upon all Israel, your people')." (The benediction is in Hebrew letters in the original.)

18. Cf. Fredriksen, *Paul*, 117.

CHAPTER 27

1. A previous version of this chapter has been published in *Reconciliation and Transformation*, 57–71.

2. For a summary of arguments for a deutero-Pauline authorship, see Martin Kitchen, *Ephesians* (New York: Routledge, 1994), 4–7. For a thorough discussion, see C. Leslie Mitton, *The Epistle to the Ephesians: Its Authorship, Origin and Purpose* (Oxford: Clarendon, 1951).

3. Moshe Halbertal, *On Sacrifice* (Princeton, NJ: Princeton University Press, 2012), 10 and 117f. There are several Hebrew words with the same root: *le-haqriv* (to carry forward, to sacrifice); *le-hitqarev* (to come near); *qerev* (interior, entrails, inner); *be-qerev* (in the middle of, inner, among); *be-qarov* (soon, impending); and *qarov* (close, relative).

4. See, e.g., Lionel J. Windsor, *Reading Ephesians and Colossians after Supersessionism: Christ's Mission through Israel to the Nations* (Eugene, OR: Cascade, 2017), 132–34.

5. See *Mishnah Middot* 2.3: *liphnim mimmenu soreg gavoha 'asarah tephachim* (On the inside [existed] a ten-cubit-high fence). For more on this unit of measurement, see 1 Kings 7:26 or Ezek 40:5 ("handbreadth").

6. For additional comments, see *The History of the Jewish People in the Age of Jesus Christ (175 B.C.–A.D. 135)*, rev. ed., ed. Geza Vermes, Fergus Millar, and Matthew Black (Edinburgh: T&T Clark, 1979), 2:285; Ernest Best, *A Critical and Exegetical Commentary on Ephesians* (Edinburgh: T&T Clark, 1998), 250–59; and Joan R. Branham, "Penetrating the Sacred: Breaches and Barriers in the Jerusalem Temple," in *Thresholds of the Sacred: Architectural, Art Historical, Liturgical, and Theological Perspectives on Religious Screens, East and West*, ed. Sharon Gerstel (Cambridge, MA: Harvard University Press, 2006), 6–24, esp. 12–16.

7. The Greek expressions are *herkion lithinou dryphaktou, dryphaktos peribeblêto lithinos*, or *ho dryphaktos*; see *Jewish Antiquities* 15.11.5 (§416f.) and *Jewish War* 5.5.2 (§193) and 6.2.4 (§124f.).

8. Acts 21:24 (emphases added).

9. See *Mishnah Pirqei Avot* 1.1.

10. Matt 5:17–48. A related question is whether the traditional term *antitheses* is applicable or whether the concept of *hypertheses* would be better (see ch. 2).

11. 1 Enoch 14:9. See Kitchen, *Ephesians*, 65f.

12. This is reminiscent of Christian presentations of texts on the rending of the temple veil in connection with the death of Jesus (see ch. 19).

13. See Andrew T. Lincoln, *Ephesians* (Nashville: Thomas Nelson, 1990): (1) Lincoln argues that Christ neutralized the negative effects of the Law (p. 142: "Christ neutralized these negative effects of the law by doing away with the law"). (2) Then he claims that Christ abolished the Law per se (pp. 142 and 144: "in order to remove the divisiveness Christ has to deal with its cause—the law itself....In his death Christ abolished the law...and terminated the old order dominated by that law, which had prevented the Gentiles from having access to salvation....The separation of the Gentiles from Israel and her election was a cleft so deep that it took the creative act of Christ's death to fill it." (3) Finally he argues that the Law was not favorable to Israel (pp. 146 and 163: "The law...separated Israel from God....Israel too was alienated from her God").

14. See, e.g., *The Koren Siddur*, 5.

15. Tet-Lim N. Yee, Jews, *Gentiles and Ethnic Reconciliation: Paul's Jewish Identity and Ephesians* (Cambridge, UK: Cambridge University Press, 2005), 158 and 160f.

16. James D. G. Dunn, "The New Perspective on Paul" (see introduction, third challenge).

17. Nelson Goodman's expression cited in Colin E. Gunton, *The Actuality of Atonement: A Study of Metaphor, Rationality and the Christian Tradition* (Edinburgh: T&T Clark, 1988), 28.

Notes

18. The word *en dogmasin* ([and] in regulations) is lacking from p[46], one of the oldest New Testament papyri, typically dated at 200 CE.

19. See, e.g., Paul's writing in 1 Cor 5:1–5 on a sexual relation that is forbidden in both Roman and Jewish law (Lev 18:8).

20. Windsor, *Reading Ephesians and Colossians after Supersessionism*, 158.

21. The name Baruch is mentioned four times in Jeremiah (ch. 32, 36, 43, and 45).

22. 2 Baruch 54.3–5. Translation by Michael E. Stone and Matthias Henze, *4 Ezra and 2 Baruch: Translations, Introductions, and Notes* (Minneapolis: Fortress, 2013), 119. See also A. F. J. Klijn's older translation, "2 (Syriac Apocalypse of) Baruch: A New Translation and Introduction," in *The Old Testament Pseudepigrapha*, vol. 1: *Apocalyptic Literature and Testaments*, ed. James H. Charlesworth (New York: Doubleday, 1983), 639: "You are the one to whom both the depths and the heights come together, and whose word the beginnings of the periods serve. You are the one who reveals to those who fear that which is prepared for them so that you may comfort them. You show your mighty works to those who do not know. You pull down the enclosure [Syriac: *suga*] for those who have no experience and enlighten the darknesses, and reveal the secrets to those who are spotless, to those who subjected themselves to you and your Law in faith." For the Syriac word that is key here, *suga* (obstacle); cf. Song of Songs 7:2: "Your navel is a rounded bowl that never lacks mixed wine. Your belly is a heap of wheat, encircled [Hebrew: *sugah*] with lilies."

23. A. F. J. Klijn, "2 (Syriac Apocalypse of) Baruch," 617; Liv Ingeborg Lied, "Those Who Know and Those Who Don't: Mystery, Instruction, and Knowledge in *2 Baruch*," in *Mystery and Secrecy in the Nag Hammadi Collection and Other Ancient Literature: Ideas and Practices*, ed. Christian H. Bull, Liv Ingeborg Lied, and John D. Turner (Leiden: Brill, 2011), 427, and Stone and Henze, *4 Ezra and 2 Baruch*, 10.

24. *Papyrus Oxyrhynchus* 3.403 contains 2 Baruch 12.1–13.2 and 13.11–14.2, see *The Oxyrhynchus Papyri: Part III*, ed. Bernard P. Grenfell and Arthur S. Hunt (London: Egypt Exploration Fund, 1903), 3–7.

25. See Lied, "Those Who Know and Those Who Don't," 427f.: "Most scholars today understand the work as a response to that destruction and as a deliberation over the situation of Jewish societies following the loss of the temple"; and Stone and Henze, *4 Ezra and 2 Baruch*, 10: "The author of *2 Baruch* wrote in response to the Roman destruction of Jerusalem in 70 CE, though the apocalypse is set factiously during and after the Babylonian sacking of Jerusalem in the year 587 BCE."

26. Emphases added.

27. Isa 25:6f. See also Zech 6:15: "Those who are far off shall come and help to build [i.e., not 'to tear down'] the temple of the Lord."

28. Benjamin D. Sommer, "Isaiah," in *The Jewish Study Bible*, ed. Adele Berlin and Marc Zvi Brettler (Oxford: Oxford University Press, 2004),

832: "When the new cosmic order emerges, the illusions that befuddle the nations will disappear, and the survivors from all nations will enjoy access to true teachings, which emanate from the God of Zion."

29. The first words are part of the song *lekha dodi*, which is sung at the Jewish worship service *qabbalat shabbat* every Friday evening.

30. In rabbinic hermeneutics we find the belief that there are no unnecessary words in the Torah (*ein bah ot yeter we-cheser* or *ein kephel ba-Miqra*). The specific meaning of each word was emphasized especially by Rabbi 'Aqivah, see, e.g., A. J. Heschel, *Heavenly Torah*, 46–64.

31. Cf. Williamson and Allen, *Interpreting Difficult Texts*, 75.

32. For a *new perspective* interpretation of the Epistle to the Ephesians, see Gary E. Weedman, "Reading Ephesians from the New Perspective on Paul," *Leaven* 14 (2006): 81–92. For an extensive post-supersessionist discussion that stresses that "Christ's blessings have come through Israel to the nations," but not at the expense of Israel's self-understanding, see Windsor, *Reading Ephesians and Colossians after Supersessionism*, 111.

CHAPTER 28

1. Cf. Moisés Silva, *Philippians*, 2nd ed. (Grand Rapids: Baker Academic, 2005), 180: "What he [i.e., Paul] once regarded highly he now finds revolting."

2. Friedrich Lang, "*skybalon*," in *Theological Dictionary of the New Testament*, ed. Gerhard Kittel and Gerhard Friedrich; trans. and ed. Geoffrey W. Bromiley (Grand Rapids, MI: Eerdmans, 1964–76 [German: 1933–49]), 7:447. (The words *pepoithenai en sarki* are written with Greek letters in Lang's article.)

3. For these explanations of Paul's *curriculum vitae*, see Michael Cook, "The Letter to the Philippians," in *The Jewish Annotated New Testament*, 2nd ed., ed. Amy-Jill Levine and Marc Zvi Brettler (Oxford: Oxford University Press, 2017), 403.

4. Peter Leithart, "Skubalon" (https://theopolisinstitute.com/leithart_post/skubalon), and Gary Manning, "Did the Apostle Paul Use Profanity?" (https://www.biola.edu/blogs/good-book-blog/2015/did-the-apostle-paul-use-profanity) (both accessed February 27, 2023). A possible wordplay is that *skybalon* is what is thrown "to the dogs" (*tois kysin*): hence, *skybalon* is *kysibalon*. It is interesting to note that dogs are actually mentioned in Phil 3:2 (cf. Matt 7:6, Luke 16:21, 2 Peter 2:22, and Rev 22:15). On the dog motif in Phil 3, see Nanos, *Reading Corinthians and Philippians within Judaism*, 111–41.

5. The *New Revised Standard Version* translates the Greek expression *tên ekklêsian tou Theou* as "the church of God." The present study, however, chooses an alternative translation, since "church" is easily (mis)understood anachronistically. Fredriksen retains the Greek original term "the ekklesia" (when translating Phil 3:2–6); see, e.g., *Paul*, 64.

6. Bruce Chilton argues that the English preposition "in" better reflects the Pauline line of thought than "to"; see *Rabbi Paul: An Intellectual Biography* (New York: Doubleday, 2004), 50f.: "The basic meaning of this language, however, is that a heavenly mystery has its cover (its -*kalupsis*) taken off (*apo*): the veil of circumstance is momentarily stripped from spiritual reality. Here the cover is removed from God's Son, who is 'in' (*en*) Paul, within his consciousness in an experience uniquely his."

7. Tomson, "*If This Be from Heaven*," 176–78.

8. For additional aspects on this rhetoric of comparison, see, e.g., William S. Campbell, *Unity and Diversity in Christ: Interpreting Paul in Context; Collected Essays* (Eugene, OR: Cascade, 2013), 212–18.

9. Charles A. Wanamaker, "Philippians," in *Eerdmans Commentary to the Bible*, ed. James D. G. Dunn and John W. Rogerson (Grand Rapids, MI: Eerdmans, 2003), 1399.

10. Christopher Zoccali, *Reading Philippians after Supersessionism: Jews, Gentiles, and Covenantal Identity* (Eugene, OR: Cascade, 2017), 105 (emphasis in the original).

11. Zoccali, *Reading Philippians after Supersessionism*, 104.

12. Zoccali, *Reading Philippians after Supersessionism*, 107. He refers to "the salvation-historical contrast" on p. 106 and to the divine economy on p. 110.

13. Zoccali, *Reading Philippians after Supersessionism*, 108. *Telos* cannot mean "end" in, e.g., 1 Tim 1:5: "But the aim [*telos*] of such instruction is love that comes from a pure heart, a good conscience, and sincere faith." Another example is 1 Peter 1:9 ("for you are receiving the outcome [*telos*] of your faith, the salvation of your souls").

14. Zoccali, *Reading Philippians after Supersessionism*, 114.

15. See, e.g., Zoccali, *Reading Philippians after Supersessionism*, 102.

CHAPTER 29

1. Matthew Jensen, "The (In)authenticity of 1 Thessalonians 2.13–16: A Review of Arguments," *Currents on Biblical Research* 18 (2019): 59.

2. David Fox Sandmel, "The First Letter of Paul to the Thessalonians," in *The Jewish Annotated New Testament*, 2nd ed., ed. Amy-Jill Levine and Marc Zvi Brettler (Oxford: Oxford University Press, 2017), 421.

3. Jeffrey S. Lamp, "Is Paul Anti-Jewish? Testament of Levi 6 in the Interpretation of 1 Thessalonians 2:13–16," *Catholic Biblical Quarterly* 65 (2003): 409f.

4. Tomson, "*If This Be from Heaven*," 175.

5. Ernest Best, *A Commentary on the First and Second Epistles to the Thessalonians* (London: Adam & Charles Black, 1979 [1972]), 114.

6. Cf. K. Stendahl, *Holy Week Preaching*, 23.

7. R. S. Ascough, *1 and 2 Thessalonians: Encountering the Christ Group at Thessalonike* (Sheffield, UK: Sheffield Phoenix Press, 2014), 27.

8. Birger A. Pearson, "1 Thessalonians 2:13–16: A Deutero-Pauline Interpolation," *Harvard Theological Review* 64 (1971): 79–94, reprinted with slight revision in B. A. Pearson, *The Emergence of the Christian Religion: Essays on Early Christianity* (Harrisburg, PA: Trinity International Press, 1997), 58–74. The first scholar to suggest that parts of 1 Thessalonians 2 is an interpolation was probably Albrecht Ritschl (1847), and this was subsequently argued also by Paul Wilhelm Schmiedel (1892), Heinrich Julius Holtzmann (1892), James Moffatt (1918), John W. Bailey (1955), S. G. F. Brandon (1957), and Karl-Gottfried Eckart (1961). Ferdinand Christian Baur referred to 2:14–16 when arguing against the authenticity of the *entire* epistle (1875).

9. No manuscripts before the fourth century contain the entire passage 2:13–16. (The papyrus fragment p^{65}, probably from the mid-third century, contains only 1:3—2:1 and 6—13.) However, 2:13–16 is not omitted in its entirety in any manuscripts.

10. Daryl Schmidt, "1 Thess 2:13–16: Linguistic Evidence for an Interpolation," *Journal of Biblical Literature* 102 (1983): 276.

11. The New Revised Standard Version translates the Greek expression *tên ekklêsian tou Theou* as "the church of God." The present study, however, prefers an alternative translation, since "church" is easily (mis)understood anachronistically.

12. Jensen, "The (In)authenticity of 1 Thessalonians 2.13–16," 72.

13. Jensen lists four arguments in favor of authenticity: text critical, contextual, traditional, and rhetorical; see "The (In)authenticity of 1 Thessalonians 2.13–16," 72.

14. Jeblae is not mentioned in the account in Genesis 34.

15. *Testament of Levi* 6.8–11 (emphasis added).

16. Lamp, "Is Paul Anti-Jewish?," 423.

17. Lamp, "Is Paul Anti-Jewish?," 427.

18. Tomson, "*If This Be from Heaven*," 174. He continues: "Paul places himself in the position of the persecuted *Jewish* minority" (emphasis added). But could he really be encouraging *Jewish* Christ followers by stating that they are being persecuted by the Jews?

19. It has been suggested that Paul uses material from a pre-Synoptic tradition, i.e., that he drew from a source that Matthew later used in his Gospel; see, e.g., R. Schippers, "The Pre-Synoptic Tradition in 1 Thessalonians II 13–16," *Novum Testamentum* 8 (1966): 231–33. But if Paul is using a pre-Synoptic source here, why does he not attribute the death of Jesus to "the Jews" elsewhere? For further comments, see Jensen, "The (In)authenticity of 1 Thessalonians 2.13–16," 74.

20. Abraham J. Malherbe, *The Letters to the Thessalonians: A New Translation with Introduction and Commentary* (New Haven, CT: Yale University Press, 2000), 179.

21. Carol J. Schlueter, *Filling up the Measure: Polemic Hyperbole in 1 Thessalonians 2:14–16* (Sheffield, UK: Sheffield Academic Press, 1993), 75.

22. Jensen, "The (In)authenticity of 1 Thessalonians 2.13–16," 76.

23. John C. Hurd, "Paul Ahead of his Time: 1 Thess. 2:13–16," in *Anti-Judaism in Early Christianity: I. Paul and the Gospels*, ed. Peter Richardson with David Granskou (Waterloo: Wilfrid Laurier University Press, 1986), 36. Similarly, Levine, *The Misunderstood Jew*, 97: "[The interpolation argument] removes from Paul the possibility that he may have changed his mind or, more pastorally, adapted his rhetoric to fit the needs of his congregations."

24. Malherbe, *The Letters to the Thessalonians*, 178.

CHAPTER 30

1. Claudia Setzer, *Jewish Responses to Early Christians: History and Polemics, 30–150 C.E.* (Minneapolis: Fortress, 1994), 100.

2. In the lectionary for the Church of Sweden, an Evangelical-Lutheran denomination with some 5.6 million members, Revelation 2:8–11 is one of the texts read on the Sixteenth Sunday after Trinity, the theme of which is "Death and Life." It does not appear in the widely used Revised Common Lectionary.

3. Colin J. Hemer, *Letters to the Seven Churches in Their Local Setting* (Sheffield, UK: JSOT Press, 1986), 66f.

4. The infamous number of the beast (666; see Rev 13:18) is probably a code (gematria) for "Emperor Nero" in Hebrew (*Neron Qisar* or *Qisar Neron*). The explanation that some manuscripts (e.g., p^{115}) have 616 instead is probably that it is based on an alternative spelling of his name (*Qisar Nero* or *Nero Qisar*). If the text is referring to Domitian, Nero's name was probably used as a code name for Domitian. Quite possibly Domitian was understood as *Nero redivivus* (Nero reborn); see, e.g., Tomson, "*If This Be from Heaven*," 374. Domitian demanded participation in the imperial cult and had himself called *Dominus et Deus* (Lord and God).

5. Robert Henry Charles, *A Critical and Exegetical Commentary on the Revelation of St. John*, 2 vols (Edinburgh: T&T Clark, 1920), 1:58.

6. G. B. Caird, *Revelation of St. John the Divine* (London: Adam & Charles Black, 1966), 53.

7. David Frankfurter, "The Revelation to John," in *The Jewish Annotated New Testament*, 2nd ed., ed. Amy-Jill Levine and Marc Zvi Brettler (Oxford: Oxford University Press, 2017), 537.

8. Frankfurter, "The Revelation to John," 537.

9. D. Moody Smith, "Judaism and the Gospel of John," 88 (emphases in the original).

10. Setzer, *Jewish Responses*, 100.

11. Frankfurter, "The Revelation to John," 543.

12. David Frankfurter, "Jewish or Not? Reconstructing the Other in Rev 2:9 and 3:9," *Harvard Theological Review* 94 (2001): 425 (emphasis in the original).

13. Frankfurter, "Jewish or Not?," 403. Gösta Lindeskog argues that those criticized are Christian schismatics ("eine Invektive gegen christliche

Sektierer"); see *Das jüdisch-christliche Problem: Randglossen zu einer Forschungsepoche* (Stockholm: Almqvist & Wiksell International, 1986), 166.

14. Frankfurter, "Jewish or Not?," 423: "Paul's Gentile followers, whether or not they embraced the label 'Jew,' were in fact nothing but '*so-called* Jews.'" Similarly, Tomson, "*If This Be from Heaven*," 376: "Under the capriciousness of Domitian's regime, they assumed a more intransigent position than certain fellow-Christians, who possibly belonged to the Pauline wing....They call themselves Jews, but they are not. The label 'Jew' has, thus, a positive connotation for John."

15. Frankfurter, "The Revelation to John," 538.

16. Walter E. Pilgrim differentiates between an *ethic of subordination* (Pauline and post-Pauline texts), an *ethic of critical distancing* (Jesus and the Gospels), and an *ethic of resistance* (Revelation); see *Uneasy Neighbors: Church and State in the New Testament* (Minneapolis: Fortress, 1999).

17. For a classic (and anti-Jewish) harmonization of these two perspectives, see Joachim Jeremias, "Paul and James," *Expository Times* 66 (1955): 368–71, esp. 371: "Paul is fighting against Jewish confidence in meritorious works, against the effort to save oneself, against the under-estimating of sin, against the over-estimating of man's power, against the self-righteousness of the pious man who has too good an opinion of himself....James has a quite different position. He is fighting against a dead orthodoxy, against a self-satisfied attitude towards grace, against an un-Christian Quietism, against a Christianity which is inwardly dying, against feigned confessors, i.e. against symptoms by which especially congregations of the Pauline type have been devastated at all times....So James ch. 2 has its full right to stand by the side of Paul. For James, also, like Paul, is repeating what Jesus said. Paul repeats Mt 5^3, James repeats Mt $7^{21\text{ff}}$. We may stress this observation—that Paul is representing the beginning, whereas James is representing the end of the Sermon on the Mount" (emphases in the original).

18. A plausible rhetorical target for John is the theology of Ignatius of Antioch, who wrote to communities that were, in the words of Ralph J. Korner, "predominantly gentile, hyper-supersessionist, neo-Pauline"; see *Reading Revelation after Supersessionism: An Apocalyptic Journey of Socially Identifying John's Multi-ethnic Ekklêsiai with the Ekklêsia of Israel* (Eugene, OR: Cascade, 2020), 64. This has previously been suggested by Elaine Pagels, "The Social History of Satan, Part Three: John of Patmos and Ignatius of Antioch; Contrasting Visions of 'God's People,'" *Harvard Theological Review* 99 (2006): 501–5.

CONCLUDING REMARKS

1. See Metzger, *A Textual Commentary on the Greek New Testament*, xiii.

2. Amy-Jill Levine, "Preaching and Teaching the Pharisees," in *The Pharisees*, ed. Joseph Sievers and Amy-Jill Levine (Grand Rapids, MI: Eerd-

mans, 2021), 421. She specifies the interpretation of the *Gospels* simply because the purpose of the book in which her article is published is to discuss the Pharisaic movement. Interpretations of Acts, the epistles, and Revelation, too, have contributed to spreading stereotyping about Jews and Judaism.

3. See, e.g., Jonathan Z. Smith, *Drudgery Divine: On the Comparison of Early Christianities and the Religions of Late Antiquity* (London: School of Oriental and African Studies, 1990), Lloyd Gaston, "The Uniqueness of Jesus as a Methodological Problem." In *Origins and Methods: Towards a New Understanding of Judaism and Christianity*, ed. B. H. McLean (Sheffield, UK: Sheffield Academic Press, 1993), and E. P. Sanders, *The Question of Uniqueness in the Teaching of Jesus: The Ethel M. Wood Lecture 15 February 1990* (London: University of London, 1990).

4. Sanders, *The Question of Uniqueness in the Teaching of Jesus*, 24 and 26.

5. Lloyd Gaston, "The Uniqueness of Jesus as a Methodological Problem," 276.

6. Davies and Allison, *The Gospel according to Saint Matthew*, 1:688.

7. See, e.g., Levine, *The Misunderstood Jew*, 23 and 119–122.

8. On the wide spectrum of christologies, see, e.g., John d'Arcy May, *Transcendence and Violence: The Encounter of Buddhist, Christian and Primal Traditions* (New York: Continuum, 2003), 139: "To continue thinking of Christ *only* in the traditional way is like sticking to the examples in a grammar book instead of *using* language freely and creatively after having assimilated the rule system of its 'generative grammar'" (emphases in the original).

9. See Jülicher, *Die Gleichnisreden Jesu*.

10. Ernst Käsemann, *New Testament Questions of Today*, trans. W. J. Montague (Philadelphia: Fortress, 1979 [German: 1965]), 184. The broadcast talk was first published in 1961.

11. Käsemann, *New Testament Questions of Today*, 186.

12. The saying was probably coined by journalist Finley Peter Dunne. It is often quoted, e.g., in the film *Inherit the Wind*.

13. Nirenberg, "Anti-Judaism as a Critical Theory" (emphases added).

14. Fredriksen, *Paul*, 109.

15. For additional aspects, see Jesper Svartvik, "'I Have Come Not to Abolish but to Fulfil': Reflections on Understanding Christianity as Fulfilment without Presupposing Supersessionism," *Religions* 13 (2022), https://doi.org/10.3390/rel13020149 (accessed April 10, 2023). John Stendahl suggests three principles of action when repudiating Christian anti-Judaism: (1) *grief-speaking*, (2) *truth-telling*, and (3) *faith-applying*; see "With Luther, Against Luther," in *Removing the Anti-Judaism from the New Testament*, ed. Howard Clark Kee and Irvin J. Borowsky (Philadelphia: American Interfaith Institute / World alliance, 2000), 165–70.

16. Krister Stendahl, "Why I Love the Bible," *Harvard Divinity Bulletin* 35 (2007) https://bulletin.hds.harvard.edu/articles/winter2007/why-i-love

-bible (accessed April 21, 2023). For the legacy of Stendahl, see Paula Fredriksen and Jesper Svartvik, eds., *Krister among the Jews and Gentiles: Essays in Appreciation of the Life and Work of Krister Stendahl* (Mahwah, NJ: Paulist Press, 2018).
    17. Cf. Fredriksen, *Paul*, 150.

BIBLIOGRAPHY

Abrahams, Israel. *Studies in Pharisaism and the Gospels*. 2 vols. Cambridge, UK: Cambridge University Press, 1917–24.

Akiyama, Kengo. *The Love of Neighbour in Ancient Judaism: The Reception of Leviticus 19:18 in the Hebrew Bible, the Septuagint, the Book of Jubilees, the Dead Sea Scrolls, and the New Testament*. Leiden: Brill, 2018.

Alexander, Philip S. "Jesus and the Golden Rule." In *Hillel and Jesus: Comparative Studies of Two Major Religious Leaders*, edited by James H. Charlesworth and Loren L. Johns, 363–88. Minneapolis: Fortress, 1997.

Alon, Gedalyahu. *Jews, Judaism and the Classical World: Studies in Jewish History in the Times of the Second Temple and Talmud*. Jerusalem: Magness, 1977.

Anderson, Benedict. *Imagined Communities: Reflections on the Origin and Spread of Nationalism*. 2nd ed. New York: Verso, 1991.

Anderson, Gary. *Sin: A History*. New Haven, CT: Yale University Press, 2009.

Anon. "The Torn Veil etc." www.youtube.com/watch?v=SU1mSKuwNN0 (accessed September 23, 2010).

Aronowicz, Annette. "Translator's Introduction." In Emmanuel Levinas, *Nine Talmudic Readings*. Translated and with an introduction by Annette Aronowicz, ix–xxxix. Bloomington: Indiana University Press, 1994.

Ascough, R. S. *1 and 2 Thessalonians: Encountering the Christ Group at Thessalonike*. Sheffield, UK: Sheffield Phoenix Press, 2014.

Attridge, Harold W. "Pharisees in the Fourth Gospel and One Special Pharisee." In *The Pharisees*, edited by Joseph Sievers and Amy-Jill Levine, 185–98. Grand Rapids, MI: Eerdmans, 2021.

Aus, Roger David. *Samuel, Saul and Jesus: Three Early Palestinian Jewish Christian Gospel Haggadoth*. Atlanta: Scholars Press, 1994.

Avery-Peck, Alan J. "The Second Letter of Paul to the Corinthians." In *The Jewish Annotated New Testament*, 2nd ed., edited by Amy-Jill Levine and Marc Zvi Brettler, 352–72. Oxford: Oxford University Press, 2017.

Avot de-Rabbi Natan....Edited by Solomon Schechter. Wien: [no publisher], [1887].

Bailey, Kenneth E. *Through Peasant Eyes*. Grand Rapids, MI: Eerdmans, 1980.
Barclay, John M. G. "2 Corinthians." In *Eerdmans Commentary on the Bible*, edited by James D. G. Dunn and John W. Rogerson, 1353–73. Grand Rapids, MI: Eerdmans, 2003.
———. *Paul and the Gift*. Grand Rapids, MI: Eerdmans, 2015.
Barclay, William. *The Parables of Jesus*. Louisville, KY: Westminster John Knox, 1999.
Barrett, C. K. *A Commentary on the First Epistle to the Corinthians*. 2nd ed. London: Adam & Charles Black, 1973.
———. *A Critical and Exegetical Commentary on the Acts of the Apostles*. 2 vols. Edinburgh: T&T Clark, 1998.
Barth, Karl. *Church Dogmatics*. Edited by Geoffrey William Bromiley, Thomas Forsyth Torrance et al. Translated by Geoffrey William Bromiley, Harold Knight, G. T. Thompson et al. Edinburgh: T&T Clark, 1957–89 (German: 1932–67).
Bauernfeind, Otto. *anapausis*. In *Theological Dictionary of the New Testament*, edited by Gerhard Kittel and Gerhard Friedrich. Translated and edited by Geoffrey W. Bromiley, 1:350f. Grand Rapids, MI: Eerdmans, 1964–76 (German: 1933–49).
Bauman, Zygmunt. "Jews and Other Europeans, Old and New." *European Judaism: A Journal for the New Europe* 42 (2009): 121–33.
Beare, Francis White. "The Sabbath Was Made for Man?" *Journal of Biblical Literature* 79 (1960): 130–36.
Bergen, Doris L. *Twisted Cross: The German Christian Movement in the Third Reich*. Chapel Hill, NC: University of North Carolina Press, 1996.
Berkovits, Eliezer. *Faith after the Holocaust*. Jerusalem: Maggid, 2019 [1973].
Bernauer, James. *Jesuit Kaddish: Jesuits, Jews, and Holocaust Remembrance*. Notre Dame: University of Notre Dame Press, 2020.
Best, Ernest. *A Commentary on the First and Second Epistles to the Thessalonians*. London: Adam & Charles Black, 1979 (1972).
———. *A Critical and Exegetical Commentary on Ephesians*. Edinburgh: T&T Clark, 1998.
Betz, Hans Dieter. *Galatians: A Commentary on Paul's Letter to the Churches in Galatia*. Philadelphia: Fortress, 1979.
———. *The Sermon on the Mount*. Minneapolis: Fortress, 1995.
Biblia Hebraica Stuttgartensia...Editio secunda emandata.... Edited by W. Rudolph and H. P. Rüger. Stuttgart: Deutsche Bibelgesellschaft, 1984.
Black, Matthew. "Does an Aramaic Tradition Underlie John 1, 16?" *Journal of Theological Studies* 42 (1941): 69f.
———. "The Parables as Allegory." *Bulletin of the John Rylands Library* 42 (1960): 273–87.
Blank, Barbara Trainin. "Portrait of Joseph Telushkin." *Hadassah Magazine* 81 (April 2000): 28–30.
Blix, Ragnar. *De 5 Aar*. Copenhagen: Berlingske Forlag, 1945.

Bibliography

Boecker, Hans Jochen. *Law and the Administration of Justice in the Old Testament and Ancient East*. Minneapolis: Augsburg, 1980.

Booth, Roger P. *Jesus and the Laws of Purity: Tradition History and Legal History in Mark 7*. Sheffield, UK: Sheffield Academic Press, 1986.

Boyarin, Daniel. *Border Lines: The Partition of Judaeo-Christianity*. Philadelphia: University of Pennsylvania Press, 2004.

———. *Carnal Israel: Reading Sex in Talmudic Culture*. Berkeley: University of California Press, 1993.

———. *Dying for God: Martyrdom and the Making of Christianity and Judaism*. Stanford, CA: Stanford University Press, 1999.

———. "Logos, A Jewish Word." In *The Jewish Annotated New Testament*, 2nd ed., edited by Amy-Jill Levine and Marc Zvi Brettler, 688–91. Oxford: Oxford University Press, 2017.

———. "The Gospel of Memra: Jewish Binitarianism and the Prologue of John." *Harvard Theological Review* 94 (2001): 243–84.

———. *A Radical Jew: Paul and the Politics of Identity*. Berkeley: University of California Press, 1994.

Branham, Joan R. "Penetrating the Sacred: Breaches and Barriers in the Jerusalem Temple." In *Thresholds of the Sacred: Architectural, Art Historical, Liturgical, and Theological Perspectives on Religious Screens, East and West*, edited by Sharon Gerstel, 6–24. Cambridge, MA: Harvard University Press, 2006.

Braun, Herbert. *Jesus: Der Mann aus Nazareth und seine Zeit*. Stuttgart: Kreuz, 1969.

Brick, Daniel. *Varför anklagar man judarna?* Stockholm: Albert Bonnier, 1944.

Brontë, Emily. *Wuthering Heights*. Hertfordshire: Wordsworth, 1992 (1847).

Brown, Peter. *The Body and Society: Men, Women and Sexual Renunciation in Early Christianity*. New York: Columbia University Press, 1988.

Brown, Raymond E. *The Birth of the Messiah: A Commentary on the Infancy Narratives in the Gospels of Matthew and Luke*. New York: Doubleday, updated ed., 1993.

———. *The Death of the Messiah: From Gethsemane to the Grave*. 2 vols. New York: Doubleday, 1994.

———. *The Gospel according to John: Introduction, Translation, and Notes*. 2 vols. New York: Doubleday, 1966–70.

Büchler, Adolf. *Der galiläische 'Am-ha 'Areṣ des zweiten Jahrhunderts: Beiträge zur innern Geschichte des palästinischen Judentums in den ersten zwei Jahrhunderten*. Wien: Hölder, 1906.

Bultmann, Rudolf. *Primitive Christianity in Its Contemporary Setting*. Translated by R. H. Fuller. London: Collins, 1960 (German 1st ed.: 1949).

Buttrick, George A. *The Parables of Jesus*. New York: Harper & Brothers, 1928.

Caird, G. B. *The Gospel of Saint Luke*. Harmondsworth: Penguin, 1963.

———. *Revelation of St. John the Divine*. London: Adam & Charles Black, 1966.
Campbell, William S. *Unity and Diversity in Christ: Interpreting Paul in Context; Collected Essays*. Eugene, OR: Cascade, 2013.
Cane, Anthony. *The Place of Judas Iscariot in Christology*. Aldershot / Burlington: Ashgate, 2005.
Cargal, Timothy B. "His Blood Be upon Us and upon Our Children: A Matthean Double Entendre?" *New Testament Studies* 37 (1991): 101–12.
Carroll, James. *Constantine's Sword: The Church and the Jews; A History*. Boston: Houton Miflin, 2001.
———. "What Donald Trump Doesn't Understand about Anti-Semitism." *The New Yorker* (February 23, 2017).
Carter, Warren. *Pontius Pilate: Portraits of a Roman Governor*. Collegeville, MN: Liturgical Press, 2003.
Cassidy, Richard J. *Four Times Peter: Portrayals of Peter in the Four Gospels and at Philippi*. Collegeville, MN: Liturgical Press, 2007.
Catalano, Rosann M. "A Matter of Perspective: An Alternative Reading of Mark 15:38." In *Seeing Judaism Anew: Christianity's Sacred Obligation*, edited by Mary C. Boys, 187–99. Lanham, MD: Rowman & Littlefield, 2005.
Cave, C. H. "Lazarus and the Lukan Deuteronomy." *New Testament Studies* 15 (1969): 319–25.
Charles, Robert Henry. *A Critical and Exegetical Commentary on the Revelation of St. John*. 2 vols. Edinburgh: T&T Clark, 1920.
Chilton, Bruce. *Rabbi Paul: An Intellectual Biography*. New York: Doubleday, 2004.
Chung, Paul S. *Karl Barth: God's Word in Action*. Eugene, OR: Cascade, 2008.
Cohen, Jeremy. *Christ Killers: The Jews and the Passion from the Bible to the Big Screen*. Oxford: Oxford University Press, 2007.
Cohen, Shaye J. D. "The Forgotten Pharisees." In *The Pharisees*, edited by Joseph Sievers and Amy-Jill Levine, 283–91. Grand Rapids, MI: Eerdmans, 2021.
———. "The Letter of Paul to the Galatians." In *The Jewish Annotated New Testament*, 2nd ed., edited by Amy-Jill Levine and Marc Zvi Brettler, 373–87. Oxford: Oxford University Press, 2017.
———. *The Significance of Yavneh and Other Essays in Jewish Hellenism*. Tübingen: Mohr Siebeck, 2010.
Cohick, Lynn. "Melito of Sardis's PERI PASCHA and Its 'Israel.'" *Harvard Theological Review* 91 (1998): 351–72.
Connelly, John. *From Enemy to Brother: The Revolution in Catholic Teaching on the Jews, 1933–1965*. Cambridge, MA: Harvard University Press, 2012.
Cook, Michael J. "The Letter to the Philippians." In *The Jewish Annotated New Testament*, 2nd ed., edited by Amy-Jill Levine and Marc Zvi Brettler, 398–406. Oxford: Oxford University Press, 2017.

———. *Modern Jews Engage the New Testament: Enhancing Jewish Well-Being in a Christian Environment*. Woodstock, VT: Jewish Lights, 2008.
Cranfield, C. E. B. *A Critical and Exegetical Commentary on the Epistle to the Romans*. 2 vols. Edinburgh: T&T Clark, 1975–79.
———. *The Gospel according to Saint Mark*. Cambridge, UK: Cambridge University Press, 1959.
Crossan, John Dominic. *In Parables: The Challenge of the Historical Jesus*. Sonoma, CA: Polebridge Press, 1992 (1973).
———. *How to Read the Bible and Still Be a Christian: Struggling with Divine Violence from Genesis through Revelation*. San Francisco: HarperOne, 2015.
———. *Jesus: A Revolutionary Biography*. New York: HarperCollins, 1994.
———. *Raid on the Articulate: Comic Eschatology in Jesus and Borges*. New York: Harper & Row, 1976.
———. "The Parable of the Wicked Husbandmen." *Journal of Biblical Literature* 90 (1971): 451–65.
———. *The Power of Parable: How Fiction by Jesus Became Fiction about Jesus*. New York: HarperOne, 2012.
Culler, Jonathan. Defining Narrative Units." In *Style and Structure in Literature: Essays in the New Stylistics*, edited by Roger Fowler, 123–42. Ithaca, NY: Cornell University Press, 1975.
Cunningham, Philip A. *Maxims for Mutuality: Principles for Catholic Theology, Education, and Preaching about Jews and Judaism*. Mahwah, NJ: Paulist Press, 2022.
Dahl, Nils Alstrup. "Der Erstgeborene Satans und der Vater des Teufels (Polyk. 7.1 und Joh 8.44)." *Apophoreta: Festschrift für Ernst Haenchen zu seinem siebzigsten Geburtstag am 10. Dezember 1964*, edited by Walther Eltester, 70–84. Berlin: Alfred Töpelmann, 1964.
Dalman, Gustaf. *The Words of Jesus: Considered in the Light of Post-biblical Jewish Writings and the Aramaic Language*. Translated by D. M. Kay. Eugene, OR: Wipf & Stock, 1997 (1902) (German: 1st ed. 1898).
Daube, David. *The New Testament and Rabbinic Judaism*. Peabody, MA: Hendrickson, reprint of 1956.
Davies, W. D. *Paul and Rabbinic Judaism: Some Rabbinic Elements in Pauline Theology*. London: SPCK, 1962.
Davies, W. D., and Dale C. Allison. *The Gospel according to Saint Matthew*. 3 vols. Edinburgh: T&T Clark, 1988–97.
deConick, April. "Why Are the Heavens Closed? The Johannine Revelation of the Father in the Catholic-Gnostic Debate." In *John's Gospel and Intimations of Apocalyptic*, edited by Catrin H. Williams and Christopher Rowland, 147–79. London: T&T Clark, 2013.
Derrett, J. Duncan M. "Fresh Light on St Luke xvi." *New Testament Studies* 7 (1960–61): 198–219.
———. *Law in the New Testament*. London: Darton, Longman & Todd, 1970.

———. "Law in the New Testament: The Story of the Woman Taken in Adultery." *New Testament Studies* 10 (1963–64): 1–26.

Dibelius, Martin, and Heinrich Greeven. *James: A Commentary on the Epistle of James*. Edited by Helmut Koester. Translated by Michael A. Williams. Philadelphia: Fortress, 1975 (German: 1964).

Dihle, Albrecht. *Die goldene Regel: Eine Einführung in die Geschichte der antiken und frühchristlichen Vulgärethik*. Göttingen: Vandenhoeck & Ruprecht, 1962.

Dodd, C. H. *The Interpretation of the Fourth Gospel*. Cambridge, UK: Cambridge University Press, 1954.

———. *The Parables of the Kingdom*. Glasgow: Collins, 1978 (1935).

Donahue, John R. "Recent Studies on the Origin of 'Son of Man' in the Gospels." *Catholic Biblical Quarterly* 48 (1986): 484–98.

Dunn, James D. G. "The New Perspective on Paul." *Bulletin of the John Rylands Library* 65 (1983): 94–122.

Eastman, Susan Grove. "Israel and the Mercy of God: A Re-reading of Galatians 6.16 and Romans 9–11." *New Testament Studies* 56 (2010): 367–95.

Ehrman, Bart. *The New Testament: A Historical Introduction to the Early Christian Writings*. 4th ed. New York: Oxford University Press, 2008.

Eisenbaum, Pamela. *Paul Was Not a Christian: The Original Message of a Misunderstood Apostle*. San Francisco: HarperOne, 2009.

Elkins, Kathleen Gallagher. "The Jews as 'Children of the Devil' (John 8:44) in Nazi Children's Literature." *Biblical Interpretation* 30 (2022): 1–17.

Ericksen, Robert P. *Theologians under Hitler: Gerhard Kittel, Paul Althaus and Emanuel Hirsch*. New Haven, CT: Yale University Press, 1985.

Fagenblat, Michael. "The Concept of Neighbor in Jewish and Christian Ethics." In *The Jewish Annotated New Testament*, 2nd ed., edited by Amy-Jill Levine and Marc Zvi Brettler, 645–50. Oxford: Oxford University Press, 2017.

Falk, Bent. *Att vara där du är: Samtal med människor i kris*. Translated by Margareta Brandby-Cöster. Stockholm: Verbum, 2005 (Danish: 1996).

Farris, Michael. "A Tale of Two Taxations (Luke 18:10–14b)." In *Jesus and His Parables: Interpreting the Parables of Jesus Today; With a Foreword by Seán Freyne*, edited by V. George Shillington, 23–33. Edinburgh: T&T Clark, 1997.

Fein, Helen. "Dimensions of Antisemitism: Attitudes, Collective Accusations, and Actions." In *The Persisting Question: Sociological Perspectives and Social Contexts of Modern Antisemitism*, edited by Helen Fein, 67–85. New York: Walter de Gruyter, 1987.

Feldman, Louis H., James L. Kugel, and Lawrence H. Schiffman, eds. *Outside the Bible: Ancient Jewish Writings Related to Scripture*. 3 vols. Philadelphia: Jewish Publication Society, 2013.

Bibliography

Feuer, Avrohom Chaim (with Nosson Scherman). *Tehillim: A New Translation with a Commentary Anthologized from Talmudic, Midrashic and Rabbinic Sources.* 2 vols. New York: Mesorah, 1985.

Filson, Floyd V. *A Commentary on the Gospel according to St. Matthew.* 2nd ed. London: Adam & Charles Black, 1971.

Fisch, Yael. "The Origins of Oral Torah: A New Pauline Perspective." *Journal for the Study of Judaism* 51 (2020): 43–66.

———. *Written for Us: Paul's Interpretation of Scripture and the History of Midrash.* Leiden: Brill, 2023.

Fischer, Lars. "Karl Barth's Letter to Friedrich-Wilhelm Marquardt (5 September 1967): 'I Am Decidedly Not a Philosemite.'" https://jnjr.div.ed.ac.uk/primary-sources/contemporary/karl-barths-letter-to-friedrich-wilhelm-marquardt-5-september-1967-i-am-decidedly-not-a-philosemite/ (accessed March 25, 2023).

Fitzmyer, Joseph A. *The Gospel according to Luke: Introduction, Translation, and Notes.* 2 vols. New York: Doubleday, 1981–85.

Flusser, David (with R. Steven Notley). *The Sage from Galilee: Rediscovering Jesus' Genius.* Grand Rapids, MI: Eerdmans, 2007.

Flusser, David. "Do You Prefer New Wine?" *Immanuel* 9 (1979): 26–31.

———. "The Parable of the Unjust Steward: Jesus' Criticism of the Essenes." In *Jesus and the Dead Sea Scrolls*, edited by James H. Charlesworth, 176–97. New York: Doubleday, 1992.

Fornberg, Tord, and Göran Larsson, ed. *Förskjutningar: Avgörande skiften i relationen mellan judar och kristna.* Skellefteå: Norma, 2022.

Frankfurter, David. "Jewish or Not? Reconstructing the Other in Rev 2:9 and 3:9." *Harvard Theological Review* 94 (2001): 403–25.

———. "The Revelation to John." In *The Jewish Annotated New Testament*, 2nd ed., edited by Amy-Jill Levine and Marc Zvi Brettler, 536–75. Oxford: Oxford University Press, 2017.

Fredriksen, Paula, and Jesper Svartvik, ed. *Krister among the Jews and Gentiles: Essays in Appreciation of the Life and Work of Krister Stendahl.* Mahwah, NJ: Paulist Press, 2018.

Fredriksen, Paula. "*Excaecati occulta justitia Dei*: Augustine on Jews and Judaism." *Journal of Early Christian Studies* 3 (1995): 299–324.

———. *From Jesus to Christ: The Origins of the New Testament Images of Jesus.* New Haven, CT: Yale University Press, 1988.

———. *Jesus of Nazareth, King of the Jews: A Jewish Life and the Emergence of Christianity.* New York: Knopf, 1999.

———. "Paul, the Perfectly Righteous Pharisee." In *The Pharisees*, edited by Joseph Sievers and Amy-Jill Levine, 112–35. Grand Rapids, MI: Eerdmans, 2021.

———. *Paul: The Pagans' Apostle.* New Haven, CT: Yale University Press, 2017.

Friedrichsen, Timothy A. "The Temple, a Pharisee, a Tax Collector, and the Kingdom of God: Rereading a Jesus Parable (Luke 18.19–14a)." *Journal of Biblical Literature* 124 (2005): 89–119.
Frymer-Kensky, Tikva. *Reading the Women of the Bible: A New Interpretation of Their Stories.* New York: Schocken, 2002.
Funk, Robert W. *Honest to Jesus: Jesus for a New Millennium.* San Francisco: HarperSanFrancisco, 1996.
———. *The Gospel of Mark: Red Letter Edition.* Sonoma, CA: Polebridge, 1991.
Furstenberg, Yair. "Defilement Penetrating the Body." *New Testament Studies* 54 (2008): 176–200.
———. "The Shared Image of Pharisaic Law in the Gospels and Rabbinic Tradition." In *The Pharisees*, edited by Joseph Sievers and Amy-Jill Levine, 199–219. Grand Rapids, MI: Eerdmans, 2021.
Gale, Aaron M. "The Gospel according to Matthew." In *The Jewish Annotated New Testament*, 2nd ed., edited by Amy-Jill Levine and Marc Zvi Brettler, 9–66. Oxford: Oxford University Press, 2017.
Garroway, Joshua D. *The Beginning of the Gospel: Paul, Philippi, and the Origins of Christianity.* Cham: Palgrave Macmillan, 2018.
Gaston, Lloyd. *Paul and the Torah.* Vancouver: University of British Columbia, 1987.
———. "The Uniqueness of Jesus as a Methodological Problem." In *Origins and Methods: Towards a New Understanding of Judaism and Christianity*, edited by B. H. McLean, 271–81. Sheffield, UK: Sheffield Academic Press, 1993.
Georgi, Dieter. *The Opponents of Paul in Second Corinthians: A Study of Religious Propaganda in Late Antiquity.* Translation supervised by Dieter Georgi. Philadelphia: Fortress, 1986 (German: 1964).
Gerleman, Gillis. "Das Übervolle Mass: Ein Versuch Mit Ḥaesaed." *Vetus Testamentum* 28 (1978): 151–64.
Gesenius, Wilhelm. *Hebräisches und Aramäisches Handwörterbuch über das Alte Testament.* 16th ed. Leipzig: Vogel, 1915.
Gibson, Margaret Dunlop. "On the Parable of the Unjust Steward." *Expository Times* 14 (1902–3): 334.
"'The Gifts and the Calling of God Are Irrevocable' [Rom 11:29]: A Reflection on Theological Questions Pertaining to Catholic-Jewish Relations on the Occasion of the 50th Anniversary of 'Nostra Aetate' [No. 4]": (https://www.vatican.va/roman_curia/pontifical_councils/chrstuni/relations-jews-docs/rc_pc_chrstuni_doc_20151210_ebraismo-nostra-aetate_en.html) (accessed March 14, 2023).
Gilad, Y. D. "On Fasting on the Sabbath." *Tarbiz* 52 (1983): 1–15 (Hebrew).
Gilmour, S. MacLean. "The Gospel according to St. Luke." In *Interpreter's Bible*, edited by George Arthur Buttrick, 8:1–434. 12 vols. New York: Abingdon-Cokesbury Press, 1952.

Bibliography

Glazer, Nahum N. *Franz Rosenzweig: His Life and Thought.* 2nd ed. New York: Schocken, 1961.

Goldberg, Michael. *Jews and Christians, Getting Our Stories Straight: The Exodus and the Passion-Resurrection.* 2nd ed. Philadelphia: Trinity Press International, 1991.

Goodman, Lenn E. *Love Thy Neighbor as Thyself.* Oxford: Oxford University Press, 2008.

Goppelt, Leonhard. *Apostolic and Post-apostolic Times.* Translated by Robert A. Guelich. Grand Rapids, MI: Baker Books House, 1970 (German: 1962).

———. *Jesus, Paul and Judaism: An Introduction to New Testament Theology.* Translated by Edward Schroeder. New York: Nelson, 1964 (German: 1954).

———. *Theology of the New Testament*, edited by Jürgen Roloff. Translated by John E. Alsup. 2 vols. Grand Rapids, MI: Eerdmans, 1981–82 (German: 1975–76).

Gordon, Robert P. *Hebrews.* 2nd ed. Sheffield, UK: Sheffield Phoenix Press, 2008.

Gould, Ezra Palmer. *A Critical and Exegetical Commentary on the Gospel according to St. Mark.* Edinburgh: T&T Clark, 1907 (1896).

Grindheim, Sigurd. "Jesus and the Food Laws Revisited." *Journal for the Study of the Historical Jesus* 31 (2020): 61–76.

Gruber, Ruth. "Allosemitism (noun)—Jews as the Perpetual 'Other.'" *Jewish Journal* (August 7, 2008) (accessed April 13, 2023).

Grundmann, Walter. *Die Geschichte Christi.* Berlin: Evangelische Verlagsanstalt, 1957.

Gunton, Colin E. *The Actuality of Atonement: A Study of Metaphor, Rationality and the Christian Tradition.* Edinburgh: T&T Clark, 1988.

Gurtner, Daniel M. *The Torn Veil: Matthew's Exposition of the Death of Jesus.* Cambridge, UK: Cambridge University Press, 2007.

Guthrie, Donald K. *Galatians.* 2nd ed. London: Marshall, Morgan & Scott, 1974.

Guttiérrez, Gustavo. *A Theology of Liberation: History, Politics, and Salvation.* 2nd ed. London: SCM, 1988 (Spanish 1st ed.: 1971).

Hagner, Donald A. *Matthew.* 2 vols. Dallas: Word Books, 1993–95.

Halbertal, Moshe. *On Sacrifice.* Princeton, NJ: Princeton University Press, 2012.

Halivni, David Weiss. *Breaking the Tablets: Jewish Theology after the Shoah.* Edited and introduced by Peter Ochs. Lanham, MD: Rowman & Littlefield, 2007.

Hamilton, Catherine Sider. *The Death of Jesus in Matthew: Innocent Blood and the End of Exile.* Cambridge, UK: Cambridge University Press, 2017.

Hays, Richard B. "'Here We Have No Lasting City': New Covenantalism in Hebrews." In *The Epistle to the Hebrews and Christian Theology*, edited by Richard Bauckham et al., 151–73. Grand Rapids, MI: Eerdmans, 2009.

Hemer, Colin J. *Letters to the Seven Churches in Their Local Setting.* Sheffield, UK: JSOT Press, 1986.

Hengel, Martin. *Crucifixion in the Ancient World and the Folly of the Message of the Cross.* Translated by John Bowden. Philadelphia: Fortress, 1977 (German: 1976).

Herzog, William R., II. *Parables as Subversive Speech: Jesus as Pedagogue of the Oppressed.* Louisville, KY: Westminster John Knox, 1994.

Heschel, Abraham Joshua. *God in Search of Man: A Philosophy of Judaism.* New York: Farrar, Straus & Giroux, 1955.

———. *Heavenly Torah: As Refracted through the Generations.* Edited and translated by Gordon Tucker with Leonard Levin. New York: Continuum, 2005 (Hebrew: 1962–65).

———. *The Ineffable Name of God: Man. Poems.* Translated from the Yiddish by Morton M. Leifman. Introduction by Edward K. Kaplan. New York: Continuum, 2004.

Heschel, Susannah, *The Aryan Jesus: Christian Theologians and the Bible in Nazi Germany.* Princeton, NJ: Princeton University Press, 2008.

———. "Race as Incarnational Theology: Affinities between German Protestantism and Racial Theory." In *Prejudice and Christian Beginnings: Investigating Race, Gender, and Ethnicity in Early Christian Studies*, edited by Laura Nasrallah and Elisabeth Schüssler Fiorenza, 211–34. Minneapolis: Fortress, 2009.

Holtz, Barry W. "Midrash." In *Back to the Sources: Reading the Classic Texts*, edited by Barry W. Holtz, 177–211. New York: Summit, 1984.

Hughes, Graham. *Hebrews and Hermeneutics: The Epistle to the Hebrews as a New Testament Example of Biblical Interpretation.* Cambridge: Cambridge University Press, 1979.

Hultgren, Arland. *The Parables of Jesus: A Commentary.* Grand Rapids, MI: Eerdmans, 2000.

Hurd, John C. "Paul Ahead of His Time: 1 Thess. 2:13–16." In *Anti-Judaism in Early Christianity: I. Paul and the Gospels*, edited by Peter Richardson with David Granskou, 21–36. Waterloo: Wilfrid Laurier University Press, 1986.

Hurt, Bruce. "2 Corinthians 3:12–14 Commentary." https://www.preceptaustin.org/2corinthians_312-14_commentary (accessed February 20, 2023).

International Council of Christians and Jews. *Reports and Recommendations of the International Conference of Christians & Jews: Seelisberg 1947.* Geneva: International Council of Christians and Jews, 1947.

Isaacs, Marie E. "Why Bother with Hebrews?" *The Heythrop Journal* 43 (2002): 60–72.

Iustini Martyris Dialogus Cum Tryphone. Edited by Miroslav Marcovich. New York: Walter de Gruyter, 1997.

Bibliography

Jackson, Bernard S. "The Problem of Exod. XXI 22–5 (Ius talionis)." *Vetus Testamentum* 23 (1973): 273–304.
Jacob, Benno. *Auge um Auge: Eine Untersuchung zum Alten und Neuen Testament*. Berlin: Philo, 1929.
———. *The Second Book of the Bible Exodus Interpreted by Benno Jacob*. Hoboken, NJ: Ktav, 1992.
Jastrow, Marcus. *A Dictionary of the Targumim, the Talmud Babli and Yerushalmi, and the Midrashic Literature*. 2 vols. New York: Judaica, 1989 (1903).
Jaubert, Annie. *La date de la Cène*. Paris: Gabalda, 1957.
Jensen, Matthew. "The (In)authenticity of 1 Thessalonians 2.13–16: A Review of Arguments." *Currents on Biblical Research* 18 (2019): 59–79.
Jeremias, Joachim. *Jerusalem in the Time of Jesus: An Investigation into Economic and Social Conditions during the New Testament Period*. Translated by F. H. Cave and C. H. Cave. London: SCM, 1969 (German: 1967).
———. *The Parables of Jesus*. Translated by S. H. Hooke. 3rd ed. London: SCM, 1972 (German: 1970).
———. "Paul and James." *Expository Times* 66 (1955): 368–71.
John Chrysostom. *Commentary on Saint John the Evangelist and Apostle: Homilies 48–88*. Translated by Sr. Thomas Aquinas Goggin. New York: Fathers of the Church, 1960.
Johnson, Bo. "Något om bibelanvändningen i latinamerikansk befrielseteologi." *Svensk Teologisk Kvartalskrift* 60 (1984): 64–70.
———. *Rättfärdigheten i Bibeln*. Gothenburg: Gothia, 1985.
Johnson, Earl S. *Hebrews*. Louisville, KY: Westminster John Knox, 2008.
Johnson, S. Lewis. "Paul and the 'Israel of God: An Exegetical and Eschatological Case-Study.'" *Master's Seminary Journal* 20 (2009): 41–55.
Johnsson, William G. "The Pilgrimage Motif in the Book of Hebrews." *Journal of Biblical Literature* 97 (1978): 239–51.
Josephus... Translated by Henry St. J. Thackeray. 10 vols. Cambridge, MA: Harvard University Press, 1926–65.
Jospe, Raphael. "'Love Your Fellow as Yourself': Universalism and Particularism in Jewish Exegesis of Leviticus 19:18." *Jewish-Christian Relations* (https://www.jcrelations.net/articles/article/love-your-fellow-as-yourself.html) (accessed April 3, 2023).
Jülicher, Adolf. *Die Gleichnisreden Jesu*. 2nd ed. 2 vols. Tübingen: Mohr Siebeck, 1910 (1st ed. 1888).
Jussem-Wilson, Nelly. "Bernard Lazare's Jewish Journey: From Being an Israelite to Being a Jew." *Jewish Social Studies* 26 (1964): 146–68.
Kahl, Brigitte. *Galatians Re-imagined: Reading with the Eyes of the Vanquished*. Minneapolis: Fortress, 2010.
———. "No Longer Male: Masculinity Struggles behind Galatians 3.28?" *Journal for the Study of the New Testament* 79 (2000): 37–49.

Kalimi, Isaac. "Targumic and Midrashic Exegesis in Contradiction to the Peshat of Biblical Text." In *Biblical Interpretation in Judaism and Christianity*, edited by Isaac Kalimi and Peter J. Haas, 13–32. New York: T&T Clark, 2006.

Kampling, Rainer. *Das Blut Christi und die Juden: Mt 27,25 bei den lateinischsprachigen christlichen Autoren bis zu Leo dem Grossen*. Münster: Aschendorff, 1984.

Kant, Immanuel. *Groundwork of the Metaphysics of Morals: With On a Supposed Right to Lie on Philanthropic Concerns*. 3rd ed. Translated by James W. Ellington. Indianapolis: Hackett, 1993 (German: 1785).

Käsemann, Ernst. *Essays on New Testament Themes*. Translated by W. J. Montague. Philadelphia: Fortress, 1982 (German: 1960).

———. *New Testament Questions of Today*. Translated by W. J. Montague; Philadelphia: Fortress, 1979 (German: 1965).

———. *The Wandering People of God: An Investigation of the Letter to the Hebrews*. Translated by Roy A. Harrisville and Irving L. Sandberg. Minneapolis: Augsburg, 1984 (German 2nd ed. 1957).

Kee, Alistair. "The Old Coat and the New Wine: A Parable of Repentance." *Novum Testamentum* 12 (1970): 13–21.

Kelly, William. *Lectures on the Gospel of Matthew*. London: Morrish, 1868.

Kilpatrick, G. D. "The Religious Background of the Fourth Gospel." In *Studies in the Fourth Gospel*, edited by F. L. Cross, 36–44. London: Mowbray, 1957.

Kimelman, Reuven. "*Birkat Ha-Minim* and the Lack of Evidence for an Anti-Christian Jewish Prayer in Late Antiquity." In *Jewish and Christian Self-Definition*, 3 vols., edited by E. P. Sanders et al., 2:226–44 and 2:391–403. Philadelphia: Fortress, 1980–82.

Kister, Menahem. "Law, Morality and Rhetoric." In *Studies in Ancient Midrash*, edited by James L. Kugel, 145–54. Cambridge, MA: Harvard University Press, 2001.

———. "The Golden Rule and Ancient Jewish Biblical Exegesis: The Pluriformity of a Tradition." *Journal of Biblical Literature* 141 (2022): 717–35.

Kitchen, Martin. *Ephesians*. New York: Routledge, 1994.

Klassen, William. *Judas: Betrayer or Friend of Jesus?* Minneapolis: Fortress, 1996.

Klawans, Jonathan. "The Law." In *The Jewish Annotated New Testament*, 1st ed., edited by Amy-Jill Levine and Marc Zvi Brettler, 515–18. Oxford: Oxford University Press, 2011.

———. "The Law." In *The Jewish Annotated New Testament*, 2nd ed., edited by Amy-Jill Levine and Marc Zvi Brettler, 655–58. Oxford: Oxford University Press, 2017.

Klein, Isaac. *A Guide to Jewish Religious Practice: A Supplement by Rabbi Joel Roth*. New York: Jewish Theological Seminary of America, 1992.

Bibliography

Klijn, A. F. J. "2 (Syriac Apocalypse of) Baruch: A New Translation and Introduction." In *The Old Testament Pseudepigrapha*. Vol. 1: *Apocalyptic Literature and Testaments*, edited by James H. Charlesworth, 615–20. New York: Doubleday, 1983.

Knight, Jonathan. *Luke's Gospel*. London: Routledge, 1998.

Koester, Craig R. *Hebrews: A New Translation with Introduction and Commentary*. New York: Doubleday, 2001.

Kohler, Kaufmann. "New Testament." In *Jewish Encyclopedia*, 12 vols., edited by Isidore Singer, 9:246–54. New York: Funk & Wagnalls, 1901–06.

The Koren Siddur: With Introduction, Translation and Commentary by Rabbi Sir Jonathan Sacks. Jerusalem: Koren, 2009.

Korner, Ralph J. *Reading Revelation after Supersessionism: An Apocalyptic Journey of Socially Identifying John's Multi-ethnic Ekklêsiai with the Ekklêsia of Israel*. Eugene, OR: Cascade, 2020.

Kosmala, Hans. "'His Blood on Us and on Our Children' (The Background of Mat. 27,24–25)." *Annual of the Swedish Theological Institute* 7 (1968–69): 99–122.

———. "The Parable of the Unjust Steward in the Light of Qumran." *Annual of the Swedish Theological Institute* 3 (1964): 114–21.

Kugel, James L. *In Potiphar's House: The Interpretive Life of Biblical Texts*. New York: HarperSanFrancisco, 1990.

———. *The Bible as It Was*. Cambridge, MA: Belknap, 1998.

Kugelman, Richard. *James and Jude*. Dublin: Veritas, 1980.

Kuyper, Lester Jacob. "Grace and Truth." *Interpretation* 18 (1964): 3–19.

Kysar, Robert. *John, the Maverick Gospel*. 3rd ed. Louisville, KY: Westminster John Knox, 2007.

Lachs, Samuel Tobias. *A Rabbinic Commentary on the New Testament: The Gospels of Matthew, Mark, and Luke*. Hoboken, NJ: Ktav, 1987.

"Lady Mobster (1998)." https://www.youtube.com/watch?v=g1u8qLM_OHc (accessed June 21, 2022).

Lamp, Jeffrey S. "Is Paul Anti-Jewish? *Testament of Levi* 6 in the Interpretation of 1 Thessalonians 2:13–16." *Catholic Biblical Quarterly* 65 (2003): 408–27.

Lang, Friedrich. "*skybalon*." In *Theological Dictionary of the New Testament*, edited by Gerhard Kittel and Gerhard Friedrich, translated and edited by Geoffrey W. Bromiley, 7:445–47. Grand Rapids, MI: Eerdmans, 1964–76 (German: 1933–49).

Langer, Ruth. *Cursing the Christians? A History of the Birkat Haminim*. Oxford: Oxford University Press, 2012.

Langmuir, Gavin I. *Toward a Definition of Antisemitism*. Berkeley: University of California Press, 1990.

Lapide, Pinchas. *Wer War Schuld an Jesu Tod?* 2nd ed. Gütersloh: Mohn, 1989.

Larsson, Göran. *Bound for Freedom: The Book of Exodus in Jewish and Christian Traditions*. Peabody, MA: Hendrickson, 1999.

———. *Fönster mot Gud: Ikonernas budskap i Svenska teologiska institutets kapell i Jerusalem*. Lund: Arcus, 2011.

Légasse, S. "L''antijudaïsme' dans l'Évangile selon Matthieu." In *L'Évangile selon Matthieu: Rédaction et théologie*, edited by M. Didier, 417–28. Gembloux: Duculot, 1972.

Lehtipuu, Outi. *The Afterlife Imagery in Luke's Story of the Rich Man and Lazarus*. Boston: Brill, 2007.

Leithart, Peter. "Skubalon" (https://theopolisinstitute.com/leithart_post/skubalon) (accessed February 27, 2023).

Lenski, Richard C. H. *Commentary on St. Matthew's Gospel 15–28*. Minneapolis: Augsburg Fortress, 1943.

Levenson, Jon D. *The Hebrew Bible, the Old Testament, and Historical Criticism: Jews and Christians in Biblical Studies*. Louisville, KY: Westminster John Knox Press, 1993.

Levine, Amy-Jill, and Marc Zvi Brettler. *The Bible with and without Jesus: How Jews and Christians Read the Same Stories Differently*. New York: HarperOne, 2020.

Levine, Amy-Jill, with Maria Mayo. *Short Stories by Jesus: The Enigmatic Parables of a Controversial Rabbi. Participant Guide*. Nashville: Abingdon, 2018.

Levine, Amy-Jill. "Preaching and Teaching the Pharisees." In *The Pharisees*, edited by Joseph Sievers and Amy-Jill Levine, 403–27. Grand Rapids, MI: Eerdmans, 2021.

———. *Short Stories by Jesus: The Enigmatic Parables of a Controversial Rabbi*. New York: HarperCollins, 2014.

———. "Supersessionism: Admit and Address Rather than Debate or Deny." *Religions* 13 (2022), https://doi.org/10.3390/rel13020155 (accessed March 23, 2023).

———. "The Gospel according to Luke." In *The Jewish Annotated New Testament*, 2nd ed., edited by Amy-Jill Levine and Marc Zvi Brettler, 107–67. Oxford: Oxford University Press, 2017.

———. *The Misunderstood Jew: The Church and the Scandal of the Jewish Jesus*. San Francisco: HarperSanFrancisco, 2006.

Liddell, Henry George, and Robert Scott. *A Greek-English Lexicon…* 9th ed. with a revised supplement. Oxford: Clarendon, 1996.

Lied, Liv Ingeborg. "Those Who Know and Those Who Don't: Mystery, Instruction, and Knowledge in *2 Baruch*." In *Mystery and Secrecy in the Nag Hammadi Collection and Other Ancient Literature: Ideas and Practices*, edited by Christian H. Bull, Liv Ingeborg Lied, and John D. Turner, 427–46. Leiden: Brill, 2011.

Lieu, Judith. *Image & Reality: The Jews in the World of the Christians in the Second Century*. Edinburgh: T&T Clark, 1996.

Lincoln, Andrew T. *Ephesians*. Nashville: Thomas Nelson, 1990.

———. *Hebrews: A Guide*. New York: T&T Clark, 2006.

Bibliography

Lindeskog, Gösta. *Das jüdisch-christliche Problem: Randglossen zu einer Forschungsepoche*. Stockholm: Almqvist & Wiksell International, 1986.

Long, Thomas G. *Hebrews*. Louisville, KY: John Knox, 1997.

Lossky, Vladimir. *The Mystical Theology of the Eastern Church*. New York: St. Vladimir's Seminary, 1976 (French: 1944).

Lowe, Malcolm. "From the Parable of the Vineyard to a Pre-Synoptic Source." *New Testament Studies* 28 (1982): 257–63.

———. "Who Were the ΙΟΥΔΑΙΟΙ? *Novum Testamentum* 18 (1967): 101–30.

Malbon, Elizabeth Struthers. "Fallible Followers: Women and Men in the Gospel of Mark." *Semeia* 28 (1983): 29–48.

Malherbe, Abraham J. *The Letters to the Thessalonians: A New Translation with Introduction and Commentary*. New Haven, CT: Yale University Press, 2000.

Mann, Jacob. "Jesus and the Sadducean Priest: Luke 10.25–37." *Jewish Quarterly Review* 6 (1916): 415–22.

Manning, Gary. "Did the Apostle Paul Use Profanity?" (https://www.biola.edu/blogs/good-book-blog/2015/did-the-apostle-paul-use-profanity) (accessed February 27, 2023).

Manson, T. W. *The Sayings of Jesus as Recorded in the Gospel according to St Matthew and St Luke Arranged with Introduction and Commentary*. London: SCM, 1949 (1937).

———. *The Teaching of Jesus: Studies of Its Form and Content*. Cambridge, UK: Cambridge University Press, 1948.

———. "The Pericope de Adultera (Joh 7,53–8,11)." *Zeitschrift für die neutestamentliche Wissenschaft* 44 (1952): 255f.

Marcus, Joel. *Jesus and the Holocaust: Reflections on Suffering and Hope*. New York: Doubleday, 1997.

Marguerat, Daniel. *Le jugement dans l'Évangile de Matthieu*. 2nd ed. Geneva: Labor et Fides, 1995.

Marmorstein, Arthur. *The Doctrine of Merits in Old Rabbinical Literature*. Oxford: Oxford University Press, 1920.

Marsh, John. *The Gospel of Saint John*. Harmondsworth: Penguin, 1968.

Martin, Troy. "Pagan and Judeo-Christian Time-Keeping Schemes in Galatians 4:10 and Colossians 2:16." *New Testament Studies* 42 (1996): 120–32.

Masters, Edgar Lee. *Songs and Satires*. London: T. Werner Laurie, 1916.

Matthews, Mary W., Carter Shelley, and Barbara Scheele. "Proclaiming the Parable of the Persistent Widow (Luke 18:2–5)." In *The Lost Coin: Parables of Women, Work and Wisdom*, edited by Mary Ann Beavis, 46–70. New York: Sheffield Academic Press, 2002.

May, John d'Arcy. *Transcendence and Violence: The Encounter of Buddhist, Christian and Primal Traditions*. New York: Continuum, 2003.

McConnell, Richard S. *Law and Prophecy in Matthew's Gospel: The Authority and Use of the Old Testament in the Gospel of St. Matthew*. Basel: Reinhardt, 1969.

McKenna, Megan. *Parables: The Arrows of God*. Maryknoll, NY: Orbis, 1994.

Meeks, Wayne A. "The Man from Heaven in Johannine Sectarianism." *Journal of Biblical Literature* 91 (1972): 44–72.
Meier, John P. *A Marginal Jew: Rethinking the Historical Jesus* (New Haven, CT: Yale University Press, 2009).
Mekilta De-Rabbi Ishmael. Edited by Jacob Z. Lauterbach. 3 vols. Philadelphia: Jewish Publication Society, 1933.
Melito of Sardis. *On Pascha and Fragments*. Edited by Stuart George Hall. Oxford: Clarendon Press, 1979.
Ménard, Jacques E. *L'Évangile selon Thomas*. Leiden: Brill, 1975.
Metzger, Bruce M. *A Textual Commentary on the Greek New Testament*…3rd ed. Stuttgart: United Bible Societies, 1975.
Midrash rabbah: 'Im kol ha-mepharshim. Jerusalem: Wagshal, (no year).
Milavec, Aaron A. "A Fresh Analysis of the Parable of the Wicked Husbandmen in the Light of Jewish-Christian Dialogue." In *Parable and Story in Judaism and Christianity*, edited by Clemens Thoma and Michael Wyschogrod, 81–117. Mahwah, NJ: Paulist Press, 1989.
Milgrom, Jacob. *The JPS Torah Commentary: Numbers*… Philadelphia: Jewish Publication Society, 1990.
Mishnayoth… Edited by Philip Blackman. 2nd ed. 7 vols. Gateshead: Judaica, 1983.
Mitton, C. Leslie. *The Epistle to the Ephesians: Its Authorship, Origin and Purpose*. Oxford: Clarendon, 1951.
Montefiore, Claude G. *The Synoptic Gospels: Edited with an Introduction and a Commentary*. 2nd ed. 2 vols. London: Macmillan, 1927.
Montefiore, Claude G., and H. Loewe. *A Rabbinic Anthology. Selected and Arranged with Comments and Introductions*. Philadelphia: Meridien / Jewish Publication Society of America, 1963 (1938).
Montefiore, Claude G., J. Edwin Odgers, and S. Schechter. "The Doctrine of Divine Retribution in the Old Testament, the New Testament, and the Rabbinical Literature." *The Jewish Quarterly Review* 3 (1890): 1–51.
Moore, George Foot. *Judaism in the First Centuries: The Age of Tannaim*. 3 vols. Peabody, MA: Hendrickson, 1960 (1927–30).
Morrison, Craig E. "Interpreting the Name 'Pharisee.'" In *The Pharisees*, edited by Joseph Sievers and Amy-Jill Levine, 3–19. Grand Rapids, MI: Eerdmans, 2021.
Morrisroe, Patrick J. "Improperia." In *Catholic Encyclopedia*, edited by Charles G. Herbermann et al., 15 vols. and index, 7:703f. New York: Encyclopedia Press, 1907–14.
Moss, Candida. "A Note on the Death of Judas in Papias." *New Testament Studies* 65 (2019): 388–97.
Mussner, Franz. *Tractate on the Jews: The Significance of Judaism for Christian Faith*. Translated by Leonard Swidler. Philadelphia: Fortress / SPCK, 1984.

Bibliography

Nag Hammadi Codex II,2-7 Together with XIII,2* Brit. Lib. Or.4926(1), and P.Oxy. 1, 654, 655...Vol. I. Gospel according to Thomas... Edited by B. Layton. Leiden: Brill, 1989.

Nanos, Mark D. *The Irony of Galatians: Paul's Letter in First-Century Context.* Minneapolis: Fortress, 2002.

———. *Reading Corinthians and Philippians within Judaism...* Eugene, OR: Cascade, 2017.

Neudecker, Reinhard. *Moses Interpreted by the Pharisees and Jesus: Matthew's Antitheses in the Light of Early Rabbinic Literature.* 2nd ed. Rome: Gregorian & Biblical Press, 2015.

Neusner, Jacob, and Bruce D. Chilton, eds. *In Quest of the Historical Pharisees.* Waco: Baylor University Press, 2007.

Neusner, Jacob, William Scott Green, and Ernest S. Frerichs, eds. *Judaisms and Their Messiahs at the Turn of the Christian Era.* Cambridge, UK: Cambridge University Press, 1987.

Newell, Jane E., and Raymond R. Newell. "The Parable of the Wicked Tenants." *Novum Testamentum* 14 (1972): 226–37.

Nineham, D. E. *The Gospel of St. Mark.* Harmondsworth: Penguin, 1969.

Nirenberg, David. "Anti-Judaism as a Critical Theory." *The Chronicle of Higher Education* (January 28, 2013): B10–B13.

———. *Anti-Judaism: The Western Tradition.* New York: Norton, 2013.

———. "Mass Conversion and Genealogical Mentalities: Jews and Christians in Fifteenth-Century Spain." *Past & Present* 174 (2002): 3–41.

Nord, Elisabet. *Vindicating Vengeance and Violence? Commentary Approaches to Cursing Psalms and Their Relevance for Liturgy.* Lanham, MD: Lexington Books / Fortress Academic, 2023.

Novak, David. "Supersessionism Hard and Soft." *First Things* (February 2019). https://www.firstthings.com/article/2019/02/supersessionism-hard-and-soft (accessed April 19, 2023).

Novenson, Matthew V. *Christ among the Messiahs: Christ Language in Paul and Messiah Language in Ancient Judaism.* Oxford: Oxford University Press, 2012.

———. *The Grammar of Messianism: An Ancient Jewish Political Idiom and Its Users.* Oxford: Oxford University Press, 2017.

Novum Testamentum Graece...Editione vicesima septima revisa..., edited by Barbara Aland and Kurt Aland et al. Stuttgart: Deutsche Bibelgesellschaft, 2004.

Odeberg, Hugo. *Pharisaism and Christianity.* Translated by J. M. Moe. St. Louis: Concordia, 1964 (Swedish: 1943).

———. "Senapskornet och surdegen." *Erevna* 11 (1954): 55–57.

Orwell, George. *Animal Farm: A Fairy Tale.* London: Secker & Warburg, 1945.

Osiek, Carolyn. "The Widow as Altar: The Rise and Fall of a Symbol." *Second Century* 3 (1983): 159–69.

The Oxyrhynchus Papyri: Part III. Edited by Bernard P. Grenfell and Arthur S. Hunt. London: Egypt Exploration Fund, 1903.

Ozarowski, Joseph. "*Keri'ah*: The Tearing of the Garment." In *Jewish Insights on Death and Mourning*, edited by Jack Riemer, foreword by Sherwin B. Nuland, 121–26. New York: Schocken, 1995 (originally published as *Wrestling with the Angel*).

Pagels, Elaine H. *The Johannine Gospels in Gnostic Exegesis: Heracleon's Commentary on John.* New York: Abingdon Press, 1973.

———. "The Social History of Satan, Part Three: John of Patmos and Ignatius of Antioch; Contrasting Visions of 'God's People.'" *Harvard Theological Review* 99 (2006): 487–505.

Pattarumadathil, Henry. "Pharisees and Sadducees Together in Matthew." In *The Pharisees*, edited by Joseph Sievers and Amy-Jill Levine, 136–47. Grand Rapids, MI: Eerdmans, 2021.

Pearson, Birger A. "1 Thessalonians 2:13–16: A Deutero-Pauline Interpolation." *Harvard Theological Review* 64 (1971): 79–94.

———. *Ancient Gnosticism: Traditions and Literature.* Minneapolis: Fortress, 2007.

———. *Gnosticism, Judaism, and Egyptian Christianity.* Minneapolis: Fortress, 1990.

———. *The Gospel according to the Jesus Seminar: Occasional Papers of the Institute for Antiquity and Christianity; Number 35.* Claremont, CA: Claremont Graduate School, 1996.

———. *The Emergence of the Christian Religion: Essays on Early Christianity.* Harrisburg, PA: Trinity International Press, 1997.

Perler, Othmar. "L'Evangile de Pierre et Méliton de Sardis." *Revue Biblique* 71 (1964): 584–90 (reprinted in *Sapientia et caritas: Gesammelte Aufsätze zum 90. Geburtstag [von] Othmar Perler*, edited by Dirk Van Damme, Otto Wermelinger, and Flavio Nuvolone, 331–37. Freiburg [Switzerland], 1990).

Perrin, Norman. *Rediscovering the Teaching of Jesus.* London: SCM, 1967.

Philo...Translated by F. H. Colson, G. H. Whitaker, and Ralph Marcus. 12 vols. Cambridge, MA: Harvard University Press, 1934.

Pilgrim, Walter E. *Uneasy Neighbors: Church and State in the New Testament.* Minneapolis: Fortress, 1999.

Piper, John. *"Love Your Enemies": Jesus' Love Command in the Synoptic Gospels and in the Early Christian Paraenesis; A History of the Tradition and Interpretation of Its Uses.* Grand Rapids, MI: Baker Book House, 1991.

Plantinga, Richard J., ed. *Christianity and Pluralism: Classic and Contemporary Readings.* Oxford / Malden: Blackwell, 1999.

Pliny. *Natural History, Volume V: Books 17–19.* Translated by H. Rackham. Cambridge, MA: Harvard University Press, 1950.

———. *Natural History, Volume VI: Books 20–23.* Translated by W. H. S. Jones. Cambridge, MA: Harvard University Press, 1951.

Bibliography

Plisch, Uwe-Karsten. *The Gospel of Thomas: Original Text with Commentary.* Translated by Gesine Schenke Robinson. Stuttgart: Deutsche Bibelgesellschaft, 2008.

Plutarch. *Moralia, Volume III: Sayings of Kings and Commanders. Sayings of Romans. Sayings of Spartans. The Ancient Customs of the Spartans. Sayings of Spartan Women. Bravery of Women.* Translated by Frank Cole Babbitt. Cambridge, MA: Harvard University Press, 1931.

Pollefeyt, Didier. "Unrevoked Covenant—Revoked Consensus—Indestructible Love? The Reception of *Nostra Aetate* 4 in Jewish-Catholic Relations." In *Res Opportunae Nostrae Aetatis: Studies on the Second Vatican Council Offered to Mathijs Lamberigts*, edited by Dries Bosschaert and Johan Leemans, 484–99. Leuven / Paris / Bristol, CT: Peeters, 2020.

Porat, Dina. *Nakam: The Holocaust Survivors Who Sought Full-Scale Revenge.* Redwood City, CA: Stanford University Press, 2022.

Porter, Stanley E. "The Parable of the Unjust Steward (Luke 16:1–13): Irony *is* the Key." In *The Bible in Three Dimensions: Essays in Celebration of Forty Years of Biblical Studies in the University of Sheffield*, edited by David J. A. Clines et al., 127–53. Sheffield, UK: Journal for the Study of the Old Testament, 1990.

Quensel, Oscar. *Judas Iskariots bild psykologiskt belyst.* Stockholm: Svenska kyrkans diakonistyrelses bokförlag, 1914.

Räisänen, Heikki. "Jesus and the Food Laws: Reflections on Mark 7:15." *Journal for the Study of the New Testament* 16 (1982): 79–100.

———. *The Torah and Christ: Essays in German and English on the Problem of the Law in Early Christianity.* Helsinki: Finnish Exegetical Society, 1986.

Reed, Annette Yoshiko. "When Did Rabbis Become Pharisees? Reflections on Christian Evidence for Post-70 Judaism." In *Envisioning Judaism: Studies in Honor of Peter Schäfer on the Occasion of His Seventieth Birthday*, 2 vols., edited by Ra'anan S. Boustan et al., 2:859–95. Tübingen: Mohr Siebeck, 2013.

Reid, Barbara E. "A Godly Widow Persistently Pursuing Justice: Luke 18:1–8." *Biblical Research* 45 (2000): 25–33.

———. "Beyond Petty Pursuits and Wearisome Widows: Three Lukan Parables." *Interpretation* (2002): 284–94.

Reim, Günter. "Joh 8.44—Gotteskinder / Teufelskinder: Wie antijudaistisch ist 'Die wohl antijudaistischste Äusserung des NT?'" *New Testament Studies* 30 (1984): 619–24.

Reinhartz, Adele. *Befriending the Beloved Disciple: A Jewish Reading of the Gospel of John.* New York: Continuum, 2001.

———. *Cast Out of the Covenant: Jews and Anti-Judaism in the Gospel of John.* Lanham, MD: Fortress Academic, 2018.

———. "'Jews' and Jews in the Fourth Gospel." In *Anti-Judaism and the Fourth Gospel*, edited by Reimund Bieringer, Didier Pollefeyt, and

Frederique Vandecasteele-Vanneuville, 213–27. Louisville, KY: Westminster John Knox, 2001.
Richardson, Peter. *Israel in the Apostolic Church*. Cambridge, UK: Cambridge University Press, 1969.
Roth, Martha T. (author), and Piotr Michalowski (ed.). *Law Collections from Mesopotamia and Asia Minor*. Atlanta: Scholars Press, 1995.
Rudolph, David J. *A Jew to the Jews: Jewish Contours of Pauline Flexibility in 1 Corinthians 9:19–2*...2nd ed. Eugene, OR: Pickwick, 2016.
Safrai, Shemuel. "Religion in Everyday Life." In *The Jewish People in the First Century: Historical Geography, Political History, Social, Cultural and Religious Life and Institutions*, 2 vols., edited by Shemuel Safrai and Menachem Stern, with David Flusser and W. C. van Unnik, 2:793–833. Assen / Maastricht / Philadelphia: Van Gorcum / Fortress, 1974–76.
Sanders, E. P. *Jesus and Judaism*. Philadelphia: Fortress, 1985.
———. "Jesus and the Constraints of the Law." *Journal for the Study of the New Testament* 17 (1983): 19–24.
———. *Jewish Law from Jesus to the Mishnah: Five Studies*. Philadelphia: SCM / Trinity Press International, 1990.
———. *Paul and Palestinian Judaism: A Comparison of Patterns of Religion*. Philadelphia: Fortress, 1977.
———. *The Question of Uniqueness in the Teaching of Jesus: The Ethel M. Wood Lecture 15 February 1990*. London: University of London, 1990.
Sanders, E. P., and Margaret Davies. *Studying the Synoptic Gospels*. Philadelphia: SCM / Trinity Press International, 1989.
Sandmel, David Fox. "The First Letter of Paul to the Thessalonians." In *The Jewish Annotated New Testament*, 2nd ed., edited by Amy-Jill Levine and Marc Zvi Brettler, 419–26. Oxford: Oxford University Press, 2017.
Sandmel, Samuel. *Anti-Semitism in the New Testament*. Philadelphia: Fortress, 1978.
Saperstein, Marc. *Moments of Crisis in Jewish-Christian Relations*. Philadelphia: SCM / Trinity, 1989.
Sarna, Nahum M. *The JPS Torah Commentary: Exodus*... New York: Jewish Publication Society, 1991.
Savage, Dorothy. "Jews and Judaism in Protestant / Christian Curriculum." In *Removing the Anti-Judaism from the New Testament*, edited by Howard Clark Kee and Irvin J. Borowsky, 157–62. Philadelphia: American Interfaith Institute / World Alliance, 2000.
Schäfer, Peter. *Judeophobia: Attitudes toward the Jews in the Ancient World*. Cambridge, MA: Harvard University Press, 1997.
Schechter, Solomon. *Aspects of Rabbinic Theology*... Woodstock, VT: Jewish Lights, 1993 (1909).
Schellenberg, Ryan S. "Kingdom as Contaminant? The Role of Repertoire in the Parables of the Mustard Seed and the Leaven." *Catholic Biblical Quarterly* 71 (2009): 527–43.

Bibliography

Schippers, R. "The Pre-Synoptic Tradition in 1 Thessalonians II 13–16." *Novum Testamentum* 8 (1966): 223–34.

Schlueter, Carol J. *Filling up the Measure: Polemic Hyperbole in 1 Thessalonians 2:14–16.* Sheffield, UK: Sheffield Academic Press, 1993.

Schmidt, Daryl. "1 Thess 2:13–16: Linguistic Evidence for an Interpolation." *Journal of Biblical Literature* 102 (1983): 269–79.

Schnackenburg, Rudolf. *The Gospel according to St John.* Translated by Kevin Smyth, Cecily Hastings, Francis McDonagh, David Smith, Richard Foley, and G. A. Kon. 3 vols. New York: Crossroad, 1990 [German: 1965–75]).

Schreckenberg, Heinz. *The Jews in Christian Art: An Illustrated History.* New York: Continuum, 1996.

Schrenk, Gottlob. "Der Segenwunsch nach der Kampfepistel" *Judaica* 6 (1950): 170–90.

———. "Was bedeutet 'Israel Gottes?'" *Judaica* 5 (1949): 81–95.

Schweizer, Eduard. *The Good News according to Luke.* Translated by David E. Green. Atlanta: John Knox, 1984 (German: 1982).

———. *The Good News according to Mark.* Translated by Donald H. Madvig. London: SPCK, 1971 (German: 1967).

———. *The Good News according to Matthew.* Translated by David E. Green. London: SPCK, 1976 (German: 1973).

Scott, Bernard Brandon. *Hear Then the Parable: A Commentary on the Parables of Jesus.* Minneapolis: Fortress, 1989.

Segal, Alan F. *Paul the Convert: The Apostolate and Apostasy of Saul the Pharisee.* New Haven, CT: Yale University Press, 1990.

Septuaginta.... Edited by Alfred Rahlfs. Stuttgart: Deutsche Bibelgesellschaft, 1979.

Setzer, Claudia. *Jewish Responses to Early Christians: History and Polemics, 30–150 C.E.* Minneapolis: Fortress, 1994.

Shamash hadash. http:/www.shamash.org/listarchives/oldflame/sheminii1.oldflame.95 (accessed January 31, 2000).

Sheeley, Steven M. "Judas Iscariot." In *Eerdmans Dictionary of the Bible*, edited by David Noel Freedman, Allen C. Myers, and Astrid B. Beck, 748f. Grand Rapids, MI: Eerdmans, 2000.

Sieffert, Friedrich. *Der Brief an die Galater. Von der 6. Auflage an neu bearbeitet.* Göttingen: Vandenhoeck & Ruprecht, 1899.

Sievers, Joseph, and Amy-Jill Levine, ed. *The Pharisees.* Grand Rapids, MI: Eerdmans, 2021.

Sifra... Edited by I. H. Weiss. Vienna: Schlossberg, 1862.

Sifrei 'al sepher Devarim... Edited by Louis Finkelstein (and Saul Horovitz). Berlin: Gesellschaft zur Förderung der Wissenschaft des Judentums, 1939.

Sifre: A Tannaitic Commentary on the Book of Deuteronomy. Translated from the Hebrew with Introduction and Notes by Reuven Hammer. New Haven, CT: Yale University Press, 1986.

Silva, Moisés. *Philippians.* 2nd ed. Grand Rapids, MI: Baker Academic, 2005.
Smith, D. Moody. "Judaism and the Gospel of John." In *Jews and the Christians: Exploring the Past, Present and Future*, edited by James H. Charlesworth, 79–96. New York: Crossroad, 1990.
Smith, Jonathan Z. *Drudgery Divine: On the Comparison of Early Christianities and the Religions of Late Antiquity.* London: School of Oriental and African Studies, 1990.
Smith, Morton, "Mt. 5.43: 'Hate Thine Enemy.'" *Journal of Biblical Literature* 45 (1952): 71–73.
Snodgrass, Klyne R. *Stories with Intent: A Comprehensive Guide to the Parables of Jesus.* Grand Rapids, MI: Eerdmans, 2008.
———. *The Parable of the Wicked Tenants: An Inquiry into Parable Interpretation.* Eugene, OR: Wipf & Stock, 2011 (1983).
Sommer, Benjamin D. "Isaiah." In *The Jewish Study Bible*, edited by Adele Berlin and Marc Zvi Brettler, 780–91. Oxford: Oxford University Press, 2004.
Soulen, R. Kendall. *The God of Israel and Christian Theology.* Minneapolis: Fortress, 1996.
Sources chrétiennes. Paris, Édition du Cerf, 1941–.
Spooner, W. A. "Golden Rule." *Encyclopaedia of Religion and Ethics*, edited by James Hastings, 10 vols., 6:310–12. New York: Charles Scribner, 1928.
Stemberger, Günter. *Introduction to the Talmud and Midrash.* 2nd ed. Translated and edited by Markus Bockmuehl. Edinburgh: T&T Clark, 1996.
Stendahl, John. "With Luther, Against Luther." In *Removing the Anti-Judaism from the New Testament*, edited by Howard Clark Kee and Irvin J. Borowsky, 165–70. Philadelphia: American Interfaith Institute / World Alliance, 2000.
Stendahl, Krister. "'And Why Is This Granted to Me?'" *Harvard Divinity Bulletin* 24 (1995): 23f.
———. "Biblical Theology, Contemporary." In *The Interpreter's Dictionary of the Bible*, edited by G. A. Buttrick, 4 vols., 1:418–32. Nashville: Abingdon Press, 1962–78.
———. *Final Account: Paul's Letter to the Romans.* Foreword by Jaroslav Pelikan. Minneapolis: Fortress, 1995.
———. *Holy Week Preaching.* 2nd ed. Philadelphia: Fortress, 1985.
———. "Kvinnan i Bibeln och Kyrkan." In *Handlingar rörande prästmötet i Stockholm den 2, 3 och 4 juni 1975*, 56–73. Stockholm: Stockholms stift, 1975.
———. "Paulus och samvetet." *Svensk Exegetisk Årsbok* 25 (1960): 62–77.
———. "The Apostle Paul and the Introspective Conscience of the West." *Harvard Theological Review* 56 (1963): 199–215.

Bibliography

———. "Why I Love the Bible." *Harvard Divinity Bulletin* 35, no. 1 (2007): https://bulletin.hds.harvard.edu/articles/winter2007/why-i-love-bible (accessed April 21, 2023).
Stendahl, Krister, and Emilie T. Sander. "Biblical Literature: New Testament Literature." In *The New Encyclopaedia Britannica (Macropaedia)*, 15th ed., 30 vols., 2:948–73. Chicago: Encyclopaedia Britannica, 1975.
Stern, David. *Parables as Midrash: Narrative and Exegesis in Rabbinic Literature*. Cambridge, MA: Harvard University Press, 1991.
Stern, Jay B. "Jesus' Citation of Dt 6:5 and Lv 19:18 in the Light of Jewish Tradition." *Catholic Biblical Quarterly* 28, no. 3 (1966): 312–16.
Stevers, Dan. "The Veil." www.youtube.com/watch?v=UcpTiV_DzVE&feature=related (accessed May 30, 2023).
Stone, Michael E., and Matthias Henze. *4 Ezra and 2 Baruch: Translations, Introductions, and Notes*. Minneapolis: Fortress, 2013.
Stroumsa, Guy G. "From Anti-Judaism to Antisemitism in Early Christianity?" In *Contra Iudaeos: Ancient and Medieval Polemics Between Christians and Jews*, edited by Ora Limor and Guy G. Stroumsa, 1–26. Tübingen: Mohr, 1996.
Sullivan, Desmond. "New Insights in Matthew 27:24–25." *New Blackfriars* 73 (1992): 453–57.
Svartvik, Jesper. *Bibeltolkningens bakgator: Synen på judar, slavar och homosexuella i historia och nutid*. 2nd ed. Stockholm: Verbum, 2022.
———. "'East is East, and West is West': The Concept of Torah in Paul and Mark." In *Mark and Paul: Comparative Essays*. Part 1: *Two Authors at the Beginnings of Christianity*, edited by Oda Wischmeyer, David C. Sim, and Ian J. Elmer, 157–85. Berlin: Walter de Gruyter, 2014.
———. "'I Have Come Not to Abolish but to Fulfil': Reflections on Understanding Christianity as Fulfilment without Presupposing Supersessionism." *Religions* 13 (2022), https://doi.org/10.3390/rel13020149 (accessed April 10, 2023).
———. *Konsten att bli vän med nåden*. Stockholm: Verbum, 2018.
———. *Mark and Mission: Mk 7:1–23 in Its Narrative and Historical Contexts*. Stockholm: Almqvist & Wiksell International, 2000.
———. "Reading the Epistle to the Hebrews without Presupposing Supersessionism." In *Christ Jesus and the Jewish People Today: New Explorations of Theological Interrelationships*, edited by Philip A. Cunningham, Joseph Sievers, Mary C. Boys, Hans Hermann Henrix, and Jesper Svartvik, 77–91. Grand Rapids, MI: Eerdmans, 2011; Italian trans. 2012.
———. *Reconciliation and Transformation: Reconsidering Christian Theologies of the Cross*. Translated by Karen Hagersten. Eugene, OR: Cascade, 2021 (Swedish: 2014).
———. "Rendering the Rending of the Veil: What Difference Does It Make?" In *Making a Difference: Essays on the Bible and Judaism in Honor of Tamara Cohn Eskenazi*, edited by David J. A. Clines, Kent Harold

Richards, and Jacob L. Wright, 257–76. Sheffield, UK: Sheffield Phoenix Press, 2012.

———. "The Children of Sarah and Hagar, and the 'Mother City' of Jerusalem." In *Enabling Dialogue about the Land: A Resource Book for Jews and Christians*, edited by Philip A. Cunningham, Ruth Langer, and Jesper Svartvik, 160–90. Mahwah, NJ: Paulist Press, 2020.

———. "The New Testament's Most Dangerous Book for Jews." *The Christian Century* (September 22, 2021), https://www.christiancentury.org/print/pdf/node/38881 (accessed May 26, 2023).

Swartley, Willard M., ed. *The Love of Enemy and Nonretaliation in the New Testament*. Louisville, KY: Westminster John Knox Press, 1992.

Talmud Bavli: 'im kol ha-mepharshim. 20 vols. Jerusalem: *Ha-Talmud ha-mephoar*, 1973.

Talmud Yerushalmi. 17 vols. Jerusalem [?]: *Tipheret*, (no year).

Targum Pseudo-Jonathan: Genesis. Translated, with Introduction and Notes by Michael Maher. Edinburgh: T&T Clark, 1992.

Taylor, Miriam S. *Anti-Judaism and Early Christian Identity: A Critique of the Scholarly Consensus*. Leiden: Brill, 1995.

Tennyson, Alfred Lord. *Poems of Tennyson....* Oxford: Oxford University Press, 1917.

Thatcher, Tom. *Greater than Caesar: Christology and Empire in the Fourth Gospel*. Minneapolis: Fortress, 2009.

Theobald, Michael. *Die Fleischwerdung des Logos: Studien zum Verhältnis des Johannesprologs zum Corpus des Evangeliums und zu 1 Joh.* Münster: Aschendorff, 1988.

Thiessen, Matthew. *Paul and the Gentile Problem*. Oxford: Oxford University Press, 2016.

Tomson, Peter J. *"If This Be from Heaven": Jesus and the New Testament Authors in Their Relationship to Judaism*. Sheffield, UK: Sheffield Academic Press, 2001.

———. *Paul and the Jewish Law: Halakha in the Letters of the Apostle to the Gentiles*. Assen: Van Gorcum / Fortress, 1990.

———. *Presumed Guilty: How the Jews Were Blamed for the Death of Jesus*. Translated by Janet Dyk. Minneapolis: Fortress, 2005.

Tosephta... Edited by M. S. Zuckermandel. Jerusalem: Wahrmann, 1970.

Trachtenberg, Joshua. *The Devil and the Jews*. New Haven, CT: Yale University Press, 1943.

Trudinger, Paul. "Exposing the Depth of Oppression (Luke 16:1b–8a)." In *Jesus and His Parables: Interpreting the Parables of Jesus Today. With a Foreword by Seán Freyne*, edited by V. George Shillington, 121–37. Edinburgh: T&T Clark, 1997.

Tyra, Gary. *Defeating Pharisaism: Recovering Jesus' Disciple-Making Method*. Colorado Springs: Authentic, 2009.

Bibliography

Tyson, Joseph B. "The Death of Jesus." In *Seeing Judaism Anew: Christianity's Sacred Obligation*, edited by Mary C. Boys, 38–45. Lanham, MD: Rowman & Littlefield, 2005.

Urbach, Ephraim E. *The Sages: Their Concepts and Beliefs*. Translated by Israel Abrahams. 2 vols. Jerusalem: Magnes Press, 1987.

Valantasis, Richard. *The Gospel of Thomas*. New York: Routledge, 1997.

van de Sandt, Huub, and David Flusser. *The Didache*. Minneapolis: Royal van Gorcum / Fortress, 2002.

VanderKam, James C. "Foreword." In Anthony J. Saldarini, *Pharisees, Scribes and Sadducees in Palestinian Society: A Sociological Approach*, 2nd ed., xi–xxv. Grand Rapids, MI: Eerdmans, 2001.

Vermes, Geza, Fergus Millar, and Matthew Black, eds. *The History of the Jewish People in the Age of Jesus Christ (175 B.C.–A.D. 135)*. Rev. ed. Edinburgh: T&T Clark, 1979.

Visi, Tamás. "John the Baptist: A Jewish Preacher Recast as the Herald of Jesus." https://www.thetorah.com/article/john-the-baptist-a-jewish-preacher-recast-as-the-herald-of-jesus (accessed March 24, 2023).

von Wahlde, Urban C. "The Johannine 'Jews': A Critical Survey." *New Testament Studies* 28 (1982): 33–60.

Walsh, Richard G. *Three Versions of Judas*. New York: Routledge, 2014 (2010).

Walzer, Michael. *Exodus and Revolution*. New York: Basic, 1985.

Wanamaker, Charles A. "Philippians." In *Eerdmans Commentary to the Bible*, edited by James D. G. Dunn and John W. Rogerson, 1394–403. Grand Rapids, MI: Eerdmans, 2003.

Watson, Francis. *Paul, Judaism and the Gentiles: A Sociological Approach*. Cambridge, UK: Cambridge University Press, 1986.

Wedderburn, A. J. M. "Sawing off the Branches: Theologizing Dangerously Ad Hebraeos." *Journal of Theological Studies* 56 (2005): 393–414.

Weeden, Theodore J. *Mark—Traditions in Conflict*. Philadelphia: Fortress, 1979 (1971).

———. "The Heresy That Necessitated Mark's Gospel." In *The Interpretation of Mark*, 2nd ed., edited by William R. Telford, 89–104. Edinburgh: T&T Clark, 1995.

Weedman, Gary E. "Reading Ephesians from the New Perspective on Paul." *Leaven* 14 (2006): 81–92.

Wenemark, Annika. "'Öga för öga, tand för tand' En biblisk vedergällningslag?" Bachelor's thesis, Lund University, 2013.

Werner, Erik. "Melito of Sardis: The First Poet of Deicide." *Hebrew Union College Annual* 37 (1966): 191–210.

Westbrook, Raymond, and Bruce Wells. *Everyday Law in Biblical Israel: An Introduction*. Louisville, KY: Westminster John Knox Press, 2009.

"What Does It Mean When Jesus Says 'My Yoke Is Easy and My Burden Is Light' (Matthew 11:30)?" https://m.youtube.com/watch?v=pOMgDwMZ1v8 (accessed April 6, 2023).

"Why Did John the Baptist Refer to the Pharisees as a Brood of Vipers?" https://www.gotquestions.org/brood-of-vipers.html (accessed June 18, 2022).

Williamson, Clark M., and Ronald J. Allen. *Interpreting Difficult Texts: Anti-Judaism and Christian Preaching*. Philadelphia: SCM / Trinity, 1989.

Wills, Laurence M. "The Gospel according to Mark." In *The Jewish Annotated New Testament*, 2nd ed., edited by Amy-Jill Levine and Marc Zvi Brettler, 67–106. Oxford: Oxford University Press, 2017.

Windsor, Lionel J. *Reading Ephesians and Colossians after Supersessionism: Christ's Mission through Israel to the Nations*. Eugene, OR: Cascade, 2017.

Woodard-Lehman, Derek Alan. "Saying 'Yes' to Israel's 'No': Barth's Dialectical Supersessionism and the Witness of Carnal Israel." In *Karl Barth: Post-Holocaust Theologian?*, edited by George Hunsinger, 67–84. London: Bloomsbury / T&T Clark, 2018.

Wright, Benjamin G., III. "Wisdom of Ben Sira." In *Outside the Bible: Ancient Jewish Writings Related to Scripture*, edited by Louis H. Feldman, James L. Kugel, and Lawrence H. Schiffman, 3 vols., 3:2208–2352. Philadelphia: Jewish Publication Society, 2013.

Wright, N. T. *Climax of the Covenant: Christ and the Law in Pauline Theology*. New York: T&T Clark, 1991.

———. *Jesus and the Victory of God*. London: SPCK, 1996.

———. *Luke for Everyone*. London: SPCK, 2001.

———. *The New Testament and the People of God*. London: SPCK, 1992.

Yee, Tet-Lim N. *Jews, Gentiles and Ethnic Reconciliation: Paul's Jewish Identity and Ephesians*. Cambridge, UK: Cambridge University Press, 2005.

Zeichmann, Christopher B. "Jesus 'ben Pantera': An Epigraphic and Military-Historical Note." *Journal for the Study of the Historical Jesus* 18 (2020): 141–55.

Zeitlin, Solomon. *Who Crucified Jesus?* New York: Harper, 1942.

Zlotowitz, Meir, and Nosson Scherman. *Pirkei Avos: Ethics of the Fathers...* New York: Mesorah, 1984.

Zoccali, Christopher. *Reading Philippians after Supersessionism: Jews, Gentiles, and Covenantal Identity*. Eugene, OR: Cascade, 2017.

Zornberg, Avivah Gottlieb. *Moses: A Human Life*. New Haven, CT: Yale University Press, 2016.

NAMES INDEX

Abarbanel, 75
Abrahams, Israel, 115
Akiyama, Kengo, 274n16
Allen, Ronald J., xliii
Allison, Dale C., 3, 9, 16, 19, 20,
  21, 23, 24, 28, 29, 38, 39, 42, 46,
  53, 54, 74, 78, 132, 133, 134,
  237, 255n11, 256n7, 256n10,
  258n35, 260n12, 262n2, 263n11,
  263n17, 264n7, 264n20, 265n26,
  270n4, 285n9
Alon, Gedalyahu, 62
Anderson, Benedict, 146
'Aqiva, Rabbi, 24, 56, 83
Arrupe, Pedro, 278n20
Ascough, Richard S., 224
Attridge, Harold W., xxiv
Augustine, 164
Aus, Roger David, 147, 148
Avery-Peck, Alan J., 296n3
'Azariah, Rabbi, 193

Bach, Johann Sebastian, 127
Bailey, John W., 306n8
Bailey, Kenneth E., 280n12
Barclay, John M. G., 182–83, 186,
  299n17
Barclay, William, 105, 278n3,
  279n5
Barrett, C. K., 176
Barth, Karl, 118–20, 143, 281n9,
  282n14
Bauckham, Richard, 277n3
Bauernfeind, Otto, 32

Bauman, Zygmunt, xvii
Baur, Ferdinand Christian, 306n8
Beare, Francis White, 38, 41
Ben 'Azzai, Rabbi, 83, 84
ben Gorion, Naqdimon, xxiii
Bergen, Doris L., 165
Berkovits, Eliezer, 292n2
Bernauer, James, xviii
Best, Ernest, 224
Betz, Hans Dieter, 206
Billerbeck, Paul, 274n15
Black, Matthew, 70, 152
Blix, Ragnvald, 116
Boecker, Hans Jochen, 12
Booth, Roger P., 268n18
Borges, Jorge Luis, 281n7
Boyarin, Daniel, 56, 58, 63, 64, 154,
  168, 269n27, 291n20, 297n12
Brandon, S. G. F., 306n8
Braun, Herbert, 59
Brick, Daniel, 258n36
Brontë, Emily, xxii
Brown, Raymond E., 125, 137, 159,
  162, 282n25, 291n3
Bultmann, Rudolf, 32, 113
Bunyan, John, xli

Caird, George Bradford, 21–22, 87,
  95, 231, 273n3, 275n8,
  275n13
Cane, Anthony, 116, 284n43
Cargal, Timothy B., 133
Carroll, James, xvii
Carter, Warren, 285n23

Catalano, Rosann M., 148, 149, 289n54
Cave, C. H., 99
Charles, Robert Henry, 231
Chilton, Bruce D., 249n44, 305n6
Chung, Paul S., 281n9
Churchill, Winston, 281n2
Claudius, 225
Clement of Alexandria, xxviii, 25
Cohen, Jeremy, 139, 141–42
Cohen, Shaye J. D., 207, 248nn35–36, 301n17
Cohick, Lynn, 142
Connelly, John, xvii
Cook, Michael J., 250n62
Cranfield, Charles E. B., 59, 205–6
Crawley, Ernest, 249n48
Crossan, John Dominic, 69, 70, 77, 280n2
Culler, Jonathan, xix
Cunningham, Philip A., 286n28

Dahl, Nils Alstrup, 167
Dalman, Gustaf, 117
Daube, David, 14–15, 84, 148, 257n19, 289n45
Davies, W. D., 3, 6, 9, 16, 19, 20, 21, 23, 24, 28, 29, 38, 39, 42, 46, 53, 54, 74, 78, 132, 133, 134, 237, 255n11, 256n7, 256n10, 258n35, 260n12, 262n2, 263n11, 263n17, 264n7, 264n20, 264n26, 270n4, 285n9
deConick, April, 167
Derrett, J. Duncan M., 96, 163, 270n9
Dibelius, Martin, 25, 261n26
Dodd, C. H., 52, 69, 70, 86, 92, 153, 154, 270n12
Domitian, 157, 231, 307n1
Donne, John, 126
Dunn, James D. G., xxxv, 212

Eastman, Susan Grove, 203, 206–7, 300n1, 301n13

Eckart, Karl-Gottfried, 306n8
Ehrman, Bart, 167, 169
Eisenbaum, Pamela, xxxiv
El'azar ben 'Azariah, Rabbi, 164
Eli'ezer, Rabbi, 103
Ericksen, Robert P., 165

Fagenblat, Michael, 83, 90, 274n18
Farris, Michael, 113
Fein, Helen, xv
Ferdinand, II, xxix
Feuer, Avrohom Chaim, 75
Filson, Floyd V., 53, 136
Fisch, Yael, 184
Fish, Stanley, 253n100
Fitzmyer, Joseph A., 92, 98, 103, 276n24, 280n14
Flusser, David, 27, 29, 31, 39, 261n8, 275n1, 276n19
Frankfurter, David, 232, 233, 234, 308n14
Fredriksen, Paula, xxiv, xxv, xxxiv, xxxvi, xxxvii, 142, 144, 148, 183–84, 241–42, 252n81, 287n22, 299n35
Freud, Sigmund, 249n48
Friedrichsen, Timothy A., 113, 114, 280n12
Frymer-Kensky, Tikva, 298n16
Funk, Robert W., 48, 51–52, 59
Furstenberg, Yair, 62–63, 64, 268nn21–26

Gaius Julius Vindex, 200
Gale, Aaron M., 133
Garroway, Joshua D., xxxiii
Gaston, Lloyd, 191, 237, 298n15
Gerleman, Gillis, 156
Gibson, Margaret D., 96
Gilmour, Samuel MacLean, 28
Goodman, Lenn E., 17, 84
Goodman, Nelson, 213
Goppelt, Leonhard, 37, 38
Gordon, Robert P., 252n89
Gould, Ezra Palmer, 59

Names Index

Greeven, Heinrich, 25, 260n26
Gressmann, Hugo, 277n3
Grindheim, Sigurd, 268n13
Gruber, Ruth, xvii
Grundmann, Walter, 274n15
Gurtner, Daniel M., 137, 143, 145–46, 287n24, 289n48
Guthrie, Donald K., 297n2
Gutiérrez, Gustavo, 278n20

Hadrian, 201
Hagner, Donald A., 137
Halbertal, Moshe, 210
Halivni, David Weiss, 283n34
Hamilton, Catherine Sider, 134, 285n14, 285n16
Hays, Richard B., xlii, 253n100
Hemer, Colin J., 231
Henze, Matthias, 214
Herod Agrippa I, 96
Herzog, William R., II, 276n21
Heschel, Abraham Joshua, xviii–xix, 148, 150, 288n26
Heschel, Susannah, 165, 174, 274n15
Hillel, 21, 24, 33, 262n8
Hitler, Adolf, xvii
Hock, R. F., 277n3
Holtzmann, Heinrich Julius, 306n8
Hultgren, Arland, 100
Hurd, John C., 229

Isaacs, Marie E., xxxix–xl
Isabella I, xxix

Jackson, Bernard S., 9
Jacob, Benno, 9
Jaubert, Annie, 261n8
Jensen, Matthew, 223, 226
Jeremias, Joachim, 53, 100, 308n17
John Chrysostom, xxiv
Johnson, Bo, 280n14
Johnson, Earl S., 252n88
Johnson, S. Lewis, 204, 205, 206, 300n2

Johnsson, William G., xlii
Josephus, xxv, 96
Jose the Galilean, Rabbi, 42
Jospe, Raphael, 17
Jülicher, Adolf, 69, 87, 238, 279n15
Jung, Carl Gustav, xxviii
Jussem-Wilson, Nelly, 246n16
Justin Martyr, 203–4, 205

Kahl, Brigitte, 196–97, 198, 199, 200, 202, 298n17, 299n18, 299n24, 299n33
Kalimi, Isaac, 257n17
Käsemann, Ernst, xli–xlii, 59, 239–40
Kee, Alistair, 27, 28, 29, 30, 261n11
Kelly, William, 143
Kimchi, David, 75
Kimelman, Reuven, 168
Kister, Menahem, 23, 24, 84, 259n5, 267n1
Klassen, William, 121, 123, 124, 125, 127, 281n7, 283n40
Klawans, Jonathan, 11, 257n16
Klijn, Albertus Frederik Johannes, 214, 303n22
Klopstock, Friedrich Gottlieb, 126
Knight, Jonathan, 92
Koester, Craig R., 252n87
Koffman, Joshua, 187
Kohler, Kaufmann, xviii
Korner, Ralph J., 308n18
Kosmala, Hans, 95, 133
Kugel, James L., 156
Kuyper, Lester Jacob, 155, 291n21
Kysar, Robert, xxxi, 151

Lachs, Samuel Tobias, 13–14, 18, 81, 254n4, 256n8, 265n1, 267n10, 270n9, 275n1
Lamp, Jeffrey S., 224, 227
Lang, Friedrich, 218
Langer, Ruth, 168
Larsson, Göran, 156
Lazare, Bernard, xvi, 246n15

Leffler, Siegfried, 174
Légasse, S., 284n5
Lenski, Richard C. H., 130–31, 284n4
Levenson, Jon D., 294n24
Levi, Rabbi, 193
Levine, Amy-Jill, xii, xxiii, 45, 49, 52, 54, 72, 89, 90, 99, 102, 103, 106, 107, 108–9, 112, 114, 115, 235, 245n2, 247n29, 256n10, 267n13, 274n12, 277n26, 277n4, 278n15, 278n22, 279n5, 279n15, 285n14, 307n23, 308n2
Lied, Liv Ingeborg, 214, 303n25
Lieu, Judith, 142
Lincoln, Abraham, 90
Llewelyn, Stephen Robert, 167
Lincoln, Abraham, 228
Lincoln, Andrew, 252n87, 254n101, 302n13
Lindeskog, Gösta, 307n13
Long, Thomas G., 253n90
Lowe, Malcolm, xxx, 72
Luther, Martin, xvi, 251n69

Macarius, 267n7
Mahler, Gustav, xxiii
Manson, T. W., xxvii, 47, 89, 91, 93, 95, 96, 162, 249n50, 274n11
Marguerat, Daniel, 131, 284n5
Marquardt, Friedrich-Wilhelm, 120
Marr, Wilhelm, xv
Marsh, John, 151–52, 290n4
Martyn, J. Louis, 167, 168, 167, 170
May, John d'Arcy, 309n8
McConnell, Richard, 59
Meeks, Wayne A., 171, 172
Meier, John P., 37, 263n2, 273n20
Melanchthon, Philipp, 251n69
Melito of Sardis, 138–41, 142, 148–49, 250n63, 286n7, 286n9
Ménard, Jacques E., 263n11
Metzger, Bruce M., xxiii
Milavec, Aaron A., 68, 72–73, 78–79, 271n34

Milgrom, Jacob, 288n44
Moffat, James, 306n8
Montefiore, Claude G., 60, 130, 148, 267n5
Moore, George Foot, 22, 84
Morrison, Craig E., xxiii
Morrisroe, Patrick J., 287n13
Moss, Candida, 123
Mussner, Franz, xxx

Nanos, Mark D., 177, 179, 180, 199, 299n18
Nero, 200, 307n4
Neudecker, Reinhard, 256n10
Neusner, Jacob, 249n44
Newell, Jane E., 71–72
Newell, Raymond R., 71–72
Nineham, D. E., 28
Nirenberg, David, xiii, 241, 288n30
Novak, David, 245n9

Odeberg, Hugo, 247n31
Orwell, George, 298n14

Pagels, Elaine, 308n18
Papias, 123, 241
Pearson, Birger A., 225, 226
Pelc, Julie Adler, 277n12
Perler, Othmar, 140
Perrin, Norman, 60
Philo of Alexandria, 25, 81, 136, 154
Piper, John, 11, 257n14
Pliny the Elder, 266n22
Plutarch, 104
Pollefeyt, Didier, 158
Polschitz, Christoph Harant Freiherr von, 298n5
Porat, Dina, 256n13
Porphyry, 176–77, 295n3

Quensel, Oscar, 117
Quisling, Vidkum, 116

Räisänen, Heikki, 60

Names Index

Reed, Annette Yoshiko, xxiii, 248n36
Reid, Barbara, 108
Reim, Günter, 167
Reinhartz, Adele, xxviii, 142, 165, 168, 169, 170, 171, 250n62
Richardson, Peter, 301n13
Ritschl, Albrecht, 306n8
Robinson, Alexandra, 167
Rosen, David, 247n29
Rosenzweig, Franz, 85
Rudolph, David J., 176, 177, 178, 179, 180

Safrai, Shemuel, 266n1
Sandauer, Artur, xvii
Sander, Emilie T., 26
Sanders, E. P., 5, 38, 39, 64, 204, 236–37, 255n11, 263n11
Sandmel, David Fox, 223, 229
Sandmel, Samuel, 250n62
Sarna, Nahum M., 257n26
Savage, Dorothy, xxxii
Schechter, Solomon, 255n12
Schellenberg, Ryan S., 45
Schippers, R., 306n19
Schlueter, Carol J., 228
Schmidt, Daryl, 226
Schmiedel, Paul Wilhelm, 306n8
Schnackenburg, Rudolf, 152
Schrenk, Gottlob, 205
Schweitzer, Albert, 249n44
Schweizer, Eduard, 11, 21–22, 28, 32, 33, 52–53, 58–59, 69, 80–81, 82, 271n1, 284n4
Scott, Bernard Brandon, 44, 100, 279n15
Segal, Alan F., 297n13
Setzer, Claudia, 230, 232
Shakespeare, William, 8
Shammai, 33, 262n8
Sievers, Joseph, xxiii, 247n29
Simlai, Rabbi, 83

Smith, D. Moody, xxix, xxxii, 168, 170, 171, 172, 173, 232, 250n59, 293n13, 295n37
Smith, Morton, 258n36
Snodgrass, Klyne R., 45, 46, 92, 100, 109, 273n7, 274n15, 276n15, 280n9
Söderbergh, Torgny, 281n2
Sommer, Benjamin D., 303n28
Soulen, R. Kendall, 245n9, 247n26, 270n2
Spooner, W. A., 21
Stendahl, John, 309n15
Stendahl, Krister, xxxiv, xxxv–xxxvii, 26, 76, 149, 174, 191, 242, 251n77, 283n8
Stern, David, 72
Stern, J. B., 82–83
Strack, Hermann L., 274n15
Strousma, Guy D., 246n19
Sullivan, Desmond, 135
Svartvik, Jesper, 248n31, 251n68, 260n12, 272n12

Taylor, Miriam S., 142
Telushkin, Joseph, 61, 64
Tertullian, 94
Thatcher, Tom, 157, 291n28
Thiessen, Matthew, 251n78
Titus, 201
Tomson, Peter J., xl, 176, 177–78, 180, 182, 224, 228, 252n81, 296n18, 297n12, 306n18, 308n14
Trachtenberg, Joshua, 166
Trudinger, Paul, 92, 95–96, 275n4, 276n21
Tyra, Gary, xxi
Tyson, Joseph B., 136

Urbach, Ephraim E., 248n33

Valantis, Richard, 70
VanderKam, James C., 247n29
van de Sandt, Huub, 261n8
Visi, Tamás, 254n10

von Bora, Katharina, 251n69
von Hase, Karl, 263n17

Walsh, Richard G., 281n7
Walzer, Michael, 169, 293n21
Wanamaker, Charles A., 221
Wassel, Blake Edward, 167
Watson, Francis, 251n77
Wedderburn, A. J. M., 253n100
Weeden, Theodore J., 73, 271n23
Weedman, Gary E., 304n32
Weigel, Gustave, xix
Wells, Bruce, 9
Wenemark, Annika, 256n12

Westbrook, Raymond, 9
Williamson, Clark M., xliii
Wills, Laurence M., 272n7
Windsor, Lionel J., 214, 304n32
Woodard-Lehman, Derek Alan, 119, 128, 282n14
Wright, Benjamin G., III, 263n15
Wright, N. T., 93, 94–95, 146, 252n85, 275n9, 275n13

Yee, Tet-Lim N., 212–13

Zoccali, Christopher, 221, 222

ANCIENT SOURCES INDEX

HEBREW BIBLE
Genesis
1:1–5	154
1:1—6:8	82
1:6	148
3	2
4:1	166
4:8	166
5:1	83
6:9—11:32	82
12:1—17:27	82
12:2	132
15:1–6	194
15:2	99
15:3	99
15:6	280n3
16:13	102
18:6	54
18:18	54
19:14	298n9
21	194
21:9	192
22	125
34	227
35:18	75
49:24	75

Exodus
4:22	76, 77
12:15	51
16:16	54
16:20	264n10
16:36	54
19:6	131
21:23–25	256n11
22:25–27	96
23:1	163
23:7	163, 262n8
24:3	135
26:31	145
26:33	145
28	74
28:12	74, 76
28:21	75
32:6	193
32:16	185
33:14	35
34:6	155, 156
34:7	156
36:26f.	185

Leviticus
1:9	246n12
11	57, 59
18:5	40, 88
18:8	303n19
19	82
19:1—20:27	82
19:18	17, 20, 22, 23, 83, 84, 90, 258n33, 260n14, 261n28, 274n16
19:23–25	70, 270n9
19:33f.	23
20:10	159
20:24–26	57
24:19f.	256n11
25:37	96

Jewish Foundations of the New Testament

Numbers	
3:6–10	273n9
12	65, 66
12:3	xxxvii, 48
15:37–41	272n17
35:31	258n26

Deuteronomy	
6	82
6:4–9	272n17
6:5	83, 84
7:7f.	210
11:13–21	272n17
12:9	xxxix
13:4	170
14	57, 59
15:11	101
15:17	101
17:7	162
19:21	256n11
22:22	159
23:19f.	96
24:9	65
25:12	257n19
30:12	103
32:35	258n30

Joshua	
2:19	284n4
15:25	117

Ruth	
2:17	54

1 Samuel	
2:8	7
12:22	205
21:1–6	40
21:2	264n18

2 Samuel	
3:28	132
13:30f.	147

1 Kings	
2:33	132
7:26	302n5

2 Kings	
2:12	147
5:18	280n7
24:4	280n7

2 Chronicles	
6:30	280n7

Ezra	
4:4	89

Job	
12:12	30
22:21	100

Psalms	
11	83
25:11	280n7
68:6 (ET 5)	105, 107
78:32	280n7
84:1f.	145
84:4	145
94:14	205
101 LXX	253n95
102:26–28	xl
104:12	47
104:29f.	186
113—18	76
118	75, 76, 77
118:17	76
118:22	74, 75, 76
125:5	207
128:6	207
133:1	187
145:16	243

Proverbs	
3:9	276n19
24:17	18
25:12f.	258n30
26:18f.	193

Song of Songs	
7:2	303n22

Isaiah	
5:1–7	71
7:14	76

8:14	75
11:1	291n26
19:24	215
25	215
25:6f.	215, 303n27
26:13	xlii
28:16	74, 75
33:15	83
43:19	252n88
49:14–16	110
51:1f.	7
54:13	75
57:19	216
58:7	101
60:1–4	215–16
66:1	83

Jeremiah
6:16	35
31:31	297n12
32	282n20, 303n21
36	303n21
43	303n21
45	303n21

Lamentations
3:42	280n7

Ezekiel
17:23	47
20:11	40, 88
31:10f.	47
31:31–33	185
40:5	302n5

Daniel
4:10f.	47
4:10–27	47
4:14	47
4:20	47
4:22	47
4:24f.	47
5:25	162
7	265n20
9:19	280n7

Amos
5:4	83

Jonah
3:1—4:1	98

Micah
6:8	83, 272n12

Habakkuk
2:4	83, 255n15, 280n3

Zechariah
6:15	303n27
11:12	122

DEUTEROCANONICAL BOOKS

Tobit
1:3	88
1:16–20	88
4:15	259n7

Sirach
6:23–38	35
9:10	30
27:4	218
35:14–19	108
35:15–17	105
51:23–27	35–36

2 Esdras
4:39f.	267n13

PSEUDEPIGRAPHA

2 Baruch
12.1–13.2	303n24
13.11–14.2	303n24
54.3–5	303n22
64.1–5	285n12

1 Enoch
14:9	302n11

4 Ezra
8.47–49	113

Testament of Benjamin
3.3 — 259n7

Testament of Issachar
5.2 — 81, 259n7
7.6 — 259n7

Testament of Levi
6.8–11 — 227, 306n15
6.11 — 228

DEAD SEA SCROLLS

The Community Rule **(1QS)**
1.4 — 259n38
1.9–11 — 18, 91, 259n38
9.21–23 — 259n38

ANCIENT JEWISH WRITERS

Josephus

Jewish Antiquities
7.2.4 — 249n45
15.11.5 — 302n7
18.1.2–6 — 249n45
18.6.3 — 96, 277n25

Jewish War
5.5.2 — 302n7
6.2.4 — 302n7

Philo

On the Decalogue
22 — 81, 272n5

Special Laws
2.15 — 272n5

NEW TESTAMENT

Matthew
1:2f. — 128
1:21 — 134
3 — 6
3:7 — 4, 254n2
3:9 — 75
5:3 — 308n17
5:16 — 49
5:17 — 19, 21, 31, 33
5:17–18 — 222
5:17–19 — 9–10
5:17–48 — 302n10
5:17—7:11 — 21
5:18 — 256n8
5:20 — 33
5:21–26 — 9, 65
5:21–48 — 9, 10
5:22 — 269n35
5:27–30 — 9
5:31f. — 9
5:32 — 40
5:33–37 — 9
5:38 — 11, 13
5:39 — 245n4
5:41 — 245n4
5:43 — 17, 18
5:43–48 — 9
5:44 — 33, 109
5:47 — 90–91, 175
6:10 — 54
6:28 — 245n6
7:1–5 — 161–62
7:6 — 304n4
7:11 — 20
7:12 — 21
7:21ff. — 308n17
8:22 — 185, 220
10:38 — 34
11:19 — 27
11:25–30 — 36
11:28–30 — 32
11:29 — 263n13
11:30 — xxvi, 245n3
12:1 — 40
12:34 — 1
12:43 — 263n13
13:3 — 53
13:35 — 53
13:45f. — 221
15 — 62, 66
15:1 — 63
15:1–20 — 58, 267n1
15:2 — xxvi, 59, 62

346

15:6	64	2:28	41
15:11	55, 60, 62, 64, 67, 267n1	3:19	121
15:20	40, 45, 62	6:30–44	54
15:21–28	122, 245n1	7	62, 66
16:6	51	7:1	63
16:6–12	53	7:1–23	58, 267n1
16:21	69	7:2	62
16:24f.	33–34	7:3	59
17:20	45, 46	7:5	xxvi
20:1–16	115	7:8	64
20:15	xii	7:15	55, 59, 60, 62, 64, 267n1
21:23–27	72	7:19	60, 63, 64
21:43	74	7:24–30	122, 245n1
21:45f.	xxv, 76	7:34	243
21:46	72	8:1–10	54
21:46f.	120	8:15	53
22:23–33	xxv	8:27—14:9	73
22:35	81, 272n6	8:31	69–70
23:4	34	8:38	16
23:33	1	11:27–33	72
24:7	74	12:6	71
24:20	40	12:12	xxv, 72, 76, 120
26:14–16	122	12:13–17	291n3
26:23	121	12:18–27	xxv
26:26–29	124, 283n30	12:26	83, 155
26:28	134	12:28	81, 272n6
26:30	76	12:31	25
26:47	121	13:8	74
26:59	45	13:14	60
26:72	127	14:10–72	73
26:73	xxx	14:11	122
26:74	127	14:20	121
26:75	127	14:22–25	124, 283n30
27:1–10	123	14:26	76
27:9	282n20	14:43	121
27:25	132, 134, 135	14:70	xxx
27:51	148	15:15	132
27:62	39	15:42	39
28:19	69, 271n27	**LUKE**	
MARK		1:6	103
1:10	137	2:29–32	97, 131
1:16—8:26	73	2:30–32	xxxviii
2:26	264n18	2:32	207
2:27	42	3	6

3:7	4, 254n2	18:8	275n6
3:8	75	18:9	111
3:21	104	18:11f.	113
3:33	128	18:12	28
4:16	43	19:8	112
4:17	66	19:9	112
5:16	104	19:13	113
5:39	29	20:1–8	72
6:4	39	20:13	71
6:12	104	20:19	xxv, 72, 76, 120
6:27	20, 109	20:27–40	xxv
6:29	16	20:37	83, 155
6:31	21	21:1–4	279n9
9:22	70	21:37f.	160
9:60	185, 220	22:1f.	160
10:25	81, 272n6	22:3	122
10:29	90	22:15–20	124, 283n30
10:36f.	91	22:21	121
11:9–13	18	22:32	104
11:24	263n13	22:47	121
12:1	51, 53	22:59	xxx
12:33	xl	23:13	284n6, 286n27
12:48	34	23:18	132
13:21	53	23:34	104, 134
13:31	249n43	23:54	39
14:26	220	24:27	277n8
14:27	34	24:44	277n8
15:3–7	108	24:53	114, 288n26
15:8–10	108		
15:13	93	**JOHN**	
16:1	93	1:14	36, 154
16:8b–13	275n4	1:16	152, 156
16:14	276n13	1:17	152
16:14f.	xxvii	2:1–12	54
16:19	98	3:1	xxiii–xxiv
16:20	98	4:1–42	86
16:21	304n4	4:9	xxx
16:30f.	103	4:22	xxix
16:31	100	4:31	88
17:6	45, 46	6:22–59	124
18:1	104	6:70	122
18:6	275n6	6:71	281n5
18:6f.	104	7:13	228
18:6–8	104	7:24	292n5
18:7	105	7:53—8:2	160

7:53—8:11	164	1:23	264n10
8	164	2:7	xxx
8:7	142	2:23	126
8:15	162	4:11	74
8:31–59	2	5:33–39	249n43
8:33	169	7:49	35
8:36	245n5	7:51f.	69
8:41	171	8:1	224
8:44	xxix, 2, 165, 166, 167, 168, 171, 173, 174, 175	15:20	260n12
		15:29	260n12
9:2	100, 277n9	16:9	xxxiii
9:22	xxix, 167, 168, 228	16:10	xxxiii
10:17f.	125	17	179
10:34	153	17:2	265n28
12:6	122	17:23	179
12:7	xxiv	18:7	177
12:24	46	21:24	302n8
12:42	167, 168	21:28f.	211
13:2	122, 281n5	21:38	117
13:26	121, 281n5	23:6	xxiv
13:27	122	28:3	2
13:34	173		
13:34f.	90	**Romans**	
14:6	209	1:17	83, 280n3
15:12f.	90	2:15	299n24
15:25	290n8	3:1	221
16:2	167, 168	3:20	299n24
17:25	153	3:21	214
18:18	127	3:27f.	299n24
18:31	161, 163	3:31	xxxvii–xxxviii
18:36	158	8:2	297n12
19:14	39	8:32	125
19:17	71	9	224
19:31	39	9—11	xxxvi
19:38	228	9:3	178, 204
19:39	xxiv	9:4f.	191, 219
19:42	39	9:5	6
20:19	xxix, 228	9:6	205, 232
20:28	157	10:4	59, 222, 268n11
20:30f.	168	11:1	224, 228
21:9	127	11:2	205
21:15–17	127	11:5	205
		11:13	xxxvi, 191, 219
ACTS		11:17–24	194
1:16–20	123	11:18–20	53

11:20	53	11	224
11:25–36	301n16	12:5–10	178
11:26	66, 206		
11:28	6	**GALATIANS**	
11:29	xli	1:13f.	219, 226
12:19–21	16–17, 229	1:13–23	225
13:8–10	23	1:14	224
14:23	39	2:7–9	199
15:7–13	207	2:8	xxxvi, 191, 219–20
		2:13	217
1 Corinthians		2:15	224, 228
2:8	224, 225	2:16	198
3:17	16	3:1	199
5:1–5	303n19	3:2	198
5:6–8	5, 295n7	3:5	198
5:11	177	3:6	217
7:17–20	239	3:10	198
8	178, 233	4	191, 195, 196
9:1–23	178	4:9	189, 198
9:19–23	176, 177, 179, 180	4:10	198
9:21	179	4:17	216, 217
9:22	176	4:19	189
9:27	109	4:21	299n24
10	178	4:21f.	191
10:7	193	4:21—5:1	189, 202
10:8	204	4:24	188, 194, 195, 201
11:1–16	186	4:25	190, 192, 194
11:23	121, 124, 225, 229	4:28f.	192
11:23–25	124, 283n30	4:29	192, 194, 197, 201
15:5	121	4:30	188, 190, 201
15:9f.	225	5:1	189, 195
15:36–40	46	5:3	189
		5:6	199
2 Corinthians		5:9	53
3	181, 184	5:11	199
3:6	182	5:14	260n14
3:8	184	6:15	198, 199, 206
3:13	185	6:16	203, 204, 205, 207
3:14	182, 185		
3:14–18	186	**Ephesians**	
3:15	185	2	214
3:16	185	2:11–22	209
5:12	184	2:15	210, 213
5:19	149	2:19	216
10:12–17	184		

Ancient Sources Index

2:20	74	8	xlii
4:29	222	8:13	xxxviii, xl, xli
		9	xlii
PHILIPPIANS		9:9	xl
1:23	xliii	9:10	xl
2:6f.	221	11—13	xlii
3:2	304n4	13:12f.	71
3:2–6	304n5	13:22	253n90
3:5	228, 232	13:24	xxxix
3:5f.	224, 225	**James**	
3:6	177, 219	1:25	25
3:7	220	2	308n17
3:10	220	2:2	230
3:14	220	2:8	24
3:16	219	3:1–12	269n34
1 Thessalonians		**1 Peter**	
1:2	226	1:9	305n13
1:3—2:1	306n9	2:6	74
1:6–13	306n9	**2 Peter**	
2	224, 306n8	2:22	304n4
2:12	226	**1 John**	
2:13	226	2:7	173
2:13–16	223, 225, 226, 229, 306n9	3:12	166
2:14–16	306n8	3:12–15	166
2:15	226	3:23	90
2:16	225, 227, 228	**2 John**	
2:17	226	5	90
1 Timothy		**Jude**	
1:5	305n13	11	166
Hebrews		**Revelation**	
1:10–12	xl	2:2–22	233
1:11	xl	2:8–11	307n2
2:17	113	2:9	231, 232
3:11	35	2:14	233
3:12—4:14	xl	2:17	232, 234
3:18	35	2:20	233
4:1	35	2:28	232
4:3	35	3:1	232
4:5	35	3:9	231, 232
4:10	35	3:15f.	230
7:14	128		

4:8	263n13	7.5	289n46
7:1	3–4	10.1	66, 90
13:8	126		
13:18	307n4	*Yadayim*	
14:4	233	3.5	56
14:11	263n13		
21:5	252n88	*Yoma*	
22:14f.	233	8.9	5–6
22:15	304n4		

RABBINIC SOURCES

Mishnah

Berakhot			
2.2	32, 263n16		
Chagigah			
1.8	264n12		
Kilayim			
2.8f.	265n1		
3.2	265n1		
Makkot			
1.10	164		
Middot			
2.3	302n5		
Mo'ed Qatan			
26a	289n46		
Nazir			
7.1	89		
Peah			
8.7	53		
Pirqei Avot			
1.1	302n9		
1.2	xxii, 248n32		
2.4	259n4		
3.5	262n1, 263n16		
4.19	259n37		
4.20	30–31		
6.2	185		
Sanhedrin			
4.5	150		

Talmud

Bavli Avodah Zarah			
5a	262n1		
Bavli Bava Metzia			
31b	250n65		
59b	103		
Bavli Bava Qamma			
25b	289n46		
83b	13, 257n20		
Bavli Berakhot			
17a	185		
64a	75, 76		
Bavli 'Eruvin			
13b	262n9		
Bavli Gittin			
90a	262n8		
Bavli Ketubbot			
16b–17a	262n8		
Bavli Makkot			
23b	83		
Bavli Megillah			
3b	273n4		
Bavli Nazir			
43b	89		
Bavli Sanhedrin			
74a	298n10		
107a	269n35		
Bavli Shabbat			
31a	259n7		
128a	264n13		

Ancient Sources Index

Bavli Sotah
22b   248n38

Bavli Yoma
85b   88, 265n22

Yerushalmi Berakhot
9.1   105

Yerushalmi Nedarim
9.4   83

Targum

Pseudo-Jonathan
Gen 4.1f.   293n7

Tosefta

Peah
1.2   269n34

Sanhedrin
7.11   297n11
13.2   90

Other Rabbinic Works

Avot de-Rabbi Natan
2.9   33
26   260n19
37   297n11

Genesis Rabbah
12.9   255n18
15.4   255n18
24.7   272n13
53.11   193

Mekhilta de-Rabbi Yishma'el
3.198   265n22–23

Pirqei de-Rabbi Nathan
26   24

Sifra
1.7   297n11

Sifra Qedushim
2.2   24, 260n20
2.4   83

Sifrei Devarim
48   30, 262n19

EARLY CHRISTIAN WRITINGS

Augustine

Questions on the Gospels
2.19   273n2

Tractate on John's Gospel
33.5   292n8

1 Clement
36:1–5   253n92

2 Clement
5.5   35

Didache
1.2   23
1.4   16
6.2   36
8.1   261n8
8.1–3   28

Eusebius

Church History
6.14.7   249n52
6.25.11–14   253n91

Gospel of Thomas
47   29, 261n1
50   263n14
60   263n14
65   70–71
76   221
90   71, 263n14

John Chrysostom

Commentary on Saint John the Evangelist and Apostle
Homily 85   249n40

Macarius

Homily
25.3   267n7

Melito of Sardis

On Pascha
79f.	287n17
82	250n63
98	289n50

Papias

Exposition of the Sayings of the Lord
book 4	123

Shepherd of Hermas
2.2.3	269n36

GRECO-ROMAN LITERATURE

Pliny the Elder

Natural History
19.54	266n22
20.87	266n22

Plutarch

Moralia
31	104

OTHER VOLUMES IN THIS SERIES

Clemens Thoma and Michael Wyschogrod, eds., *Understanding Scripture: Explorations of Jewish and Christian Traditions of Interpretation* (1987; ebook only)

Bernard J. Lee, *The Galilean Jewishness of Jesus: Retrieving the Origins of Christianity (Conversation on the Road Not Taken, Vol. I)* (1988; ebook only)

Clemens Thoma and Michael Wyschogrod, eds., *Parable and Story in Judaism and Christianity* (1989)

Eugene J. Fisher, ed., *Interwoven Destinies: Jews and Christians through the Ages* (1992; ebook only)

George M. Smiga, *Pain and Polemic: Anti-Judaism in the Gospels* (1992; ebook only)

Anthony J. Kenny, *Catholics, Jews, and the State of Israel* (1993; ebook only)

Eugene J. Fisher, ed., *Visions of the Other: Jewish and Christian Theologians Assess the Dialogue* (1994; ebook only)

Vincent Martin, *A House Divided: The Parting of the Ways between Synagogue and Church* (1995; ebook only)

Leon Klenicki and Geoffrey Wigoder, *A Dictionary of the Jewish-Christian Dialogue* (1995; ebook only)

Frank E. Eakin Jr., *What Price Prejudice? Christian Antisemitism in America* (1998)

Philip A. Cunningham and Arthur F. Starr, eds., *Sharing Shalom: A Process for Local Interfaith Dialogue between Christians and Jews* (1999)

Ekkehard Schuster and Reinhold Boschert-Kimmig, *Hope against Hope: Johann Baptist Metz and Elie Wiesel Speak Out on the Holocaust* (1999)

Mary C. Boys, *Has God Only One Blessing? Judaism as a Source of Christian Self-Understanding* (2000)

Johannes Reuchlin; translated and edited by Peter Wortsman, *Recommendation Whether to Confiscate, Destroy and Burn All Jewish Books: A Classic Treatise against Anti-Semitism* (2000)

Avery Dulles and Leon Klenicki, *The Holocaust, Never to Be Forgotten: Reflections on the Holy See's Document* We Remember (2001)

Philip A. Cunningham, *A Story of Shalom: the Calling of Christians and Jews by a Covenanting God* (2001; ebook only)

Philip A. Cunningham, *Sharing the Scriptures: The Word Set Free, Volume 1* (2003)

Dina Wardi, *Auschwitz: Contemporary Jewish and Christian Encounters* (2003)

Michael Lotker, *A Christian's Guide to Judaism* (2004)

Edward H. Flannery, *The Anguish of the Jews: Twenty-Three Centuries of Antisemitism* (Revised and Updated) (2004)

Lawrence Boadt, CSP, and Kevin di Camillo, eds., *John Paul II in the Holy Land: In His Own Words: With Christian and Jewish Perspectives by Yehezkel Landau and Michael McGarry, CSP* (2005)

James K. Aitken and Edward Kessler, eds., *Challenges in Jewish-Christian Relations* (2006)

Steven C. Boguslawski, OP, *Thomas Aquinas on the Jews: Insights into His Commentary on Romans 9–11* (2008)

George M. Smiga, *The Gospel of John Set Free: Preaching without Anti-Judaism* (2008)

Daniel J. Harrington, SJ, *The Synoptic Gospels Set Free: Preaching without Anti-Judaism* (2009)

Richard C. Lux, *The Jewish People, the Holy Land, and the State of Israel: A Catholic View* (2009)

Cardinal Jean-Marie Lustiger, edited by Jean Duchesne, *Cardinal Jean-Marie Lustiger on Christians and Jews* (2010)

Pope Benedict XVI, *Pope Benedict XVI in the Holy Land* (2010)

Thomas G. Casey and Justin Taylor, eds., *Paul's Jewish Matrix* (2011)

Franklin Sherman, ed., *Bridges—Documents of the Christian-Jewish Dialogue: Volume One—The Road to Reconciliation (1945–1985)* (2011)

Eugene J. Fisher, eds., *Memoria Futuri: Catholic-Jewish Dialogue Yesterday, Today, and Tomorrow; Texts and Addresses of Cardinal William H. Keeler* (2012)

Mary C. Boys, *Redeeming Our Sacred Story: The Death of Jesus and Relations between Jews and Christians* (2013)

Celia M. Deutsch, Eugene J. Fisher, and James Rudin, eds., *Toward the Future: Essays on Catholic-Jewish Relations in Memory of Rabbi León Klenicki* (2013)

Franklin Sherman, ed., *Bridges—Documents of the Christian-Jewish Dialogue: Volume Two—Building a New Relationship (1986–2013)* (2014)

Ronald Kronish, ed., *Coexistence and Reconciliation in Israel: Voices for Interreligious Dialogue* (2015)

Elena G. Procario-Foley and Robert A. Cathey, eds., *Righting Relations after the Holocaust and Vatican II: Essays in Honor of John Pawlikowski, OSM* (2018)

Paula Fredriksen and Jesper Svartvik, eds., *Krister among the Jews and Gentiles* (2018)

Carol Rittner, Stephen D. Smith, and Irena Steinfeldt. *The Holocaust and the Christian World: Reflections on the Past, Challenges for the Future*, 2nd ed. (2019)

Philip A. Cunningham, Ruth Langer, and Jesper Svartvik, eds., *Enabling Dialogue about the Land: A Resource Book for Jews and Christians* (2020)

Philip A. Cunningham, *Maxims for Mutuality: Principles for Catholic Theology, Education, and Preaching about Jews and Judaism* (2022)

Teresa Pirola, *Catholic-Jewish Relations: Twelve Key Themes for Teaching & Preaching* (2023)

Murray Watson, *Restoring the Gospels' Jewish Voice: André Chouraqui and the Intersection of Biblical Translation and Interfaith Dialogue* (2023)

STIMULUS BOOKS are developed by the Stimulus Foundation, a not-for-profit organization, and are published by Paulist Press. The Foundation wishes to further the publication of scholarly books on Jewish and Christian topics that are of importance to Judaism and Christianity.

The Stimulus Foundation was established by an erstwhile refugee from Nazi Germany who intends to contribute with these publications to the improvement of communication between Jews and Christians.

Books for publication in this Series will be selected by a committee of the Foundation, and offers of manuscripts and works in progress should be addressed to:

The Stimulus Foundation
c/o Paulist Press
997 Macarthur Boulevard
Mahwah, NJ 07430
www.paulistpress.com